URBAN FORTUNES

URBAN FORTUNES

THE POLITICAL ECONOMY OF PLACE

John R. Logan
Harvey L. Molotch

UNIVERSITY OF CALIFORNIA PRESS

Berkeley   Los Angeles   London

University of California Press
Berkeley and Los Angeles, California

University of California Press, Ltd.
London, England

©1987 by
The Regents of the University of California

Library of Congress Cataloging-in-Publication Data

Logan, John R., 1946-
  Urban fortunes.

  Bibliography: p.
  Includes index.
  1. Sociology, Urban—United States. 2. Cities and
towns—United States—Growth. 3. Human ecology—
United States. 4. Real property, Exchange of—United
States. 5. Urban economics. I. Molotch, Harvey Luskin.
II. Title.
HT123.L645 1987   307.7'6   85-23229
ISBN 0-520-05577-2 (alk. paper)

Printed in the United States of America

1   2   3   4   5   6   7   8   9

Contents

Preface

We met by an unusual route. The editors of the *American Journal of Sociology* made the match. Having decided to publish papers by each of us in their September 1976 issue (Molotch's growth machine essay and Logan's study of stratification of suburbs), they organized an impromptu debate. Alongside each article, they published the author's commentary on the other's work. Molotch urged Logan to look beyond the suburbs to larger arenas of stratification (including those at the national and international level) as well as to hierarchies of power and wealth within places. Logan urged Molotch to elaborate the growth machine model to account for variations in the growth strategies of different kinds of places and to recognize more directly the participation of national corporations in local growth politics.

Both authors were convinced that local conflicts over growth are central to the organization of cities, a view that provides the starting point of this book. This position clearly separates us from the conventional approach to urbanization, which we criticize as excessively deterministic, in the mode of neoclassical economics. It also distinguishes us from the mainstream of the neo-Marxian approach to the city, which tends in still another way to treat development as inexorable, flowing in this case from the macrostructure of the "means of production." We are investigating how various kinds of people and institutions struggle to achieve their opposing goals in the creation of the metropolis. And compared to the other two approaches, we stress not only the economic imperatives of the larger system but also the strivings of parochial elites to make money from development and ordinary people to make community a resource in their daily lives. The long tradition of community sociology, including the ethnographies of neighborhood life ignored by ecologists and neo-Marxians,[1] thus has a valued role in our analysis.

Although the prolific output of talented scholars has extended what was supposed to have been a one-year project into a five-year labor, it has been a stimulating time in which to write. Urban theory has been revitalized (even as we worked) by scores of social scientists who have seen the promise of linking the city to larger structures of economy and power, following the leads of Marx and Weber into more contemporary intellectual and empirical domains. Wherever we saw use for a concept or a finding, we made it our own, giving credit where we could. Much of this recent work has been devoted to a rebuilding of urban theory. Scholars have been willing to risk mistakes in return for boldness, and often in this book we, too, have made assertions for which the evidence is inadequate. Nevertheless, we have striven to be concrete, to use concepts with transparent links to everyday experience, and to indicate by examples the kinds of phenomena that would validate our assertions. By avoiding the abstractions sometimes achieved by both neoclassical economics and Marxism, we make more obvious the points at which the evidence is weak and the kinds of studies that are needed. We believe that the central task of the next decade is to design and carry out the research that will evaluate the theoretical gains apparently made in the past decade.

Colleagues have been good to us. We acknowledge assistance from Robert Alford, Greg Allain, Richard Appelbaum, Richard Flacks, Riley Dunlap, Robert Klausner, Richard Kolodin, Margit Meyer, John Pipkin, Chris Smith, Todd Swanstrom, Richard Walker, Maurice Zeitlin, and the late Nigel Taylor. Maureen Jung read the first horrible draft from beginning to end and gave us an honest critique. Steven Clayman provided able research assistance, and the staff of the Santa Barbara Sociology Department

---

1. We distinguish between neo-Marxians, who, in our terminology, adhere to Marx's analytic frame, and neo-Marxists, who actively advance Marx's political program (the two groups often, but don't always, overlap).

(led by Chris Allen) provided every assistance to help us produce drafts and discs. Carolyn Horowitz checked and rechecked our bibliography to make our citations accurate and complete. Full readings and detailed suggestions were provided by our friends G. William Domhoff, Roger Friedland, Albert Hunter, and Michael Schwartz. We are very grateful to them.

The 1983 Albany Conference on Urban Theory and National Urban Policy provided many ideas that found their way into our work, and we acknowledge the help of participants as well as the State University of New York and the American Sociological Association for supporting that conference. Research grants from the National Science Foundation and National Institute of Child Health and Human Development supported Logan's research on suburban growth. Molotch was helped by the academic senate grants program of the University of California, Santa Barbara, the Harry Frank Guggenheim Foundation, and the Center for Urban Affairs and Policy Research of Northwestern University.

1

The Social Construction of Cities

The earth below, the roof above, and the walls around make up a special sort of commodity: a place to be bought and sold, rented and leased, as well as used for making a life. At least in the United States, this is the standing of place in legal statutes and in ordinary people's imaginations. Places can (and should) be the basis not only for carrying on a life but also for exchange in a market. We consider this commodification of place fundamental to urban life and necessary in any urban analysis of market societies.

Yet in contrast to the way neoclassical economists (and their followers in sociology) have undertaken the task of understanding the property commodity, we focus on how markets work as *social* phenomena. Markets are not mere meetings between producers and consumers, whose relations are ordered by the impersonal "laws" of supply and demand. For us, the fundamental attributes of all commodities, but particularly of land and buildings, are the social contexts through which they are used and exchanged. Any given piece of real estate has both a use value and an exchange value.[1] An apartment building, for example, provides a "home" for residents (use value) while at the same time generating rent for

1. We derive the distinction between use and exchange values from Marx's original formulation, as clarified through David Harvey's (1973, 1982) writings.

the owners (exchange value). Individuals and groups differ on which aspect (use or exchange) is most crucial to their own lives. For some, places represent residence or production site; for others, places represent a commodity for buying, selling, or renting to somebody else. The sharpest contrast (and the most important in this book) is between residents, who use place to satisfy essential needs of life, and entrepreneurs, who strive for financial return, ordinarily achieved by intensifying the use to which their property is put.

The pursuit of exchange values in the city does not *necessarily* result in the maximization of use values for others. Indeed, the simultaneous push for both goals is inherently contradictory and a continuing source of tension, conflict, and irrational settlements.[2] This book explores the conflict between use and exchange values in cities, enumerates and examines the forms of this contradiction, and analyzes how it is ordinarily managed. In our view, this conflict closely determines the shape of the city, the distribution of people, and the way they live together. Similarly, in light of this tension we can better understand the political dynamics of cities and regions and discover how inequalities in and between places—a stratification of place as well as of individuals and groups—are established and maintained.

This method of analysis is particularly appropriate to the urban system in the United States, a country that is unusual, even among Western industrial societies, in the extent to which places are the sites of struggles over use and exchange goals. The United States, as Harvey (1982:346) observes, "is the one country in which land, from the very beginning, was treated in a manner that came closest to that dictated by purely capitalistic considerations." The chronic protests of entrepreneurs notwithstanding, the numerous layers of the American government do relatively little to interfere with the commercial manipulation of land and buildings. This extreme commodification of place touches the lives of all and influences virtually every cultural, economic, and political institution that operates on the urban scene.

2. Unlike traditional geographers who blandly treat "locational conflicts" as essentially technical difficulties, Cox (1981), like ourselves, traces them to a "commodification" of the communal living space, which pits residents against property entrepreneurs over issues of land development and finance.

There is another distinguishing characteristic of the U.S. market environment. Local officials have extensive authority and fiscal responsibility for land use, revenues, and levels of urban services. This autonomy together with the enforced self-sufficiency of localities raises the stakes for an individual "choosing" a place to live or invest in, as well as what rides on local decision making. Life chances of all sorts, including the ability to make money from property, are significantly determined by what goes on at the local level. The tools of place manipulation are within reach (or at least appear to be), and this motivates individuals and groups to pursue their interests at the local level, particularly by influencing local government. The ensuing conflict between those seeking gain from exchange values and those from use values is by no means a symmetrical one, for differently equipped contenders mobilize their individual, organizational, and class resources on behalf of place-related goals. The ability to manipulate place successfully, including altering the standing of one place compared to that of another, is linked to an individual's location in the stratification system generally. The two systems of stratification (place and individual) thus penetrate one another.

Although these conditions make U.S. cities an appropriate focus for a study of the social nature of markets in land and buildings, our analysis applies to other societies to the degree that they approximate the U.S. situation of private real estate markets and local government autonomy. Virtually all market societies bear some resemblance to the U.S. case, but all also vary in ways that may make our conclusions fit only more or less closely. Nevertheless, we offer the basic hypothesis that all capitalist places are the creations of activists who push hard to alter how markets function, how prices are set, and how lives are affected. Our present goal is to learn how this is done in the United States, specifying the roles various social groups and institutions play.

In making this our central urban question, we draw upon much previous research and analysis from diverse intellectual traditions. We rely heavily upon the steady stream of recent advances in neo-Marxian political economy (from sociologists, economists, geographers, political scientists, and planners) but extensively use more traditional materials in human ecology and community studies as well. We do not conceive of this book as either a summary or a synthesis, although there are elements of both. Rather, we use what we need from a number of traditions to explain the city as a meeting ground of use and exchange values. In making the case for an interest-driven social construction of cities, our aim is not to negate the results of other approaches but to draw upon them as the basis for a new way of conducting an urban sociology.

In the remainder of this chapter, we clarify how our approach differs from the two main traditions that have influenced our thinking. We then present the substance of our argument and indicate how we will provide, chapter by chapter, evidence for and elaboration of our central argument.

Human Ecology and Its Successors

The centrality of markets and the assumption of a free market system have been major elements in the reasoning of urban social science since it first began (Thomlinson, 1969:129), although this is usually not explicitly acknowledged. As sociologists, we are most familiar with the Chicago school of human ecology, a school of thought so deeply immersed in free market reasoning that its practitioners seem not to have been aware that there was even an alternate approach. Perhaps because of this reliance on a closed set of market assumptions, the human ecology school maintained a theoretical consistency enjoyed by few other schools within social science. This distinctive perspective has been expertly exploited over several generations, yielding hundreds of studies, theoretical refinements, and policy recommendations. Most important, and the precedent we strive to emulate in this book, the Chicago school of human ecology actually possessed a "real object" (Castells, 1976:73) and a research strategy that distinguished it from other social science approaches.

In human ecology, spatial relations are the analytical basis for understanding urban systems, including the physical shape of cities, relations among people, and economic and social relations between urban areas. Regardless of the degree to which this spatial emphasis caused so much to be left "behind in the dust" (Michelson, 1976:3), the ecology school did impose a worthwhile discipline on the topic. Within the human ecology framework, urban sociology cannot be expanded to the study of all phenomena found in the city (which is virtually all phenomena). Human ecology provided a theory, a focus on the subject matter, and an agenda for ordering research priorities.

The Chicago ecologists explained urban development through a "biotic" determinism. Like all other living things, human beings must first find a spatial niche in the larger habitat. This gives rise to a struggle, benignly competitive in the ecologists' formulation, in which each type of land user ends up in the location to which the user is best adapted. In a social Darwinism of space, the geographical allocation of human types maximizes efficiency for the community as a whole. The biggest bank naturally gains access to a site in the center of town because that's the point from which it can most efficiently serve its customers, who are located everywhere around it. An auto repair garage is appropriately displaced to a less crucial spot on the periphery. The bank and garage are not at war with one another, but are linked through symbiotic competition. Just as the mighty redwood tree does not wantonly "exploit" the ferns that live in the shade it provides, the dominant and less dominant within the human ecological community are mutually adaptive, contributing to the sustenance of the total habitat (see Hawley, 1950:66–68). Each subarea takes on its own character stemming from the kind of role (for example, banking center or rooming house district) it best plays.

In contrast to other species whose behaviors are genetically fixed, human beings have an equilibrating force in the property market and its price system. Although the ecological theorists did not make detailed statements about their market assumptions, their formulations necessarily assume free competition for space among users, resolved according to the relative desirability of particular locations and the buying power of competing land users. The "supplies" consist of land and buildings, which entrepreneurs add to the market in proportion to consumers' demand. Both buyers and sellers are autonomous individuals: Property entrepreneurs try to satisfy space needs of consumers, and consumers "vote" their preferences by choosing among products as their taste dictates, always free to substitute one product for another if price, quality, or utility should change. In good market fashion, buyers use their money to bid up the price of the most useful properties, which, because of their high cost, then go to the "fittest" of consumers.

We thus end up in the ecological perspective with a "hidden hand" that secures the greatest good for the greatest number as a natural outcome of the market mechanism. In the world of human beings, money reflects fitness for dominance and provides the access to a given niche; price reflects the inherent desirability of a particular piece of property to those who can put it to the "best" use. High prices "signal" producers to mark out new land and create buildings to meet additional needs; consumers follow the same signals in determining where to live or set up shop. The market, in a biological metaphor, shapes the urban landscape and, because of the social adaptations it demands, determines the relations of people within the city.

The result is an optimal ordering of human settlement, in which the only real interests are the shared ones of keeping the market system functioning smoothly. Inequality is inevitable, but benign. In Park's words (1952:161), "the process results in the regulation of numbers, the distribution of vocations, putting every individual and every race into the particular niche where it will meet the least competition and contribute most to the life of the community." For the prominent ecologist Amos Hawley, inequality among places is even more explicitly construed as a natural consequence of differentiation. "A hierarchy of power relations emerges among differentiated (geographic) units . . . inequality is an inevitable accompaniment of functional differentiation. Certain functions are by their nature more influential than others; they are strategically placed in the division of labor and thus impinge directly upon a larger number of other functions . . . functional differentiation necessitates a (geographic) centralization of control" (Hawley, 1950:221).

Like differences within cities, differences between cities are based on a functional symbiosis that distributes growth and development across nations and world regions (Bogue, 1951, 1971; Duncan et al., 1960). Cities thus grow because they are able to make a positive contribution in the larger system of cities. Successful cities have special advantages like a deep water port (New York City) or a centrality and therefore easy access to markets and raw materials (Chicago). New York thus becomes the U.S. center of world trade, Chicago the meatpacking capital of America. Extensive lists of such attributes, primarily physical advantages, are used to claim ecological superiority and to explain the consequent urban growth (see White and Foscue, 1964).

Dominance both within and between places thus follows necessarily from the inherent differences among places and sustains efficiency of the system, an efficiency that follows more or less automatically. Hawley relegates politics to the role of maintaining the market mechanism.[3] As Mingione (1981:64) remarks on ecologists generally, they avoid "any connection between urban social structures and the general class structure of society, and between the urbanization process and the capital accumulation process."[4] There is nothing essentially problematic in the view that, as Park and Burgess (1921:712) put it, "the modern city . . . is primarily a convenience of commerce and it owes its existence to the marketplace around which it sprang up."[5]

Besides their impact within sociology, the basic precepts of the Chicago school of human ecology live on in other fields. The Chicago school had been stimulated by, and helped to foster, complementary intellectual programs in urban economics and urban geography.[6] Indeed, unencumbered by the constraints imposed by close observation of the real behavior of human beings, these spe-

3. On this point see the criticisms made by Alihan (1938), Hollingshead (1947), and Firey (1945). Zorbaugh ([1926] 1961) specifically discounted the sociological relevance of what he called administrative areas. Not all the Chicago ecologists excluded political factors. McKenzie ([1926] 1961), in fact, counted "political and administrative measures" among the "ecological factors" that shape the spatial relations among persons. Elsewhere McKenzie (1933:158–70) explicitly considered the competition among cities for favorable positions in an increasingly interdependent system of cities and such phenomena as local boosterism and conflicts over federal tax and expenditure policies. Yet even McKenzie was primarily interested in the economic forces leading toward system integration, seeing political competition as a subsidiary phenomenon. As a rule, human ecologists have failed to see geopolitical units as representing vested interests.

4. In Mingione's formulation (1981:21), "a) territory is a map of social relations of production because it is fundamental to all those relationships; b) territory is itself a means of production c) territory is a consumer good in short supply."

5. Maureen Jung (1983) pointed out this passage.

6. There is the pioneering work of von Thunen (1826) and Christaller (1933), through the more modern formulations of Alonso (1964) and Muth (1969). Such doctrines as central place theory, rank-size rules, the self-driven dynamics of agglomeration economies, the bid-rent curve, and the hierarchy of urban places share the free market economic determinism implicit in the ecological model.

cialties could go on to achieve especially impressive technical refinement and logical consistency. They retain, indeed reify, a vision of place as market-ordered space, to which human activity
responds.

Beyond the assumption that humans are individualistic strivers,
scholars in these fields have no interest in either entrepreneurs or
place users as social actors. Entrepreneurs merely compete with
one another to provide place products, the price of which is determined by buyers seeking to maximize their own individual efficiencies. Price itself is analytically interesting only because it indicates an equilibrium outcome; price measures real value of one
place compared to another and is a handy *reflection* of the efficiencies of location. By reading the price of parcels, one gains the
crucial information of the urban social system.

Many social scientists have not accepted such assumptions,
whether expressed in the economists' terminology we have just
used or in the biotic language of the ecologists. A minority of
economists—"institutional economists"—have insisted that social organization routinely interferes with market functioning and
must be treated as an empirical problem (Clawson, 1972). Many
sociologists, even those with close ties to the ecologists, wince at
the determinism that excludes human volition, cultural folkways,
and political activities as real factors in human affairs (see Alihan,
1938). Much work has been done in urban sociology, particularly
"community studies," with little or no reference to the ecological
framework.

Indeed, the shortcomings of the ecology school seem to have
given sociologists license to study almost anything taking place in
the city and to call it urban sociology. After dismissing the spatial
determinism and market assumptions of the ecologists, these sociologists have offered no clear alternative for an analytical discipline. As long as it had a city address, the urban research topic
could be poor families or rich ones, a halfway house or a dance
hall. Subjects like juvenile delinquency, poverty, or mental illness
were all "urban." In our terminology, there was anecdotal preoc-
cupation with the struggle *among* those striving for use values,
largely without systematic attention to the exchange value context. To be sure, there were certain recurrent themes (like whether
or not urban conditions "depersonalize" human interaction) to be

tested in a hundred different places at a hundred different times (see Hauser, 1967; Fischer, 1984:25–28 passim). But these were, at best, hypotheses within a topic, not the boundary of a field or the basis for an intellectual agenda. In the 1960s, when a new era of political reform demanded an urban studies "relevant" to the "urban crisis," virtually any question having to do with race, ethnicity, social class, deprivation, or human handicap was subsumed by the fashionable field of urban studies.

Our goal is to avoid this topical wandering, even while acknowledging that people and their institutions do "count." We can do this by doing more than noticing that the market-driven schools like ecology have "left out" human culture. The real flaw of such schools is that they ignore that markets themselves are the result of cultures; markets are bound up with human interests in wealth, power, and affection. Markets *work through* such interests and the institutions that are derived from and sustain them. These human forces *organize* how markets will work, what prices will be, as well as the behavioral response to prices.

People draw upon their emotional and social resources to build lives and develop entrepreneurial schemes around the opportunities available to them in a particular place. In brief, *price is sociological* and sociology is needed to analyze its determination as well as its consequence. By showing, in effect, how social factors shape prices of places and humans' response to those prices, we can understand the physical and social shape of cities. We will continue to study land "markets," retaining thereby the "real object" of the ecologists, but we will throw out the limiting and untenable assumptions about how those markets operate. Whereas the key behavioral assumption of economist thinking is that people are inherently individualistic with aggregate efficiency following as a result, our behavioral assumption is that people tend, in their market behavior as everywhere else, toward coalition and organization. It is the efficiency of results that is open and problematic.

Put still another way, we see places as *vital* units, not goods on a rack. Both property entrepreneurs and residents make great efforts, often organized ones, to guarantee that various kinds of production and consumption occur in one place and that other activities occur in another place. Among the consequences of these efforts are changes in prices, which then lead to still more social effects in other realms. Geographical communities are not mere containers of activities, some of which happen to have price results or respond to price cues. Rather, community is accomplished through concrete, practical activities of individuals (see Romes, forthcoming), who, regardless of where they live, work, or invest, see place as the vehicle for meeting significant needs. In the prescient words of William Form (1954:317), there is active manipulation of place itself through "the institutional pressures which maintain the ecological order."

The Marxian Approach to the City

Marx gave relatively little attention to space as an analytical problem (Qadeer, 1981:176) and treated the owners of real estate as an essentially reactionary residue of a disappearing feudal order. Marx appears, in his writing, to be "extraordinarily reluctant to admit of any positive role for the landlord under capitalism" (Harvey, 1982:331). Contemporary Marxian scholars have thus applied the more general Marxian framework to urban issues, using the productive system—the accumulation process—as their primary explanatory apparatus. Thus, in throwing out the economistic assumptions of optimizing markets, the neo-Marxians have tended toward their own set of limiting assumptions. Whereas for the ecologists the city results from a happy market equilibrium, for the Marxians it is a dismal consequence of the logic of capital accumulation. In the ecological formulation, urban people are little more than various species of land users; for the Marxians residents are "labor" whose urban role is to be "reproduced" as a factor of production. Whatever exists in the urban realm, as in any other, must be there because it serves the exploitation of workers by capitalists. Under such reasoning, for example, suburbia developed merely to provide capital with a new realm in which to invest and to stimulate additional demand for consumer goods. This verges on a Marxian version of functionalism, a "fudging" (Giddens, 1984a) that avoids working through how human activities actually give social structures their reality.

David Harvey, the most important of the Marxian urban scholars and the author of much work that has inspired our own, has sometimes generalized in ways that would seem to cut off a great deal of useful thinking and research. Harvey writes (1976:289, as quoted in Domhoff, forthcoming):

> Conflicts in the living space are, we can conclude, reflections of the underlying tension between capital and labor. Appropriators and the construction faction mediate the forms of conflict—they stand between capital and labor and thereby shield the real source of tension from view. The surface appearance of conflicts around the built environment—the struggles against the landlord or against urban renewal—conceals a hidden essence that is *nothing more* [our emphasis] than the struggle between capital and labor.

Similarly, another important Marxian writer, Richard Walker (1981:385), even as he discusses use values, defines the problem as a need to understand how the city is "constructed and continually reconstituted to assure the reproduction of capital (accumulation) and capitalist social relations (holding class struggle in check)."

The topics of an urban sociology come dangerously close to merging with Marxian political economy, generally, and the analytical exercises become as predictable as those carried out by economist market theorists.[7] Once again, the "real object" of an urban sociology may be lost as analysis of all phenomena fixes on the accumulation process. The only actors who matter, if any actors matter at all, are the corporate capitalists, whose control of the means of production appears to make them, for all practical purposes, invincible.

Much of our work tries to show *how* human activism is a force in cities. We strive to follow a more recent dictum of David Harvey in which, though rejecting the ecologists' treatment of "geometric properties of spatial patterns as fundamental," he ac-

---

7. The parallel between ecological and Marxist thinking was acknowledged by Castells, who argued in *The Urban Question* that

the results obtained by ecology have more value for the establishing of a theory of space than a mass of sociocultural correlations, for they reflect this primary determination by the productive forces and the relations of production that stem from them (Castells, 1979:122–23).

knowledges the "opposite danger" of seeing "spatial organization as a mere reflection of the processes of accumulation and class reproduction." We also try to "steer a middle course" and "view location as a fundamental material attribute of human activity but recognize that location is socially produced" (Harvey, 1982:374; see also Duncan, 1961).[8]

To carry out this effort, we give primary attention to the strategies, schemes, and needs of human agents and their institutions at the local level. People dreaming, planning, and organizing themselves to make money from property are the agents through which accumulation does its work at the level of the urban place. Social groups that push against these manipulations embody human strivings for affection, community, and sheer physical survival. The boundaries of our urban sociology are drawn around the meeting place (geographical and analytical) of these two struggles.

Our focus on parochial actors is not meant to slight the obviously crucial linkages between these local urban phenomena, on the one hand, and cosmopolitan political and economic forces, on the other.[9] But for the sake of manageability, our urban sociology must focus on the local manifestations of those linkages. Then, however, analysis should work "outward" toward macro concerns of world systems theorists, as well as "inward" toward micro psychic understandings, since both feed into, and are shaped by, activities at the land-use nexus. Our focal point is always the meeting of use and exchange values on the urban ground, which then directs how the inward and outward investigations should proceed.

8. Our view closely corresponds to Storper and Walker's (1983) conception of "structural realism." A model of employment, in their terms, "involves both underlying 'structural' relations and their logic, of which the human actors are largely unaware, and human agency and contingent circumstances. . . . Together, structures and agency/contingency generate the actual events of everyday life. Such a conception necessarily includes the flow of history, indeterminate (nonpredictable) outcomes, and contradictory outcomes, including those so severe as to threaten the reproduction of either the actors or the social system itself." This approach is akin to Giddens's (1984b) conception of "structuration" as a call to end the dualism in which social structure and human action are juxtaposed as different "things."

9. Thus we cannot abide the happy populism that seems to characterize Castells's (1983) recent work because it seems oblivious to the structures through which social action receives its challenges (see Molotch, 1984).

The Building of Cities

The chapters that follow are an effort to construct a sociology of cities on the basis of a sociology of urban property relations. Chapter 2 presents our perspective on the markets of places, emphasizing the ways in which the sociological qualities of real estate make conventional market reasoning especially inappropriate for understanding how social relations are ordered around it. We identify people and organizations with interests in places and how those interests affect use and exchange values. We emphasize the ongoing effort of place entrepreneurs to increase local rents by attracting investment to their sites, regardless of the effects this may have on urban residents. We argue that these strivings for exchange value create a competition among place entrepreneurs to meet the preferences of capital investors. This is our way of showing how local actors link parochial settings with cosmopolitan interests, making places safe for development. It is a system, we indicate, that stratifies places according to the ease with which they can attract capital—a stratification that then alters the life chances of local individuals and groups. The remainder of the book is devoted to more detailed and empirically based elaborations of these themes.

In chapter 3 we argue that the pursuit of exchange values so permeates the life of localities that cities become organized as enterprises devoted to the increase of aggregate rent levels through the intensification of land use. The city becomes, in effect, a "growth machine." The growth ethic pervades virtually all aspects of local life, including the political system, the agenda for economic development, and even cultural organizations like baseball teams and museums. Moving beyond previous analyses (Molotch, 1967, 1976, 1979), we argue that these growth machines are historical, dating from frontier America, but take different forms and have different impacts depending upon time and context. Although growth is often portrayed as beneficial to all residents of all places, in reality the advantages and disadvantages of growth are unevenly distributed. The nature of the growth machine, including its tactics, organization, and effects on local populations, has been little investigated by students of community power, and we therefore sketch a picture of growth machines in action.

How neighborhood life is affected by and in turn affects the growth system is analyzed in chapter 4. Neighborhood stability, we argue, is dependent on an area's strategic utility to the growth machine apparatus. Neighborhoods whose obliteration would better serve growth goals are subject to the strongest pressure; unless their residents and organizations are high enough in the hierarchies of power to resist, neighborhoods are sacrificed to the growth goal. Such neighborhood attributes as the mode of interpersonal supports, the presence or absence of an indigenous business class, and race and racism also help shape specific outcomes.

In chapter 5 we evaluate the ways government, at various levels, has intervened in the distribution of use and exchange values. In contrast to the use value rhetoric that regularly cloaks government policy making, the policies themselves routinely bolster exchange gains for the powerful. In zoning, planning, environmental protection, and, more broadly, national urban policies, the overall thrust of urban programs has been to bolster development and rents, and rarely to enhance use values. Even in the case of suburban local government, often portrayed as the bastion of "local control," the development process is dominated by the search for rent and profit with the very creation of suburbs guided by such goals. The result is a patchwork of governmental jurisdictions that appears to reflect urban chaos, but actually *organizes* inequalities among jurisdictions and their residents.

New tensions are emerging in the growth machine system, and in chapter 6 we investigate these and other signs that the well-worked-out mechanisms for integrating residents, entrepreneurs, and capital may be faltering. In particular, instances of use value revolt, primarily in the form of environmental movements, are potential threats to rents and capital mobility. At the same time, new modes of linking locality to the needs of capital seem to be emerging, such as a tendency for corporate officials to participate more directly in both the real estate business and local politics.

Finally, in chapter 7 we describe changes in the macroeconomic system that are increasingly impinging upon localities, including upon the struggles for use and exchange values going on within them. New sorts of cities, distinguished by their specialized role in the international economic system, are giving rise to distinctive relations among their component social groups. As cities are increasingly altered by forces outside local boundaries, there are new challenges for residents straining to gain a degree of control over local processes of development. We argue that neighborhood parochialism will have to be supplanted by a broader vision of how the *system* of places works, and how intelligent action in one place can complement (but not necessarily replicate) actions in others.

These are our themes and their order of presentation. To the extent possible, we have tried to muster empirical evidence for our points, sometimes utilizing illustrative detail and in other instances relying on more fully developed research programs. Because we try to trace an argument through analytical levels and in a way that makes sense overall, our evidence is not always as deep or as complete as we would have liked. Our way of formulating urban problems has not been widely followed among social scientists and for that reason we have had to rely upon research materials generated by those with agendas different from our own. But in the holes and troughs in our evidentiary base, there is an opportunity for new work, by ourselves and by others as well.

Although we are seldom explicit about it, we are also describing a program for the American community, comparable to more frequently pronounced national strategies on such issues as defense, economic development, and industrial policy. Local communities are both the site of people's life gratifications and the only arena in which most citizens can take any meaningful action. We hope that the ideas and evidence contained in this book can help, however indirectly, to clarify how and why localities matter, and embolden people to take more informed and effective actions on behalf of the lives they collectively lead.

2

Places as Commodities

For us, as for many of our intellectual predecessors, the market in land and buildings orders urban phenomena and determines what city life can be. This means we must show how real estate markets actually work and how their operations fail to meet the neoclassical economists' assumptions. In short, we will find the substance of urban phenomena in the actual operations of markets. Our goal is to identify the specific processes, the *sociological* processes, through which the pursuit of use and exchange values fixes property prices, responds to prices, and in so doing determines land uses and the distribution of fortunes. Since economic sociology is still without a clear analytical foundation (Stinchcombe, 1983:6), we must begin our work in this chapter by laying a conceptual basis for the empirical descriptions that will be presented later.

Special Use Values

People use place in ways contrary to the neoclassical assumptions of how commodities are purchased and consumed. We do not dispose of place after it has been bought and used. Places have a certain *preciousness* for their users that is not part of the conventional concept of a commodity. A crucial initial difference is that place is indispensable; all human activity must occur somewhere. Individuals cannot do without place by substituting another product. They can, of course, do with less place and less desirable place, but they cannot do without place altogether.

Even when compared to other indispensable commodities—food, for example—place is still idiosyncratic. The use of a particular place creates and sustains access to additional use values. One's home in a particular place, for example, provides access to school, friends, work place, and shops. Changing homes disrupts connections to these other places and their related values as well. Place is thus not a discrete element, like a toy or even food; the precise conditions of its use determine how other elements, including other commodities, will be used. Cox (1981:433) speaks of "home" as a vested interest "spilling out of the individual household and its dwelling and projecting itself onto neighbors, streets, local businesses, schools and other institutions." Any individual residential location connects people to a range of complementary persons, organizations, and physical resources.[1]

The stakes involved in the relationship to place can be high, reflecting all manner of material, spiritual, and psychological connections to land and buildings. Places represent "the focusing of experiences and intentions onto particular settings . . . full with meanings, with real objects, and with ongoing activities" (Relph, 1976:141). Numerous scholars—from Anderson (1976) to Whyte (1943)—have shown that given places achieve significance beyond the more casual relations people have to other commodities. Although the connection to place can vary in intensity for different class, age, gender, and ethnic groups, individual relationships to place are often characterized by intense feelings and commitments appropriate to long-term and multifaceted social and material attachments.

This special intensity creates an asymmetrical market relation between buyers and sellers. People pay what the landlord demands, not because the housing unit is worth it, but because the property is held to have idiosyncratic locational benefits. Access to resources like friends, jobs, and schools is so important that residents (as continuous consumers-buyers) are willing to resort

1. These linkages are analogous to the mutually reinforcing advantages that businesses gain from *their* special relations to complementary land uses—"agglomeration economies." Roger Friedland drew this analogy from an earlier draft of this chapter.

to all sorts of "extramarket" mechanisms to fight for their right to keep locational relations intact. They organize, protest, use violence, and seek political regulation. They strive not just for tenure in a given home but for stability in the surrounding neighborhood as well.

Location establishes a special collective interest among individuals. People who have "bought" into the same neighborhood share a quality of public services (garbage pickup, police behavior); through these forms of "collective consumption" (Castells, 1983), residents have a common stake in the area's future. Residents also share the same fate when natural disasters such as floods and hurricanes threaten and when institutions alter the local landscape by creating highways, parks, or toxic dumps. Individuals are not only mutually dependent on what goes on inside a neighborhood (including "compositional effects"); they are affected by what goes on *outside* it as well. The standing of a neighborhood vis-à-vis other neighborhoods creates conditions that its residents experience in common. Each place has a particular political or economic standing vis-à-vis other places that affects the quality of life and opportunities available to those who live within its boundaries. A neighborhood with a critical voting bloc (for example, Chicago's Irish wards in the 1930s) may generate high levels of public services or large numbers of patronage jobs for its working-class residents, thereby aiding their well-being. A rich neighborhood can protect its residents' life styles from external threats (sewer plants, public housing) in a way that transcends personal resources, even those typically associated with the affluent. The community in itself can be a local force.

Neighborhoods organize life chances in the same sense as do the more familiar dimensions of class and caste. Giddens (1973:108–10) notes the importance of spatial segregation as a "proximate factor of class structuration . . . an aspect of consumption rather than production which acts to reinforce the separations" produced by unequal market capacity. Richard Peet emphasizes that "each social group operates within a typical daily 'prism,' which for the disadvantaged closes into a 'prison of space and resources.' . . . Deficiencies in the environment—limitations on mobility and the density and quality of social resources—must clearly limit an individual's potential" (Peet, 1975:484–85, cited in Dear, 1981). Like class and status groupings, and even more than many other associations, places create "communities of fate" (Stinchcombe, 1965:181). Thus we must consider the stratification of places along with the stratification of individuals in order to understand the distribution of life chances. People's sense of these dynamics, perceived as the relative "standing" of their neighborhood, gives them some of their spiritual or sentimental stake in place—thus further distinguishing home from other, less life-significant, commodities.

Contrary to much academic debate on the subject, we hold that the material use of place cannot be separated from psychological use; the daily round that makes physical survival possible takes on emotional meanings through that very capacity to fulfill life's crucial goals. The material and psychic rewards thus combine to create a feeling of "community." Much of residents' striving as members of community organizations or just as responsible neighbors represents an effort to preserve and enhance their networks of sustenance. Appreciation of neighborhood resources, so varied and diffusely experienced, gives rise to "sentiment." *Sentiment* is the inadequately articulated sense that a particular place uniquely fulfills a complex set of needs. When we speak of residents' use values, we imply fulfillment of all these needs, material and non-material.

Homeownership gives some residents exchange value interests along with use value goals. Their houses are the basis of a lifetime wealth strategy (Perin, 1977). For those who pay rent to landlords, use values are the only values at issue. Owners and tenants can thus sometimes have divergent interests. When rising property values portend neighborhood transformation, tenants and owners may adopt different community roles (see chapter 4); but ordinarily, the exchange interests of owners are not sufficiently significant to divide them from other residents.

Although residents are the foremost example of people who pursue use values through property, others also pursue use values through property, and these people also operate in a manner different from what the market model would imply. Retailers, for example, depend on geographical context and often develop enduring connections to a given location. Proximity to customers can be their most important locational resource. Moreover, their prospects are affected by some of the same factors important to residents: physical amenities, community services, and a social network supporting the makeup of the neighborhood, including the shops. A retailer may depend not only on a substantial number of people nearby but on a certain type of residential enclave. A kosher butcher needs Jews; an exclusive boutique needs the trendy rich. Thus merchants have an ongoing stake in a particular social makeup of place. Retailers, like residents, may or may not welcome nearby development, which could mean new competitors as well as an expanded market. These indeterminacies cause retailers, as a group, to have mixed interests; they may serve an intermediate social role in conflicts that arise between residents and place entrepreneurs. Their role is not easily predictable, however, since it is contingent on the specific form of retailing and whether or not the present residential population will enhance or inhibit future profit making (see chapter 4). Retailers may also own extensive property themselves, further complicating their interests in a neighborhood.

Producers of goods, or capitalists in our terminology, derive their own use values from place. Whatever the basis for corporate locational decisions (conventionally described as maximizing access to raw materials, markets, and labor), firms do not, in principle, depend on intensification of adjacent land for the success of their own operations. They may benefit from a nearby assortment of business support services that will deliver "agglomeration economies," but there is no inherent need for land-use intensification per se. Of course, such firms can also simultaneously own land and buildings; and this ownership may eventually override other considerations. Corporations principally involved in productive enterprise may later find their real estate holdings their greatest asset. At that point their interest shifts from the use values of a place to its exchange value, once again blurring the neatness of our distinctions (see chapter 6 for a case description).

In contrast to our extensive information about residents (based on hundreds of ethnographies and mountains of survey results), we know little about corporations' attachments to place. There is substantial research on the business image of various places and on factors considered important by executives when choosing a site. But the study of "corporate culture" has only recently gained much attention and has rarely included an analysis of that culture in relationship to specific places (but see Galaskiewicz, 1985). We have legends about the loyalty of plutocrats to a particular place: John D. Rockefeller's Midwest boosterism, for example, was supposedly behind his creation of the University of Chicago (Storr, 1966). But we know little about how such factors enter into decision making, how sentiment and "culture" might coexist with material strategies to sustain allegiance to particular places. We know that "other factors" besides dollar efficiency do indeed matter (executives' social networks may determine the location of new plant sites), but research on such topics is still in an early, although promising, stage (see Gordon, 1976; Pred, 1976, 1977, 1980; Walker, 1981).

We can therefore proceed only tentatively, but we make three general observations about capitalists' attachments to place. First, compared to those of residents, the satisfaction that capitalists derive from place is less diffuse. Their paramount interest is the profitability of their operations; concerns with place turn heavily on how well land and buildings serve that overarching goal. Second, capitalists, at least compared to residents, have greater opportunity to move to another place should conditions in one place cease to be appropriate. Free of at least some of the constraints holding residents, such as sentimental ties to family and access to schools and jobs, corporations can exit more easily. Firms that have not committed major facilities to a given location (sunk costs) are particularly mobile. Finally, capitalists' use of place is less fragile than that of residents. Capital can adapt to changes such as noise, odor, and ethnic succession, whereas the effect of such change on residents is more immediate and more serious. Of course, some forms of capital do have specific locational needs, but these are ordinarily upset only by the most extreme changes (for example, the closing of a port or the destruction of a communication line).

Although residents vary in their attachment to a neighborhood (Janowitz, 1951), capitalists' attachment to place is much weaker overall. This adds to the difficulties of those, like government officials or neighborhood leaders, who might try to control them. At the other extreme are residents like the elderly poor who are permanently and intensely tied to the place they use. The most vulnerable participants in place markets are those with the fewest alternatives.

Special Exchange Values

Exchange values from place appear as "rent." We use the term broadly to include outright purchase expenditures as well as payments that home buyers or tenants make to landlords, realtors, mortgage lenders, real estate lawyers, title companies, and so forth. As with use values, people pursue exchange values in ways that differ from the manner in which they create other commodities. Suppliers cannot "produce" places in the usual sense of the term. All places consist, at least in part, of land, which "is only another name for nature, which is not produced by man" (Polanyi, 1944:72) and obviously not produced for sale in a market. The quantity is fixed. It is not, says Harvey (1982:357), "the product of labour." This makes the commodity description of land, in Marx's word, "fictitious"; Storper and Walker (1983:43) describe land, like labor, as a "pseudocommodity." Even conventional economists acknowledge that "the urban land market is a curious one" (Dowall, 1984:111).

Place as Monopoly

Perhaps the fundamental "curiosity" is that land markets are inherently monopolistic, providing owners, as a class, with complete control over the total commodity supply. There can be no additional entrepreneurs or any new product. The individual owner also has a monopoly over a subsection of the marketplace. Every parcel of land is unique in the idiosyncratic access it provides to other parcels and uses, and this quality underscores the specialness of property as a commodity. Unlike widgets or Ford Pintos, more of the same product cannot be added as market demand grows. Instead the owner of a particular parcel controls all access to it and its given set of spatial relations. In setting prices and other conditions of use, the owner operates with this constraint on competition in mind.

Property prices do go down as well as up, but less because of what entrepreneurs do with their own holdings than because of the changing relations among properties. This dynamic accounts for much of the energy of the urban system as place entrepreneurs strive to increase their rent by revamping the spatial organization of the city. Rent levels are based on the location of a property vis-à-vis other places, on its "particularity" (Losch, 1954:508). In Marxian conceptual terms, entrepreneurs establish the rent according to the "differential" locational advantage of one site over another. Gaining "differential rent"[2] necessarily depends on the fate of other parcels and those who own and use them (see Gaffney, 1961). In economists' language, each property use "spills over" to other parcels and, as part of these "externality effects," crucially determines what every other property will be. The "web of externalities" (Qadeer, 1981:172) affects an entrepreneur's particular holding. When a favorable relationship can be made permanent (for example, by freezing out competitors through restrictive zoning), spatial monopolies that yield even higher rents—"monopoly rents" in the Marxian lexicon—are created. But all property, as Qadeer (1981:172) succinctly states, tends to have a "monopolistic character." This

> makes land relatively impervious to economic laws of supply and demand, and it alters assumptions about the operation of land markets. . . . [The] uniqueness of individual parcels and their monopolistic character arise from situational and contextual factors, and it is not the product of an entrepreneur's inventiveness.

Nevertheless, property owners can and do inventively alter the *content* of their holdings. Sometimes they build higher and more densely, increasing the supply of dwellings, stores, or offices on their land. According to neoclassical thinking, this manner of increase should balance supply and demand, thus making property respond to market pressures as other commodities supposedly do.

2. For discussions of differential rent as well as the other Marxian rent categories, see Walker (1974); Harvey (1982:349–57); and Lamarche (1976).

But new construction has less bearing on market dynamics than such reasoning would imply. New units on the same land can never duplicate previous products; condominiums stacked in a high-rise building are not the same as split-levels surrounded by lawn. Office space on the top floor of a skyscraper is more desirable than the same square footage just one floor lower. Conversely, the advantages of street-level retail space cannot be duplicated on a floor above. Each product, old or new, is different and unique, and each therefore reinforces the monopoly character of property and the resulting price system.

Another curious aspect of the real estate market is its essentially "second-hand" nature (Turner, 1977:39). Buildings and land parcels are sold and resold, rented and rerented. In a typical area, no more than 3 percent of the product for sale or rent consists of new construction (Markusen, 1979:153). Not only land, but even the structures on any piece of land can have infinite (for all practical purposes) lives; neither utility not market price need decrease through continuous use. Indeed, "successive investments . . . can often build upon rather than devalue each other" (Harvey, 1982:356). Moreover, since the amount of "new" property on the market at any given moment is ordinarily only a small part of the total that is for sale, entrepreneurs' decisions to add to this supply by building additional structures will have a much more limited impact on price than would the same decisions with other types of commodities (Markusen, 1979). Indeed, recent studies indicate that U.S. cities with more rapid rates of housing construction have higher, not lower, housing costs, even when demand factors are statistically controlled (Appelbaum and Gilderbloom, 1983). Similarly, relatively high vacancy rates are not associated with lower rent levels (Appelbaum and Gilderbloom, 1983), which suggests that new construction "leads" local markets to a new, higher pricing structure rather than equilibrating a previous one. Given the fixed supply of land and the monopolies over relational advantages, more money entering an area's real estate market not only results in more structures being built but also increases the price of land and, quite plausibly, the rents on previously existing "comparable" buildings. Thus higher investment levels can push the entire price structure upward.

Neoclassical economists have developed models with exquisite precision to show how locational advantages lead to *rent differ-entials* in a city or region. But few social scientists have tried to identify the specific factors that determine aggregate rents or the basic price that *anyone* must pay for the use of place. Marxian theorists have exhaustively treated the exploitation of labor by capital but have given almost no attention to explaining the amount that either labor or capital must pay simply for being somewhere.[3]

All societies have a way to organize rents. From a broad historic and geographic vantage, we know that the proportion of income paid for rent has differed considerably. Elites have forced peasants and workers to produce varying amounts of surplus beyond subsistence; the proportion of that surplus taken for rent has also varied. In most instances householders pay the going rate and adjust their other expenditures accordingly. Whether through tithe, tribute, tax, or mortgage payment, owners exact what the institutional framework allows (see Keyfitz, 1965; Pearson, 1957). In the modern era peasants in some parts of the world give one-half to two-thirds of their crop yields for the right to work their lands (Keyfitz, 1965:278). Even in a rich country like the United States, some residents only subsist (eat and reproduce) after paying like proportions of their incomes for the right to tenancy—rather than the fourth or third now held to be the reasonable standard. There is nothing inevitable about the current rent-wage split. Indeed, periodic regional and historical shifts in the ratio (for example, California's extreme housing inflation in the late 1970s) represent still another face of the use versus exchange struggle on the modern urban scene.

North Americans do not pay tribute to barons and bishops; instead they pay banks and savings institutions, real estate brokers, and landlords. In the modern context, as in the ancient and feudal, the amount of rent is not determined by any balance between supply and demand or by what people can "afford" to pay. Instead price is driven by competitive bidding on a fixed resource by investors who assume that the future price will be greater than the present one. This is the essence of speculation, and any invest-

3. Conceptually, at least, it comes up in the analysis of the Marxian category "absolute rents."

ment that turns on such an envisioned outcome is by our definition speculative. For fictitious commodities like real estate, investment levels are set by anticipated social outcomes, by "expectations" (Dowall, 1984:111) of what other people will do, rather than by more traditional business criteria such as the efficiency of a given firm, the quality of a product, or the cunning of a firm's marketing strategy. And like other objects of speculation (diamonds, Boehm birds, or old masters, for example), the real estate bubble can sometimes burst. But no principle, theoretical or empirical, can explain when this will happen or even if it will happen at all (Thurow, 1985). Meanwhile people *do* pay the price of place as investors' bidding drives up the cost of being somewhere. The "wild" exigencies of social organization (and its anticipated changes) set rent levels; and everyone must deal with what Sir Isaac Newton called, in trying to analyze people's financial speculations, "the madness of human beings" (Thurow, 1985:7).

Omnipresent "Regulation"

Newton's diagnosis of madness is not entirely correct. Investors consider a number of concrete factors that could potentially alter future property prices—and a key one is government activity. Public decisions crucially influence which parcels will have the highest rents as well as the aggregate rent levels for the whole region or society. Rents are made possible in the first place through government stipulations regarding rights and privileges among market participants (for example, deeds, leases, and sales contracts). Without such government "regulation" there could be no exchange of place at all. The State actively sustains the commodity status of land. At present in the United States, the courts forbid government's "taking" of property without just compensation. Legislative and judicial actions preclude a rent control or zoning law that would eliminate a "reasonable return" on investments.

Similarly, building and maintaining urban infrastructures *must* involve government, and such involvement determines market outcomes. Few property entrepreneurs, however shrewd, can do better than the person who owns the alfalfa field next to the plot of land earmarked by the city council for a new jetport. Government activity thus distributes and redistributes rents among owners. Walker (1974) has added to the Marxian lexicon of rent types the category "redistributional rent," referring to the substantial rent increments that come with specific government activity. Indeed, virtually all modern rent is in part redistributed rent.

Such institutional involvement in the use and exchange of places is endemic to human settlement. It does not result, as has often been assumed, from the peculiarly high densities and complex arrangements of modern cities. Nor does it result, as Mollenkopf (1983:216) seems to argue, from the modern proliferation of federal government programs, such as urban renewal, that have mandated new forms of political intervention. The mixing of markets and regulation can be traced at least as far back as the English enclosure laws, which ushered in the industrial revolution, the modern State, and the property commodity. In the New World, regulation was as necessary to form the settlement at Plymouth as it was to make the desert bloom into modern Phoenix. As Polanyi remarks, "Regulation and markets, in effect, grew up together" (1944:68). The form of regulation changes, but not its omnipresence and necessity.

We can now summarize the peculiarities of the place commodity: Just as real estate cannot be consumed privately, it cannot be produced privately. Just as there are limits to users' abilities to substitute alternative commodities, producers cannot add new products to satisfy demand. In fact, because of its durability, place is not really consumed at all, and because of its origin in nature, it is not produced. Both "producers" and "consumers" must inevitably contend with and use extraordinary "extramarket" forces, like government activity and support from neighbors, to gain value from place. Taken together, these characteristics indicate that place products, and their use and distribution, are not a simple reflection of the summed preferences of discrete consumers bidding freely for the wares of autonomous producers. Locational behavior cannot be explained as responses to price "signals" without an awareness of the institutional forces that continuously organize prices and structure people's ability to escape paying them. Both buyers and sellers use nonmarket resources as they pursue their separate urban goals. A given market is their tool or their encumbrance; it is not, as orthodox economics would imply, their guide.

A Social Typology of Entrepreneurs

Place entrepreneurs, the people directly involved in the exchange of places and collection of rents, have the job of trapping human activity at the sites of their pecuniary interests. The special qualities of the real estate commodity distinguish their activities from those of other business operators. Place entrepreneurs are a special group among the privileged: modern urban *rentiers,* somewhat analogous to their feudal landholding predecessors. Not merely a residue of a disappearing social group, as the classic Marxian position would imply, rentiers persist as a dynamic social force.

We identify three types of contemporary place entrepreneurs, each with different social relationships to the place commodity and each generating different kinds of rent; we discuss each entrepreneurial type in turn.

Serendipitous Entrepreneurs

Some rentiers are only very marginally entrepreneurs at all, having become rent collectors by inheriting property or by some other fortuitous circumstance. Thus they derive returns from a product not "made" by anybody, and not even brought under control by any of their own efforts. Or again, the real estate may have been acquired for one purpose (for example, farming) but was found to be more valuable when sold or rented for other uses. The farmer may have worked hard on the land, but the real fortune grew while the farmer slept. Quite often, of course, the farmer is bilked by the more sophisticated operator ("city slicker"), who better understands the nature of changed property values (the Indians' "sale" of Manhattan to the Dutch is an apocryphal case in point). The serendipitous entrepreneur (common in recent years even among ordinary homeowners in some areas) is essentially passive, following the behavior of the classic rentier, who lived off family entitlements.

Active Entrepreneurs

Some individuals seek out the right place to be in the future. These entrepreneurs, who anticipate changing use values from place, speculate on the future of particular spots. Such active entrepreneurs seek rent by gaining control over locations likely to become more strategic over time. They strive to capture differential rents by putting themselves in the path of the development process. This is active speculation, based on predicting development trends (regardless of their source) and gambling on accurate predictions. Once again the needed business talent is special: the entrepreneur needs skill, not in the production of a good or service, but in the estimation of the geographical movements of others, including those who do produce goods and services. Small-scale or medium-scale investors are the prototypical actors; they try to monitor others' investments, using local social networks to learn who is going to do what and where. The more sophisticated among them may also use principles of human ecology or urban economics in their efforts to discern future growth patterns.

Structural Speculators

Some place entrepreneurs do not rely solely on their capacity to estimate future locational trends; they supplement such intelligence by intervening in that future. These entrepreneurs speculate on their ability to change the relationships of a given place to other places—that is, they attempt to determine the patterns through which others will seek use values from place. Like the commodities traders who speak of their market-rigging activities as "creating a situation" (Copetas, 1984), place entrepreneurs seek to alter the conditions that structure the market. Their strategy is to *create* differential rents by influencing the larger arena of decision making that will determine locational advantages. They may attempt, for example, to influence the location of a defense plant, to alter a freeway route, or to encourage government subsidizing of a private business that is likely to move to their property. They lobby for or against specific zoning and general plan designations.

Given the extraordinary price impacts of government actions, structural speculators realistically seek redistributive rents. They may also strive for monopoly rents, again often through the use of government to fix for themselves a unique locational advantage (e.g., monopoly zoning). Like other forms of successful structural speculation, monopoly rents help minimize the risks related to the vagaries of urban development. But it takes substantial skill, resources, and ongoing vigilance to sustain political decisions that preserve a given set of spatial relations.

These three ways of generating material gain from place (serendipitous, active, and structural entrepreneurship) reflect different degrees of intentionality and institutional control, and a range of social consequences. Compared to structural speculators, when serendipitous entrepreneurs acquire their land, they are ignorant of its eventual use and do not envision government authority playing a role; active entrepreneurs represent a middle case. There is also a difference in the degree of parochialism; the serendipitous entrepreneur's habits and fortunes are most closely tied to a specific local parcel, whereas the structural speculator has the most cosmopolitan field of operation. Again, the active entrepreneur falls between these two. Finally, there is also a range of rent types sought. The structural speculator ambitiously strives for monopolistic and redistributive rents, not merely rents that are serendipitous or differential. Precisely because they do understand the social nature of property prices, sophisticated entrepreneurs are driven to the *organizational manipulations* that will boost their returns. Each type of entrepreneurial activity tends to affect different sorts of neighborhoods and to involve distinct kinds of organizational efforts.

Organizing for Exchange and Use

Among the entrepreneurial types, the structural speculators are the most important; their behaviors reverberate through every aspect of the urban scene. People out to structure markets tend not to work in isolation; they work together in organized groups. Let us here consider how the collective efforts to pursue exchange values are carried out; then we shall turn to the larger economic and governmental contexts of such attempts. Finally, we shall discuss how community organization becomes a counter-response on behalf of use value goals.

Growth Machines

Those seeking exchange value often share interests with others who control property in the same block, city, or region. Like residents, entrepreneurs in similar situations also make up communities of fate, and they often get together to help fate along a remunerative path.

Whether the geographical unit of their interest is as small as a neighborhood shopping district or as large as a national region, place entrepreneurs attempt, through collective action and often in alliance with other business people, to create conditions that will intensify future land use in an area. There is an unrelenting search, even in already successful places, for more and more. An apparatus of interlocking progrowth associations and governmental units makes up what Molotch (1976) calls the "growth machine." Growth machine activists are largely free from concern for what goes on within production processes (for example, occupational safety), for the actual use value of the products made locally (for example, cigarettes), or for spillover consequences in the lives of residents (for example, pollution). They tend to oppose any intervention that might regulate development on behalf of use values. They may quarrel among themselves over exactly how rents will be distributed among parcels, over how, that is, they will share the spoils of aggregate growth. But virtually all place entrepreneurs and their growth machine associates, regardless of geographical or social location, easily agree on the issue of growth itself.

They unite behind a doctrine of *value-free development*—the notion that free markets alone should determine land use. In the entrepreneur's view, land-use regulation endangers both society at large and the specific localities favored as production sites. Just as markets in neoclassical reasoning are, in general, the only legitimate mechanisms for choosing *what* is to be produced (with no need for collective evaluation), so markets should also be the invisible hand that determines *where* and *how* production should occur. When the two value-free doctrines are joined at the local level, communities forfeit control over both the content and location of production. Communities do not evaluate a product by its social worth, a machine in terms of its human value (Goodman and Goodman, 1947), a locational decision by its social consequence. Instead they invite capital to make virtually anything—whether buttons or bombs, toasters or tanks—in their own back yards. Aggregate growth is portrayed as a public good; increases in economic activity are believed to help the whole community. Growth, according to this argument, brings jobs, expands the tax base, and pays for urban services. City governments are thus wise to do what they can to attract investors.

Many academic experts also hold this view, even those outside such fields as real estate economics (where developers and professors have notoriously close ties). The prominent political scientist Paul Peterson (1981:20–21) equates the "well-being" of cities with their levels of capital investment because such investment is to the "benefit of all residents." It is, Peterson argues, "in the interest of cities" (as opposed to specific groups within cities) to avidly pursue developmental policies. Peterson equates virtually all capital growth projects (including those that must be publicly subsidized) as net gains—at least on the fiscal front. Otherwise, Peterson (1981:42, 43) implies, why would local officials ever have "judged" them a good idea? In his view small-time political corruption (e.g., hands in the till) is the only source of "economically regressive" policies at the local level; development programs, almost of any sort, have only positive consequences for a city overall. Thus Peterson concludes that problems of the type we raise (the costs of development) "have little theoretical relevance" for the fortunes of places and their people.

Long before academics presented such arguments, local rentiers had them down pat. Modern rentiers have long functioned as intermediaries between the corporate elite and the local citizenry, playing the stabilizing role of a "third tier" (Wallerstein, 1979: 223). For this reason, perhaps, a class that, as Marx said, can find no "morally edifying rationalisation for its continued existence" (Harvey, 1982:359) is nevertheless permitted to persist under capitalism. Rentiers not only perform the "ideological and legitimizing function" for private property generally (Harvey, 1982:360) but also coordinate the needs of corporate elites with the behavior of local government and citizens' groups. Even though rent payments reduce capitalists' profits, rentiers' presence is useful in the accumulation process. Rentiers mute local opposition to capitalists' projects. Any threat to the growth machine apparatus thus endangers the ongoing system through which sites are prepared for capital under more or less ideal conditions.[4]

Contrary to the arguments of such scholars as Peterson, we are certain that local economic growth does not *necessarily* promote the public good. Even in terms of helping the fiscal condition of the city, the long-term consequence of growth can be negative. We find much that is "theoretically relevant" in the regressive effects of development. Development projects that increase the scale of cities and alter their spatial relations inevitably affect the distribution of life chances. When capital moves from one place or economic sector to another, the "action" always has potential for redistributing wealth and changing the allocation of use and exchange values within as well as across places.

In other words, human activities generate costs and benefits, some of which are borne by those who create them (they are "internalized") and some of which are not (they are "externalized"). People who share control of places try to trap growth. They join together in order to shift internal costs of activities to other areas or to others in their own area, and to capture the benefits of those activities, particularly rents, for themselves. This behavior, when replicated across the country, involves exploiting virtually every institution in our political, economic, and cultural systems. Actors from all these spheres participate in a complex "ecology of games" (Long, 1958) sustained by growth elites' struggle for private fortunes through the development process.

Government for Growth

Because of the limited amount of mobile capital, the growth apparatus in each area must compete with that of other areas to attract scarce investment. Coalitions of interest, recruited

---

4. For other conceptions of the "confused and confusing affair" of the analytic status of landed property under capitalism, see Harvey (1982:346, 359–67).

and organized along territorial lines, becoming working cooperative units, even if on other grounds their members have divergent goals. Thus if one form of truly urban conflict is the internal struggle between use and exchange values, a second is the external battle of place elites against one another—the battle of the growth machines. This contest goes on at all geopolitical levels, with competitive systems nested within one another. Owners of a commercial block compete against owners of the next block, but they unite when their business district competes against other business districts in the same city. The owners of all the business districts in one city stand together in competition with other cities.

Sometimes the arenas and units of competition correspond to formal government entities, such as incorporated cities, states, and nations. In other instances the entities are more informal, such as national regions, and only voluntary associations (for example, a local Chamber of Commerce) act on their behalf. These varying degrees of formal authority determine in part the influence of each level on the competitions on the lower tiers. Because the nation-state is the strongest political unit in the modern world, the institutions of this unit ordinarily determine the formal channels of competition of places within the national system. In the international system, where place competition is only loosely regulated by international constraints, capital operates in a different, more open, environment (see chapter 7).

If a given territory has a government corresponding in jurisdiction to the geographical borders of the territory, the elite can mobilize the government to bolster growth goals. When residents' claims on behalf of use values threaten to undermine growth, government can turn back the challenge, either by invoking police power or by distracting dissidents with payoffs (for example, relocation allowances to displaced tenants). Governments can also help coordinate the roles of diverse members of the growth coalition, securing the cooperation of local entrepreneurs in ambitious growth projects and even disciplining those who will not cooperate. Similarly, government can help overcome entrepreneurs' resistance to accommodations with dissenting residents. Growth elites' larger, long-term interests can sometimes be best served by selectively granting concessions to those in opposition, and public authorities are often ideally suited to do this.

Finally, access to a government can help in generating resources from tiers above. From the perspective of a growth coalition, it must have influence not only at the level of daily at-hand operations but also beyond the local level to the higher levels that determine large geographical patterns of public investments, pollution controls, and government procurement spending. Participants in a growth coalition must be concerned with both the substantive decisions made at those higher levels (for example, Will money be allocated for a freeway?) and the procedural questions (for example, Which jurisdiction—the city, county, or state—will make the routing decision?). If local elites have a government unit through which to operate, they have access to publicly paid staffs, consultants, and powers of "home rule" to use against a higher authority. By working through a local government, moreover, the efforts of an elite gain the appearance of a civic campaign waged on behalf of a legal entity and its citizens, rather than of a conspiracy of vested interests. Nevertheless, elites are sometimes better off operating independently, relying on informal mechanisms for influencing others. Optimally, both strategies should be available, to be used according to the issue at hand and conditions of time and place.

The degree of authority found in each level of a system is not static, but rather, as part of the political process, varies according to the struggles among competing interests. For example, rentiers who have good control over local government tend to favor "home rule" when it comes to land-use zoning; environmentalists who think they have a better chance of achieving their goals on a higher tier may strive to enact "state standards" that preempt local decision making. The limits of home rule thus expand and contract (Walker and Heiman, 1981) in response to the power shifts among competing structural speculators, other entrepreneurs, and their use value opponents. The same dynamics also determine the degree to which authority is centralized or dispersed among smaller geographical units. Thus there has been, within the United States and around the globe, a historical seesaw between calls for devolution on the one hand and trends toward centralized institutions on the other (for example, metropolitan authorities, common markets, or world government). These efforts represent strategic manipulations of the sites of decision making in order to influence distributional outcomes among and within places.

Although we obviously have an interest in such issues as government authority, centralization, and fragmentation, our focus means that our treatment of these topics will differ from that in traditional political science. Rather than evaluate which institutional format is more or less efficient, more or less democratic, more or less universalistic, we will examine how jurisdictional entities are purposively enacted and then gradually altered through the struggles over use and exchange. We argue, for example, that the great urban reform movements of this century, which brought us such innovations as the suburban towns and professional land-use planning, owe their existence more to entrepreneurs seeking higher investment returns than to residents trying to build better lives. Indeed, this is true for the way city boundaries were carved out of the hinterland as well as for the administrative roles and land-use functions given to the city. The legal creation and regulation of places have been primarily under the domination of those searching, albeit sometimes in the face of use value counterdemands, for exchange value gains.

Community Organization

Because the competition for growth does not ordinarily work on their behalf, residents often use organization of their own to sustain the places in which they live. Maintenance of "home" in the largest sense of the term motivates people to come together in block clubs, neighborhood groups, and other associations that have place-related use values as at least one of their central concerns. These organizations may take such diverse actions as pressuring the local planning commission to uphold zoning restrictions or blocking the sale of a home to someone who is considered a threat to the neighborhood's "good standing." Community organizations that strive to alter the distribution of exchange values and to influence the kinds of use values that can be gained from place are, for us, "urban" phenomena. Their frequent clash with those striving for higher rents results in urban conflict. This is not simply one of many social stresses played out on the stage of the city, but a distinctive conflict over place values themselves.

The traditional academic literature on the topic tends to equate the "community organization" with progressive social forces generally and to see all such groups as analytically equivalent because they are from the "grass roots" and help "empower" local people. Castells's (1983) recent version of this doctrine treats virtually all neighborhood groups—ethnic clubs, job-training programs, civil rights groups, peace activists, the YMCA, and so forth—as grass-roots, spatially oriented "urban social movements." But many of these movements and organizations are not essentially urban, regardless of their physical location, and it can be very misleading to reduce them to local conflicts over land use (Molotch, 1984). Similarly, there is no justification for treating progressive movements as an urban phenomenon and simply ignoring reactionary ones (Are all reactionary groups "rural"?). Civil rights groups are no more or no less urban than anti–civil rights groups, ethnic associations no more or no less urban than religious cults. Even movements for welfare services, medical care, or other forms of collective consumption may have little to do with the social organization of property and space; hence they may, depending on specific local circumstance, also lie outside our urban purview. Although there may be good reasons to cast the organizational net broadly, doing so undermines efforts to hold fast to an urban analytical object.

Movements found in the city may change their nature over time, in terms of both their specific urban roles and their essential urbanness. Associations formed to oppose development may acquiesce after entrepreneurs and political figures co-opt their leadership. Sometimes community groups move from a concern with place-related use values to management of service delivery (for example, running mental health clinics), which would similarly remove them from our analytical interest. But our category of "urban" is wide enough to embrace social movements that are often excluded because they are not progressive. Even if most urban movements are "liberal" in that they frequently oppose entrepreneurs' schemes, some are racist and reactionary (for example, exclusive suburbs), but they do not therefore cease to be urban.

Just as there are different types of place entrepreneurs, there are different kinds of neighborhoods and neighborhood organizations according to the kinds of challenges they confront and the tools at their disposal. Rich neighborhoods, for example, are better able to protect themselves through "working within the system"; poor neighborhoods are particularly vulnerable to disruptions from the surrounding exchange system.

Residents' organizational efforts are greatly enhanced when their cause is joined by at least a portion of the entreprenurial sector, just as the entrepreneurs' goals are facilitated when residents become part of the development consensus. Efforts to achieve such effective coalitions (see Gamson, 1968) mobilize the full range of instruments of communication, education, and social control. The success or failure of entrepreneurs in their rent competition with other places sometimes depends upon their ability to put a wide array of community units behind them. Similarly, the survival and prosperity of neighborhood organizations may require them to join with at least some of their potential entrepreneurial adversaries. Thus local growth machines may successfully mobilize, through the vehicle of neighborhood organization, the affectional ties of a residential community, and do so on behalf of exchange goals. Conversely, communities of sentiment may conceivably enlist the aid of a segment of land-based entrepreneurs, who may, for examples, conclude that the survival of some "local color" will enhance their new development nearby. Part of the tension of the urban drama consists in this making and unmaking of coalitions among neighborhood and entrepreneurial actors.

Migration

Instead of expending energy on organizing the place they are in, people can move their residence or their investments. Indeed, commentators like to describe urban life as fast paced and fluid. But a more useful description is that the basic ingredients of urban existence—money, labor, and investments in factories and land—move about with different degrees of ease and speed. Holland (1975) has defined a continuum of investment "velocities" that formalizes some of the variations. "Portfolio" investments—assets in the form of money, stocks, and other financial forms—are the most mobile. Owners can transfer such wealth almost instantaneously across city, state, and, increasingly, national boundaries. The growing internationalization of capital (in the form of cross-national finance, marketing, and production arrangements) keeps boosting that velocity. Investment in plants and equipment, however, is less mobile. It takes foresight and patience to depreciate these assets over time. Firms accomplish such disinvestment *gradually* through cutbacks in maintenance and modernization (Bluestone and Harrison, 1982). Local rentiers, with their investments in land and buildings, have the most limited mobility of all the entrepreneurs. The place speculator's knowledge of local markets and connections to community political and financial networks are not easily transferable to other locales. But it is possible to "bail out," and if done at the right time, the entrepreneur can get out with enough to start over somewhere else.

Of all the factors of urbanization, labor is the least mobile. Ordinary people's resources are too small to easily carry them through the uncertainty of migration, and their residential use values, important for survival, are tied to a particular setting. That is why workers are often left behind and appear as the leaders of the rear guard fight for stability. Although some residential moves are no doubt welcomed changes in life chances, many are forced hardships caused by land clearance, eviction, and steep rent increases. The ability to move is radically constrained by a world of risks, many of which cannot be anticipated. For every proud pioneer memorialized in a town square, there is probably another who died on the trek.

Besides the "internal" inhibitions on residential movement, there are also external barriers imposed by authorities. Visa, passport, and citizenship requirements obviously obstruct people's movement between countries. Even within a relatively open country such as the United States, there are institutional constraints on mobility. Because of the peculiarities imposed by the federal system, rights of citizenship are provided in part by states or even cities rather than by the national government. Access to certain forms of welfare benefits, including medical care, low-cost college tuition, public housing, and unemployment compensation, are often contingent on satisfying residence rules. Beyond these inhibitions, localities also erect barriers to certain kinds of migrants through large-lot zoning and poor enforcement of laws that might protect unwanted newcomers (such as laws prohibiting racial discrimination in housing and employment). Whereas the courts have frequently overturned local legislation that interferes with "interstate commerce," they have allowed many constraints on residential migration to stand. Ordinary people may overcome political barriers and even manage to cross borders of barbed wire and murky rivers, but the desperation of their "choice" reflects not so much their ability to move as the intensity of the "push" that sent them on their way.

These constraints on mobility contradict urban migration models that presume individuals can freely pick and choose the places that best serve their needs. In the neoclassical migration theory of Charles Tiebout (1956), the assumed freedom of people to move leads places to compete to attract them. In writings of a generation ago, but which have influenced more recent work (Bish, 1971; Peterson, 1981), Tiebout likened towns and cities to products—packages of benefits and costs from which consumers make their choices. Each town establishes its own standards for taxes and its level and mix of services. Members of the public, as residential buyers, then choose the package that most suits their preferences. Thus people for whom high-quality public education is a valued good will—according to this theory—choose to live in a city where this is provided, even if that means paying higher taxes or forgoing another valued urban service. Over time the competition of places to attract residents produces a rich variety of packages as each place stakes out its own market segment. The result is a happy placement of each according to taste, since sovereign consumers vote with their feet to select the package of their choice.

Our critique should by now be predictable: The free, autonomous action assumed by market theories fails to acknowledge people's bonds to place, entrepreneurs' collusion, and the regulatory function—all inherent in real estate markets. To think of whole towns and cities as "products" and residents as "shoppers" truly strains the market metaphor.

People looking for a place to live are, as we have reiterated, tightly grounded by forces that local government can do little to alter. First and foremost, people must reside where they can get work, making corporate investment—not residential preference—the critical lead factor in urban development. Similarly, differences in housing costs and ethnic composition are obviously far more significant than variations in local government expenditures in determining residential movements (see Rossi, 1955). People also strive to live near friends and family.

Looking at the other half of the Tiebout market system equation (the city as a "seller" of service bundles), we find that packaging to please potential *residents* has little bearing on most government decisions on raising or allocating tax money. Public choice theorists like Tiebout do not recognize the internal cleavages within cities or the competing designs of outsiders on the management of cities. They think of local policies as mere summations of citizen-residents' preferences—particularly of potential residents who might be attracted through the right service mix. But we find it easy enough to demonstrate that such land-use democracy is an exception rather than the rule in determining how local governments operate; the politics of place is about *whose* interests government will serve. The growth machine dynamic is a crucial part of the process that pushes people from one residential location to another, from one city to another. Cities, regions, and states do not compete to please people; they compete to please capital—and the two activities are fundamentally different.

Some places do indeed end up with nicer packages than others, but these are for the most part nicer for *anybody*. The real differences between jurisdictions—between good schools and lousy ones, smooth streets and rutted ones, well-connected neighbors or powerless ones—are intercorrelated and determined primarily by social class. The public choice model trivializes the inequalities that develop among places by treating these inequalities as differences in taste. Obscuring the inequality among the packages also obscures the consequences of such place differences. To the degree that people's fates are tied to the places in which they live, this becomes a critical error. People individually disadvantaged because of the nature of their location have less ability to move to a better place. They are tied down by the surrounding social net, which they also need to survive. Residential location affects the ability to move somewhere else, once again reflecting the unique quality of the place "product." Initial "choice" of residential location (often determined by an accident of birth) is both involuntary and self-sustaining in a way that one's choice of, say, a pickle brand is not.

Once again capital is the contrasting case. It comes much closer to the "shopper model" of a consumer ever alert to the best deal. Especially in the context of a more fully integrated world economic system, capital can choose another town, state, or country as need dictates. Such geographical shifts determine which cities will grow and which will decline, which social groups (skilled or unskilled workers, citizens or noncitizens, land owners and so forth) will be hurt or helped, who will migrate, and who will be left behind. Neoclassical reasoning sees nothing analytically or socially problematic in such increased velocities of capital and pays little attention to the possibility that other types of actors may lack the same mobility. In conventional economics, more speed for capital means more perfect markets, and human mobility follows as a matter of course. All forms of migration, whether of people or of capital, are the inevitable and natural mechanisms for smoothing out temporarily uneven distributions of resources and labor. The impersonal market apparatus guides technologies, populations, and resources—as passive "things"—toward optimum and equilibrated deployment.

In contrast, we rely on the alternative perspective: Places achieve their reality through social organization in the pursuit of use and exchange values. Resources of all sorts—human, technological, and material—are exploited and moved around in the process. The different mobilities of capital and labor become still another contingency in the struggle over use and exchange within and between places. There is nothing necessarily optimizing in the purposive and conflictual strategies by which this process goes on.

The Reality of Places

Places are not simply *affected* by the institutional maneuvers surrounding them. Places *are* those machinations. A place is defined as much by its position in a particular organizational web—political, economic, and cultural—as by its physical makeup and topographical configuration. Places are not "discovered," as high school history texts suggest; people construct them as a practical activity.

The very boundaries of place, as well as the meaning of those boundaries, are a result of the intersecting searches for use and exchange values. Others have pointed out that boundaries and place identifications are social constructions (Hunter, 1974; Lynch, 1960). People and institutions repeatedly name and define boundaries in anticipation of specific consequences. If Beverly Hills, for example, should move its city line to include three additional blocks to the east, the mere change in an intellectual and legal construct will enhance the status of the new territory, raising property values as well as levels of urban services for residents. And to some degree the area within the earlier boundaries of Beverly Hills may be "cheapened" (resources will be diluted) by the inclusion of such lower-income-generating properties. As another instance of how boundaries affect use and exchange values, structural speculators may need to be included in one kind of special planning district (for example, a redevelopment zone) and excluded from another to benefit from development subsidies.

Sometimes "boundary work" is more informal; a realtor may advertise a property as located within a certain prestigious area when it is actually "just outside." Repetitions of such incorrect designations may eventually alter perceived boundaries to include the parcels involved. (There usually are good reasons for such conventional "errors"; see Garfinkel [1967, chap. 6].) Residents also may strive to manipulate boundaries in order to improve their standing in the larger social world, laying claim to participating in the prestigious daily round that corresponds to a given community. Of course, if political boundaries can be changed, the reverberations are louder and last longer. When one person's favored boundaries are marked off by a political authority, that person's gains are institutionalized.

Incorporated suburban towns sometimes owe their very creation to the effort of local entrepreneurs to increase their property's urbanization prospects. Such cases create problems for central city residents, who would have lost less if the new development, especially if it is tax rich, had been annexed to the existing city instead. Failing annexation, central cities try to force suburbs to carry "their fair share" of public service burdens through such devices as city payroll taxes or compensatory state aid. In effect the cities strive to redefine the meaning of the suburban boundary line. If central city advocates can cause federal aid to be based on the number of poor in a city (as it was under certain Great Society programs), the city line loses some of its significance and the poor become less of a burden and more of a resource. The meaning of the boundary lines and what they enclose is changed, with important implications for the well-being of specific neighborhood groups and growth elites.

Once again we see that the attributes of place are achieved through social action, rather than through the qualities inherent in a piece of land, and that places are defined through social relationships, not through nature, autonomous markets, or spatial geometry. Such factors as topography and mineral resources do matter, but they interact with social organization; the social and physical worlds mutually determine the reality of one another.[5]

The socially contingent quality of place can be more dramatically illustrated with large-scale examples. Let us consider the state of Alaska and the oil being exploited from its subsurface. Although we do not often view it in this way, the institutional nature of the oil helps determine the nature of Alaska, just as the nature of the state will determine the nature of the oil. Alaskan oil is more truly "Alaskan" if the headquarters of oil companies are located in Juneau than if they are located in New York. If located in Juneau, mineral exploitation leads to growth in the white-collar, professional, and service economy within Alaska; otherwise that form of development occurs elsewhere. Let us look at this example from the standpoint of how the nature of Alaska affects the nature of the oil. If federal law permits the state to tax its own mineral production, Alaska will be a fiscally rich place. Under those conditions the state will do all it can to ensure the exploitation of oil. If there were neither fiscal nor rent benefits to be derived from the oil, the Alaskans would probably prefer to keep the

---

5. The relationship, as mediated through human consciousness, is indexical and reflexive (Garfinkel, 1967).

oil in the ground. That would make Alaskan oil, as a commodity, nonexistent.

Indeed, in the precolonial territories, before penetration by the nascent market societies, minerals were a noncommodity. As these resources were commodified, they were perceived to be "in" the European empires, not "in" the tribal lands where they were physically found. Existence of resources for native gain (as local profits, rents, or public goods) could happen only after liberation. In the clear-cut case of South Africa, diamonds and gold did not exist as commodities before their exploitation by the colonial powers. The minerals of South Africa do much for the white minority but serve as a hindrance for the blacks, whose country the resources are "in." South Africa is a nation of social arrangements designed to support the exploitation of its resources, just as those arrangements cause the resources to exist in their current form.

The contextual dependence of the nature and location of every single element is also applicable to labor. In some societies guest workers are employed in factories and fields but have no rights of citizenship. There are "in" a place, but only in a sense. In other parts of the world, the status of "illegal" immigrants is constantly under judicial review, often in the hope of creating the right legal conditions that will enable capital to secure them as labor without paying the social costs of their presence. When rich countries offer permanent citizenship only to those Third World migrants with high levels of skill, the effect, not coincidentally, is to increase the level of inequality between places as the rich societies reap the investments in training made by poor nations. These international arrangements mean that during their training the future émigrés are less than full members of their native society, incipiently oriented toward membership in their ultimate destination. Their anticipatory socialization makes them, to a degree, émigrés even before their departure. At the same time the creation of such identities and the related migrations reinforce the nature of the societies involved: the poor country becomes poorer as the rich grows richer.

American citizens who retire to Mexico to stretch their U.S. pensions are "in" which place? Welfare recipients who have recently moved to another state take on ambiguous locational status for the jurisdictions that serve them. University students, soldiers, and the homeless similarly have problematic locational statuses that are important to taxing bodies, voting officials, and welfare organizations.

Political turmoil in various parts of the world puts people in explicitly contested locational statuses: the Palestinians in the Israeli-held territories conquered from Jordan, the Protestants of Northern Ireland, the Basques of Spain, El Salvador refugees in the United States. Although these people add up to millions throughout the world, the main point is not their demographic significance, but rather, as the intense conflicts of the examples show, that placeness is negotiated with concrete consequences in view. Locational status is inextricably tied to the definitions and redefinitions imposed by state authorities, citizens' movements, and exchange value pressures. Always at stake are the name, boundaries, and meanings of location, and who and what should be "in" and who and what should be "out."

The reality of place is always open, making its determination an inherently social process.[6] In the United States, in a world apart from most of the world's ethnic and national struggles over territory, the widespread acceptance of an impersonal, self-equilibrating market obscures the socialness of place. Such organizational determinants of cities as entrepreneurs' coalitions, government's redistribution of rents, and the negotiated citizenship of all residents recede from view. Efforts to make place serve use values are therefore noticeable as "interfering" in the "normal" urban processes. Whereas buying and selling real estate needs no special justification, regulating that buying and selling for the benefit of residents requires special political action and ideological mobilization.

Most people generalize from the microeconomic meeting of buyer and seller making a deal to the larger market system. They divorce the microexchange from the social organization that permeates each economic act. Because attitudes toward markets are so myopic, any social intervention in those contexts runs a heavy risk of generating hostility. This lack of understanding of markets leads to an ongoing ideological asymmetry between those strug-

6. This view is consistent with the social-psychological maxim that the more ambiguous the stimulus, the more do social factors intervene in perception.

gling over use and exchange, with those pursuing exchange having the advantage. Through their institutional power and a potent ideological context, entrepreneurs have the hegemonic edge in making U.S. places.

Conclusion: The Social Place

The reality of places is constructed through political action, with the term *political* encompassing both individual and collective efforts, through both informal associations and institutions of government and the economy. In explaining individual stratification and occupational hierarchy, scholars have offered a familiar wisdom (Davis and Moore, 1945) that unequal occupational rewards inspire those with the most individual talent (brains, wit, persistence) to do the most difficult (and highest-paying) work, making the whole system more productive as a result. Systems of places have also been portrayed (by the ecologists) as differently endowed, some having such inherent advantages as centrality, mineral resources, or intersecting trade routes. Such qualities make them rise to the top among the places, becoming bigger and higher priced than their inferior competitors. By extending the functionalist thinking, we can link the two stratification theories: The most talented individuals rise to the top as they use their skills to develop the best places to maximize geographical potential. People migrate to those areas that can best use their particular skills, which includes the migration of the most talented people to the most crucial spots. The overall system secures the triumphs of the fittest people and the fittest places, resulting in a maximally efficient society. It all works because, given unfettered occupational and geographical mobility, the best people help society get the most out of the best locations.

We have a different way of explaining the two systems of hierarchy and how they are connected. Markets among individuals are socially structured (given oligopoly, racism, inheritance, and so forth). Rich people use wealth to send their children to good schools, to provide themselves with excellent health care, and to keep others from usurping their privileges. This leads to longer lives, higher IQ scores, and happier days (Bradburn and Caplovitz, 1965). As a result, they do better in the individual competition. The inequality among individuals thus not only results from differentiation but also causes it. Similarly, place inequality is both cause and consequence of differences among places. Those in control of the top places use place status to maintain privileges for their locations, often at the expense of the lesser locales. Often with the help of place-based organizations, they manipulate transportation routes, secure desired zoning, and keep out unwanted social groups.

The two systems of hierarchy are connected through the tendency for individual and place status to reinforce each other. Advantage in one can be used to develop advantage in the other. High status within the social hierarchy can bring access to the most desirable places (for residence or investment) and a guarantee of a rewarding future for whatever place one controls. At the same time a high status for one's geographical place means the availability of resources (rents, urban services, prestige) that enhance life chances generally.

We seek to understand how these two intersecting systems of hierarchy constitute human settlements. We explore the urban fortunes of people: entrepreneurs tie their futures to the manipulation of exchange values, which then affect the fortunes of residents using place to live another day. We explore the urban fortunes of places: places achieve their standing through internal social conflicts and the struggles of actors, local and remote, trying to generate profits, rents, and use values. We seek to show that the nature of human settlement, including its market organization, is a product of social arrangements and a force in the lives of people. We seek, in other words, to move systematic urban analysis away from both the neoclassical economists (of whatever discipline) and the Marxian determinists. We strive to develop an authentic urban sociology.

3

The City as a Growth Machine

Traditional urban research has had little relevance to the day-to-day activities of the place-based elites whose priorities affect patterns of land use, public budgets, and urban social life. It has not even been apparent from much of the scholarship of urban social science that place is a market commodity that can produce wealth and power for its owners, and that this might explain why certain people take a keen interest in the ordering of urban life.

Research on local elites has been preoccupied with the question "Who governs?" (or "Who rules?"). Are the politically active citizens of a city split into diverse and competing interest groups, or are they members of a coordinated oligarchy? Empirical evidence of visible cleavage, such as disputes on a public issue, has been accepted as evidence of pluralistic competition (Banfield, 1961; Dahl, 1961). Signs of cohesion, such as common membership in voluntary and policy groups, have been used to support the alternative view (see Domhoff, 1970).

We believe that the question of who governs or rules has to be asked in conjunction with the equally central question "For what?" With rare exceptions (see Smith and Keller, 1983), one issue consistently generates consensus among local elite groups and separates them from people who use the city principally as a place to live and work: the issue of growth. For those who count, the city is a growth machine, one that can increase aggregate rents and trap related wealth for those in the right position to benefit. The desire for growth creates consensus among a wide range of elite groups, no matter how split they might be on other issues. Thus the disagreement on some or even most public issues does not necessarily indicate any fundamental disunity, nor do changes in the number or variety of actors on the scene (what Clark [1968] calls "decentralization") affect the basic matter. It does not even matter that elites often fail to achieve their growth goal; with virtually all places in the same game, some elites will inevitably lose no matter how great their effort (Lyon et al., 1981; Krannich and Humphrey, 1983).

Although they may differ on which particular strategy will best succeed, elites use their growth consensus to eliminate any alternative vision of the purpose of local government or the meaning of community. The issues that reach public agendas (and are therefore available for pluralists' investigations) do so precisely because they are matters on which elites have, in effect, agreed to disagree (Molotch and Lester, 1974, 1975; see Schattschneider, 1960). Only under rather extraordinary circumstances is this consensus endangered.

For all the pluralism Banfield (1961) uncovered in Chicago, he found no disagreement with the idea that growth was good. Indeed, much of the dissension he did find, for example, on where to put the new convention center, was part of a dispute over how growth should be internally distributed. In his studies of cities on both sides of the southern U.S. border, D'Antonio found that when community "knowledgeables" were "asked to name the most pressing problems facing their respective cities," they cited finding sufficient water for both farming and urban growth (Form and D'Antonio, 1970:439). Whitt (1982) found that in formulating positions on California transportation policies, elites carefully coordinated not only the positions they would take but also the amount of money each would give toward winning relevant initiative campaigns. Thus on growth infrastructure, the elites were united.

Similarly, it was on the primacy of such growth and development issues that Hunter found Atlanta's elites to be most unified, both at the time of his first classic study and during its replication twenty years later (Hunter, 1953, 1980). Hunter (1953:214) reports, "They could speak of nothing else" (cited in Domhoff, 1983:169). In his historical profiles of Dallas and Fort Worth, Melosi (1983:175) concludes that "political power in Dallas and Fort Worth has typically been concentrated in the hands of those people most willing and able to sustain growth and expansion." Finally, even the ecologically oriented scholars with a different perspective, Berry and Kasarda (1977:371), have remarked, "If in the past urbanization has been governed by any conscious public objectives at all, these have been, on the one hand, to encourage growth, apparently for its own sake, and on the other hand, to provide public works and public welfare programs to support piecemeal, spontaneous development impelled primarily by private initiative." And even Hawley (1950:429) briefly departs from his tight ecological schema to remark that "competition is observable . . . in the struggle for transportation and communication advantages and superior services of all kinds; it also appears in efforts to accelerate rates of population growth."

All of this competition, in addition to its critical influence on what goes on *within* cities, also influences the distribution of populations throughout cities and regions, determining which ones grow and which do not. The incessant lobbying, manipulating, and cajoling can deliver the critical resources from which great cities are made. Although virtually all places are subject to the pervasive rule of growth boosters, places with more active and creative elites may have an edge over other areas. In a comparative study of forty-eight communities, Lyon et al. (1981) indeed found that cities with reputedly more powerful elites tended to have stronger growth rates. This may mean that active elites stimulate growth, or it may mean that strong growth emboldens elites to actively maintain their advantage. Although we suspect that both perspectives are valid, we stress that the activism of entrepreneurs is, and always has been, a critical force in shaping the urban system, including the rise and fall of given places.

Growth Machines in U.S. History

The role of the growth machine as a driving force in U.S. urban development has long been a factor in U.S. history, and is nowhere more clearly documented than in the histories of eighteenth- and nineteenth-century American cities. Indeed, although historians have chronicled many types of mass opposition to capitalist organization (for example, labor unions and the Wobblie movement), there is precious little evidence of resistance to the dynamics of value-free city building characteristic of the American past. In looking back we thus have not only the benefit of hindsight but also the advantage of dealing with a time in which "the interfusing of public and private prosperity" (Boorstin, 1965:116) was proudly proclaimed by town boosters and their contemporary chroniclers. The creators of towns and the builders of cities strained to use all the resources at their disposal, including crude political clout, to make great fortunes out of place. The "lively competitive spirit" of the western regions was, in Boorstin's view (1965:123), more "a competition among communities" than among individuals. Sometimes, the "communities" were merely subdivided parcels with town names on them, what Wade (1959) has called "paper villages," on whose behalf governmental actions could nonetheless be taken.[1] The competititon among them was primarily among growth elites.

These communities competed to attract federal land offices, colleges and academies, or installations such as arsenals and prisons as a means of stimulating development. These projects were, for many places, "the only factor that permitted them to outdistance less favored rivals with equivalent natural or geographic endowments" (Scheiber, 1962:136). The other important arena of competition was also dependent on government decision making and funding: the development of a transportation infrastructure that would give a locality better access to raw materials and markets. First came the myriad efforts to attract state and federal funds to link towns to waterways through canals. Then came efforts to subsidize and direct the paths of railroads (Glaab, 1962). Town leaders used their governmental authority to determine routes and subsidies, motivated by their private interest in rents.

The people who engaged in this city building have often been celebrated for their inspired vision and "absolute faith." One historian characterizes them as "ambitious, flamboyant, and imaginative" (Fuller, 1976:41). But more important than their person-

---

1. The same phenomenon is found today in Chicago suburbs formed principally to benefit from state fiscal codes.

alities, these urban founders were in the business of manipulating place for its exchange values. Their occupations most often were real estate or banking (Belcher, 1947). Even those who initially practiced law, medicine, or pharmacy were rentiers in the making. These professional roles became sidelines: "Physicians became merchants, clergymen became bankers, lawyers became manu-facturers" (Boorstin, 1965:123). Especially when fortunes could be made from growth, the elite division of labor was overwhelmed and "specialized skills . . . had a new unimportance" (Boorstin, 1965:123). Speaking of the early settlers' acquisition of specula-tive lands through the preemption regulations of the 1862 Home-stead Act, Leslie Decker remarks that "the early comers to any town—from lawyers to doctors to merchants, to just plain town developers—usually diversified in this fashion" (quoted in Wolf, 1981:52; see also Swierenga, 1966).

The city-building activities of these growth entrepreneurs in frontier towns became the springboard for the much celebrated taming of the American wilderness. As Wade (1959) has argued, the upstart western cities functioned as market, finance, and ad-ministrative outposts that made rural pioneering possible. This conquering of the West, accomplished through the machinations of "the urban frontier," was critically bound up with a coordinated effort to gain rents. In order for town leaders to achieve their goals, there was "ingenious employment of the instruments of po-litical and economic leverage at [their] disposal" to build the cit-ies and regions in which they had made investments (Scheiber, 1962:136).

Perhaps the most spectacular case of urban ingenuity was the Chicago of William Ogden. When Ogden came to Chicago in 1835, its population was under four thousand. He succeeded in becoming its mayor, its great railway developer, and the owner of much of its best real estate. As the organizer and first president of the Union Pacific (among other railroads) and in combination with his other business and civic roles, he was able to make Chicago (as a "public duty") the crossroads of America, and hence the dominant metropolis of the Midwest. Chicago became a cross-roads not only because it was "central" (other places were also in the "middle") but because a small group of people (led by Ogden) had the power to literally have the roads cross in the spot they chose. Ogden candidly reminisced about one of the real estate deals this made possible: "I purchased for $8,000, what 8 years thereafter, sold for 3 millions of dollars" (Boorstin, 1965:117). The Ogden story, Boorstin says (p. 118), "was re-enacted a thousand times all over America."

This tendency to use land and government activity to make money was not invented in nineteenth-century America, nor did it end then. The development of the American Midwest was only one particularly noticed (and celebrated) moment in the total process. One of the more fascinating instances, farther to the West and later in history, was the rapid development of Los Angeles, an anomaly to many because it had none of the "natural" features that are thought to support urban growth: no centrality, no harbor, no transportation crossroads, not even a water supply. Indeed, the rise of Los Angeles as the preeminent city of the West, eclipsing its rivals San Diego and San Francisco, can only be explained as a remarkable victory of human cunning over the so-called limits of nature. Much of the development of western cities hinged on access to a railroad; the termination of the first continental railroad at San Francisco, therefore, secured that city's early lead over other western towns. The railroad was thus crucial to the fortunes of the barons with extensive real estate and commercial interests in San Francisco—Stanford, Crocker, Huntington, and Hopkins. These men feared the coming of a second cross-country railroad (the southern route), for its urban terminus might threaten the San Francisco investments. San Diego, with its natural port, could become a rival to San Francisco, but Los Angeles, which had no comparable advantage, would remain forever in its shadow. Hence, the San Francisco elites used their economic and political power to keep San Diego from becoming the terminus of the southern route. As Fogelson (1967:51, 55) remarks, "San Diego's supreme asset, the bay, was actually its fatal liability," whereas the disadvantage of Los Angeles—"its inadequate and unprotected port—was its saving grace." Of course, Los Angeles won in the end, but here again the wiles of boosters were crucial: the Los Angeles interests managed to secure millions in federal funds to construct a port—today the world's largest artificial harbor—as well as federal backing to gain water (Clark, 1983:273, 274).

The same dynamic accounts for the other great harbor in the

Southwest. Houston beat out Galveston as the major port of Texas (ranked third in the country in 1979) only when Congressman Tom Ball of Houston successfully won, at the beginning of this century, a million-dollar federal appropriation to construct a canal linking landlocked Houston to the Gulf of Mexico (Kaplan, 1983:196). That was the crucial event that, capitalizing on Galveston's susceptibility to hurricanes, put Houston permanently in the lead.

In more recent times, the mammoth federal interstate highway system, hammered out by "a horde of special interests representing towns and cities" (Judd, 1983:173), has similarly made and unmade urban fortunes. To use one clear case, Colorado's leaders made Denver a highway crossroads by convincing President Eisenhower in 1956 to add three hundred miles to the system to link Denver to Salt Lake City by an expensive mountain route. A presidential stroke of the pen removed the prospects of Cheyenne, Wyoming, of replacing Denver as a major western transportation center (Judd, 1983:173). In a case reminiscent of the nineteenth-century canal era, the Tennessee-Tombigbee Waterway opened in 1985, dramatically altering the shipping distances to the Gulf of Mexico for many inland cities. The largest project ever built by the U.S. Corps of Engineers, the $2 billion project was questioned as a boondoggle in Baltimore, which will lose port business because of it (Maguire, 1985), but praised in Decatur, Alabama, and Knoxville, Tennessee, which expect to profit from it. The opening of the canal cut by four-fifths the distance from Chattanooga, Tennessee, to the Gulf, but did almost nothing for places like Minneapolis and Pittsburgh, which were previously about the same nautical distance from the Gulf as Chattanooga.

Despite the general hometown hoopla of boosters who have won infrastructural victories, not everyone gains when the structural speculators of a city defeat their competition. It is too easy, and misleading, to say that "the public benefits . . . because it got the railroads" (Grodinsky, as cited in Klein, 1970:294).[2] Given

2. We were struck by the naive wording used by one historian in commenting upon the life of an urban booster-lawyer: "*despite* [our emphasis] his extensive business career, Brice delved deeply into politics as well. His devotion to the State [Ohio] and its economic interests won him wide popularity there" (Klein, 1970:110).

the stakes, the rentier elites would obviously become engulfed by the "booster spirit." But despite the long-held supposition of an American "antiurban bias" (White and White, 1962), researchers have made little effort to question the linkage between public betterment and growth, even when they could see that specific social groups were being hurt. Zunz reports that in industrializing Detroit, city authorities extended utility service into uninhabited areas to help development rather than into existing residential zones, whose working-class residents went without service even as they bore the costs (through taxes) of the new installations. There was a "bias in favor of speculators and against the working class" (Zunz, 1982:116). Even the great urban reformers, such as Detroit's Mayor Hazen Pingree, while working to change this "standard practice" for financing growth (Zunz, 1983:118), were doing so in order to increase the overall efficiencies of urban services and hence "engineer growth better" (Zunz, 1983:111). "Real estate specialists and builders were more involved in the city-building process," Zunz (1982:162) says, "than anybody else." Reviewing urbanization from 1850 to 1930, Lewis Mumford observed: "That a city had any other purpose than to attract trade, to increase land values, and to grow is something, if it uneasily entered the mind of an occasional Whitman, never exercised any hold on the minds of our countrymen" (quoted in Mollenkopf, 1983:14).

This is the consensus that must be examined, particularly in light of recent urban development. Let us turn now to a description of the ingenious modern incarnations of the growth machines and to an analysis of how they function, a task made more difficult for modern times because the crucial participants seldom speak so openly as did Mr. Ogden.

The Modern-day Good Business Climate

The jockeying for canals, railroads, and arsenals of the previous century has given way in this one to more complex and subtle efforts to manipulate space and redistribute rents. The fusing of public duty and private gain has become much less acceptable (both in public opinion and in the criminal courts); the replacing of frontiers by complex cities has given important roles to mass media, urban professionals, and skilled political entrepreneurs. The growth machine is less personalized, with fewer local heroes, and has become instead a multifaceted matrix of important social institutions pressing along complementary lines.

With a transportation and communication grid already in place, modern cities typically seek growth in basic economic functions, particularly job intensive ones. Economic growth sets in motion the migration of labor and a demand for ancillary production services, housing, retailing, and wholesaling ("multiplier effects"). Contemporary places differ in the type of economic base they strive to build (for example, manufacturing, research and development, information processing, or tourism). But any one of the rainbows leads to the same pot of gold: more intense land use and thus higher rent collections, with associated professional fees and locally based profits.

Cities are in a position to affect the "factors of production" that are widely believed to channel the capital investments that drive local growth (Hawley, 1950; Summers et al., 1976). They can, for example, lower access costs of raw materials and markets through the creation of shipping ports and airfields (either by using local subsidies or by facilitating state and federal support). Localities can decrease corporate overhead costs through sympathetic policies on pollution abatement, employee health standards, and taxes. Labor costs can be indirectly lowered by pushing welfare recipients into low-paying jobs and through the use of police to constrain union organizing. Moral laws can be changed; for example, drinking alcohol can be legalized (as in Ann Arbor, Mich., and Evanston, Ill.) or gambling can be promoted (as in Atlantic City, N.J.) to build tourism and convention business. Increased utility costs caused by new development can be borne, as they usually are (see, for an example, Ann Arbor, Michigan, Planning Department, 1972), by the public at large rather than by those responsible for the "excess" demand they generate. Federally financed programs can be harnessed to provide cheap water supplies; state agencies can be manipulated to subsidize insurance rates; local political units can forgive business property taxes. Government installations of various sorts (universities, military bases) can be used to leverage additional development by guaranteeing the presence of skilled labor, retailing customers, or proximate markets for subcontractors. For some analytical purposes, it doesn't even matter that a number of these factors have little bearing on corporate locational decisions (some certainly do; others are debated); just the *possibility* that they might matter invigorates local growth activism (Swanstrom, 1985) and dominates policy agendas.

Following the lead of St. Petersburg, Florida, the first city to hire a press agent (in 1918) to boost growth (Mormino, 1983: 150), virtually all major urban areas now use experts to attract outside investment. One city, Dixon, Illinois, has gone so far as to systematically contact former residents who might be in a position to help (as many as twenty thousand people) and offer them a finder's fee up to $10,000 for directing corporate investment toward their old home town (*San Francisco Chronicle,* May 10, 1984). More pervasively, each city tries to create a "good business climate." The ingredients are well known in city-building circles and have even been codified and turned into "official" lists for each regional area. The much-used Fantus rankings of business climates are based on factors like taxation, labor legislation, unemployment compensation, scale of government, and public indebtedness (Fantus ranks Texas as number one and New York as number forty-eight). In 1975, the Industrial Development Research Council, made up of corporate executives responsible for site selection decisions, conducted a survey of its members. In that survey, states were rated more simply as "cooperative," "indifferent," or "antigrowth"; the results closely paralleled the Fantus rankings of the same year (Weinstein and Firestine, 1978: 134–44).

Any issue of a major business magazine is replete with advertisements from localities of all types (including whole countries) striving to portray themselves in a manner attractive to business. Consider these claims culled from one issue of *Business Week* (February 12, 1979):

> New York City is open for business. No other city in America offers more financial incentives to expand or relocate. . . .

The state of Louisiana advertises

> Nature made it perfect. We made it profitable.

On another page we find the claim that "Northern Ireland works" and has a work force with "positive attitudes toward company loyalty, productivity and labor relations." Georgia asserts, "Government should strive to improve business conditions, not hinder them." Atlanta headlines that as "A City Without Limits" it "has ways of getting people like you out of town" and then details its transportation advantages to business. Some places describe attributes that would enhance the life style of executives and professional employees (not a dimension of Fantus rankings); thus a number of cities push an image of artistic refinement. No advertisements in this issue (or in any other, we suspect) show city workers living in nice homes or influencing their working conditions.

While a good opera or ballet company may subtly enhance the growth potential of some cities, other cultural ingredients are crucial for a good business climate. There should be no violent class or ethnic conflict (Agger, Goldrich, and Swanson, 1964:649; Johnson, 1983:250–51). Rubin (1972:123) reports that racial confrontation over school busing was sometimes seen as a threat to urban economic development. Racial violence in South Africa is finally leading to the disinvestment that reformers could not bring about through moral suasion. In the good business climate, the work force should be sufficiently quiescent and healthy to be productive; this was the rationale originally behind many programs in work place relations and public health. Labor must, in other words, be "reproduced," but only under conditions that least interfere with local growth trajectories.

Perhaps most important of all, local publics should favor growth and support the ideology of value-free development. This public attitude reassures investors that the concrete enticements of a locality will be upheld by future politicians. The challenge is to connect civic pride to the growth goal, tying the presumed economic and social benefits of growth in general (Wolfe, 1981) to growth in the local area. Probably only partly aware of this, elites generate and sustain the place patriotism of the masses. According to Boorstin, the competition among cities "helped create the booster spirit" as much as the booster spirit helped create the cities (1965:123). In the nineteenth-century cities, the great rivalries over canal and railway installations were the political spectacles of the day, with attention devoted to their public, not private, benefits. With the drama of the new railway technology, ordinary people were swept into the competition among places, rooting for their own town to become the new "crossroads" or at least a way station. "The debates over transportation," writes Scheiber (1962:143), "heightened urban community consciousness and sharpened local pride in many western towns."

The celebration of local growth continues to be a theme in the culture of localities. Schoolchildren are taught to view local history as a series of breakthroughs in the expansion of the economic base of their city and region, celebrating its numerical leadership in one sort of production or another; more generally, increases in population tend to be equated with local progress. Civic organizations sponsor essay contests on the topic of local greatness. They encourage public celebrations and spectacles in which the locality name can be proudly advanced for the benefit of both locals and outsiders. They subsidize soapbox derbies, parade floats, and beauty contests to "spread around" the locality's name in the media and at distant competitive sites.

One case can illustrate the link between growth goals and cultural institutions. In the Los Angeles area, St. Patrick's Day parades are held at four different locales, because the city's Irish leaders can't agree on the venue for a joint celebration. The source of the difficulty (and much acrimony) is that these parades march down the main business streets in each locale, thereby making them a symbol of the life of the city. Business groups associated with each of the strips want to claim the parade as exclusively their own, leading to charges by still a fifth parade organization that the other groups are only out to "make money" (McGarry, 1985:II:1). The countercharge, vehemently denied, was that the leader of the challenging business street was not even Irish. Thus even an ethnic celebration can receive its special form from the machinations of growth interests and the competitions among them.

The growth machine avidly supports whatever cultural institutions can play a role in building locality. Always ready to oppose cultural and political developments contrary to their interests (for example, black nationalism and communal cults), rentiers and their associates encourage activities that will connect feelings of community ("we feelings" [McKenzie, 1922]) to the goal of local growth. The overall ideological thrust is to deemphasize the connection between growth and exchange values and to reinforce the link between growth goals and better lives for the majority. We do not mean to suggest that the only source of civic pride is the desire to collect rents; certainly the cultural pride of tribal groups predates growth machines. Nevertheless, the growth machine coalition mobilizes these cultural motivations, legitimizes them, and channels them into activites that are consistent with growth goals.

The Organization of the Growth Coalition

The people who use their time and money to participate in local affairs are the ones who—in vast disproportion to their representation in the population—have the most to gain or lose in land-use decisions. Local business people are the major participants in urban politics (Walton, 1970), particularly business people in property investing, development, and real estate financing (Spaulding, 1951; Mumford, 1961). Peterson (1981:132), who applauds growth boosterism, acknowledges that "such policies are often promulgated through a highly centralized decision-making process involving prestigious businessmen and professionals. Conflict within the city tends to be minimal, decision-making processes tend to be closed." Elected officials, says Stone (1984:292), find themselves confronted by "a business community that is well-organized, amply supplied with a number of deployable resources, and inclined to act on behalf of tangible and ambitious plans that are mutually beneficial to its own members."

Business people's continuous interaction with public officials (including supporting them through substantial campaign contributions) gives them *systemic* power (Alford and Friedland, 1975; Stone, 1981, 1982). Once organized, they stay organized. They are "mobilized interests" (Fainstein, Fainstein, and Armistead, 1983:214). Rentiers need local government in their daily money-making routines, especially when structural speculations are involved. They are assisted by lawyers, syndicators, and property brokers (Bouma, 1962), who prosper as long as they can win decisions favoring their clients. Finally, there are monopolistic business enterprises (such as the local newspaper) whose futures are tied to the growth of the metropolis as a whole, although they are not directly involved in land use. When the local market is saturated with their product, they have few ways to increase profits, beyond expansion of their surrounding area. As in the proverbial Springdale, site of the classic Vidich and Bensman (1960:216) ethnography of a generation ago, there is a strong tendency in most cities for "the professionals (doctors, teachers, dentists, etc.), the industrial workers, the shack people and the lower middle-class groups [to be] for all intents and purposes disenfranchised except in terms of temporary issues."

Because so much of the growth mobilization effort involves government, local growth elites play a major role in electing local politicians, "watchdogging" their activities, and scrutinizing administrative detail. Whether in generating infrastructural resources, keeping peace on the home front, or using the city mayor as an "ambassador to industry" (Wyner, 1967), local government is primarily concerned with increasing growth. Again, it is not the only function of local government, but it is the key one.

In contrast to our position, urban social scientists have often ignored the politics of growth in their work, even when debates over growth infrastructures were the topic of their analyses (see Banfield, 1961; Dahl, 1961). Williams and Adrian (1963) at least treat growth as an important part of the local political process, but give it no priority over other government issues. There are a number of reasons why growth politics is consistently undervalued. The clue can be found in Edelman's (1964) distinction between two kinds of politics.

The first is the "symbolic" politics of public morality and most of the other "big issues" featured in the headlines and editorials of the daily press: school prayer, wars on crime, standing up to communism, and child pornography, for example. News coverage of these issues may have little to do with any underlying reality, much less a reality in which significant local actors have major stakes. Fishman (1978) shows, for example, that reports of a major crime wave against the elderly in New York City appeared just at a time when most crimes against the elderly were actually on the decline. The public "crime wave" was created by police officials who, in responding to reporters' interest in the topic, provided "juicy" instances that would make good copy. The "crime wave" was sustained by politicians eager to denounce the perpetrators, and these politicians' pronouncements became the basis for still more coverage and expressions of authoritative police concern. Once this symbiotic "dance" (Molotch, 1980) is in motion, the story takes on a life of its own, and fills the pages and airwaves of news media. Such symbolic crusades provide the "easy news" (Gordon, Heath, and leBailly, 1979) needed by reporters pressed for time, just as these crusades satisfy the "news needs" (Molotch and Lester, 1974) of politicians happy to stay away from issues that might offend growth machine interests. The resulting hubbubs often mislead the general public as well as the academic investigator about what the real stuff of community cleavage and political process might be. To the degree that rentier elites keep growth issues on a symbolic level (for example, urban "greatness"), they prevail as the "second face of power" (Bachrach and Baratz, 1962), the face that determines the public agenda (McCombs and Shaw, 1972).

Edelman's second kind of politics, which does not provide easy news, involves the government actions that affect the distribution of important goods and services. Much less visible to publics, often relegated to back rooms or negotiations within insulated authorities and agencies (Caro, 1974; Friedland, Piven, and Alford, 1978), this is the politics that determines who, in material terms, gets what, where, and how (cf. Lasswell, 1936). The media tend to cover it as the dull round of meetings of water and sewer districts, bridge authorities, and industrial development bonding agencies. The media attitude serves to keep interesting issues away from the public and blunt widespread interest in local politics generally. As Vidich and Bensman (1960:217) remark about Springdale, "business control rests upon a dull but unanimous political facade," at least on certain key issues.

Although there are certainly elite organizational mechanisms to inhibit them (Domhoff, 1971, 1983; Whitt, 1982), cleavages within the growth machine can nevertheless develop, and internal disagreements sometimes break into the open. But even then, because of the hegemony of the growth machine, *its* disagreements are allowable and do not challenge the belief in growth itself. Unacceptable are public attacks on the pursuit of exchange values over citizens' search for use value. An internal quarrel over where a convention center is to be built, Banfield (1961) shows us, becomes the public issue for Chicago; but Banfield didn't notice that there was no question about whether there should be a convention center at all.

When elites come to see, for example, that inadequate public services are repelling capital investment, they can put the issue of raising taxes on the public agenda. Trillin (1976:154) reports on Rockford, Illinois, a city whose school system was bankrupted by an antitax ideology. Initially, local elites opposed taxes as part of their efforts to lure industry through a low tax rate. As a result, taxes, and therefore tax money for schools, declined. Eventually, the growth coalition saw the educational decline, not the tax rate, as the greatest danger to the "economic vitality of the community." But ironically, elites are not able to change overnight the ideologies they have put in place over decades, even when it is in their best interests to do so.[3] Unfortunately, neither can the potential *opponents* of growth. As the example of Rockford shows, even such issues as public school spending can become subject to the growth maximization needs of locality. The appropriate level of a social service often depends, not on an abstract model of efficiency or on "public demand" (cf. Tiebout, 1956), but on whether the cost of that service fits the local growth strategy (past and present).

By now it should be clear how political structures are mobilized to intensify land uses for private gain of many sorts. Let us look more closely, therefore, at the various local actors, besides those directly involved in generating rents, who participate in the growth machine.

3. Trillin remarks that rejection of high taxes by the citizens of Rockford is "consistent with what the business and industrial leadership of Rockford has traditionally preached. For years, the industrialists were considered to be in complete control of the sort of local government industrialists traditionally favor—a conservative, relatively clean administration committed to the proposition that the highest principle of government is the lowest property tax rate" (Trillin, 1976:150).

Politicians

The growth machine will sustain only certain persons as politicians. The campaign contributions and public celebrations that build political careers do not ordinarily come about because of a person's desire to save or destroy the environment, to repress or liberate the blacks or other disadvantaged groups, to eliminate civil liberties or enhance them. Given their legislative power, politicians may end up doing any of these things. But the underlying politics that gives rise to such opportunities is a person's participation in the growth consensus. That is why we so often see politicians springing into action to attract new capital and to sustain old investments. Even the pluralist scholar Robert Dahl observed in his New Haven study that if an employer seriously threatened to leave the community, "political leaders are likely to make frantic attempts to make the local situation more attractive" (quoted in Swanstrom, 1981:50).

Certainly, politicians differ in a number of ways. Like Mayor Ogden of Chicago, some are trying to create vast fortunes for themselves as they go about their civic duties on behalf of the growth machine. Robert Folson, the mayor of Dallas, has direct interests in over fifty local businesses, many of which have stakes in local growth outcomes. When the annexation of an adjacent town came up for a vote, he had to abstain because he owned 20 percent of it (Fullinwider, 1980). Another Texan, former governor John Connally, has among his holdings more than $50 million in Austin-area real estate, property slated to become its county's largest residential and commercial development ("Austin Boom," *Santa Barbara News Press,* June 24, 1984, p. B-8). According to Robert Caro (1974), Commissioner Robert Moses was able to overcome opposition to his vast highway and bridge building in the New York City area in part because the region's politicians were themselves buying up land adjacent to parkway exits, setting themselves up for huge rent gains. Most of Hawaii's major Democrat politicians, after winning election on a reform platform in 1954, directly profited as developers, lawyers, contractors, and investors through the zoning and related land-use decisions they and their colleagues were to make over the next thirty years of intensive growth and speculation (Daws and Cooper, 1984). Machine politics never insulated candidates from the development process; builders, railroaders, and other growth activists have long played crucial roles in boss politics, both in immigrant wards (Bell, 1961) and in WASP suburbs (Fogelson, 1967:207). All this is, as George Washington Plunkitt said in 1905, "honest graft" as opposed to "dishonest graft" (quoted in Swanstrom, 1985:25).[4]

Although a little grease always helps a wheel to turn, a system can run well with no graft at all—unless using campaign contributions to influence elections is considered graft. Virtually all politicians are dependent on private campaign financing (Alexander, 1972, 1980, 1983; Boyarsky and Gillam, 1982; Smith, 1984), and it is the real estate entrepreneurs—particularly the large-scale structural speculators—who are particularly active in supporting candidates (see chapter 6 for additional documentation). The result is that candidates of both parties, of whatever ideological stripe, have to garner the favor of such persons, and this puts them squarely into the hands of growth machine coalitions. Thus many officeholders use their authority, not to enrich themselves, but to benefit the "whole community"—that is, to increase aggregate rents. Again, this does not preclude politicians' direct participation in property dealing on occasion and it certainly does not preclude giving a special hand to particular place entrepreneurs with whom a politician has a special relationship.

Elected officials also vary in their perception of how their authority can best be used to maximize growth. After his thorough study of the Cleveland growth machine, Swanstrom (1985) concluded that there are two types of growth strategists: the "conservative" and the "liberal." The former, paramount during the city's age of steel, favor unbridled exploitation of the city and its labor force, generally following the "free economy" political model. Programs of overt government intervention, for purposes of planning, public education, or employee welfare, are all highly suspect. The liberal growth machine strategy, in contrast, acknowledges that longer-term growth can be facilitated by overt

4. Local planning officials also sometimes get in on some of the corruption; they may make real estate investments of their own. Los Angeles Planning Director Calvin Hamilton was pressured to resign after twenty years on the job in part because of revelations that he accepted free rent from developers for a side business and had other conflicts of interest (Clifford, 1985d).

government planning and by programs that pacify, co-opt, and placate oppositions. This is a more modern form of growth ideology. Some politicians, depending on place and time, tend to favor the hard-line "unfettered capitalism" (Wolfe, 1981); others prefer the liberal version, analogous to what is called, in a broader context, "pragmatic state capitalism" (Wolfe, 1981; see also Weinstein, 1968). These positions became more obvious in many regions when urban renewal and other federal programs began penetrating cities in the postwar period. Especially in conservative areas such as Texas (Melosi, 1983:185), elites long debated among themselves whether or not the newfangled growth schemes would do more harm than good.

On the symbolic issues, politicians may also differ, on both the content of their positions and the degree to which they actually care about the issues. Some are no doubt sincere in pushing their "causes"; others may cynically manipulate them to obscure the distributional consequences of their own actions in other matters. Sometimes the results are positive, for example, when Oklahoma City and Dallas leaders made deliberate efforts to prevent racist elements from scaring off development with "another Little Rock." Liberal growth machine goals may thus help reform reactionary social patterns (Bernard, 1983:225; Melosi, 1983:188). But despite these variations, there appears to be a "tilt" to the whole system, regardless of time and place. Growth coalition activists and campaign contributors are not a culturally, racially, or economically diverse cross section of the urban population. They tend to give a reactionary texture to local government, in which the cultural crusades, like the material ones, are chosen for their acceptability to the rentier groups. Politicians adept in both spheres (material and symbolic) are the most valued, and most likely to have successful careers. A skilled politician delivers growth while giving a good circus.

The symbolic political skills are particularly crucial when unforeseen circumstances create use value crises, which can potentially stymie a locality's basic growth strategy. The 1978 Love Canal toxic waste emergency at Niagara Falls, New York, reveals how local officials use their positions to reassure the citizens and mold local agendas to handle disruptive "emotional" issues. In her detailed ethnographic account, Levine (1982:59) reports that "the city's chief executives, led by the mayor, minimized the Love Canal problem in all public statements for two years no matter how much personal sympathy they felt for the affected people whose health was threatened by the poisons leaking into their homes" (see also Fowlkes and Miller, 1985). Lester (1971) reports a similar stance taken by the Utah civic leadership in response to the escape of nerve gas from the U.S. military's Dugway Proving Grounds in 1969 (see also Hirsch, 1969). The conduct of politicians in the face of accidents like the leakage of poison into schoolyards and homes in Niagara Falls or the sheep deaths in Utah reveal this "backup" function of local leaders (Molotch and Lester, 1974, 1975).

Still another critical use of local politicians is their ability to influence higher-level political actors in their growth distribution decisions. Although capital has direct links to national politicians (particularly in the executive office and Senate, see Domhoff [1967, 1970, 1983]), rentier groups are more parochial in their ties, although they may have contact with congressional representatives. Hence, rentiers need local politicians to lobby national officials. The national politicians, in turn, are responsive because they depend on local political operators (including party figures) for their own power base. The local politicians symbiotically need their national counterparts to generate the goods that keep them viable at home.

The goods that benefit the local leaders and growth interests are not trivial. The develoment of the Midwest was, as the historical anecdotes make clear, dependent on national decisions affecting canal and railroad lines. The Southwest and most of California could be developed only with federal subsidies and capital investments in water projects. The profound significance of government capital spending can be grasped by considering one statistic: Direct government outlays (at all levels) in 1983 accounted for nearly 27 percent of all construction in the United States (Mollenkopf, 1983:43). The figure was even higher, of course, during World War II, when federal construction expenditures laid the basis for much of the infrastructural and defense spending that was to follow.

Local Media

One local business takes a broad responsibility for general growth machine goals—the metropolitan newspaper. Most newspapers (small, suburban papers are occasionally an exception) profit primarily from increasing their circulation and therefore have a direct interest in growth.[5] As the metropolis expands, the newspaper can sell a larger number of ad lines (at higher per line cost), on the basis of a rising circulation base; TV and radio stations are in a similar situation. In explaining why his newspaper had supported the urbanization of orchards that used to cover what is now the city of San Jose, the publisher of the *San Jose Mercury News* said, "Trees do not read newspapers" (Downie, 1974:112, as cited in Domhoff, 1983:168). Just as newspaper boosterism was important in building the frontier towns (Dagenais, 1967), so today "the hallmark of media content has been peerless boosterism: congratulate growth rather than calculate consequences; compliment development rather than criticize its impact" (Burd, 1977:129; see also Devereux, 1976; Freidel, 1963). The media "must present a favorable image to outsiders" (Cox and Morgan, 1973:136),[6] and only "sparingly use their issue-raising capacities" (Peterson, 1981:124).

American cities tend to be one-newspaper (or one-newspaper company) towns. The newspaper's assets in physical plant, in "good will," and in advertising clients are, for the most part, immobile. The local newspaper thus tends to occupy a unique position: like many other local businesses, it has an interest in growth, but unlike most others, its critical interest is not in the specific spatial pattern of that growth. The paper may occasionally help forge a specific strategy of growth, but ordinarily it makes little

5. Although many suburban newspapers encourage growth, especially of tax-generating businesses, the papers of exclusive suburban towns may instead try to guard the existing land-use patterns and social base of their circulation area. Rudel (1983:104) describes just this sort of situation in Westport, Connecticut. There are a number of reasons for this occasional deviation from the rule we are proposing. When trying to attract advertising dollars, newspapers prefer a small, rich readership to a larger but poorer one. Maintaining exclusivity is itself occasionally a growth strategy for smaller communities. Opposition to growth in these cases is consistent with the desires of local elites.

6. Cox and Morgan's study of British local newspapers indicates that the booster role of the press is not unique to the United States.

difference to a newspaper whether the additional population comes to reside on the north side or the south side, or whether the new business comes through a new convention center or a new olive factory. The newspaper has no ax to grind except the one that holds the community elite together: growth.

This disinterest in the specific form of growth, but avid commitment to development generally, enables the newspaper to achieve a statesmanlike position in the community. It is often deferred to as a neutral party by the special interests. In his pioneering study of the creation of zoning laws in New York City in the 1920s, Makielski (1966:149) remarks, "While the newspapers in the city are large landholders, the role of the press was not quite like that of any of the other nongovernmental actors. The press was in part one of the referees of the rules of the game, especially the informal rules, calling attention to what it considered violations." The publisher or editor is often the arbiter of internal growth machine bickering, restraining the short-term profiteers in the interest of more stable, long-term, and properly planned growth.

The publishing families are often ensconced as the most important city builders within the town or city; this is the appropriate designation for such prominent families as Otis and Chandler of the *Los Angeles Times* (see Clark, 1983:271; Halberstam, 1979); Pulliam of the *Arizona Republic* and *Phoenix Sun* (see Luckingham, 1983:318); and Gaylord of the *Daily Oklahoman* (see Bernard, 1983:216). Sometimes these publishers are directly active in politics, "kingmaking" behind the scenes by screening candidates for political office, lobbying for federal contracts and grants, and striving to build growth infrastructure in their region (Fainstein, Fainstein, and Armistead, 1983:217; Judd, 1983:178). In the booming Contra Costa County suburbs of the San Francisco Bay Area, the president of the countywide organization of builders, real estate investors, and property financiers was the owner of the regional paper. In his home county, as well as in the jurisdictions of his eleven other suburban papers, owner Dean Lesher ("Citizen Lesher") acts as "a cheerleader for development" who simply kills stories damaging to growth interests and reassigns unsympathetic reporters to less controversial beats (Steidtmann, 1985). The local newspaper editor was one of the three "bosses" in Springdale's "invisible government" (Vidich and Bensman, 1960:217). Sometimes, the publisher is among the largest urban landholders and openly fights for benefits tied to growth in land: The owners of the *Los Angeles Times* fought for the water that developed their vast properties for both urban and agricultural uses. The editorial stance is usually reformist, invoking the common good (and technical planning expertise) as the rationale for the land-use decisions the owners favor. This sustains the legitimacy of the paper itself among all literate sectors of society and helps mask the distributive effects of many growth developments.

The media attempt to attain their goals not only through news articles and editorials but also through informal talks between owners and editors and the local leaders. Because newspaper interests are tied to growth, media executives are sympathetic to business leaders' complaints that a particular journalistic investigation or angle may be bad for the local business climate, and should it nevertheless become necessary, direct threats of advertising cancellation can modify journalistic coverage (Bernard, 1983:220). This does not mean that newspapers (or advertisers) control the politics of a city or region, but that the media have a special influence simply because they are committed to growth per se, and can play an invaluable role in coordinating strategy and selling growth to the public.

This institutional legitimacy is especially useful in crises. In the controversy surrounding the army's accidental release of nerve gas at the Dugway Proving Grounds, Lester found that the Utah media were far more sympathetic to the military's explanations than were media outside Utah (Lester, 1971). The economic utility of the Dugway Proving Grounds (and related government facilities) was valued by the local establishment. Similarly, insiders report that publicizing toxic waste problems at Love Canal was hindered by an "unwritten law" in the newsroom that "a reporter did not attack or otherwise fluster the Hooker [Chemical Company] executives" (Brown, 1979, cited in Levine, 1982:190).

As these examples indicate, a newspaper's essential role is not to protect a given firm or industry (an issue more likely to arise in a small city than a large one) but to bolster and maintain the predisposition for general growth. Although newspaper editorialists may express concern for "the ecology," this does not prevent them from supporting growth-inducing investments for their regions. The *New York Times* likes office towers and additional industrial installations in the city even more than it loves "the environment." Even when historically significant districts are threatened, the *Times* editorializes in favor of intensification. Thus the *Times* recently admonished opponents to "get out of the way" of the Times Square renewal, which would replace landmark structures (including its own former headquarters at 1 Times Square) with huge office structures (*New York Times,* May 24, 1984, p. 18). Similarly, the *Los Angeles Times* editorializes against narrow-minded profiteering that increases pollution or aesthetic blight—in other cities. The newspaper featured criticism, for example, of the Times Square renewal plan (Kaplan, 1984:1), but had enthusiastically supported development of the environmentally devastating supersonic transport (SST) for the jobs it would presumably lure to Southern California. In an unexpected regional parallel, the *Los Angeles Times* fired celebrated architectural critic John Pastier for his incessant criticisms of Los Angeles's downtown renewal projects (Clark, 1983:298), and the *New York Times* dismissed Pulitzer Prize winner Sydney Schanberg as a columnist apparently because he "opposed civic projects supported by some of New York's most powerful interests, particularly those in the real estate industry" (Rosenstiel, 1985:21).

Although newspapers may openly support "good planning principles" of a certain sort, the acceptable form of "good planning" does not often extend to limiting growth or authentic conservation in a newspaper's home ground. "Good planning principles" can easily represent the opposite goals.

Utilities

Leaders of "independent" public or quasi-public agencies, such as utilities, may play a role similar to that of the newspaper publisher: tied to a single locale, they become growth "statesmen" rather than advocates for a certain type of growth or intralocal distribution of growth.

For example, a water-supplying agency (whether public or private) can expand only by acquiring more users. This causes utilities to penetrate deep into the hinterlands, inefficiently extending lines to areas that are extremely costly to service (Gaffney, 1961; Walker and Williams, 1982). The same growth goals exist within central cities. Brooklyn Gas was an avid supporter of the movement of young professionals into abandoned areas of Brooklyn, New York, in the 1970s, and even went so far as to help finance housing rehabilitation and sponsor a traveling slide show and open houses displaying the pleasant life styles in the area. All utilities seem bent on acquiring more customers to pay off past investments, and on proving they have the good growth prospects that lenders use as a criterion for financing additional investments. Overall efficiencies are often sacrificed as a result.

Transportation officials, whether of public or private organizations, have a special interest in growth: they tend to favor growth along their specific transit routes. But transportation doesn't just serve growth, it creates it. From the beginning, the laying-out of mass transit lines was a method of stimulating development; indeed, the land speculators and the executives of the transportation firms were often the same people. In part because of the salience of land development, "public service was largely incidental to the operation of the street railways" (Wilcox, quoted in Yago, 1983:44). Henry Huntington's Pacific Electric, the primary commuting system of Los Angeles, "was built not to provide transportation but to sell real estate" (Clark, 1983:272; see also Binford, 1985; Fogelson, 1967; Yago, 1983). And because the goal of profitable transportation did not guide the design and routing of the system, it was destined to lose money, leaving Los Angeles without a viable transit system in the end (Fogelson, 1967).

Transit bureaucrats today, although not typically in the land business, function as active development boosters; only in that way can more riders be found to support their systems and help pay off the sometimes enormous debts incurred to construct or expand the systems. On the national level, major airlines develop a strong growth interest in the development of their "hub" city and the network it serves. Eastern Airlines must have growth in Miami, Northwest Airlines needs development in Minneapolis, and American Airlines rises or falls with the fortunes of Dallas-Fort Worth.

Auxiliary Players

Although they may have less of a stake in the growth process than the actors described above, certain institutions play an auxiliary role in promoting and maintaining growth. Key among these auxiliary players are the cultural institutions in an area: museums, theaters, universities, symphonies, and professional sports teams. An increase in the local population may help sustain these institutions by increasing the number of clients and support groups. More important, perhaps, is that such institutions often need the favor of those who are at the heart of local growth machines—the rentiers, media owners, and politicians, who can make or break their institutional goals. And indeed, cultural institutions do have something to offer in return.

Universities

The construction and expansion of university campuses can stimulate development in otherwise rural landscapes; the land for the University of California at Los Angeles (UCLA) was originally donated for a state normal school in 1881 "in order to increase the value of the surrounding real estate" (Clark, 1983:286). Other educational institutions, particularly the University of California campuses at Irvine and Santa Barbara, had similar origins, as did the State University of New York at Stony Brook and the University of Texas at San Antonio (Johnson, 1983). Building a university campus can be the first step in rejuvenating a deteriorated inner-city area; this was the case with the Chicago branch of the University of Illinois (Banfield, 1961), the expansions of Yale University in New Haven (Dahl, 1961; Domhoff, 1978), and the University of Chicago (Rossi and Dentler, 1961). The use of universities and colleges as a stimulus to growth is often made explicit by both the institution involved and the local civic boosters.

The symbiotic relationship between universities and local development intensified in the 1980s. Drawing on the precedent of Silicon Valley (with Stanford University as its intellectual center) and Route 128, the high-tech highway, in the Boston area (with MIT as its intellectual center), many localities have come to view universities as an infrastructure for cutting edge industrial growth.

Universities, in turn, have been quick to exploit this opportunity to strengthen their local constituency. A clear illustration is the Microelectronics and Computer Technology Corporation (MCTC), a newly created private firm with the mission of keeping the United States ahead of Japan in the microelectronics field. Jointly funded by twelve of the most important American firms in advanced technology, the new company had to build, at its founding, a $100 million installation. Austin, Texas, won the project, but only after the local and state governments agreed to a list of concessions, including subsidized land, mortgage assistance for employees, and a score of faculty chairs and other positions at the University of Texas for personnel relevant to the company mission (Rivera, 1983a).

The Austin victory reverberated especially through California, the location of the runner-up site. A consensus emerged, bolstered by an MCTC official's explicit statement, that faltering support for California higher education had made Texas the preferred choice. The view that a decline in the quality of higher education could drive away business may have been important in the fiscally conservative governor's decision to substantially increase allocations to the University of California in the following year. Budget increases for the less research-oriented state college system were at a much lower level; the community college system received a decrease in real dollar funding. The second and third groups of institutions play a less important role in growth machine strategies. As the president of the University of Texas said after his institution's victory, "The battle for national leadership among states is being fought on the campuses of the great research universities of the nation" (King, 1985:12).

Museums, Theaters, Expositions

Art and the physical structures that house artworks also play a role in growth strategies. In New York City, the art capital of the country, the arts generate about $1.3 billion in annual economic activity, a sum larger than that contributed by either advertising or computer services (Pittas, 1984). In Los Angeles, another major art center, urban redevelopment funds are paying for the new Museum of Contemporary Art, explicitly conceived as a means of enhancing commercial success for adjacent downtown residential, hotel, and office construction. Major art centers are also being used as development leverage in downtown Miami, Tampa (Mormino, 1983:152), and Dallas. The new Dallas Museum of Art will be the central focus of "the largest downtown development ever undertaken in the United States" (Tomkins, 1983:92). Whatever it may do to advance the cause of artists in Texas, the museum will do much for nearby rents. According to a Dallas newspaper report, "The feeling persists that the arts have been appropriated here primarily to sell massive real estate development" (quoted in Tomkins, 1983:97).

Other sorts of museums can be used for the same purpose. Three Silicon Valley cities are locked in a battle to make themselves the site for a $90 million Technology Museum that "is expected to draw one million visitors a year, boost hotel occupancy and attract new business" (Sahagun and Jalon, 1984:1). Two of the competing cities (Mountain View and San Jose), in promising millions in subsidies, would use the museum as a focal point for major commercial developments. In a not dissimilar, though perhaps less highbrow effort, the city of Flint, Michigan ("the unemployment capital of America") invested city money in a Six Flags Auto World Theme Park that displayed cars (old and new) and used the auto as a motif for its other attractions. The facility was situated so as to boost the city's crumbling downtown; unhappily, gate receipts were poor and the park was closed, and the $70 million public-private investment was lost (Risen, 1984).

Theaters are also being used as a development tool. Believing that the preservation of the legitimate theater will help maintain the "vitality" of Midtown Manhattan, city officials are considering a plan to allow theater owners to sell the "development rights" of their properties, which the dense zoning in the theater district would otherwise permit. The buyer of these rights would then be allowed bonus, or greater, densities on other nearby sites, thereby protecting the theaters' existence while not blocking the general densification of the area (*New York Times,* September 19, 1983, p. 1). In many parts of the country, various individuals and groups are encouraging (and often subsidizing) the construction and rehabilitation of theaters and concert halls as growth instruments. Downtown churches are looking to the heavens for financial returns, arranging to sell air rights over their imposing edifices to developers of nearby parcels.

These programs allow cultural institutions, in effect, to collect rents they otherwise could gain only by tearing down their structures. The arrangement heads off any conflict between developers and those oriented to the use values that theaters and historic buildings might provide and helps to maintain these "city treasures" that help sustain the economic base. But aggregate levels of development are not curtailed.

Still another kind of cultural institution involved in the growth apparatus is the blue-ribbon committee that puts together local spectaculars, like annual festivals and parades, or a one-shot World's Fair or Olympics competition. These are among the common efforts by Chambers of Commerce and Visitors Bureaus to lure tourists and stimulate development. There are industrial expositions, music festivals, and all manner of regional annual attractions. Such events are considered ways of meeting short-term goals of generating revenue, as well as ways of meeting long-term goals of attracting outside businesses. They show off the locality to outsiders who could generate additional investments in the future. Los Angeles business leaders, for example, "created the Rose Parade to draw national attention to Southern California's balmy weather by staging an outdoor event with fresh flowers in the middle of winter" (Clark, 1983:271).

The short-term results of big events can mean billions of dollars injected into the local economy, although costs to ordinary citizens (in the form of traffic congestion, higher prices, and drains on public services) are notoriously understated (Clayton, 1984; Shlay and Gilroth, 1984). To help gain the necessary public subsidies for such events, the promoters insist that "the community" will benefit, and they inflate revenue expectations in order to make trickle-down benefits at least seem plausible (Hays, 1984). The 1983 Knoxville World's Fair, one of the few World's Fairs to actually produce a profit on its own books, nevertheless left its host city with $57 million in debts (Schmidt, 1984), a debt large enough to require an 8 percent increase in property taxes in order to pay it off. The 1984 New Orleans World's Fair showed a $100 million loss (Hill, 1984). Other spectaculars, like the Los Angeles Olympics, do come out ahead, but even so, certain costs (like neighborhood disruption) are simply not counted.

Clearly, a broad range of cultural institutions, not often thought of in terms of land development, participate closely as auxiliary players in the growth process for many reasons. Some participate because their own organizational goals depend on local growth, others because they find it diplomatic to support the local rentier patrons, others because their own properties become a valuable resource, and still others because their boards of directors are closely tied to local elites. Whatever the reasons, the growth machine cuts a wide institutional swath.

Professional Sports

Professional sports teams are a clear asset to localities for the strong image they present and tourist traffic they attract (Eitzen and Sage, 1978:184). Baseball, the American pastime, had its beginning in amusement parks; many of the team owners were real estate speculators who used the team to attract visitors to the subdivisions they offered for sale. Fans would ride to the park on trolley lines that the team owner also owned (Roderick, 1984). In more recent years, baseball and football stadia and hockey and basketball arenas have been used by local *governments* to provide a focus for urban renewal projects in Pittsburgh, Hartford, Minneapolis, and other cities (Roderick, 1984). New Orleans used the development of the Superdome "to set the stage for a tourist-based growth strategy for the future development of downtown" (Smith and Keller, 1983:134). The facility ended up costing $165 million (instead of the projected $35 million), and has had large annual operating losses—all absorbed by the state government.

St. Petersburg, Florida, seems to be following the example of New Orleans. The Florida city has agreed to invest $59.6 million in a new stadium *in the hope* that it will lure a major league franchise to a city that woefully lacks the demographic profile necessary to support major league sports. So far the project has required displacement of four hundred families (primarily black) and saddled the city with a huge debt. A city official insists it will be worth it because

When you consider what it would mean in new business for hotels, jobs, pride, tourism—then it's a real good deal. We believe for every dollar spent inside a stadium, seven are spent outside. [Roderick, 1984:24.]

In an even more dubious effort, the city of Albany, New York, gained popular support (and some state funding) for a $40 million multipurpose downtown civic center on the grounds that it *might* attract a hockey team to the city (D'Ambrosio, 1985). Like the New Orleans project, this plan puts sports boosters behind a project that will help local business with its other events (such as conventions), regardless of its success in attracting a professional team.

Local teams are an industry in themselves. Atlanta's professional sports organizations have been estimated to be worth over $60 million annually to the local economy (Rice, 1983:38). But a local team does much more than the direct expenditures imply: It helps a city's visibility, putting it "on the map" as a "big league city," making it more noticeable to all, including those making investment decisions. It is one of "the visible badges of urban maturity" (Rice, 1983:38). Within the city, sports teams have an important ideological use, helping instill civic pride in business through jingoistic logic. Whether the setting is soccer in Brazil (Lever, 1983) or baseball in Baltimore, millions of people are mobilized to pull for the home turf. Sports that lend themselves to boosting a locality are the useful ones. Growth activists are less enthusiastic about sports that honor individual accomplishment and are less easily tied to a locality or team name (for example, tennis, track, or swimming). Only when such sports connect with rent enhancement, for example, when they are part of an Olympic competition held on home ground, do they receive major support.

The mobilization of the audience is accomplished through a number of mechanisms. Money to construct stadia or to attract or retain the home team is raised through public bond issues. About 70 percent of current facilities were built with this tool, often under conditions of large cost overruns (Eitzen, 1978). Enthusiastic corporate sponsorship of radio and TV broadcasts greatly expands public participation (and by linking products with local heroes this form of sponsorship avoids any danger of involving the corporate image with controversial topics). Finally, the news media provide avid coverage, giving sports a separate section of the newspaper and a substantial block of broadcast time during the period designated for the news (including the mention of the city name on national news). No other single news topic receives such consistent and extensive coverage in the United States.

The coverage is, of course, always supportive of sports itself and the home team in particular. There is no pretense of objectivity. It is all part of the ideological ground for other civic goals, including the successful competition of cities for growth-inducing projects. Professional teams serve many latent social functions (Brower, 1972); sustaining the growth ideology is clearly one of them.

Organized Labor

Although they are sometimes in conflict with capitalists on other issues, labor union leaders are enthusiastic partners in growth machines, with little careful consideration of the long-term consequences for the rank and file. Union leadership subscribes to value-free development because it will "bring jobs," particularly to the building trades, whose spokespersons are especially vocal in their support of development. Less likely to be openly discussed is the concern that growth may bring more union members and enhance the power and authority of local union officials.[7]

Union executives are available for ceremonial celebrations of growth (ribbon cuttings, announcements of government contracts, urban redevelopment ground breakings). Entrepreneurs frequently enlist union support when value-free development is under challenge; when growth control was threatened in the city of San Diego in 1975, three thousand labor union members paraded through downtown, protesting land-use regulations they claimed were responsible for local unemployment (Corso, 1983: 339). Labor leaders are especially useful when the growth machine needs someone to claim that development opponents are "elitist" or "selfish." Thus, in a characteristic report on a growth

---

7. Unions oppose growth projects that bring nonunion shops; the UAW did not welcome Japanese-owned auto plants that would exclude the union.

control referendum in the city of Riverside, California, Neiman and Loveridge (1981:764–65) found that the progrowth coalition "repeated, time and again, that most of organized labor in the area opposed Measure B, firms wishing to locate in Riverside were being frightened away . . . and thousands of voters would lose their jobs if Measure B passed." Although this technique apparently worked in Riverside at the polls and in San Diego in the streets, it is doubtful that the majority of the rank and file share the disposition of their leaders on these issues (a point to be documented in chapter 6). Nevertheless, the entrepreneurs' influence over the public statements and ceremonial roles of union leaders, regardless of what their members think, helps the rentiers in achieving their aggressive growth policies.

The co-optation of labor leadership is again evident in its role in national urban policy. Labor essentially is a dependable support of growth—anywhere, anytime. Although its traditional constituency is centered in the declining areas of the country, the unions' national hierarchy supports policies little more specific than those that provide "aid to the cities." The active campaign by the United Auto Workers (UAW) for increased investment in Detroit and other sections of the country's "automotive realm" (Hill, 1984) is an exception. Although unions may be especially concerned with the future of the declining areas, they have not tried to develop an effective strategy for directing investment toward these places, at the expense of other places. Labor cannot serve the needs of its most vulnerable and best organized geographical constituency because it won't inhibit investment at any given place. The inability of labor to influence the distribution of development within the United States (much less across world regions) makes organized labor helpless in influencing the political economy of places. Labor becomes little more than one more instrument to be used by elites in competing growth machines.

Self-employed Professionals and Small Retailers

Retailers and professionals ordinarily have no clear interest in the generation of aggregate rents. The stake of these groups in growth depends on their particular situation, including the possibility that growth may displace a clientele upon which they are dependent. Any potential opposition from these groups is, how-ever, blunted by a number of factors, two of which are especially important. Retailers need customers and this often leads them to equate aggregate growth in a locality with an increase in sales and profits for themselves. They also have social ties with local rentier groups, whose avid growth orientation may have a strong influence.

By contrast, larger but locally based retailing chains with substantial local market shares have a direct interest in local growth. They can grow more cheaply by expanding in their own market area (where media and other overhead costs can be spread among existing stores) than by penetrating distant regions. But a larger population base also draws new competitors, since retailing is more competitive than most other businesses. In particular, on reaching a certain size, markets become more attractive to higher-volume, national retailers, such as McDonald's or chain department stores and the malls that house them. Large operations are especially drawn to fast-growing areas in which an early decision to locate can preempt other national competitors. Department stores and chain restaurants displace an enormous number of smaller entrepreneurs (Friedland and Gardner, 1983). Despite these prospects, small retailers are often supporters of local growth machines, even when it means bringing in directly competitive operations. In this instance, ideology seems to prevail over concrete interests and the given record.

Well-paid professionals such as doctors and lawyers sometimes invest their own high salaries in property syndicates (often unprofitable ones) that are put together for them by brokers and financial advisers. This gives the professionals the direct stake in growth outcomes that we ordinarily associate with place entrepreneurs. As social peers of the rentiers, and as vague supporters of value-free production generally, these professionals are often sympathetic to growth. They seem less supportive than business groups, but more supportive than lower-paid professionals or members of the working class (Albrecht, Bultena, and Hoiberg, forthcoming). A critical issue for the affluent professionals is whether their own use of places—to live, shop, and earn money—is compatible with growth. Professionals can avoid the dilemma by investing at a distance from their own homes. As we will see in the next two chapters, professionals not tied to the growth machine make particularly effective citizen opponents of the growth coalition.

Corporate Capitalists

Most capitalists, like others whose primary attachment to place is for use values, have little direct interest in land-use intensification in a specific locality. They are in business to gain profits, not rents. Particularly when local corporate leaders are division heads of multilocational firms, there is little reason for direct involvement (see Schulze, 1961). In his report on Houston's historical development, Kaplan quotes a local observer who remarks that the "pro-growth faction" consists of people "whose very good livelihoods depend on a local government that will continue to make the 'right' policy decisions." "Surprisingly," Kaplan comments (1983:204), "the oil and gas industry remains aloof from local Houston politics, preferring to concentrate on the national and international policies crucial to its interests." This disinterest of the large industrials is not a surprise to us.

Nevertheless, corporate actors do have an interest in sustaining the growth machine ideology (as opposed to the actual growth of the area surrounding their plant). This ideology helps make them respected people in their area. Their social worth is often defined in terms of "size of payroll," and their payroll in turn helps them get land-use and budget policies consistent with corporate needs. As long as the rentiers dominate locality, capitalists and their managers need not play a direct role. They may choose to do so anyway, particularly when they are natives of the locale (not branch plant functionaries) with ties to rentier groups (Friedland and Palmer, 1984; Galaskiewicz, 1979a, 1979b). But the absence of corporate officials in local politics (especially branch plant managers), repeatedly observed by various investigators (see Banfield and Wilson, 1963; Dahl, 1961; Schulze, 1961), is not a sign of their lack of power. It can instead be evidence that the local agenda is so pervasively shaped by their interests that they have no need to participate. Like good managers generally, they work through others, leaving their relative invisibility as a sign of their effectiveness. Only when there is a special opportunity, as in modern-day company towns (see chapter 5), or when ordinary hegemonic mechanisms fail (see chapter 6), do we find corporate functionaries again active in urban politics.

The Effects of Growth

By claiming that more intensive development benefits virtually all groups in a locality, growth machine activists need pay no attention to the distinction between use and exchange values that pervades our analysis. They assert that growth strengthens the local tax base, creates jobs, provides resources to solve existing social problems, meets the housing needs caused by natural population growth, and allows the market to serve public tastes in housing, neighborhoods, and commercial development. Similarly, Paul Peterson speaks of development goals as inherently uncontroversial and "consensual" because they are aligned with the "collective good" (1981:147), "with the interests of the community as a whole" (1981:143). Speaking in characteristically sanguine terms even about urban renewal (widely known by then for its detrimental effects on cities), Peterson says in his celebrated book: "Downtown business benefits, but so do laborers desiring higher wages, homeowners hoping house values will rise, the unemployed seeking new jobs, and politicians aiming for reelection" (1981:147).

Some of these claims, for some times and places, are true. The costs and benefits of growth depend on local circumstance. Declining cities experience problems that might be eased by replacement investments. Even in growing cities, the costs of growth can conceivably be limited by appropriate planning and control techniques. Nevertheless, for many places and times, growth is at best a mixed blessing and the growth machine's claims are merely legitimating ideology, not accurate descriptions of reality. Residents of declining cities, as well as people living in more dynamic areas, are often deceived by the extravagant claims that growth solves problems. These claims demand a realistic evaluation.

Fiscal Health

Systematic comparative analyses of government costs as a function of city size and growth have found that cost is positively related to both size of place and rate of growth, at least for middle-size cities (see Appelbaum, 1976; Follett, 1976). Of course, the *conditions* of growth are important. The overall fiscal state of a city depends on the kind of growth involved (industrial versus residential, and the subtypes of each) and the existing capacities of the local infrastructure. In general, most studies (see Stuart and Teska, 1971) conclude that housing development represents a net fiscal loss because of the service costs that residents require, although housing for the rich is more lucrative than housing for the poor. Industrial and commercial growth, on the other hand, tends to produce net benefits for the tax base, but only if the costs of servicing additions to the local labor force are omitted from the calculations. If local government provides special tax incentives or other sorts of subsidies to attract new industries, the fiscal costs of development will obviously be higher.

Growth can also at times save a local government money. A primary factor in this possibility is the existence of "unused capacities." If a town has a declining birth rate and thus a school district with empty classrooms, officials may try to attract additional families to increase the efficient use of the physical plant and thereby reduce the per capita costs. If a city is paying off a bonded debt on a sewer plant that could serve double its present demand, officials may seek additional users in order to spread the costs to a larger number and thus decrease the burden for current residents.

Under other conditions, however, even small increases in demand can have enormous fiscal costs if the increases entail major new public expenditures. In many cases infrastructures must be built "all at once"; these are "lumpy" costs. Additional water supplies can sometimes be gained only by constructing a vast aqueduct system that can transport 100,000 acre feet annually as easily as a single acre foot. The costs of such utility investments are usually shared equally by all users; the "new people" don't have to pay more because of the extraordinary costs their presence creates. The developer of a "leap frog" housing tract (one that jumps

beyond existing urban development) doesn't pay more than previous entrepreneurs to run utilities a greater distance, despite the
higher costs entailed by the location. This pricing system, in
which each user pays the same amount regardless of when or how
the user joined the client group, tends to mask the cost of additional growth (or the irrationalities of its distribution). These costs
can be especially high because the cheap sources of water, power,
and highway rights of way are the first ones tapped; expansion
thus tends to be increasingly expensive.

Costs to existing residents can be particularly high if the anticipated growth does not materialize. In what Worster (1982:514)
calls the "infrastructural trap," localities that place bets on future
growth by investing in large-scale capacities then must move
heaven and earth to make sure they get that growth. Whether
through deceitful plot or inadvertent blunder, the results can be a
vicious cycle of crisis-oriented growth addiction as various infrastructures collapse from overuse and are replaced by still larger
facilities, which then can only be paid for with additional growth
that again creates another crisis of overuse.

All of this resembles the infrastructure crises of much earlier
efforts at growth inducement in the nineteenth century. Scheiber
(1973) reports absurd redundancies in the canal-building spree of
the state of Ohio as each politically powerful land group demanded a linkage to the great waterways. The scenario was repeated with turnpikes and railroads, leading to absurd overcapac-
ity and the "intolerable indebtedness" that led to bond defaults by
several states (Goodrich, 1950). Costs of construction were considerably increased through corrupt management, and the viability of the completed projects was eroded by duplication and irrational routings. The result was "bitter disillusionment" (Scheiber,
1973:138) when prosperous towns did not materialize where expected (almost everywhere) and the costs of overbuilt infrastructures remained as a continuous drain on public budgets.

It is less likely today that a single project could bring about
such a fiscal disaster, although the nuclear power bankruptcy in
1983 of the major utility in the state of Washington is one case in
point, just as similar nuclear power problems threaten other rate-
payers elsewhere. In most instances, growth spending corrodes
subtly, slowly eroding fiscal integrity as the service costs of new

developments outweigh the revenues they generate. Some localities have demanded "hard looks" at the precise cumulative costs,
and have come up with striking results. A 1970 study for the city
of Palo Alto, California, found that it would be cheaper for that
city to purchase its privately owned undeveloped foothills at full
value, rather than allow the land to be developed and enter the tax
rolls (Livingston and Blayney, 1971). Again, a study of Santa
Barbara, California, demonstrated that service expenditures for
virtually any population growth would require raising property
taxes and utility rates, with no compensatory public service benefits for local residents (Appelbaum et al., 1976). Similar conclusions on the costs of growth have resulted from studies of Boulder,
Colorado (cited in Finkler, 1972), and Ann Arbor, Michigan (Ann
Arbor, Michigan, Planning Department, 1972). In their review of
case studies of the effects of industrial growth in small towns,
Summers and Branch (1984) report that increments to the local
tax base were in most cases outweighed by added service burdens,
except when industrial development was not subsidized by local
government and new employees lived in other communities.

The kinds of cities that have undertaken these studies, primarily university towns, are by no means typical U.S. places; in the
declining cities of the frostbelt, the results might well be different.
And cities can, in reality, manipulate the fiscal consequences of
growth to benefit them. Here we want to stress that growth cannot,
just because it "adds to the tax base," be assumed beneficial to a
city's fiscal well-being. Only a careful analysis of the details can
yield accurate conclusions about a specific place at a given time.
We suspect that the promised benefits of growth would be found,
more often than not, to have been greatly exaggerated by the local
growth activists, who, while portraying themselves as the prudent
guardians of the public purse, often lead their cities into terrible
fiscal troubles.

Employment

A key ideological prop for the growth machine, especially in appealing to the working class, is the assertion that local
growth "makes jobs." This claim is aggressively promulgated
by developers, bankers, and Chamber of Commerce officials—

people whose politics otherwise reveal little concern for problems of the working class. The emphasis on jobs becomes a part of the statesmanlike talk of media editorialists. Needless to say, the benefits in profits and rents are seldom brought up in public.

The reality is that local growth does not make jobs: it only distributes them. In any given year the United States will see the construction of a certain number of new factories, office units, and highways—regardless of where they are put. Similarly, a given number of automobiles, missiles, and lamp shades will be made in this country, regardless of where they are manufactured. The number of jobs in this society, whether in the building trades or in any other economic sector, will therefore be determined by rates of return on investments, national trade policy, federal decisions affecting the money supply, and other factors unrelated to local decision making. Except for introducing draconian measures that would replicate Third World labor conditions in U.S. cities (not as remote a possibility as we might think; see chapter 7), a locality can only compete with other localities for its share of newly created U.S. jobs. Aggregate employment is unaffected by the outcome of this competition among localities to "make" jobs. The bulk of studies that search, either through cross-sectional or longitudinal analysis, for relations between size or growth of places and unemployment rates fail to show significant relationships (Applebaum, 1976; Follett, 1976; Garrison, 1971; Greenberg, n.d.; Hadden and Borgatta, 1965:108; Samuelson, 1942; Sierra Club of San Diego, 1973; Summers et al., 1976; Summers and Branch, 1984; but see Eberts, 1979).

Despite the pain and difficulty often associated with interurban migrations, there is enough worker mobility, at least within national boundaries, to fill jobs at geographically distant points, including even the wilds of Alaska. When jobs develop in a fast-growing area, workers from other areas are attracted to fill the developing vacancies, thus preserving the same unemployment rate as before the growth surge. Indeed, especially in cases of rapid, "boom town" growth, enthusiastic media coverage can prompt large numbers of workers to migrate, much in excess of immediate job openings. A large surplus of workers results when the boom comes to its inevitable end, often with many of the infrastructural costs still to be paid (Markusen, 1978). The human strain of migration—people forced to leave their relatives and neighborhood behind—may prove to have been for nothing. Unemployment rates in the state of Alaska, a boom region for many years, exceeded the national average from 1972 to 1982 every year except one. In 1978, even before oil prices began their precipitous fall, the national unemployment rate was 6.1 percent and the Alaska rate was 11.2 percent.

Similarly, just as "new jobs" may not change the aggregate *rate* of unemployment (either locally or nationally), they may also have little affect on unemployed *individuals* in a given place. For example, cities that are able to reverse chronic economic decline and stagnation, as Atlantic City has done through its recent gambling boom, often provide new jobs primarily for suburbanites and other "outsiders," rather than for the indigenous working class in whose name the transformation was justified (Sternlieb and Hughes, 1983a; see also Greenberg, n.d.; Summers et al., 1976). Summers and Branch (1984) draw the same conclusion in their review of the effects of growth on small towns, reporting that typically less than 10 percent of new industrial jobs are filled by persons who were previously unemployed (of whatever residential origin). Evidently, the new jobs are taken by people who already have jobs, many of whom are migrants.[8] Summers observes that "newcomers intervene between the jobs and the local residents, especially the disadvantaged," because they possess "more education, better skills, or the 'right' racial heritage" (as quoted in Bluestone and Harrison, 1982:90).

It is still possible that certain patterns of growth may stimulate employment without attracting migrants. New jobs that bring underemployed women or youths into the work force may have this effect. It is also true that certain categories of workers can be especially penalized if local labor markets fail to expand, for example, those immobilized by ill health, family commitments, or other factors that limit mobility. But overall, even though local growth may sometimes have beneficial effects on specific individuals and subgroups, both the weight of empirical evidence and the logic of the process indicate that net benefits do not follow as a

8. Further, new industrial investment in one city often eliminates jobs at another city, with no net gain. This process is detailed in chapter 7.

matter of course. Indeed, our conclusions reinforce what has been called the "unanimous" agreement among economists that "the only jurisdiction that should be concerned with the effects of its policies on the level of employment is the Federal government. Small jurisdictions do not have the power to effect significant changes in the level of unemployment" (Levy and Arnold, 1972:95).

The real problem is that the United States is a society of constant joblessness, with unemployment rates conservatively estimated by the Department of Commerce at 4 to 11 percent of the work force defined as ordinarily active. A game of musical chairs is being played at all times, with workers circulating around the country, hoping to land in an empty position when the music stops. Redistributing the stock of jobs among places may move the chairs around, but it does not alter the number of chairs available to the players.

Job and Income Mobility

Related to the issue of unemployment is the question of occupational mobility in general. It seems obvious that only in the largest places is it possible to attain the highest incomes in the lucrative occupations; for individuals with such ambitions, large may be the only option. Other than moving (the more efficient mechanism), growth of place is the only answer. In general, studies that have compared wage rates among places have found that urban areas with more people have higher wages rates, although the differences between places are small (Alonso, 1973; Appelbaum, 1978; Fuchs, 1967; Hoch, 1972).

More relevant in the present context than the issue of how size affects wages is the issue of how income is influenced by urban *growth*. In his study of matched "self-contained" cities, Appelbaum (1978) found that there was indeed a positive relation between family income and rate of urban growth (see Eberts [1979] for similar results using Northeast counties). But the size and growth effects together had a small *net* effect: controlling for other variables, size and growth explained about 8 percent of the variance in income among places. More crucially, we don't learn in these studies whether growth tends to merely attract higher-wage workers from other areas (which then "decline" in median income as a result), or growth itself benefits indigenous populations.

Also complicating the interpretation of the growth-related income difference is evidence that larger places (and in particular fast-growing ones) have higher living costs, which offset the higher wages. The degree to which this occurs is a matter of debate (Appelbaum, 1978; Hoch, 1972; Shefer, 1970). Although most evidence suggests that *size* has little effect on living costs, *growth* has a much greater effect. This is especially true for housing costs; the effects of growth on prices are especially strong for both single-family houses and apartments (Appelbaum, 1978:36–37; Appelbaum and Gilderbloom, 1983). Because so many detrimental effects of growth on costs are not reflected in these studies of household income—for example, the effects of pollution on health care and building maintenance expenses—we must conclude that growth does not benefit a family in terms of net income or quality of life.

An alternative way of investigating the connection between growth and the personal income of local populations is through case studies of how growth has affected the wages of specific social and occupational groups in given places. Greenberg (n.d.) carried out such a study with a special focus on low-wage groups and, in particular, poor blacks in southern counties of three subregions that were experiencing different patterns of development. Although all the areas in her study experienced rates of growth exceeding the national growth rate between 1960 and 1980, the economic basis of that growth was different in each place and had distinct consequences for specific labor groups. There were three different patterns: (1) growth in service industry in an area of declining low-wage manufacturing; (2) invasion of manufacturing jobs into an agricultural zone; and (3) major expansion of government jobs in an area with a mixed economy.

In the first case, found in Durham, North Carolina, the transition from a manufacturing to a service economy meant "that blacks simply exchanged low wage jobs in low growth sectors of the economy for low wage jobs in high growth sectors" (Greenberg, n.d.:23). In the second pattern, found in the area outside Durham, in which manufacturing invaded a former agricultural zone, Greenberg found that incoming industrialization did not bring higher living standards: "The transition from agriculture to low wage manufacturing has done little to improve the relative economic position of blacks in most types of nonagricultural employment. Whites also earn substantially less than their counterparts in the adjacent urban counties" (Greenberg, n.d.:24). In Greenberg's third growth pattern, there were substantial gains for blacks and, presumably, the poor in general. In Wake County, the growth in employment was based heavily on expansion by the government. The number of blacks in high-level jobs increased and their wage gains outpaced the national average for blacks during this period. Although Greenberg attributes these gains for blacks to the increased "diversity" of the economy that government employment provided, we might put equal stress on the civil service and affirmative action requirements of government hiring and promotion (see Baron and Bielby, 1980).

Whatever the specific reasons for the differences among places, Greenberg's findings indicate that "growth *per se* is no panacea for urban poverty" (Greenberg, n.d.:26). Instead, the issue is the *kind* of growth that is involved, and the degree (ordinarily, limited) to which local residents are given an advantage over migrants in the competition for jobs. Otherwise, local growth may be only a matter of making the local rich even richer, or, alternatively, of moving those already privileged in their jobs from one part of the country to another part of the country. To stay with our metaphor of musical chairs, the number of *comfortable* chairs and the basis for allocating them does not change; only their *location* is altered. As Summers and Branch conclude on the basis of their own growth studies, "Industrial location has a small or even negative effect on the local public sector and on economically disadvantaged citizens" (1984:153; see also Garrison, 1971). This is hardly consistent with the myth of opportunity promoted by supporters of the growth machine.

Eliminating Social Problems

The idea that an increase in numbers and density leads to severe social pathology has been, at long last, thoroughly discredited (see, for example, Fischer, Baldasarre, and Ofshe, 1975). We do believe, however, that size and rate of growth have a role in creating and exacerbating urban problems such as segregation and inequality.

The great population explosions that marked America's industrial cities earlier in this century cannot be said to have increased levels of either equality or class and racial integration. Instead, greater numbers seem to have increased spatial and social segregation between rich and poor, black and white (Lieberson, 1980; Zunz, 1982). In a more contemporary context, Sternlieb and Hughes (1983a) have studied the social effects of the growth of gambling in Atlantic City, New Jersey—the revitalization of a service sector industry. Sternlieb and Hughes report that the consequences have been extremely negative for existing residents. The growth boom has set up "walled off universes" of casino-generated wealth, with the old people and poor finding their former "dismal comforts being swept away," without the compensation of better jobs.[9] The original residents are not participating in the new economy, except at the bottom (as is consistent with Greenberg's findings, discussed above), and the overall effect of the gambling boom on the community is to exacerbate visible cleavages between the rich and the poor (see also Markusen, 1978).

More generally, growth may not be the cause of problems, but increases in scale make it more difficult to deal with those that do exist. Racial integration is more difficult when members of a minority are concentrated in large ghettos within a vast, and often politically divided, region. It becomes harder to accomplish school integration without busing pupils over long distances and across jurisdictional lines. Busing generates controversy and high costs to public budgets as well as taking up children's time. In small places, racially and economically diverse social groups can more easily end up in the same schools, as well as the same shopping, recreation, and work settings. Whether through fortuitous movements of people or through managed intervention programs, small places can be more easily integrated, racially and economically. Under current jurisdictional and ecological patterns, growth tends to intensify the separation and disparities among social groups and communities.

9. "Atlantic City Hurt by Gambling, Study Finds," *Los Angeles Times*, November 2, 1983, sec. I, p. 11.

Growth likely increases inequality within places through its effects on the distribution of rents. Increases in urban scale mean larger numbers of bidders for the same critically located land parcels (for example, the central business district or the site for a freeway intersection), inflating land prices relative to wages and other wealth sources. Although growth expands the center zone (as well as stimulating other pockets in the area) the critical locations remain unique. Hence we see the familiar pattern of an intense use of critical spots (for example, Wall Street or Rodeo Drive) with a sharp drop in rent levels just outside their boundaries. Growth disproportionately increases the value of strategic parcels, generating monopoly effects for their owners. Thus, in terms of rental wealth, urban growth likely increases inequality.

There is some empirical evidence showing greater income disparities within larger and faster-growing places, whether from monopoly rent effects or another factor (Haworth, Long, and Rasmussen, 1978; but see Walker, 1978). Other studies, however, find little or no impact of size or growth rates on wealth distribution (Alonso, 1973; Appelbaum, 1978; Betz, 1972). Our own conclusion is that growth mainly hurts those in its direct path whose primary tie to place is for its residential use value. When tracing the effect of growth, we must look at how particular groups, at a given time and place, are affected by development (a task we take up in the next chapter).

Environment

Growth has obvious negative consequences for the physical environment; growth affects the quality of air and water, and the ease of getting around in a town or city. Growth obliterates open spaces and damages the aesthetic features of a natural terrain. It decreases ecological variety with a consequent threat to the larger ecosystem.

Though sometimes viewed as trivial concerns of an idle middle class ("rich housewives," according to the stereotype), these blows to the physical environment most heavily affect the less well to do. A high-quality physical environment constitutes a free public good for those who have access to it (Harvey, 1973). Those who are unable to buy amenities in the market lose most from the unavailability of such resources. More concretely, since the poor are most likely to live and work in close proximity to pollution sources, the poor are more affected by growth-induced environmental decay than are the rich.

Perhaps nowhere are the effects of environmental decline more dramatically displayed than in those places with the most rapid growth experiences. Feagin (1983a), for example, has compiled a list of Houston's problems that have accompanied that city's emergence as "capital of the sunbelt." These include crises in sewage disposal, toxic dumps, water supplies, and transportation. In addition to the visible increases in pollution and congestion, past environmental sins will entail vast cleanup costs—what Worster (1982:514) calls "ecological backlash." By 1983, Houston was second only to New York City in per capita bonding liability. Environmental decline, here as elsewhere, can exacerbate fiscal problems and inequality of life chances among rich and poor.

Accommodating Natural Increase

Growth activists incessantly raise the problem of providing "homes and jobs for our children." To avoid the forced exile of their youth, towns and cities might reasonably have as a goal the maintenance of economic expansion sufficient to provide jobs and housing for new generations. These expansions would be modest in scale, given the low rates of birth that are characteristic of U.S. urban populations. The difficulty is "reserving" the right openings for the right youths, a goal that is unrealistic given the nature of the hiring queue and the constitutional limitations on restraint of trade. Virtually no local growth policy could effectively guarantee local jobs for local people. Many of the young prefer, of course, to leave their home town anyway, and this in itself probably eliminates the problem of having to create large numbers of jobs to accommodate local youth.

Satisfying Public Taste

The current pattern of urbanization is not necessarily a response to people's wishes. As Sundquist has remarked,

The notion commonly expressed that Americans have "voted with their feet" in favor of the great cities is, on the basis of every available sampling, so much nonsense. . . . What is called "freedom of choice" is, in sum, freedom of employer choice or, more precisely, freedom of choice for that segment of the corporate world that operates mobile enterprises. The real question, then, is whether freedom of corporate choice should be automatically honored by government policy at the expense of freedom of individual choice where those conflict. [1975:258.]

Most evidence suggests that people prefer living in small places or rural areas (Appelbaum et al., 1974:4.2–4.6; Finkler, 1972:2, 23; Hoch, 1972:280; Mazie and Rowlings, 1973; Parke and Westoff, 1972). Although only 8 percent of Americans in 1977, for example, lived in small towns and farm areas, 48 percent gave such places as their residential preference (Fischer, 1984:20). The larger the metropolis, the greater the proportion of people (in both the central city and suburbs) who express a desire to move away (Gallup, 1979:85). If people's responses to surveys are any indication, a substantial portion of the migration to the great metropolitan areas of the postwar decades was more in spite of tastes than because of them.

Growth Trade-offs

Although there is clear evidence on some of the effects of growth, urban size is fundamentally a political or value issue in which one person's criteria are lined up against another's (see Duncan, 1957). It may, for example, be necessary to sacrifice clean air to build a population base large enough to support a major opera company. If one loves music enough, the price may be worth paying. But in reality, differential material interests influence the trade-offs. If one happens to be on the winning side of the rent intensification process (or in the opera business), the pleasures of cleaner air or lower taxes will be easier to forgo.

Besides the variations between individuals and groups, the actual price to be paid for growth and the willingness to pay it will vary somewhat. Having an opera house is probably more important to the Viennese than to the residents of Carmel, California, and in the same way the preferred trade-offs in population size will vary. On more prosaic grounds, certain places may need additional population to absorb the costs of existing road and sewer systems, however misguided the initial commitment to build them. People in some small towns may want a population increase in order to make rudimentary specialization possible in their public school system. In other instances, a past history of outmigration may have left behind a surplus of unused capacities, which would easily accommodate additional growth and provide public benefits of various sorts.

These variations notwithstanding, the evidence on fiscal health and economic or social problems indicates clearly that the assumptions of value-free development are false. In many cases, probably in most, additional local growth under current arrangements is a transfer of wealth and life chances from the general public to the rentier groups and their associates. Use values of a majority are sacrificed for the exchange gains of the few. To question the wisdom of growth for any specific locality is to threaten a benefit transfer and the interests of those who gain from it.

4

Homes: Exchange and Sentiment in the Neighborhood

The push for growth and rents is not the only force on the urban scene; there are also efforts, individual and collective, to enhance use values. The two processes together determine the patterns of neighborhood life—the ways in which people grow up, live, and die, interconnect with one another, and defend (or offend) the places in which they live. "Sentiment" is indeed at work in structuring the city, but this sentiment is "refracted" (Storper and Walker, 1983:25) through a larger system of material production and manipulation of rents. People's feelings about their daily round, their psychological attachments to place, and their neighborhood ethnic solidarities are very real to them, but these feelings are bound up with forces originating outside residents' immediate milieus, far beyond the social and geographical boundaries of their routines. Sentiment and structure cohere in various ways in "generating the actual events of everyday life" (Storper and Walker, 1983:27), in different places at different times. The city is a setting for the achievement of both exchange values and use values; and the neighborhood is the meeting place of the two forces, where each resident faces the challenge of making a life on a real estate commodity. From the point of view of residents, the creation and defense of the use values of neighborhood is the central urban question, and it is our topic in this chapter.

The Residual Neighborhood

Within the Marxian framework, neighborhood is essentially a residual phenomenon (Molotch, 1979). Since it is merely a site for the reproduction of labor (see Castells, 1976; Lamarche, 1976)—that is, for the daily sustenance of the working class—the neighborhood receives its shape and qualities from the dynamics of the accumulation process. The locations of neighborhoods and the goings-on within them are consequences of the needs of accumulation; accumulation is not, for example, a consequence of the location of the neighborhood. The needs of production come first.

Such notions of the residual quality of neighborhoods and the primacy of the production apparatus were also among the assumptions of the Chicago ecologists. Knowledge of neighborhood life could be derived from the subsocial, "biotic" level of reality. For Ernest W. Burgess, Homer Hoyt, Robert E. Park, and many of their followers in neo-Chicago location theory, the land commodity market allocates to the most strategic locations those uses most critical to the basic economy. These strategic locations are not going to be the residential areas of ordinary people, who find their "niches" in the interstices between more dominant uses.

It followed, therefore, in the classic Burgess concentric-zone model, that the "zone of transition" (in part, a neighborhood of last resort for the otherwise homeless) would *naturally* be "invaded" by business district expansion, just as the next ring (workingmen's homes) would then be replaced by the mixed uses of the former zone of transition. To this day, even in most instances of officially planned land use, such as programs of urban renewal and redevelopment, contemporary planning professionals assume that these zones of transition are crying out for the same sort of "higher and better uses" of the next transition.

More culturally oriented social scientists, some working at the same time and place as the Chicago ecologists, were also in search of general urban laws: they still chose, however, to derive their propositions from ecological foundations. In Louis Wirth's celebrated formulation of "urbanism as a way of life," inherited folkways of more traditional social orders give way, in the face of "numbers, density, and heterogeneity," to more bureaucratic and formalistic modes of interpersonal relations. It is a vision of "community lost" (Wellman, 1979) under the press of demographic circumstance. The urban *gemeinschaft*, in which immediate locality is the basis of spiritual as well as material sustenance, is replaced by the community of limited liability (Janowitz, 1951). Neighborhood becomes only one of a number of bases for managing daily life—alongside the job, school, and extended kin groups located elsewhere. The result is a decrease in personal investment in, and in vulnerability to, locality—a limiting of liability that parallels the limiting of interpersonal commitment characteristic of the impersonal, *gesellschaft* social order generally. The city becomes an arena for the blasé individualistic strivings of its residents. It is essentially a container (at most a "crucible"), a function that complements the general patterns of social and geographical mobility that urbanism and modernity imply. In its boldest form, the classical position holds that a quality of urbanism itself, rather than nineteenth-century American capitalism or class structure, for example, leads to a universal form of modern life. But this is an inadequate theoretical basis for explaining why, for example, working-class Italian-American homeowners live one way, barrio Chicanos live another, and affluent professionals live still another.

Although Marxian scholars have given less attention to neighborhood life, they have also assumed a homogeneity among almost all neighborhoods, regardless of race, ethnicity, or location. At least for the great mass of working people, alienation from the productive apparatus colors their lives with one another and provides little basis for neighborhood variation. In a more recent variant, Marxian scholars argue that residents' shared dependence on the same urban services and other forms of collective consumption generate similar dynamics throughout neighborhoods (Castells, 1979, 1983).

Despite all the efforts at theorizing a general law, empirically based community studies have continuously exposed a variety of cultural patterns that directly challenge monolithic views. Beginning with Wirth's important contribution (1928) and the classic ethnographies of the pre–World War II period, the tenacity of neighborhood sentiment and its rich varieties have been appreciatively recorded. Gans (1962) found in the late 1950s Italian inner-city residents very much tied to their neighborhood in a manner akin to a village culture. Even in suburban Levittown, whose residents were far less folklike in their observable ties to turf, Gans found at least the potential for "an intense identification with the community" that might have arisen "should something have threatened the community as a whole" (Gans, 1967). Scholars have numerous opportunities in contemporary settings to witness expressions of intense place identification: when routines are disrupted by school busing (Rubin, 1972), zoning changes (Rudel, 1983), oil spills (Molotch, 1970), toxic leaks (Levine, 1982), or other threats to residential tenancy (Fried and Gleicher, 1961; Trillin, 1979). Though only part of the story, residential place has meaning and significance for people and they act, sometimes passionately, on that meaning.

One concrete empirical observation runs counter to our concern for neighborhood: the high rate of residential mobility characteristic of urban residents. Seventeen percent of the U.S. population changes residence each year (U.S. Bureau of the Census, 1983a). But again, this mobility may not be *intrinsic* to urbanism, but instead contingent on the market mechanisms that induce, or coerce, mobility. The rootless "organization man," as a general personality description, may be a similarly misleading characterization.

The data supporting the main observation need to be examined more closely. Although there are a lot of moves each year, there are fewer movers. Certain kinds of people move a lot, in particular, young adults, who have approximately a 50 percent higher mobility rate than people over thirty-five.[1] Further, most people who do move look for housing near the place where they live. Over the 1975–1980 five-year census period, only 20 percent of Americans moved to a different *county*. A random sample of movers drawn from a University of Michigan panel study concluded that "movement across jurisdictional boundaries even within the same SMSA [standard metropolitan statistical area] is relatively rare" (Newman and Owen, 1980). Research by the National Insti-

---

1. Population figures are from U.S. Bureau of the Census (1983b:16), and U.S. Bureau of the Census (1983a:377).

tute for Advanced Studies on those displaced from a San Francisco neighborhood found that almost half moved to another house within either the same or an adjacent planning district, and only 9 percent moved to another city (see Schill and Nathan, 1983). There is thus substantial residential stability in the United States, and this is especially true among certain age groups. Less than 5.0 percent of those over 65 move each year; for the 45 to 64 age group, only 7.7 percent move. Those between 35 and 44 have a 13 percent annual mobility rate. And within all these groups, a good number are people who move only reluctantly, clinging to their place almost for dear life.

The specific meaning residents give to place is shaped by the ways they use the material and social resources at hand to make their daily round. Ethnic identity, inherited folkways, or more modern moral codes can, depending on the specific neighborhood, group within it, and historical time, be the appropriate tools for survival. Given the wide variety of possible urban circumstances, the lives of urban peoples must come to differ. Even neighborhoods of similar social class can vary on all these issues in part because of how racial and ethnic characteristics are shaped in the struggle against exchange pressures. Let us look more closely, therefore, at the different kinds of use values people gain from neighborhood and at the drive for rents that makes instability a constant threat to the successful use of neighborhood.

Types of Use Values

Each neighborhood has its own individual mix of use values, forged through the historic develoment of its physical structure, ethnic and class relations, and connections to outside institutions. We discern six categories of use values—six factors that make up the basis of neighborhood.

The Daily Round

The place of residence is a focal point for the wider routine in which one's concrete daily needs are satisfied. Neighborhoods provide a place for shopping (particularly for food and other essentials), schooling, child care, and routine health needs. For some, the locality is also a place of work. For others, it is a point of departure to a work place, affording access to appropriate means of transportation. Defining a daily round is gradually accomplished as residents learn about needed facilities, their exact locations and offerings, and how taking advantage of one can be efficiently integrated into a routine that includes taking advantage of others. Routes and timings have to be carefully worked out to achieve maximum benefits. The development of an effective array of goods and services within reach of residence is a fragile accomplishment; its disruption, either by the loss of one of the elements or by the loss of the residential starting place, can exact a severe penalty.

Informal Support Networks

Place of residence is the potential source of an informal network of people who provide life-sustaining products and services (Wellman, 1979). Examples range from friends and neighbors who baby-sit, do yard work, or shovel snow to friends, neighbors, and acquaintances who offer aid that can alter a way of life, such as referrals for an available job, a political connection to solve a problem, a welfare benefit, or lucrative criminal contact. Sometimes gains are achieved through an informal marketplace among proximate beneficiaries, in which money may change hands but more commonly operates according to a barter system. Reciprocity rules the loaning of cups of sugar or the minding of children (Stack, 1974). These, too, are hard-won gains; and along with other attributes of neighborhood, they form "the bonds people build with one another that enable them to rely on one another" (Mollenkopf, 1981:320).

Especially for the poor, this income "in kind" represents a crucial resource and it is made possible only by a viable community. In order to situate themselves to capture such advantages, working-class people tend to live near their relatives and to draw their friends from a proximate group of neighbors (Komarovsky, 1962; Rainwater, Coleman, and Handel, 1959; Rubin, 1976). Though they have fewer friends than people in other classes (Fischer, 1982:93), they seem to depend upon their network more than do people in affluent areas (Fischer, 1984:131; Foley, 1950; Fried, 1963; Oliver, 1984). Since the community of poor people is less spatially "liberated" (Wellman, 1979) than that of the well-to-do, poor people's use values are particularly damaged when their neighborhood is disrupted. Even if it is only a "place on the corner" to hang out, home location can be the crucial foundation for making a life for those otherwise lacking standing in the larger metropolis (Anderson, 1976).

Security and Trust

A neighborhood also provides a sense of physical and psychic security that comes with a familiar and dependable environment. There are "eyes on the street" from friendly onlookers (Jacobs, 1961, chap. 2) and a variety of "social landmarks," individuals and institutions accepted as dependable, predictable actors with known reputations. Gerald Suttles (1968), in his effort to construct a general theory of urban life, or at least "the" social structure of the slum, portrays neighborhoods as bastions "defended" against the perceived dangers of interlopers drifting in from adjacent areas. Signs of commonality (skin color, diction, gait in walking) serve as a *prima facie,* if imperfect, basis for categorizing others as either members or nonmembers of the neighborhood circle of mutual trust. This process of "categoric knowing" (Lofland, 1973) is reinforced by various mechanisms in daily life that maintain the distinction between insiders and interlopers. Residents recognize it by their own sense of insecurity when they move around outside the neighborhood, by the contrasting responses of shopkeepers to "intimates" and outsiders, by the youth gangs' defense of turf, and by the periodic acts of incivility and violence for which the outsiders get more than their proper share of blame. Reassured by shared symbols, common cultures, kinship ties, and personal reputations, residents experience a sense of relative security, a sense they sorely need in the larger contexts of physical danger and, we would emphatically add to Suttles's picture, threats from the exchange system that surrounds them. Neighborhood can provide the benefit of *membership* in a social space that is viewed as orderly, predictable, and protective.

Although not as dependent on the local security net as the poor, the well-to-do also have a round of routines that cannot be reproduced overnight. Again, the affluent may less often depend upon neighborhood networks to get jobs, but face-to-face interaction still has its uses. Even in the highest circles, proximity matters; that's why we find that memberships on corporate boards of directors so frequently overlap within regions, rather than across them (see Mintz and Schwartz, 1985; Palmer, Friedland, and Roussell, 1985). Business executives' networks of clubs and other social settings, some of which are based in neighborhoods, are part of the trust system that facilitates not only developing a mundane routine but also sharing strategic corporate information, shaping mutual understandings of ethical boundaries, and eliciting peer consensus on business and larger policy issues (Domhoff, 1970; Kanter, 1977; Koenig and Gogel, 1981; Mills, 1956; Ratcliff, Gallagher, and Ratcliff, 1979). More specifically, face-to-face contact in community settings can help executives avoid written correspondence ("paper trails") that can later be used in lawsuits, media exposés, or criminal proceedings. Even phone conversations can be dangerous; some surreptitiously recorded executive phone talk has ended up as courtroom evidence.[2] Sometimes the best place to discuss delicate business is the clubhouse or locker room.

For women with families, regardless of social status, neighborhood use values have special significance (see Hayden, 1981). Women must construct a path to appropriate schools, lessons, a job, shops, and friends. They must be "in so many places at a time." Involved are hours of daily work and a great deal of automobile driving or time on the bus (DeVault, 1984; Markusen, 1980; Shlay and DiGregorio, 1983). Working women's double burden of managing family life and employment (Berk, 1985) makes the neighborhood resource base that much more critical. Some women are involved in the largely "invisible work" of vol-

2. One telling example is a taped phone conversation in which the president of American Airlines proposed an air fare price-fixing scheme to the president of Braniff Airlines. The Braniff president turned the recording over to authorities for legal action. Perhaps with tighter social bonds, this corporate mishap would not have occurred; at least the tape-recording would have been less feasible had the conversation occurred at the country club (Sing, 1985).

unteer activities, which, while providing free resources to their community, build on women's knowledge of the unmet needs in the nearby life space (Daniels, 1986). Although often the basis for silly television stories, the work by women indicates a special connection to neighborhood, and this in turn is reflected in women's attitudes and behaviors toward location. Women have a greater aversion to moving, and women homeowners are apparently less eager than men to cash in on house equity when the opportunity arises (see Shlay and DiGregorio, 1983).

Identity

A neighborhood provides its residents with an important source of identity, both for themselves and for others. Neighborhoods offer a resident not only spatial demarcations but social demarcations as well. In the United States, people use place names to identify the general social standing of themselves and others. To do this people must have a sense of neighborhood boundaries and the connotations of names of other areas. Hunter reports that between 80 and 90 percent of his Chicago respondents were able to define clear boundaries for their place-named communities and, more important here, tended to manipulate these names and boundaries to increase or protect their own status. For example, "lower status individuals attempt through a 'halo' effect to become identified with a neighboring area of higher status," whereas those of higher status attempt to prevent this sort of borrowing of their status (Hunter, 1974:78). The linkage people make between their location and their social standing means that residents' stakes in place go well beyond the actual material conditions of a given place (for example, public services or park amenities), and involve the symbolic meanings that real estate takes on. These connotations are sustained through the evaluations of outsiders as perceived by residents and strangers alike. As Hunter and Suttles (1972:51) note, "Residential identities . . . are imbedded in a contrastive structure in which each neighborhood is known primarily as a counterpart to some of the others" (see also Logan and Collver, 1983).

This contrastive structure also means that community resources are desired not just to secure better material conditions, like nice parks, but to display success compared to other neighborhoods seeking the same resources. That is one reason why it is impossible for city governments to satisfy neighborhood claims; since public facilities are needed for competitive advantage over other areas, the needs are infinite and insatiable. Resources are needed not only to sustain a daily round but also to sustain a daily identity. This is not simply a matter of a vague psychic reward; it is—in a competitive market society—also a way of gaining access to other rewards by establishing one's credentials, by demonstrating that one comes from a good place. This truth is sensed by urban people and helps fuel the rational fires of turf defense, which analysts have sometimes mistaken for vestiges of irrational, primordial folkways.

Agglomeration Benefits

A shared interest in overlapping use values (identity, security, and so on) in a single area is a useful way to define neighborhood. A neighborhood is far more than a mere collection of houses; rather, it is a shared experience of an agglomeration of complementary benefits.

The concentration of a large number of similar people stimulates the development of agglomerations especially appropriate to their needs. For example, the presence of many Mexican-Americans in one place provides the necessary base for a bodega, which then attracts still more Mexican-American residents, who then provide the still larger base needed to support a Spanish-language movie theater. These institutions become symbols of belonging and control, enhancing the feeling of turf security, which reinforces the base on which the ethnic businesses depend. Potentially at least, a successful indigenous business class can then play a supporting role in defending the neighborhood against external threats. Local business and social life become intertwined in a single support system.

All urban residents do not live in such "full" neighborhoods (Keller, 1968; Wellman, 1979), but most residential areas have some of the aspects described above, and a good number have them all. When a neighborhood is threatened by exchange value machinations, the precise makeup of this "neighborhoodness" will have a bearing on the costs of residential displacement and on the ability of people to block it.

Ethnicity

Not infrequently, these benefits are encapsulated in a shared ethnicity. Everybody you need is a member of your ethnic group. When this occurs, ethnicity serves as a summary characterization of all the overlapping benefits of neighborhood life. Ethnicity works for these purposes because it does often accurately represent a shared life style, similar needs in the daily round, and the social boundaries for providing service and gaining interpersonal support. Ethnicity works because of its simple practicality; it neatly demarcates large numbers of people with a single term and, with greater or lesser degrees of accuracy, categorizes them on the basis of only a few gross indicators (such as skin color or diction). Ethnicity is a powerful force because it is part of the solution of many real problems, but also because it underlies many other problems. While one group uses common traits to mark off an arena of trust, another group uses the same traits to identify individuals to be feared, hated, or excluded. The two versions of reality ultimately meet and alter the perceptions of *both* groups and how they use the city.

This interaction suggests that ethnicity as a cognitive tool for organizing and sensing security is a real, but contingent, feature of urban life that, as Bonacich says, "must be constructed and activated" and not taken for granted by scholars as a natural phenomenon (Bonacich, 1980:11; see also Steinberg, 1981). For us, the critical point in understanding the construction of ethnicity is, not the interaction of ethnic groups on the streets, but the exchange and production forces that touch all groups and thereby help shape those interactions.

This raises the question of how ethnicity was influenced by the circumstances that first gave rise to America's neighborhoods. Compared to the European working classes, American workers lacked proletarian political organization and maintained a sharp separation between the work realm and the neighborhood. This gave to residential space a more central life focus and to the American worker a more "divided consciousness" than would be found elsewhere (Katznelson, Gille, and Weir, 1982:231; also Katznelson, 1981). Again in contrast to other industrial countries, the U.S. system provided little security backup in the form of an income maintenance system, public medical care, or stable (nonmarket) housing. The social insecurities of particularly heterogenous inner cities were compounded by a lack of security overall and by the active promotion of a complementary ideology of consumerist individualism (Ewen, 1976). Heterogeneity, in a context of such disruption and challenge, is pregnant with potential for the kind of daily anxiety and intergroup hostility that has been much observed by urban ethnographers. With no *systematic* policies to help immigrants as human beings (they were merely labor), it was perhaps inevitable that immigrants' struggle for residential space, jobs, and security would lead them to interethnic conflict.

The resulting ethnic patterns in American cities are clearly not a mirror of Old World cultures. Although population movements have slower velocities than capital (see chapter 2), *cultures* have the slowest velocity of all. Indeed time as well as distance defeats them, making their complete and wholesale transplanting a virtual impossibility. Our evidence of ethnic solidarity in the city, whether turf-linked gang violence or ethnic neighborhood festivals, is part of the current effort to derive use values from the circumstances at hand.

Summary: Neighborhood Use Values

Regardless of how they come about, the overlapping and intersecting methods of solving daily problems take on a life of their own. Bound up with the fears and triumphs of family life, safety at night, and daily sustenance, these patterns achieve emotional significance and go to the core of the human psyche. It may be that in any realm there is no absolute distinction between practical purposes and emotional attachments (see Hochschild, 1983; Leach, 1976); certainly when it comes to constituting a neighborhood, diffuse sentiment and concrete needs are intimately bound together.

The Exchange Value Threats to Neighborhood

Threats to neighborhood, forces with the potential for overturning the local systems of material and psychic accomplishment, vary according to time and place. Parting with the Wirthian tradition, we do not see "the city" or the "urban" as ipso facto undermining a neighborhood culture. Certainly we do not consider the unpredictability of outsiders from another gang or turf as the critical threat (cf. Suttles, 1968). For us, the major challenge to neighborhood, as a demographic-physical construct as well as a viable social network, comes from organizations and institutions (firms and bureaucracies) whose routine functioning reorganizes urban space. The stranger to fear may not be the man of different ethnicity on the street corner, but a bank president or property management executive of irrelevant ethnicity far from view. In their large-scale study of a national sample of neighborhoods, Schill and Nathan (1983) found that a large proportion of movers (22%) were, in effect, forced out by rent increases, property renovation or conversion, or the landlord's sale of the property. A study of locational conflicts in a large Canadian city (Janelle, 1977) found that over 60 percent resulted from development initiatives that were opposed by individual citizens and resident associations (rather than by competing entrepreneurs or government agencies). Studies like these receive little attention among urban sociologists despite omnipresent daily newspaper coverage of the same phenomena across North America.

Sometimes, of course, these changes can represent a use value gain; despite initial hardships from adjustment to even forced moves, many people end up with housing they judge to be at least as good as what they started with (Schill and Nathan, 1983:112, 115). And some commercial manipulations contribute to use values; residents may come to value their new grocery store on the corner or the new factory down the road. Nevertheless, residents ordinarily have little *control* over such changes and this contributes to the general anxiety resulting from the fact that market mechanisms, as currently structured, may well serve to undermine neighborhood.

The very nature of a neighborhood, including its future prospects, is shaped by its connection to the commodity system including, crucially, the place of the neighborhood within the system as a commodity. The daily round, informal networks, agglomeration benefits, and even ethnic identities take their form from this exchange value context. Robert Park (1967:40) described the city as "a mosaic of little worlds that touch but do not interpenetrate." We agree there are "little worlds," but some of them are routinely capable of penetrating the others. Neighborhoods become vulnerable to exchange pressures for specific reasons. The commodity status of an area within the larger urban system, combined with its internal organization, will determine the fortune of a neighborhood.

"Reviving" Poor Neighborhoods

Poor people's neighborhoods are the most vulnerable to social and physical transformation, both by government bureaucrats and by property entrepreneurs. The poor are more likely than other groups to be displaced, and at least for the unemployed and those who have always had trouble finding a stable place to live, dislocation tends to result in higher rates of overcrowding and poorer housing (Schill and Nathan, 1983:57, 59, 111).[3] Some must move several times before finding even a semipermanent place to live, and a large proportion of the displaced try to move back into their old area when they can (Stanfield, 1977).

The crux of poor people's urban problem is that their routines—indeed their very being—are often damaging to exchange values. Low-income people pay less rent than the affluent. Poor people's low buying power makes them disfavored customers and the rich, who do have money to spend, don't want to live near them. Some institutions, for example, elite universities and high-

3. In virtually all studies of the displaced, researchers encounter a severe methodological problem in their inability to interview the poorest and most marginal residents. With general response rates of only between 10 and 35 percent for all groups, researchers must consistently understate the social costs of displacement for those at the bottom. Even when samples are matched by income (respondents and nondisplaced controls), that individuals are unavailable for the follow-up interview may be a sign of a special hardship, particularly homelessness (see Schill and Nathan, 1983:66–69).

tech firms, similarly find their goals thwarted by proximity to low-income neighborhoods. Local officials often adopt an active role, therefore, in eliminating the daily round of the poor, even though the pawnshops, taverns, bookie joints, and so forth are as important to those without money as the analogous boutiques, restaurants, and corporate office complexes are to the rich. Indeed, efforts at urban "revival" are often schemes to break, through either wholesale land clearance or selective destruction, just this chain of complementary relationships within poor areas. The only strong debate revolves around strategy: whether to close the tavern, arrest the prostitutes, relocate the mission, or destroy a group of physical structures that serve a use for the useless.

Often justified by planning officials' misleading cost-benefit analyses that show that the disruption of poor people's neighborhoods will create the least loss in taxes and land values, the life life chances of the poor are sacrificed on behalf of profits and rents enjoyed by people living elsewhere (see chapter 5).

The special vulnerability of poor people's neighborhoods also stems from the low standing of their residents in the larger systems of economic and political power, not only because of their poverty but also because of the relative ineffectiveness of the organizations that represent their interests. It takes very little to set destabilizing actions into motion, and the entrepreneur has little to fear from defenders of the poor. If an entrepreneur can make only a small profit by adding a wall or tearing one down, there is little standing in the way.

Locating Infrastructure.   As cities grow and government bureaucrats seek sites for devalued projects (for example, sewage plants, jails, and halfway houses), they look first—if they have any occupational competence at all—to poor people's neighborhoods (cf. Meyerson and Banfield, 1955; Seley and Wolpert, 1975). In addition to meeting a larger urban need, new projects located in a slum can clear out some "decay" and thus do "double duty." In Houston, Texas, whose population is 28 percent black (although blacks occupy less than 28 percent of the area), over three-fourths of the city-owned garbage incinerators are located in black neighborhoods, as are all city-owned garbage dumps (Bullard, 1983). Or again, Harlem was created as a black ghetto by the dislocation of Midtown Manhattan blacks to make way for Pennsylvania Station (Osofsky, 1963:93). Poor people are double losers; they have the least to gain from the infrastructural development and much to lose by the choice of its location.

Urban Renewal.   The postwar urban renewal programs (lasting into the late 1960s) were truly, in James Baldwin's phrase, "Negro removal," so frequently was residential clearance to afflict poor, black people's communities. Urban renewal used government authority and subsidy to make large-scale private investment attractive in areas where the potential payoff was too low to attract investors. The results were overwhelming in their costs to poor neighborhoods. In Atlanta, one in six city residents was dislocated through urban renewal, the great majority of whom were poor (Stone, 1976). For the country as a whole, urban renewal contributed substantially to the total "disruption rate" of the 1960s: the proportion of U.S. urban housing removed from the housing stock. Ten percent of all central city residences occupied by whites and 20 percent of units occupied by blacks were lost over the decade (Dahmann, 1982). This disruption rate does not include the displacement, beginning during the urban renewal years and continuing into the present, brought about by more routine market forces (evictions, rent increases).

The fact that a "neighborhood" cannot be rebuilt in a short period means that the disruption persists as an ongoing penalty in people's lives. The *threat* of disruption affects an even larger number. Whether it comes to imagining a family, a job search, or starting a small business, confronting the reality of residential instability must have at least some detrimental effect on the way people think about their lives together and make plans. And such "official disruptions" are only one of the forces making it difficult for low-income people to hold onto place. Marginality in the job market, vulnerability to changing welfare rules, and inability to cope with unexpected financial emergencies cause poor people to miss rent payments and be evicted from their dwellings. In her study of slum life in a midwestern city, Stack (1974) reports that one man killed his wife as the final result of the tension and family chaos stemming from an eviction. Stack describes a never-ending struggle of kin and friendship groups to maintain geographical proximity in the face of the many difficulties imposed by economic marginality.

Gentrification.   Poor neighborhoods are directly threatened by "gentrification," the "reinvasion" (London, 1980) of the central city by affluent young "urban pioneers," who displace the less affluent from urban locations. Real estate firms or individual buyers acquire buildings, which they upgrade, either for their own use or for sale to another. The neighborhood is often taken gradually, building by building, block by block, but the outcome—in which a certain kind of neighborhood is destroyed—can be just as complete as in wholesale urban renewal (see Newson, 1971; Tournier, 1980).

Sometimes neighborhood residents, particularly homeowners, help the process along. Touched by exchange value interests, these insiders forsake sentimental attachment in the face of newly discovered exchange value potential. Only one needs to sell to open the neighborhood to the process. Gentrification implies sales to affluent outsiders, and their very presence generates the kind of neighborhood effects (such as increased property value) that make it increasingly likely that other residents will make deals with outsiders. Renters, with no property to sell, but higher rents to pay, are, as is the usual course, victimized.

Notwithstanding the harm often done to poor people's lives in the process and the real possibility of fiscal losses to the city caused by the pioneers' high service demands (see chapter 5), gentrification is not ordinarily seen as an urban problem. Whereas a "good neighborhood" into which poor people move (especially black poor) is usually considered a tragic example of urban decline, the invasion of affluent whites is considered—among the press, the public bureaucracies, and the entrepreneurs—grounds for celebration. They celebrate because this sort of transformation builds rents and is thought to make the city more attractive for other investments, including growth-driving additions to the basic economy. "Blockbusting" that "upgrades" a neighborhood into a more affluent residential zone or growth-promoting corporate center is no urban sin. The lack of disapproval means that violence against the blockbusters will not be tolerated by the police, that real estate regulatory agencies will not discipline brokers who participate, and that those who sell their homes to outsiders will feel little shame for their disloyalty to neighbors, including renters who have no profits to make.

Racial Change

Neighborhood racial change resembles gentrification in its gradual nature, although it differs from gentrification as well as from other types of neighborhood transformation in its implications for rent returns and in the social groups it damages and helps. Blacks, including poor ones, make gains as whites, after evaluating their options, cede the neighborhood to black residency.

Departing white homeowners are often caught in a conflict between their local reputations and sentimental ties to neighborhood, on the one hand, and their desire for a good sale price, on the other. The trouble arises because general racist discrimination makes housing available to both races worth more to blacks than to whites; whites can choose from any housing in the metropolitan area but blacks cannot (Molotch, 1972; see also Osofsky, 1963:92; Philpott, 1978:149). One St. Louis study (Yinger et al., 1978) found that blacks paid 15 percent more than whites for similar housing in the same neighborhood, with overall housing costs 25 percent higher in black neighborhoods than their white counterparts. That means that although white sellers may not want to upset their neighbors by selling to blacks, they have no choice if they want to sell for the maximum price.

As the discrepancy grows between what whites and blacks will pay in a transitional area, white resistance is broken down by the "economic facts," and the process of racial change in the neighborhood, without any "white flight," becomes inexorable (Molotch, 1972; see also Taeuber and Taeuber, 1965). Even as local public policy and sentiment rail against the alleged "blockbusters," the special ways in which commodification intersects with ethnicity mean that resegregation occurs (albeit with new racial borders) and past patterns of discrimination, dual markets, and segregation are sustained. Racial change, the most common mechanism through which black housing opportunities are expanded, is the only known market process in which property entrepreneurs are commonly denounced (and even on occasion legally disciplined) for their transforming activities.

Site Assemblage

In contrast to the gradual nature of racial change and much gentrification, some forms of neighborhood change involve large-scale entrepreneurial land assemblage. Again, the conversion of much of Atlantic City from a decaying retirement and working-class residential zone into a gambling resort is a useful illustration. Developers of hotel-casino projects faced the time-consuming process of bargaining separately with each small homeowner. In this process developers run a major risk: holdouts can demand premium prices from desperate entrepreneurs. Trillin (1979) has poignantly described a technique for heading off such an eventuality, a method that, in effect, turns the social bonds of neighborhood into a force supporting the developer's goals. A large corporation wished to construct a casino-hotel on a street of individually owned working-class homes adjacent to the city's Boardwalk. In order to assemble the land, the corporation simultaneously offered each owner a price substantially above market value. But there was one special condition of the sale: the price was good only if *every* householder sold by a specified date. The younger families, seduced by the money, wanted out and were willing to give up the neighborhood benefit, but there were residents who did not want to sell at any price. Some of the old people had "nowhere to go," not because there would not be enough money for a new place, but because proximity to the daily round would be lost. For the old, the tie was less to the housing value than to the social network. Death was viewed as the alternative. The developer's strategy was to use the exchange value interest of the young as a lever against the social investment of the old. According to Trillin's account, the once placid little community became a battle zone as great pressures were put on the elderly holdouts by members of their own neighborhood. The two bases of neighborhood commitment are brought into vivid contrast as entrepreneurs manipulate homeowners' exchange value interest to overcome lingering sentimental ties.

A similar dynamic operates in the more affluent suburban context when the land on which houses sit becomes valuable enough for more intense use. When suburban land outside Atlanta began selling for as much as $1.3 million per acre in 1984, various groups of residents began offering their homes as a group to prospective developers (Schmidt, 1984). In the Dunwoody community, owners of upscale houses (worth $100,000 each) moved their homes to other parcels to make way for more intensive development. At the Lake Helm subdivision, houses sold for approximately twice their market value ($225,000) because their owners were able to offer all parcels as a single assemblage for development (*Changing Times,* 1985). Similar sales have been reported for the Courtlands neighborhood in Arlington, Virginia (22 homes), and the Ernie Pyle subdivision in Oak Brook, Illinois (46 homes). It especially helps when the neighbors get their land rezoned ahead of time and thus offer not only a package of contiguous parcels but also one for which the zoning and permit wars have already been fought and won for the developers. Other residents, like tenants with nothing to sell or homeowners not directly in the path of urban expansion, have little to gain by such deals. Those opposed to the changes come together and, using the environmental review process, may strive to protect their daily round. Indeed, one group of homeowners sued to block rezonings for one of the Atlanta assemblages and fought the reelection of local officials who supported it (Schmidt, 1984).

Suburbanization

Although not ordinarily considered an urban neighborhood issue, the transformation of rural areas into suburban residential zones involves similar patterns of collusion between insiders and outsiders, with specific results for various internal groups. The urbanization process means great rewards for the serendipitous speculators who happen to own property; the near-in farmers, the owners of land with the greatest profit potential, gain most from the conversion of properties to residential and industrial uses. Again, loss of community becomes easier to bear when substantial rents are in the offing. These "farmer-developers" (Rudel, 1983), taking advantage of their "old-timer" status and well-established political and social connections, are able to overcome any competing local interests supporting preservation (see Mans-

bridge, 1980; Rudel, 1983). They may be able to use their considerable political power, apparently preeminent in the rural setting
(see Vidich and Bensman, 1960:218; Rudel, 1983), to forestall
zoning controls and tight building regulations until their own
property is subdivided and sold. For the unpropertied locals, suburbanization means that they will lose their status as insiders belonging to a small community and become leftover "hicks." The
urban newcomers' ideas on schooling, religion, neighborliness,
and consumption overwhelm the old folk patterns. In their effort
to gain exchange value, the serendipitous entrepreneurs sell their
fellow country people down the river; and the renters gain no compensatory rewards for the environmental degradation, higher
taxes, and alteration of the cultural climate of the locality.

The newcomers often face troubles of their own. They must
also contend with environments built with little concern for long-
term livability. Lax controls allow the obliteration of virtually all
open space, the destruction of irreplaceable recreational sites, and
the construction of homes on flood plains, on unstable hillsides,
and even adjacent to toxic dumps (Levine, 1982). New owners
can find themselves living on sites where topsoil has been stripped
away, adjacent to collapsing roadways, and with flooding base-
ments and houses built with shoddy construction and cheap materials (Rudel, 1983). All of this is especially likely to occur in
low-end neighborhoods built for unwary young families, whose
former experience as apartment dwellers gave them few skills in
detecting building defects. In what appears to be a general pattern
in the suburban politics of land use (Rudel, 1983), the newcomers
then demand land-use and building code reform, but at a late stage
in the process. Besides paying for the individual defects in their
homes, they are faced with the high taxes necessary to deal with
the many irresponsible prior government decisions. One kind of
life routine has been destroyed, and those trying to build another
have to pay an extra price because their rentiers were uncontrolled
in their place manipulations.

Defiling Affluent Neighborhoods

The well-to-do, least dependent on neighborhood networks, can buy many of their needed services and draw upon the
whole city and region for their friendships. If they should have to

move for any reason, they may already have contacts in the new place; sometimes their corporate employers ease the transition into a new community with housing and school "tips," Welcome Wagon teas, and club introductions (Friedmann and Wolff, 1982:317). Nevertheless, the affluent do face certain distinctive challenges in protecting the sizable financial investments in their houses and in the social standing and networks that their neighborhood confers. The rich choose to live, as Suttles cogently puts it, "where the character of fellow residents is assured by the costs of living there and the presumed reputability of people so heavily rewarded by society" (Suttles, 1972:236). They oppose public housing, dense residential development, or any other land-use change that might lower the "tone" of their area. They favor large-lot zoning, which not only provides each family with the amenity of lawns and privacy but also produces a neighborhood of vast acreage, ipso facto isolating all but those who must live along the edges from contact with anyone who is not affluent. When physical distance is not feasible, as in dense inner-city zones, the affluent purchase social distance by paying for doormen, chauffeurs, and electronic security systems.

Affluent people's daily round is lucrative for those owning the property and businesses with which they make contact. The rich have a midas touch on geography. Affluent people as well as those who supply their provisions pay a lot of rent. They may get better value than the poor for their money (Caplovitz, 1963), but they do pay, in absolute terms, a lot. Clusters of high-spending consumers inflate the value of retail property, both within and adjacent to affluent neighborhoods. Although rentiers are always pressing for still more people with affluence, it is basically in the interests of rentiers and many retail businesses to sustain the character of these areas. This is the most important source of neighborhood power for the rich.

More broadly still, deluxe neighborhoods are often thought to be an asset for the urban growth machine; these "good places to live" can help sell outside executives on the local metropolis as a place in which to invest. "Showpiece" neighborhoods also serve as symbols of general urban vitality, and are occasionaly featured in business magazine advertisements touting the local business climate. All in all, the rich neighborhood has a potential role to play in both micro and macro growth strategies. The well-to-do community thus can rely upon "the protective shield provided by city administrators, highly placed politicians, and the leaders in certain businesses . . .[and] police policy toward trespassers" (Suttles, 1972:237). Community defense is substantially provided by the larger political structure within which the affluent routinely seek to institutionalize privilege, but probably less because of residents' personal wealth than the role their place plays in the geopolitical economy.

This also means that even the rich neighborhoods can decline as their function in the local urban system shifts. Expansion of the basic economy (itself a result of growth machine strategies) attracts migrants who, inconvenient as it may be, must be put somewhere. The growth machine sets in motion classic residential succession sequences, which, as in the case of postwar ghetto expansions, impinge on neighborhoods throughout the metropolis (Duncan and Duncan, 1957; Taeuber and Taeuber, 1965). In addition to this "push" against the affluent areas, there is also the "pull" of a better life in the wealthy suburbs, enthusiastically marketed by rentiers using all manner of legal and financial instruments to make their speculative profits in the hinterlands. As the subsidized suburbanization process drains more and more of the affluent from the city, there are simply not enough of the rich (or even middle class) to go around, leaving the stragglers high and dry in a newly devalued and disrupted social environment.

A different problem for affluent areas comes from the extraordinary rents that can be collected by those able to intensively develop parcels of land within or adjacent to such ordinarily lower-density neighborhoods. There are several classic scenarios: high-rise apartments adjacent to mansions (along the Winnetka-Wilmette border outside Chicago); resort hotel complexes near the second homes of the wealthy (characteristc of some development in Palm Beach and Boca Raton, Florida); large-scale shopping centers near the towns of well-to-do (almost every posh suburb in America faces this pressure). The town politics of Beverly Hills, California, is driven by a constant effort by developers to overcome controls on hotel, retail, office, and apartment expansion (see Mitchell, 1984). To one degree or another, such battles have compromised use values in many affluent towns, like Purchase,

New York, Greenwich, Connecticut, and La Jolla, California. The political tensions in such areas represent the increasing disparity between the rent payoff of parcels under current low densities and the rent potential of the same parcels if they are turned over to more intensive uses. Exchange value pressures are sometimes so great that no community can withstand them, no matter how much wealth it has.

In the limited space we have here, we cannot explain why specific affluent areas seem able to withstand exchange value threats, but others fall more readily to this force. Although we reject the mechanistic determinism of the classical ecologists (under which all areas must give way to subsocial demographic expansion), we are also suspicious of those who would attribute stability to a vague, "ineffable, and at times overpowering coerciveness" tied to primordial attachments (Geertz, 1963:109). Firey's (1945) classic analysis of Boston's centrally located, but historically rich, Beacon Hill, for example, is often used to argue that precisely this sentimentality is sufficient to preserve a neighborhood in the face of all manner of pressures on it. But more than "sentiment" was involved in Beacon Hill's preservation. Firey described the political struggle through which its affluent residents protected themselves from those "insiders" who might have sold out, and also noted that much of the working-class North End, no less of a sentimental community, was completely wiped out by an expressway. It wasn't just sentiment; it was sentiment of organized and powerful people.

There also may have been an element of economic accident in the preservation of Beacon Hill, just as there is in other instances of preservation. The newly discovered precious historic districts of the country, such as Baltimore's Federal Hill, New Orleans's French Quarter, and many quaint Maine villages, were saved not so much by sentiment as by their decline in economic vitality. Modernization passed them by through no efforts of their own residents. Neighborhoods may be ignored because the costs of conversion exceed the rent anticipated through private redevelopment. This can give an area a breathing period during which, ignored by the active speculators and challenged only by the rain, wind, and poor, it can survive, to one day "come back" as an architectural gem, yielding higher rents than anyone ever dreamed.

Our assumption is that virtually all neighborhoods are subject to *potential* threats from the rent intensification process. Rich neighborhoods are more capable of institutional resistance and this means that disrupting them requires a concomitantly greater economic divergence between current and potential rents to set disruptive change in motion. This gives the affluent one more reason to sleep soundly in their beds at night, but not without an edge of concern.[4]

All of our examples are meant to show that, whether among rich or poor neighborhoods, in the central city or urban fringe, neighborhood futures are determined by the ways in which entrepreneurial pressures from outside intersect with internal material stakes and sentimental attachments. The exchange value interest of some residents in their neighborhood property can generate the kind of commitment to neighborhood that not only can help to preserve a way of life but also can undermine it. The potential rent increase, along with neighborhood differences in ethnic solidarities, age, and gender, is important in determining which form the commitment will take. The simultaneous presence of both exchange and use values (often among different groups of people, such as homeowners and tenants) makes even internal neighborhood politics diverse.

We cannot deduce a rule, therefore, that will predict the outcome in all cases. Instead, we can only reiterate the critical determinants: (1) the strategic value of neighborhood in the larger system of places (i.e., its changing utility in the rent generation process); (2) the nature of the internal pressures for exchange value returns and the particular strategies used; (3) the power and status of residents in the larger political economy; and (4) the sentiments and cultural systems of residents that guide the pursuit of local use values. The conditions and fate of any neighborhood stem from the way these factors come to be arrayed. Let us apply

4. For some problems, wealth is less of a solution; for example, the rich are victims of ransom kidnapping and jewel theft. In general, of course, they are much less likely to be victims of crime than the poor, particularly young black men, whose murder victimization rate is by far the highest of any group.

these notions to the neighborhood whose existence poses the most vexing analytical and political issues of U.S. society, the black ghetto.

The Dilemma of the Ghetto

Just as there has been substantial variation in the rate and degree to which different immigrant and racial groups have acquired "a piece of the pie" (Lieberson, 1980), so there are variations in the ways these groups' neighborhoods function in the larger systems of individual and area stratification. At least since the turn of the century, there has been a "pattern of unequal autonomy" (Zunz, 1982:87) among minority neighborhoods. Some have been able to provide their residents with a stable daily round and strong informal support systems, with reliable political and economic linkages, including ties to the outside world. The neighborhood has been an effective melding of sentimental, economic, and political opportunities, an autonomous "proving ground" for developing ways to build both psychological and economic security. The word *quarter* (following Levine, 1980) or *enclave* (following Portes, 1981, 1982) describes these places. The prototypical cases are the neighborhoods of the immigrant Italians and Jews. For the contrasting case, in which autonomy is much more limited, we reserve the term *ghetto* (originally applied to Jewish areas of European cities). It still implies that castelike discrimination isolates people from other geographical settings as well as from mainstream economic roles. The neighborhoods of U.S. blacks, a people whose slave origins make them "immigrants" only by an awkward extension of language, are the exemplars.

There was at least an element of choice in the appearance of the European immigrants in the United States; they must have arrived with some hope and with kinship ties and other sorts of basic "human capital" intact. They took places in industrial job queues only partially rigged against them, found apartments, and built homes in areas more or less in line with their economic resources. For some, local political structures became avenues of mobility, providing lucrative municipal contracts for their own business firms and stable careers for cronies and kin (Bell, 1961; Cornwall, 1969; Handlin, 1951; Wilson, 1980). They built neighborhood economies through which they employed coethnics, particularly relatives; some functioned as "middlemen," trading goods and brokering services among other groups (Bonacich, 1973). Within the neighborhoods, as streams of ethnographic accounts have indicated, the bulk of retailing and service trade was controlled by locals of the same ethnicity, with many businesses held intergenerationally (see Gans, 1962; Suttles, 1968; Whyte, 1943; Wirth, 1928). Some, like the Italian restaurants and Jewish delis, became "famous" and brought in outside money and fostered local pride. Others, like the Italian building firms and Irish insurance companies, were large enough to draw wealth from the entire metropolis and operate on a wide scale. Many residents owned their own homes, even in poor areas like the Polish workers' district of Detroit (Zunz, 1982:173). A significant number of residents became interested in place for its exchange returns as well as its use values. As long as these exchange interests did not lend themselves to schemes of profiting from neighborhood transformation, owners' parochial interests unproblematically called for preservation of neighborhood. This provides a system that binds residents to their own neighborhood while at the same time connecting neighborhood to its surrounding metropolis.

Although only approximating an ideal "multiple institutional" neighborhood model (Warren, 1963),[5] such arrangements did exist, and even now persist among new immigrant groups, with consequences that are again quite real. Portes (1981), in examining the occupational structure of the Miami Cuban community (in 1976), found that about one third of the immigrants worked for other Cubans in the enclave economy; in San Francisco's Chinatown, the proportion is one half (Mar, 1984; Takagi, 1985). Portes remarks that although wages paid to workers under these conditions are low, they foster an indigenous bourgeoisie and a community of overlapping functions and allegiances. "The principle of ethnic solidarity, which enterpreneurs invoke to extract labor from new arrivals, may also cause them to promote and support the economic initiatives of other immigrants" (Portes, 1982:109;

5. This is the medieval ideal (Pirenne, 1925; Sjoberg, 1955), in which the town quarter contains "the major institutions of work, religion, family, leisure and, to a considerable degree, government and social control" (Yancey, Ericksen, and Juliani, 1976:395).

see also Portes, 1981; Wilson and Portes, 1980, but see Mar, 1984).[6] This manner of autonomous exploitation seems to be a factor in upward mobility for the Koreans in Los Angeles (Bonacich, Light, and Wong, 1977), Arabs in Detroit (Abraham and Abraham, 1983), and Vietnamese in a number of areas (Nguyen and Henkin, 1982), just as it was once the pattern for Germans in Milwaukee (Conzen, 1976) and Jews in New York (Howe and Libo, 1979).

This is the portrait of immigrant experience that dominates the imagination of both the lay public and the urban scholars as *the* trajectory against which the "performance" of other groups, particularly blacks, is measured (see Glazer, 1971; Rosen, 1959; Sowell, 1981). By this methodology, blacks don't do well and various characterological attributes are often used to explain the "failure" of the black "immigrant" group. The alternative is to see these groups as not parallel at all, and view each ethnic group (and each of its cohorts) as having different experiences in what Goering (1978:81) terms the "constantly shifting network of exchange and competition among rival interests and institutions." There were, even at the outset of the process, differences in internal resources, in external sources of opportunity and in levels of imposed degradation. And this brings us to the crucial point. If the trajectory of upward and outward social and geographical movement is identified as an intrinsic "immigrant" phenomenon, then institutional factors in the market structure, in the political system, and in the cultural realm *did not allow blacks to be immigrants*. The task, which can only be touched on here, is to learn how a slave past in the United States, intersecting with evolving internal and external forces, has led to current patterns of ghetto life—to a neighborhood ethnicity that has "emerged" (Yancey, Ericksen, and Juliani, 1976), like all aspects of ethnicity, out of conditions in the new settlement as much as conditions in the old (see Blauner, 1972; Oliver and Glick, 1982:513).

The distinctive oppression of blacks, plausibly rooted in the material and ideological needs of European colonialism (Cox, 1948; Frazier, 1957; Jordon, 1974; Novak and Udry, 1983), has

---

6. Mar (1984) presents contrary data indicating that aggregate mobility is not increased among the San Francisco Chinese, although some do indeed become quite prosperous. Mar argues that class divisions within the ethnic community are sustained through the enclave wage structure.

been replicated under successive capitalist orders, including those that formed the modern U.S. city. Compared to blacks, no other urban workers were so excluded by the emerging industrial firms from core employment, paid at levels so much lower than prevailing wage scales, or so totally excluded from craft union membership. Although racism was by no means invented by U.S. industrialists, it was useful enough to be left intact by them. Henry Ford's exclusion of blacks from both work on his assembly lines and residence in his company town was probably a help to his "labor relations." Industrial firms actively promoted racial segregation within their work forces by creating separate lunch areas, washrooms, and toilets (Zunz, 1982:321). These racial manipulations, including the widespread use of blacks as scabs, had the considerable benefit (not coincidental) of restraining labor militance (Allen, 1974; Bonacich, 1973, 1980; Gutman, 1976), and shifting tension to the residential arena.

The pattern of institutional behavior in the larger metropolis had specific consequences for the black neighborhood. The immigrant scenario of mutually reinforcing individual mobility and community building was denied to blacks. This does not mean that the black neighborhood was *disorganized,* but instead that it was organized differently. Clues from the early phase of the development of ghettos in the United States indicate the nature of the differences. Black urban residents had a distinctive sex ratio (many men, few women), even compared to the immigrant groups. Blacks had extraordinarily high rates of infant mortality and low fertility rates, well below those of other poor urban people (Zunz, 1982:379). The earliest black urban elites in business and the professions tended to have white clients and to live in white neighborhoods. The imposition of urban segregation destroyed these social contacts and economic relationships. In another unusual twist, black segregation *increased* during the period of rapid industrialization (1910–1930), just when the residential concentrations of Italians and Poles, for example, were breaking up (Lieberson, 1980:268–70).[7] As Zunz remarks, "Blacks lived

---

7. Lieberson (1980) argues that segregating blacks was a way to sustain the traditional low degree of white contact with blacks in neighborhood contexts. When there were few blacks in the urban North, the whiteness of the daily round remained even with a dispersed black population. But as black numbers grew, segregation was rigidly and blatantly imposed to sustain separation.

history in reverse" (1982:398). Blacks who had earlier lived among whites became, as the need arose, "the victims of many forms of terrorism . . . the ghetto sprang up, in part, as a reaction to a xenophobic violence which no other group of migrants to the city [of Detroit] had ever experienced" (Zunz, 1982:373; for the Los Angeles case, see Oliver and Johnson, 1984:68; Spaulding, 1946). And the location of these ghettos seems to have continuously placed black residential areas far from the factories and offices ("sunrise industries") of their day (Osofsky, 1963; Zunz, 1982).

Blacks' efforts to build equity in property and sustain indigenous business enterprises faced analogous challenges. We know very well that in settings otherwise governed by free market ideologies arbitrary forces can be unleashed against minority group members striving for business success. Markets are restructured for personal gain by socially dominant groups. The Japanese-Americans suffered severe material losses at the time of their detention during World War II (Broom and Riemer, 1973), just as Chinese-Americans were intermittently harassed long before that point (Saxton, 1971). The California Mexican-Americans lost their vast cattle ranches through lack of credit during periods of drought and price decline, as well as through the propensity of Anglo officials and "shyster" (Pitt, 1966) lawyers to reinterpret land deeds and tax laws to force property transfers to Yankee immigrants (Camarillo, 1979; Pitt, 1966).

New evidence from the South (Johnson and Roark, 1984a, 1984b) shows the tenuous threads by which the wealthy colored entrepreneurs and landowners of the mid-nineteenth century held on to their real estate enterprises, always wary that a wrong social move, a slight offense of etiquette, might bring ruin at the hands of offended whites. In the North, one of the few lucrative businesses open to blacks, real estate, was difficult and dangerous: entrepreneurs who tried to sell property outside the ghetto faced threats to their lives and repeated bombings of their homes and offices (Philpott, 1978:177). Blacks had little capacity to manipulate zoning and other political institutions on behalf of their enterprises. Structural speculation was precluded. More generally, black entrepreneurs consistently lacked access to credit, which tended to "wash out" black enterprises during downturns in the business cycle (Osofsky, 1963:102).[8] Even much of the corruption in the ghetto, such as the "policy" and other gambling rackets, was controlled by whites, particularly the machine political bosses (Drake and Cayton, 1945:483). Black business, like black mobility generally, was "curtailed by traditional attitudes toward colored persons and by the vested economic interests of white occupational groups" (Drake and Cayton, 1945:437). It is significant that black West Indian immigrants have been most active as entrepreneurs, "legendary in their frugalness and thrift" (Drake and Cayton, 1945:133), for they have had the *least* exposure to the debilitating mores of the U.S. caste system. Although it may be true that the black American "lacks a business tradition or the experience of people who, over generations, have engaged in buying and selling" (Frazier, 1962:139), there were (and are) good reasons to keep such a tradition from developing.

Indeed, on almost all fronts, racist discrimination persists even in contemporary times, albeit at lower levels of intensity. Black job applicants are still disfavored by white employers (Alexander and Sapery, 1973; Bloom, Fletcher, and Perry, 1972; Butler, 1976), sometimes facing the same simple "door in the face" discrimination as in the past (Feagin, 1982:125–32). The same pattern is found in housing. Careful investigations of instances in which applicants matching in every way except race apply for the same housing vacancies reveal that black applicants are far less likely to be successful than whites (Wienk et al., 1979; see also Molotch, 1972; Pearce, 1976). Financial institutions take more money out of black neighborhoods (as deposits) than they put back in (as home mortgages), and finance a disproportionately small number of home buyers compared to the total amount of home purchasing in black areas (Taggart and Smith, 1981). These practices along with the redlining of whole sections of the city have detrimental effects on housing costs, homeownership rates,

8. Self-employed black farmers experience a similar squeeze today (although small-scale white farmers are also under pressure). In 1910, black farmers operated 15 million acres of land; in 1978 ownership was down to 4.7 million acres. The crisis was exacerbated by the agricultural downturn of the early 1980s, which may shake out virtually the last of the black farmers. The irony is that black farmers do as well as whites on a gross-return-per-acre basis, but because they have difficulty obtaining credit and have small farms, they are less able to survive cyclical downturns (Brooks, 1984).

and people's chances of using house equity to "trade up" to better areas (Bradbury, Downs, and Small, 1982; Darden, 1980). Similarly, blacks continue to suffer from the disruption of the neighborhoods they do occupy; even after the demise of urban renewal, the loss of black residential units continued in the 1970s, at 80 percent of the rate in the 1960s, while the white rate declined to the much lower levels of the 1950s (Dahmann, 1982).

The evidence clearly points to a pattern of ghetto dependency. Homeownership rates are low among urban blacks; 64 percent of U.S. whites owned their own homes in 1980; only 44 percent of blacks owned their own homes, with rural, small-town, or Southern blacks accounting for the bulk of black owners (U.S. Bureau of the Census, 1982b:110). Further, blacks are far more likely than whites to be paying rent to people of a different race and to people who live outside their neighborhood. This has other, indirect, impacts on use values. As Molotch (1972) observed in his study of the changing South Shore neighborhood of Chicago, through interviews with three hundred landlords throughout the metropolis, property owners and management firms often see racial change as a signal to cut back property maintenance and reinvestment in structures. The most efficient route to maximize exchange value is, if not a "milking" of the property for short-term gain, at least a decrease in maintenance. The pattern is strong enough to make black neighborhoods of high rates of homeownership virtually the only ones in which properties are maintained in a safe and respectful fashion.

We find the same patterns in business: blacks have a low rate of ownership. Even in black Harlem during the Negro Renaissance of the 1920s, blacks owned far fewer of the ghetto businesses than whites (about 20 percent of Harlem businesses). In 1938 in Chicago, blacks owned almost half of all businesses in the black belt, but because these establishments were small, 90 percent of all shoppers' money spent in the area went to the white entrepreneurs (Drake and Cayton, 1945:438).[9] As in earlier decades, black businesses continued in the postwar years to be con-

---

9. The outside ownership pattern has an ethnic quality as well; in 1938 in Chicago, three-fourths of white-owned ghetto businesses were owned by Jews; in New Orleans Italians were the major entrepreneurs (Drake and Cayton, 1945:432).

centrated in personal services (barbershops, clothes cleaners, restaurants), which cannot easily be "exported" to other groups. Whites owned the groceries and clothing and furniture stores (Frazier, 1962:53; Osofsky, 1963:137; see also Drake and Cayton, 1945:438). As of 1977, less than 1.5 percent of the U.S. black labor force was employed by other blacks, a very low rate compared to the rates for other large ethnic groups (Brown, 1984; U.S. Bureau of the Census, 1979). For every 1,000 blacks in the United States, only 9.2 businesses are owned by blacks; for Hispanics the rate is 19.5; for Asians, 28.8 (U.S. Minority Business Development Agency, 1982).

These patterns of discrimination and deprivation are obviously not the result of recent trends like suburbanization or high-tech displacement. These patterns represent a historically consistent, sequentially reinforcing practice of repression. The only people lower than blacks in their contemporary economic standing are the Native Americans (Sowell, 1981), also not "immigrants" but subjected, as despised "savages," to the harshest repression (indeed, genocide). Today, they live in residential areas that, whether as remote reservations or urban slums, have high levels of dependence on outside bureaucracies and a weak "business tradition." This situation, like that of the blacks, implies something about the difference between immigration and subjugation, not arrival times.

The ghetto is, *in the exchange value context of U.S. urban life,* "institutionally incomplete" (Breton, 1964), with, as Oliver (1984:24) states bluntly, "the dominant social institutions being churches and liquor stores." Donald Warren (1975:11) has observed that ghetto leaders rise to their positions "in social bureaucracies—church, welfare, drug-abuse programs, public schools, etc.—which are . . . consumption rather than production 'industries.'" Leaders of such institutions cannot provide economic links within the neighborhood, or exercise much clout outside it. Even the black churches, an important part of black neighborhood life (Frazier and Lincoln, 1973; Ley, 1974), cannot make up for the absence of an indigenous exchange value engine. No church organization is ever of crucial importance in metropolitan dynamics (except occasionally as a tourist site). And the black church, unlike the Catholic or Protestant churches of the immigrants, is not itself closely tied to the religious organizations of the dominant white groups. Not only are black ministers not considered important to growth goals, they are also irrelevant to the personal salvation of white leaders.[10]

Taken together, the many examples of exclusion and harassment give rise in the contemporary ghetto to ways of dealing with this geographically organized vulnerability. Amid a special "forthrightness and camaraderie" (DeZutter, 1981; Kochman, 1981), there has evolved an extraordinary coping system built upon mutual exchange and reciprocity (Anderson, 1976; Liebow, 1967; Stack, 1974; Valentine, 1978, but see Fischer, 1982:254). There is a network of interpersonal support, and a density of internal organization that can be higher than that in white areas (Warren, 1975). But rich interpersonal relationships within the neighborhood may be relatively inconsequential for community defense if there are no effective extralocal ties (Guest, 1985). Hunter (1974) reports that Chicago's black residents have a "localized" and "primary group" orientation toward neighborhood, one that does not facilitate mobilization on instrumental issues (see also Greer, 1962:138; Rudzitis, 1982–83). Blacks' local networks are not able to profitably link their participants' everyday lives with the economic and political structures that provide mobility and neighborhood defense.

The critical fact is that in the ghetto, the pursuit of exchange values is almost totally in the hands of outsiders; the daily round is worth little to anyone with an exchange interest and the resources needed to back up those interests. The people who own and control the ghetto, through their market holdings or their bureaucratic positions, live elsewhere and thus have little stake in enhancing the use values of residents. The "mixed allegiance" to both use and exchange values characteristic of some small-scale retailers and resident property owners in other areas is missing and

10. Similarly, increased black participation in the union rank and file does not easily translate into a neighborhood resource. In the steel communities studied by Kornblum (1974), black steelworkers were unique among ethnic groups in their lack of stable ties to a specific community that could be used to build reputations and help in advancement in union politics; this, in turn, meant "one of their own" was not visible as a worker whose union connections at the plant could be used by neighbors as a basis for job advancement. Reputations built in the plant could not, as they did for the other groups, serve as a basis for furthering neighborhood solidarity.

cannot function to restrain exchange goals. This weakens the indigenous group's capacity to secure the turf against outsiders' entrepreneurial and bureaucratic schemes. To build upon Zeitlin's formulation (1984a; Zeitlin, Neuman, and Ratcliff, 1976), the personification of use value is distinct from the personification of exhange value.[11] This, through an indirect route, is one of the key neighborhood consequences of the racist subjugation of black Americans.

A conspicuous minority of ghetto residents, those with the weakest entitlements to a secure place, are more than mobile; their inability to pay rent makes them drifters, or, in the words of the streets, "hoodlums" or, if they drink, "wineheads" (Anderson, 1976). Their street corner is the starting point of their daily round, a round that is devalued by almost everyone except themselves. The presence of such people and related ghetto conditions makes it more difficult for a critical mass of respectability to develop and take spatial form, for the daily round of *anyone* to be consistently sanctioned as "decent" (see Wilson, forthcoming). It is not simply a matter of poor public services, high levels of air pollution, and decaying absentee-owned buildings. People may not put flowerpots on the housing project balcony, knowing that their very residence is stigmatized and that the pot will probably be knocked over by a vandal anyway. Residents may not worry about their trash; they may relate to public areas in the same way as higher-income groups treat their rooms at the Airport Hilton, showing little perception of shared responsibility with other "guests," the housekeeper, or the management. The litter and graffiti are taken as signs that many residents betray the tenets of middle-class "civility" (Lewis and Maxfield, 1980; Lewis and Salem, 1983); rates of violence are known to be higher, prison records more common, and welfare dependence more prevalent. These differences cannot

11. Zeitlin and his associates, in their analysis of class cleavage in Chile, argue that the conflict between the *roles* of landed aristocracy and bourgeoisie was muted because the families with large landholdings overlapped with members of the corporate elite; "contradictory interests and social cleavages did not coincide" (Zeitlin, Neuman, and Ratcliff, 1976:1025). The two forces coalesced in the form of persons with family ties to both spheres. The prominent political role played by such persons meant that State policy had to take into account both landlord and corporate interests, thus facilitating long-term political stability. (Michael Schwartz suggested the parallel to our work.)

be denied through a liberal doctrine that "we are all the same" (in Kochman's terms, a "politeness conspiracy"),[12] or obscured by mechanistic searches for a general description of urban life. But these conditions, resulting from the larger pattern of historical relations in production and rent collection, can then be mistaken by outsiders to mean that there is nothing worth preserving in the ghetto, making almost all black people's homelands appropriate candidates for any reuse that will serve the growth needs of the metropolis. Blaming the victims helps justify destroying their community.

Paradoxes of Community Organization

The inherent instability of U.S. places leads to the founding of neighborhood community organizations (COs); these voluntary organizations typically exist to enhance use values, often in the face of exchange threats. They are created to deal with problems that, in the residents' view, are beyond the reach of existing governmental and single-focus civic associations, an accurate perception in most cases, since the government and most civic agencies are linked to the growth machine system (see chapter 3). Many scholars, from Tocqueville to more modern commentators, have noted the tendency of Americans to join and support associations generally. This can be at least partially explained by the extreme degree to which land is treated as a commodity in the United States, which destabilizes places, and the decentralization of government authority, which puts growth tools as well as regulating controls within at least apparent reach of local citizens. Nevertheless, because use values rather than exchange values guide most urban residents' actions, they are "naturally disorganized" (Friedland and Palmer, 1984:396); only extraordinary circumstances bring them into effective play against business elites, who are, as they tend their speculations, "naturally organized" (Stone, 1982).

12. Higham (1975:115) puts it as an invitation: "Instead of washing all the specific color out of our ethnic fabric in our fear of propagating stereotypes, let us look for the realities behind them" (as cited in Zunz, 1982:7).

Though they need it least, residents of affluent areas are more likely than others to join community organizations, and to have organizations that achieve unity and become effective (Crenson, 1983:297–300; see also Ley and Mercer, 1980; Rich, 1980). People of higher socioeconomic status participate more in local issues (Burnett, 1983; Goodman and Clary, 1976), and show a stronger link between "sensing a problem" and "becoming active" (Cox and McCarthy, 1980). We attribute these class differences, not to personality attributes of race, class, or ethnic groups, but to the larger set of interrelated advantages of wealthy neighborhoods, which contribute to successful mobilization: financial and political resources, residential stability, social homogeneity, and an array of organizations long in place (Henig, 1982). Neighborhood collective action is particularly strategic for the affluent when political conflict over land use becomes inescapable and the mode of conflict shifts from individual clout to more organized (and public) forms of action. When land development matters are the bone of contention in affluent areas (which they often are), the result is that "well-organized homeowners face well-financed developers" with each side "spending liberally for legal counsel and technical expertise" (Rudel, 1983:114). There may be constant litigation as one entrepreneur after another strives for the bonanza that can result if opposition can be overcome.

When defending their turf, the rich don't have to invoke their own use values. Instead, they can enthusiastically argue that preservation of their neighborhood is consistent with the needs of the whole city (including its growth "vitality"), or even of civilization itself. Citizens of places like Pebble Beach, California, or Beacon Hill can claim that their turf is unique in the world and must be "saved," as if it were an endangered species. And given the propensity of the affluent to choose their neighborhoods well and then lavish money and attention on them, their arguments are not without a grain of truth. Joined by many others, including sympathetic outsiders of lower social status but elevated aesthetic sensibilities, the rich can often mobilize enough political muscle to bring about protective government action.

Poor people, in contrast, are not in a position to effectively claim that their neighborhood, *as used by them,* is either a national resource or useful for attracting capital. Instead they must make a more "emotional," a less "public-regarding" (Banfield and Wilson, 1963) case for their rights to their homes and shops. Their claims can be dismissed as idiosyncratic, even if understandable, efforts to intervene in legitimate market and governmental planning processes. Given such problems and the general lack of internal resources needed to ward off disruption, community organization seems on its face to be one of the few viable defense strategies. It is no wonder, therefore, that so many analysts have looked to the urban poor as the natural wellspring for this, as well as so much other, effective organizational opposition. Whether in the radical populist tradition of Alinsky (1969), the more conventional practices of social workers, or the urban social movements of Castells (1983), poor people's neighborhoods are where most of the action is supposed to be.

The paradox, of course, is that the neighborhoods with the most serious need for community organizations are those with the least capacity to create and sustain them. A neighborhood's general standing affects its *internal* material and social workings, which in turn affect the likelihood of effective community organization. A critical problem, again especially common in ghetto areas, is the absence of local business leaders (retailers, service providers, and property owners) who might supply material resources as well as connections with outside entrepreneurs and political organizations. Although this helps prevent unholy alliances between internal entrepreneurs and outsiders, it also means that the internal coalitions upon which community organizations typically depend cannot take form either. It becomes more difficult to achieve simple goals like getting a stop sign, blocking a sewer plant, or having the police evict unruly neighbors without burning down the whole neighborhood in the process. This is what happened in Philadelphia in the 1985 eviction of MOVE cultists; through the authorities' "grossly negligent behavior" eleven people were killed and sixty-one homes destroyed (Secter, 1986:8).

Low-income people are difficult to mobilize; their day-to-day marginality makes it hard for them to contribute time or funds. And since they have little or no money after meeting basic needs, combining internal resources can represent little more than multiplying zero times zero; the result is still zero.[13] Moreover, when organizations do somehow manage to get hold of some resources, the frequent result in a context of so much shortage is destructive internecine squabbles over the few available crumbs (Katz and Mayer, 1985:16). Particularly in ghetto areas, it is difficult even to identify a stable constituency because of high rates of mobility and a certain heterogeneity that brings the underclass into the daily round of even the affluent.

This kind of instability and heterogeneity seems to work against the residents' commitment to a spatially demarcated organization. Research on community attachment (Kasarda and Janowitz, 1974) has demonstrated the strong positive effect of residential stability. Reactionary neighborhood defense organizations, like the Boston antibusing movement studied by Useem (1980), as well as more progressive organizations, require a stable local base. Greer (1962:147) suggests that suburban stability and social homogeneity are major sources of political consensus among residents, and Guest and Oropesa (1984:839) report that homogenous communities in the Seattle area are the most able to support ongoing community organizations.

In some degree of contrast, black ghettos produce a form of urbane sophistication, a stigmatized cosmopolitanism that comes from having economic fates tied to distant and somewhat arbitrary institutions. Just as Jencks (1983:38) was forced to the "painful conclusion" that chronic exclusion, instability, and poverty inhibit blacks' performance in school or at work, we think these same disadvantages provide difficulties, not assets, for a community organizer looking for an enthusiastic constituency upon which to build a base.

Under conditions of meager neighborhood resources and obvious overall deprivation, people must find alternatives to traditional community organization. Organization in the ghetto has taken a pan-neighborhood form that makes comprehensive demands for the benefit of all blacks in the metropolis. Ghetto organizers took the offensive against the larger urban system (for example, city hall or the school board) or the national govern-

---

13. John McKnight provided this formula in a conversation with Molotch.

ment. Ghettos are organized less as attempts to defend the ongoing social and institutional patterns of a specific neighborhood and more as assaults on the larger social order that denies basic resources to all deprived places and the people in them. It is organization around victimization (Warren, 1975; see also Pahl, 1970:63).[14]

Black people's access to use values was so casually and pervasively left to the whim of the exchange value apparatus (whether in labor or property markets) that opposition to the pattern had to be as comprehensive as the threat. At least during the time of the most energetic activity in poor black areas (the 1960s and early 1970s), the activist thrust was against the larger system, which was correctly perceived to be the source of both individual and neighborhood troubles. Both the special vulnerability of black neighborhoods to outside penetration and the difficulties of organizing around turf issues are caused by racist patterns of exploitation, exclusion, and stigma. The movements for black liberation were thus not "urban social movements" (Castells, 1983), but part of a worldwide crusade against caste oppression, albeit a rebellion that, like many in the modern age, occurs primarily in the city (Tilly, 1974; Tilly, Tilly, and Tilly, 1975).

The energy needed to fight on these larger and more diffuse grounds is difficult to sustain. The struggle requires a more profound ideology than that behind the immediate and concrete interests of protecting one's property values or daily round. Ironically, it is the latter sort of activity as carried out by the affluent that has been misleadingly identified as altruistic and "public-regarding." But the movements of the ghetto poor require the more thorough transcendence of competing "selfish" demands of everyday life (Flacks, 1976, forthcoming) and precisely for that reason are more difficult to sustain over long periods.

The strategy of broad-based, disruptive attack on the centers of power was appropriate given the ghetto's extreme *social* distance from those centers but close *geographical* proximity to them. Some black activists, following the Alinsky (1969) advice, resorted to "rubbing raw the sores of discontent" in order to make

14. As Pahl (1970:63) says, a community can take its form from "a common disaster or common restriction on freedom" as much as from a shared advantage.

the troubles of ghetto people felt as troubles in the larger system. The geographical proximity of blacks to sensitive elite places (central business districts, prestige medical centers, and universities) positions blacks to threaten the stability of the surrounding urban system (Hicks and Swank, 1983; Piven and Cloward, 1971), including its long-term growth prospects. This spatial configuration was part of the "organizational substructure of disorderly politics" (Von Eschen, Kirk, and Pinard, 1971). Ghetto residents' insurrections create the unstable conditions that imply a poor investment climate for the nearby areas; if protest and mayhem go too far, a liberal growth machine may emerge to seek accommodation (as an alternative to draconian repression). This was the explicit goal of civic leaders in Atlanta, Georgia, and other cities (see chapter 3) who proposed to the rest of the white citizenry that their city was, in the slogan of the day, "too busy to hate" (Rice, 1983). The goal appears to have been especially characteristic of cities with major corporate headquarters, where much was at stake in the outcome (Friedland, 1982).

Organizing the Organizers

All community organizations have vulnerabilities; even the most militant can be shaped by elites toward a *modus vivendi* that reestablishes urban routines. There are even ways in which community groups, including radical protest organizations, can be used to help the process of growth intensification, or at least to remove any acute threat.

Neighborhood Management

Community organizations are not moneymakers and have to struggle for the funds needed to survive—to pay staff and cover expenses. One way to survive is to abandon insurrection. Parallel to the classic process of co-optation (Selznick, 1949), community organizations and insurrectionary movements adapt to "the real world," especially to a liberal growth machine strategy that holds out a peaceful hand.

An example is The Woodlawn Organization (TWO) of Chicago, accurately credited with stopping the University of Chicago and city hall from taking over its turf in the 1960s for campus expansion and a highway (Fish et al., 1966). TWO has evolved in the decades since its founding into an administrative funnel for government programs (job training, community mental health, and others), performing adjunct functions to the still-centralized welfare system. The organization's leaders have taken on the role of a locally based bourgeoisie: through government subsidies as well as the participation of outside private firms, the community organization operates a few modest retail businesses (such as the neighborhood supermarket) and sponsors housing rehabilitation and construction. A similar pattern is found in Boston and San Francisco, in which former activists were "tamed" (Mollenkopf, 1983:191) as their organizations evolved into alternative social service providers; "political leaders become program administrators [and] their constituents . . . become clients" (Mollenkopf, 1983:97). For blacks, it is by now a familiar pattern: upward mobility is made possible by being in charge of "social control programs specifically designed to deal with 'black issues'" (Allen, 1970, as cited in Oliver and Glick, 1982:521). It is much like the way rich countries relate to Third World societies. Government supports high-risk private capital, which then enters into partnership with indigenous elites. These elites' participation in turn helps stabilize the investment, and they share in the returns accordingly. The linkage of the external power structure to the ghetto remains paternalistic and ad hoc, with the black leadership possessing no structural leverage over the system (see Seley and Wolpert, 1975:281).

By the scale of neighborhood standards—an economy of groceries, taverns, and barbershops—such organizations are significant components of community life, although by metropolitan standards of corporate headquarters and world-class museums they are trivial. They are substantial enough, perhaps, to inject at least a simulated enclave provincialism into the ghetto: for those who have careers tied to the community organization and its various operations, there is a turf-related basis for getting ahead and making a life. With a parochial interest to defend, the leaders of the community organization become a force for stability—a stability that translates into a system of accumulation and rent collection outside the neighborhood that can proceed unimpeded. The old goals of opposition, of "smashing the state," of "power to the people" are displaced by the need to build turf and the institutions to which one's life chances are tied. This transformation from offensive urbanity to reactionary provincialism mitigates the insurrectionary threat.

Vanguard of the Bourgeoisie

When exchange value conditions are right, community organizations can facilitate the reuse of poor people's neighborhoods for more lucrative purposes. Operating through the community organization mechanism, the "better element" in an otherwise disadvantaged area can function as a vanguard for change. These higher-class elements can be leftovers from a previous transition, or pioneers in a new one, or they may simply be drawn into a community by conveniently adjusting boundary lines to "borrow" some desirables from an adjacent turf. Whatever their origins, these people can end up as an organizational leadership to "speak for the community" on behalf of "higher standards" and the sort of land uses that might facilitate them.

Not surprisingly, those who ordinarily join and become leaders in a community organization tend to be the middle-class (or aspiring middle-class) homeowners, even if present only in small numbers in any neighborhood. Those who are better-off can routinely take over even a longstanding community organization, not as a result of a coup or a conspiracy, but merely as a result of devoting their energy and resources to it. Their presence can be a wedge through which outsiders can introduce and foster transformation.

Sometimes, gentrifying pioneers, in forming their community organizations, come to be taken as primary neighborhood representatives. In defending their own financial and psychological investments, these volunteers strive to make the entire neighborhood more closely resemble their own way of life. They use community organization, in lieu of sufficient funds to buy into an affluent area, to create a critical mass of pleasant amenity. Often remaking their homes with their own "sweat equity," these people are notorious for their organizational hard work; like speculators who have only exchange value interests, they are "naturally organized" because their small-scale structural speculation forces them to be. They have bet on a land parcel by betting they can use organizational clout to make a new social structure become real.

Front Organization

A community organization can so completely identify with those who wish to recycle the neighborhood that the organization comes to owe its very existence to outsiders' efforts. In the renewal of the Hyde Park-Kenwood community in Chicago, the University of Chicago established and funded the Southeast Chicago Commission (Rossi and Dentler, 1961), a purported community group headed by a leader of the university community (and brother of the dean of the Law School).[15] In the case of the transformation of Boston's South End, Mollenkopf (1983:175) reports an intimate connection between city authorities and the neighborhood "leadership." The Boston Redevelopment Authority, in finding "a group of elite homeowners and tenants who aspired to make the South End a respectable middle-class neighborhood," was able, in effect, "to organize the community in behalf of its own bureaucratic interests" (Mollenkopf, 1983:175).

Neighborhood leaders are useful in testifying in support of rezoning, redevelopment subsidies, or tax abatements for a favored project. They can also be used to dampen internal neighborhood opposition to entrepreneurs' development projects. In Santa Barbara, local growth elites have created a community group called Santa Barbara Futures, whose members routinely testify on growth-related projects. Exxon oil, in order to win one of its many land-use battles with the community, in 1985 paid for the creation of an organization called County Citizens for Local Control, a thinly disguised political arm of its own campaign effort to industrialize the area.

Community organizations are not always cynical expressions of outsiders' entrepreneurial interests. In the Chicago South

15. The organization's director was Julian Levi, whose brother Edward then went on to become president of the university and attorney general of the United States. The Southeast Chicago Commission was rival to the Hyde Park-Kenwood Community Conference, a grass-roots community group more representative of the area's embattled middle-class residents.

Shore, the community organization was the stimulus for efforts to build an industrial park that might, it was hoped, lure a higher class of resident to the area. Some entrepreneurs, watching these organizations in action, make grateful financial contributions. In some instances, the community organization becomes a legally constituted Local Development Corporation that acts as a recipient of government development funding, becoming the official agency for packaging new subsidized projects for developers (Katz and Mayer, 1985). The boundaries between community organizations and at least some elements of entrepreneurial growth virtually disappear.

White Integrator

Much of the work of community organizations focuses on the goal of racial integration; many neighborhood associations owe their very existence to this pursuit. Although people can have any of a number of reasons for supporting racial integration, one reason supported in particular by rentier and political elites is that whites are thought to be more effective than blacks in the rent intensification process. Even when not stated explicitly, this belief is part of the background against which media and public discourse proceeds.

There are two ways in which integration enters the agenda of a community organization. First, black migration into a previously white neighborhood raises the prospect of the neighborhood becoming a ghetto. Under these conditions, integration means preserving a substantial white presence. Second, through gentrification or "spot" redevelopment, white migrants move in. Here integration can be a method of bringing the advantages of white presence to a previously "abandoned" area.

Regardless of the context, whites become the prize and thus the group whose needs come first. Similarly, in both contexts, blacks are either displaced (when whites are coming in) or actively discouraged (when whites are moving out). Honor goes to whites; stigma to blacks. In both instances, organizational success effectively decreases the supply of housing available to blacks, thereby increasing the prices they will have to pay in the less desirable neighborhoods, which they must then turn to. The community

organization dynamic, with its pleasant connotations of democratic self-determination, links up with the growth machine's de-
valuation of black residents. The result undermines black people's
use values by weakening their ability either to hold onto old turf
or to claim new ground upon which to build their community.

The Iron Law of Upgrading

The temptation to partake in the social "upgrading" of a
neighborhood is present even in the most progressive organizations; in the context of the tough problems of crime, poverty, and
funding crises, the sincere yearning of the "decent" residents is
seductive; and it is easy to exclude the winos, homeless, and
hoodlums as a constituency. Given a realistic understanding of the
dynamics that created the difficulties of the underclass, the finite
resources of *any* community organization seem useless for helping
such people. The most efficient way to solve neighborhood problems is perhaps through a triage system in which the best-off receive some attention, the poorest are abandoned, and the middle
group receive the most. Raising the neighborhood's social class,
even if only by a little, enables a community organization to show
progress in "cleaning up the neighborhood." Just as even the rich
neighborhoods strive, albeit subtly, to attract even more affluent
residents, every slum needs a better class of slum dweller.[16] And
as the community organization itself builds a stake in local businesses and becomes an accepted voice of the community, its leaders need more local buying power to sustain the investments. They
may also want a stronger and more dignified social base to represent. Once again, the community organization has reasons to support changes in land use and social climate that outside growth
elites desire. Improving the use values of the better-off (at the
expense of the poor) fits well with the rent intensification goals of
outsiders, whose prospective projects need more socially benign

16. Donald Cressey was once asked to suggest the best way to ease the threat
of riots in U.S. penitentiaries. Cressey replied that we needed a better class of
prisoner. His point was this: A system that generates so many hardened criminals
and then locks them up together is going to have to face some very unpleasant
events within the walls. Cressey's remark applies to neighborhoods that perform
an analogous role.

surroundings. Thus there may be a fruitful basis for coalition. From the standpoint of the community organization, and this is indeed another paradox, it becomes necessary to destroy at least part of the neighborhood in order to save it.

The methods and the stakes vary from place to place, but the organizational push of urban life tends to be the same in rich and poor areas: to discourage those who damage identities, who lower rents, who are not appropriate constituents of viable organizations. Although there may be some resistance to these changes, rooted in sentiment, ethnicity, and charity, overall they will be implemented. As Cox (1981:438) succinctly puts it, "The community can only be saved by treating [it] as *commodity*" (our emphasis). That is why we so rarely witness effective community organization (especially with government support) to halt social upgrading, or to actually encourage the filtering down of a neighborhood to the downtrodden social groups that need it most. Instead, the community organization commonplace (as opposed to the celebrated exception) is preserving rich neighborhoods for the affluent, helping young professionals pioneer an inner-city conversion, or ridding a striving ghetto of its worst element. For neighborhoods, in all such cases, there is nowhere worth going but up. And going up means attracting, from a finite supply, the prized land users. This locks communities (even poor ones) into the same zero-sum competition across the cityscape. Neighborhoods thereby become wedded to the general rent intensification dynamic, making at least some of them receptive to the entrepreneurs' occasional offers of "revitalization."

The result is a sort of Burgess-succession process in reverse, in which the system's energy is provided, not by general upward social mobility and outward geographical movement, but by a thrusting away—in all places in which it is feasible—of those most marginal. There is no inevitable march of development from the center to the hinterlands, or in any other direction. It is perhaps a reflection of new modes of economic organization of society (to be outlined in chapter 7) that the relevant land-use problem ceases to be a question of how to deploy vast migrations of success-oriented workers and becomes instead a problem of determining which locations will have to deal with those for whom there is least use.

At stake in the outcome of these and the other struggles we have been describing is the stability of life and its quality within the neighborhoods. Again, the likelihood of transformation and its direction vary by kind of neighborhood as well as type of city, the moment in history, and the presence or absence of urban programs that affect the form and durability of community organization. Also significant are the changing intraelite power configurations that give advantage to one particular structural speculator's development scheme, and not another's. One way or the other, the residents' quality of life results from the way in which their individual and collective standing intersects with the potential use of their turf in the larger process of production and rent generation.

5

How Government Matters

Social forces are always at work structuring markets; and sometimes the means to regulate the use and exchange of a commodity are governmental. The official apparatus for managing land and buildings includes departments of planning, zoning, urban development, and the like. In this chapter, we focus on two ways in which government affects urban fortunes: first, formal and quasi-formal planning at various governmental levels and, second, the home-rule mechanism, which disperses planning authority into thousands of separate jurisdictions, particularly the legally incorporated suburban towns. Government matters; and here we explain how.

U.S. Planning "Exceptionalism"

Compared to most other industrial societies, the United States organizes land use in a unique manner, both in the extent of authority given to private developers and in the extreme independence of local government agencies. Among market societies, Sweden perhaps offers the strongest contrast, with local authority exercised by metropolitan-wide agencies and a great share of property investment (and therefore locational choice) made directly by the State. In the 1960s, a boom decade of housing growth in Stockholm, for example, 65 percent of all housing was publicly built. The metropolitan government owns virtually all undeveloped land in Stockholm as well as extensive tracts beyond the city, where it builds additional housing as the need arises. Two-thirds of the rental housing is out of the market system (Appelbaum, forthcoming). The State supplies 90 percent of all housing loans whether for private or for public construction (Anton, 1975:138).

In Great Britain, governmental control over development decisions is also more pervasive than in the United States (for a review, see Hall, 1973). A large share of new residential housing is provided by public agencies (65 percent in the years 1945–1960, although dropping to 45 percent in later periods). The planning agencies of county and metropolitan governments have had extensive authority over growth proposals, including fine details of design and layout. The national Ministry of Housing and Local Government hears appeals on local land-use matters and can reverse lower-level decisions; this gives the national government a key role in laying down guidelines for local development (Pahl, 1969; Rex and Moore, 1967).

Perhaps more important from our vantage point, the tax system in the post–World War II period has restrained speculative profits in the land market (Drewett, 1973:225). Under the 1947 British Town and County Planning Act, any increase in land values that resulted from the granting of planning permission was subject to a development charge of 100 percent of the gain—even if no sale of the property was involved (this levy was reduced to 80 percent in 1976 and 60 percent in 1979). As a further constraint on speculation, government can purchase property at a market price dictated by its present uses, regardless of its potential use.

There is also a "curious Anglo-American contrast" (Cox, 1978) in the extent of competition among local groups over land development and fiscal resources. In Cox's view, "fiscal mercantilism" (the competition among local governments for growth in the property tax base) is virtually unknown in Britain and neighborhood activism on any kind of issue is not common (see also Agnew, 1978; Burnett, 1983). One reason for this is that local services in Britain are heavily subsidized from national tax resources, decreasing motivation to politicize locational issues. Local service levels do not so directly rise or fall according to the kind of development an area experiences.

None of this makes Britain completely devoid of the land-use politics found in the United States. According to Williams's (1976) intensive study of the real estate market in Islington (London), large real estate firms are actively engaged in structural speculations, acting to depress the inner-city housing market during one period in order to reap the profits from subsequent gentrification. Young and Kramer (1978) cite numerous reports of suburban land-use conflicts based on exclusionary motivations and residents' concerns over preservation of social status and fiscal security. These similarities notwithstanding, there are still strong differences between the two countries in the *degree* that land use is politicized at the local level. A strong land-use authority vested in the national government combined with the central financing of local services and the heavy taxing of speculative transactions undermines some of the energy of a growth machine system. Central government, working closely with elites in the production sphere, has relatively greater direct impact on the distribution of development than is the case in the United States, where parochial rentiers have a more central role.

With its federal system and lack of control over speculation, Germany seems to resemble the United States. But the match is only approximate. Yago (1984) reports that the strong development controls imposed by Frankfurt in the late nineteenth century responded to the interests of a growing corporate sector that sought "economic expansion and rationalized urban development, deemphasizing the profit-making interests of land and transit speculators" (Yago, 1984:86). Such concern for production over rentier interests was to continue as an influence into more modern times. Yet Evers (1976) suggests that modern German localities must tolerate disparities in services and employment opportunities and compete for growth in their tax base, despite the central government's relatively strong authority in planning and financing. Yago argues that after 1960, the Social Democrats in control of local governments promoted economic growth despite increasing neighborhood protests over highway expansion and intensive land development—again in the service of corporate interests. Thus planning was a conscious tool for overcoming local resistance to development. The interventions of the State are mobilized tools in service of "rationalization": to eliminate the smallest governmental units, to orient investments to places with the greatest development potential, and to improve the technical level of planning (Evers, 1976). We would therefore expect to find much active speculation in Germany as well as efforts to manipulate government to gain redistributive rents. In other words, conditions are ripe for many of the same growth machine dynamics that we have observed in the United States, although they would operate in Germany in conjunction with a stronger tradition of government planning and intervention.

Finding parallels to the United States seems to be most difficult in the nonmarket societies, although there may be more resemblances than first appear. In the socialist countries, where government planning authority is complete, place can still be used to better one's standing in the stratification system, although the institutional mechanisms differ from those found in the West. Szelenyi (1983) observes, in his general survey of urban policy in Eastern Europe, that although the market is replaced by administrative allocation, the networks and political skills of residents in affluent neighborhoods nevertheless give them advantages over those in poorer areas in obtaining services. Conflicts at this level yield differences in use values, and those in turn reinforce class stratification.

The more general problem in applying our model to socialist countries is identifying interests that are analogous to the pursuit of exchange values, which are at the heart of the U.S. growth machine. Since "location has no official value" (Szelenyi, 1983: 123), there is no pressure for intensive development of central locations. The questions we must ask are these: What *are* the bases of land-use preference? What land-use purposes are promoted by such diverse officials as factory managers, local party secretaries, and central economic planners? How do the land-use interests of ordinary people intersect with the strategies of such production-oriented actors? The general instabilities and anxieties Americans experience because of the commodity system are replaced, perhaps, by insecurities that come from bureaucratic decision making. Land-use planning, a strong feature of these societies, must somehow take into consideration the interests of bureaucracies managing production, residential groups of varying degrees of influence, and those who institute land-use decisions affecting both. In this sense, then, our basic analytical problem is relevant everywhere, although without more research we cannot specify solutions in such a broad context.

The Thrust of Reform

In contrast to the explicit government intervention that has marked other societies, the United States became an industrial nation with relatively little constraint placed upon the wheeling and dealing that distributed populations and business activities across the land. Of course, the necessity of government participation in the development of the infrastructure (railroads and utilities) and the conniving relations between real estate speculators and officials belie claims that a "free" market was ever at work. But the belief was there and that meant that virtually any proposals for explicit intervention, at least on behalf of use values, were anathema.

Increasingly, however, the maturing of the industrial city, in both physical and social terms, made such doctrines problematic. The sheer increase in size and complexity threatened congestion, confusion, and mayhem. Cities were choking on their own growth, endangering long-term rentier interests as well as residential use values. If for no other reason than to counter the spread of infectious disease, influential people had to alter the situation of the masses. Immigrants also needed to be socialized and controlled, especially since their sheer numbers now threatened to lead to their political dominion over the whole city. Although capital was to eventually work out a satisfactory *modus vivendi* with the ethnic machines (Peterson, 1981; Royko, 1971), the emerging style of urban politics did not augur well for smoothly functioning industrial infrastructures or for urban services in respectable neighborhoods (Weinstein, 1968:95).

From these concerns came the reform spirit of the early twentieth century (Hays, 1964). For land-use issues, reformism drew upon a diverse set of middle-class and upper-class actors (the working class was more active in demands for municipalization of services and other, more radical changes). The "city beautiful movement" wing had a constituency among affluent women and professionals eager to enhance appearances; rentier and local capitalist groups sometimes sensed that handsome public works (such as Chicago's lake-front museums and monuments) would attract outside attention and boost local growth. Other city-planning enthusiasts focused on ambitious waterworks, roadways, and railroad depots, which more directly served growth goals. At the same time, there were reformers anxious to enhance use values for ordinary people. Frederick Olmsted, the designer of New York's Central Park, wanted public parks in order to bring qualities of the countryside into the lives of the poor, and Jane Addams's settlement house movement tried to ease the squalor of slum life (Gans, 1968:231–32). Such reformers looked to regulation as a means of protecting neighborhoods, securing safer buildings, and preserving historic structures (Delafons, 1969; Ervin et al., 1977). In a pattern that was to become a virtual hallmark of the urban reform process (see Edelman, 1977), their diligence, imagination, and altruism became an important political and ideological element in urban coalitions. Their presence also helped obscure the more pecuniary interests that were always at work.

The ideological umbrella for such diverse interests was the call for technocratic meritocracy on all levels of urban government (Fogelson, 1967, chap. 10; Holli, 1969). In the giddy positivism of the day (Rothman, 1971), reformers and growth activists could agree on the need for objective and dispassionately rational solutions to urban ills. Some of the country's wealthiest families (the Rockefellers, Rosenwalds, Harrimans) helped create an "urban policy planning network" (Domhoff, 1978:160) made up of such organizations as the National Municipal League and the International City Managers Association. These organizations encouraged cities to adopt approved administrative standards and procedures (Domhoff, 1978:160–69; Hays, 1964). Thus came civil service to regulate personnel practices, competitive bidding to control procurement, the city manager form of government to systematize decision making, and at-large elections to dilute the voting power of the working classes (Alford and Lee, 1968; Davidson and Korbel, 1981; Fogelson, 1967:218). More directly relevant for our analysis was the advent of systematic land-use controls: zoning, planning, and transportation authorities.

All along the way, however, as reform efforts were reaching their peak, the city itself was leaking beyond its boundaries—first into areas annexed to the existing city, then into regions that were later incorporated as separate suburban towns. At times the thrust of reformers was to block this fragmentation; at others, reform simply took hold—or better hold (Goodall, 1968:60–61)—in at least some of these outlying urban towns where homogenous populations could more easily secure "businesslike," clean government. Regardless of the outcomes of the struggles to reform the city itself, the suburban city could become a haven from the excesses of industrialism and the unwashed immigrants. Whether or not reform worked in the city, it would certainly work in the suburbs, where home rule and enlightened civic virtue would facilitate good planning principles. One way or the other, rational planning "science" would provide order for the urban system. In each sphere, there would plausibly be new instruments to bolster the interests of citizens against the tyranny of both the marketplace and the political machine.

This faith in a technocracy of urban expertise has been widely accepted, with planning and local government efficiency accepted as neutral forces leading to public betterment. But this view omits several considerations. Parallel to the struggle over use and exchange values in other realms, people struggled over planning and the conditions of government autonomy because of the results they might bring. Planning, virtually from its inception in the United States, has primarily been at the service of the growth machine. Similarly, home rule, whether at the city or suburban level, takes its form only through the surrounding growth machine dynamics. In such a context, autonomy becomes a lead weight for the majority of cities, with only the most affluent towns able to create privilege from their formal independence. The political autonomy of places, as well as the planning power this entails, reproduces and exaggerates the inequalities between places rather than leveling them. Local control and the planning apparatus that is part of this becomes a Trojan horse in the American city.

Planning to Grow

Intervention in land use in the United States has never been meant to replace the operation of the property marketplace, only to smooth out its functioning. Even though individual entrepreneurs may balk at specific decisions or even denounce the entire planning process when they lose a particular contest, entrepreneurs throughout the twentieth century have come to appreciate that selective intervention can yield, in the end, benefits for the growth process (Schultze, 1977; Shonfield, 1965; Wilson, 1980). In this sense, the necessity for the "relative autonomy of the State" percolates down to the local level: In order to keep the property market rising, government must act on behalf of the market.

Given the controversy inherent in the interventions that must take place, advocates of planning have surrounded the planning apparatus with "strategic rituals" (Tuchman, 1972) that connote expertise and efficiency. There is a great deal of jargon, use of quantitative data, and a fetish for map displays and other visual presentations. But the planning process is, of course, inherently political; any land-use designation distributes use and exchange values. Whether building a public amenity or allowing a high-rise office tower, officials making decisions on location, parking, security, and access to transportation will affect the balance between public and private gains. A city park sandwiched between two convention hotels, for example, will do less for local citizens (but more for rentiers) than one built in a dense residential area. Similarly, increasing the allowable density at one site absorbs investment demand that might bid up prices at other locations; our public park may increase the value of the convention hotels, but decrease the likelihood of similar price inflation at other commercial sites. In the earthy formulation of a sunbelt journalist, "The route of a sewer line is a trail of power."[1]

In making decisions, government officials operate with both sticks (regulations) and carrots (incentives) to structure local markets. The sticks are regulations and punishments, albeit mild, that fall upon developers who break the existing rules; the carrots take the form of financial rewards for those whose activities serve a putative public purpose.

Regulatory Programs

Zoning. Regulatory programs, such as zoning, growth control, and environmental report requirements, serve to distrib-

---

1. Personal letter from Joe Goodman to G. William Domhoff, December 4, 1985.

ute use and exchange values throughout the urban system. They are the mild sticks of government.

Although much of the rationale for modern zoning has been couched in use value language—for example, zoning is the defense of "collective rights"—from its inception in the United States, zoning has served as a tool for safeguarding and increasing rents. The precursors to modern zoning were "nuisance laws," regulations that protected individual property owners from proximate dangers to the use of their land. Thus, a slaughterhouse could not operate without regard to its impact on the property rights of an adjacent owner. In the Supreme Court decision that sustained a city's right to impose zoning (*Euclid v. Ambler Realty Co.*, 1926), there was similar concern for property rights, although much of the language of the decision also stressed use value goals, such as "safety and security of home life" and "a more favorable environment to raise children."

In his detailed analysis of the reformers' enactment of the country's first comprehensive zoning ordinance—by New York City in 1916[2]—Makielski (1966) concludes that the law was developed to guard the exclusive Fifth Avenue shopping district from the invasion of harmful land uses like garment manufacture. Another key motivation was to sustain Midtown Manhattan's role as the dominant commercial and corporate center of the city. More comprehensively, the "general business groups," to whom zoning reformers had to

> continuously make concessions, approached zoning from an economic viewpoint. . . . Their economic interest in the city gave them a stake in a "healthy, growing community" where tax rates were not prohibitive, where city government was "efficient," and where some of the problems of the urban environment—a constricting labor force, congestion, and lack of space—were being attacked. When a new zoning proposal was offered, these groups were inclined to test it against these criteria. [Makielski, 1966:141.]

In Makielski's view, these findings are evidence of pluralistic governance in New York because there was much bargaining among

---

2. Although New York was the first city to have a *comprehensive* zoning law, Los Angeles was the first to implement some form of zoning. This was "district zoning," which placed only broad land-use designations on large city areas.

competing land entrepreneurs, and because "no single actor or set of actors was able to totally dominate zoning policy making" (Makielski, 1966:185). For us, the important clue to what was really going on is contained in the goal of a "healthy, growing community" to which the reformers also subscribed. Health and growth were closely equated and the growth of the dominant area was to be the centerpiece of growth overall. Indeed, the actual outcome of the process, the successful defense of Fifth Avenue and Manhattan's hegemony, indicates that the most powerful business groups succeeded in using the planning apparatus to achieve their goals.

After investigating the history of zoning in Los Angeles, another of the country's first cities to enact land-use control, Fogelson (1967:257) concludes:

> Originally conceived as a means of sound and strong land-use regulation, it was compromised in its formulation and emasculated in its implementation . . . it was changed into a method of promoting property interests through political influence. . . . Far from guiding the expansion of the metropolis, [zoning] merely sanctioned the preferences of private enterprise.

This use of planning to support the interests of dominant actors has not changed appreciably in the intervening years. The purpose of zoning is primarily to *distribute* growth and rents within a metropolitan area, ideally in such a way that the sustainable totals will be increased (Babcock, 1969). But since the techniques for doing this are not derived from any real scientific principles, the way is open for property entrepreneurs to influence the zoning decisions. Shifts in power among the entrepreneurs as well as shifts in the rent opportunities that arise result in changes in zoning and land-use plans. "Highest and best use" is the conveniently vague phrase so often invoked by planning professionals as a rationale for their recommendations. Because "highest and best use" means whatever the market circumstance dictates—if it means anything at all—the phrase serves to align the work of planning officials with the needs of local growth machines. As the planning professionals like to say, their demarcations are not "set in concrete" and are "living" documents that must, necessarily, be altered as unforeseen opportunities present themselves. The result has been that "if zoning restricts development much below market price, ordinances have been quickly changed and/or variances given" (Sabatier and Mazmanian, 1983; see also Babcock, 1969; Mandelker, 1971). Amendments to general plans, changes in zoning ordinances, or special exceptions are provided as new entrepreneurial needs are anticipated. That is why virtually all significant urban areas in the United States are zoned for population and industrial increases double or triple their current levels and why, if history is any guide, those levels will in turn be raised if growth approaches those ceilings.

Zoning restrictions provide for "symbolic rituals" (Perin, 1977:183) in a "zoning game" (Babcock, 1969) that inconveniences, but typically does not thwart, the entrepreneurs willing to invest time and money in the local political process (see Gottdiener, 1977). The practice of zoning inserts planning professionals, politicians, and a cumbersome bureaucracy into the rent generation process. This forces rentiers into the role of structural speculators who must influence government decisions if they are to maximize returns from their holdings. They must also make campaign contributions (or bribes) to public officials; the result can be the corruption of the entire political system (Balk, 1966; Delafons, 1962).[3]

Houston, Texas, is the only major American city with no zoning. Although its indifference to planning may be bringing it more than the usual degree of infrastructural chaos (Feagin, 1983b), certain aspects of Houston's overall land-use patterns are not very different from those of other cities (Babcock, 1982:23; Willhelm, 1962). It has homogenous deluxe neighborhoods, working-class areas with jumbles of mixed land uses, and a booming downtown with spectacular skyscrapers. Houston's overall similarity to other cities is sometimes interpreted to mean that market mechanisms *on their own* result in rationally organized cities, making governmental regulation an unnecessary burden to developers and citizens alike.

3. Although we shall never have "good data" on the number of bribes and illicit contributions to politicians, officeholders often seem to face criminal indictment on the basis of conduct tied to land use. In perhaps the most important case, criminal charges based on land-use corruption led to the resignation of Vice-President Spiro Agnew. Such incidents of corruption, it is often said, are like cockroaches: For each one you see, there are a thousand more in the woodwork.

A more accurate alternative conclusion is that Houston differs in its land-use regulation from other cities much less than appears. First, as we have already pointed out, zoning in other cities is often without integrity, responding primarily to entrepreneurial pressures. Second, in Houston there are over ten thousand deed restrictions that cover two-thirds of the city, mostly devoted to ensuring neighborhood homogeneity. The "zoning" is built into the deeds. If these restrictions were fully enforced, Houston would be the most regulated big city in the United States. But citizens must go to court to stop owners from ignoring deed restrictions. The pattern of enforcement is thus uneven; residents of the rich neighborhoods file lawsuits to block attempts to sully their areas, whereas the poor, who can't pay for lawyers, must put up with whatever comes their way. A telling instance is the oil company that planned to build a gas station on a lot in an upper-class neighborhood that happened not to be protected by a deed covenant. A neighborhood protest forced the gasoline company to abandon its plans (Babcock, 1982:22). Going beyond deed restrictions, the city also formed a "neighborhood analysis committee" to ensure that government-subsidized housing was built in appropriate areas—with the result that "Houston managed to practice exclusionary zoning even without a zoning ordinance" (Babcock, 1982:23). The various social classes, with zoning laws or without them, with deed restrictions or without them, are unequally able to protect their environmental interests. This inequality is the force that, present everywhere, gives cities so much of their similarity.

Zoning as a technical tool *for* development can encourage certain projects in one place and not in another. Shlay and Rossi (1981) have reported that the zoning designations of census tracts in the Chicago area were somewhat useful in predicting actual patterns of development over the 1960–1970 decade, although the authors don't indicate if developers followed the zoning or the zoning designations were themselves anticipations of entrepreneurs' intentions.

Zoning also seems to function as an effective tool for manipulating social deviance. Boston has used zoning to restrict much of its pornography and prostitution to a single area, the "combat zone"; Los Angeles is using zoning to keep bondage sex clubs out of specific neighborhoods (Braun, 1984). Zoning does sometimes help head off certain gross land-use blunders (see Popper, 1981), such as mindlessly destroying precious historic districts, building housing in a flood plain, or putting a school playground on top of a leaking toxic dump, which was done at Love Canal, New York (see Levine, 1982). Because it is possible to channel growth without detracting from the overall level of growth, governments in some areas have taken the broader view, sometimes producing use value gains in the process. Nevertheless, the efficacy and integrity of zoning have been greatly exaggerated by both supporters and critics, with exchange value purposes of zoning consistently understated.

Growth Control.   A more direct threat than zoning to the growth process is controls that put overall limits on development. Densities of all projects may be effectively reduced through planning techniques such as open space requirements or utility access restrictions; bolder controls are massive downzoning or placing annual caps on the amount of new construction.[4] By 1975, growth control of various sorts was in effect in over three hundred jurisdictions (Cohn, 1979:18). Critics have claimed that these development limits have inhibited the growth of entire metropolitan areas, so distorting the property market that the cost of doing business or establishing a residence has substantially risen (Case and Gale, 1981; Dowall, 1984; Frieden, 1979a; Priest, 1980). Tight controls force home buyers to compete for a fixed supply, thus raising prices; and discouraged investors take their factories elsewhere, thereby destroying local economies.

It is important at this point not to overgeneralize these cases to the whole country, to exaggerate the degree of control, or to misinterpret the *kind* of control that exists even in areas where growth regulation seems to prevail most completely. So far, the evidence on growth control communities suggests that rapidly growing areas impose regulation policies after the fact. These areas do not

---

4. Frieden (1979b) usefully catalogs a large number of techniques with potential for discouraging growth, particularly in housing.

impose regulations at a time when they could limit future growth. That is the conclusion drawn from a survey of growth control areas by Baldasarre and Protash (1982).

Let us consider as an example the notorious program of suburban Petaluma (north of San Francisco), termed "world famous" as a "symbol of hostility to growth" (Frieden, 1979a:32). Despite the rhetoric, the Petaluma program has had little overall effect on regional development. The residential building quotas established under the Petaluma plan have never been "built out" in any year of the program's existence (Freitas, 1980). Although new housing units built in Petaluma have become larger and more "deluxe" since the growth control system was imposed, even this change should probably be attributed to the general upgrading of the overall suburban region in past years rather than to the quota system. Neighboring Rohnert Park, for example, has no growth controls, but has experienced as much price inflation over the same period (Schwartz et al., 1979; Wolf, 1981).

Even growth controls affecting large parts of a metropolis may have little impact on overall development. The Santa Barbara area of California is blanketed with environmental and growth control schemes said to be among the strongest and most comprehensive in the country (Appelbaum, 1985; Editors, 1975; Frieden, 1979a; Hill, 1978). But there is little evidence that overall development (industrial or residential) has been significantly affected. After carefully examining the local housing market, taking into account such factors as changes in consumer demand, interest rates, and other trends, Appelbaum (1985) concluded that although growth controls apparently had slightly discouraged overall housing construction rates, area sales prices and rents were unaffected (see also Molotch and Kasof, 1981).[5] In the main, regulation probably diverts different kinds of growth from one location to another within the region, "market reorientation" and "spillover" in Do-

5. Mercer and Morgan (1982) found a significant "shortfall" in Santa Barbara area housing and they attribute it to growth controls. But the Mercer and Morgan study failed to examine secular development trends in the Southern California region coinciding with their study period; they thus attribute the general collapse of the U.S. housing industry to Santa Barbara regulation. See additional discussion in chapter 7, particularly note 11, for review of other studies.

wall's (1984) terms, but does not alter the overall market structure.

Once again, growth regulation has a limited impact in part because the housing market consists primarily of existing structures; ordinarily the number of new products on the market is too small a proportion of the total to have much consequence (Markusen, 1979). Further, growth regulation fails to limit development in part because adjacent unregulated areas take care of the demand and because there are many "loopholes" even within the controlled jurisdictions. Water hookup moratoria are bypassed by converting agricultural water meters to urban uses. Private water wells are drilled to avoid dealing with local water board restrictions. Claims of "special hardships" are presented in order to gain density variances; allowable densities are increased because a developer sets aside a number of units as "affordable housing." Sometimes, density restrictions are waived if the developer provides special amenities, such as restoration of natural stream beds.

Houston, Texas, offers several examples of how particular growth restrictions can be avoided by creative rentiers. Although notorious for nonplanning, Houston has since 1974 formally restricted the issuance of sewer permits. In large parts of the city, sewer capacity has been exhausted, and no new permits are being issued. Unused sewer rights, on the other hand, can be freely bought and sold, giving rise to Houston's "Great Sewer Swap" (King, 1983). Even the owners of cemeteries, it turns out, may have unused permits based on building lots recorded on old subdivision maps. "Every realtor in town has a briefcase full of sewer letters," says a local developer. "Guys are running around with all this sewer capacity in their briefcases" (quoted in King, 1983:18), with a 1984 price of $3,000 to $5,000 per sewer hookup. The sewer limitation has meant, in effect, that properties without immediate development potential are still worth something because of their sewer rights; government restriction cuts their owners in on a piece of the development action they would otherwise lack. It is a subtle case of redistributional rent.

In still other instances of development controls, the loopholes are more openly written into the controlling legislation. State development restrictions sometimes exclude entire industries in this way. Florida exempts its hotel industry from key restrictions, even though the encroachment of hotels on fragile environments was one of the main reasons environmentalists pressed for reform. Vermont excludes farming (its largest industry) as well as utilities, probably the state's biggest environmental offender (Popper, 1981:102).

Perhaps the most crucial fact about growth control is that it tends to target residential construction rather than industrial expansion. Increase in basic economic functions, the growth most critical for regional elite's goals, is not altered. Beyond fostering loud but largely symbolic debates, growth control programs have had little effect; at most they have influenced the distribution of some residential development, with regulation deflecting the affluent toward places improved through the restrictions. None of this means that *eventually* the seesawing between developers and growth controllers won't be more definitely resolved, and with important use and exchange value consequences (this possibility is discussed in chapters 6 and 7). For now, the ingenuity of both sides has led to a standoff in certain areas, with some entrepreneurs inconvenienced here and there and the affluent, as always, making some gains.

Environmental Impact Reports.   Among recent environmental regulations is the requirement that, at least in the case of a large or "controversial" development, an environmental impact report (EIR) must be prepared. First enacted in 1969 by the federal government for projects of the national government, the requirements of the National Environmental Policy Act have since been adopted by the states for a much wider range of private and public developments. Reports required by this act are supposed to specify all relevant benefits and costs of a given project. Local government is typically mandated to reject projects with severe disadvantages. But like zoning and growth controls, the EIR requirement has not had the dramatic consequences attributed to it by either advocates or critics. In the end, the EIR affords the public certain *procedural* rights, but once an agency or court rules that the procedures have been followed, almost anything can be approved—no matter what an EIR contains (Benveniste, 1981).

EIRs are usually provided by private consulting firms, often chosen by, or in consultation with, the entrepreneur who pays the fees. Perhaps because of this administrative arrangement, EIRs have several features that tend to encourage development. First is the narrow scope of the typical analysis. The emphasis is placed on fiscal losses or benefits to local (only local) government; if the cost for a needed public infrastructure can be paid by state or federal sources, EIRs usually treat the project as fiscally sound. Second, costs and benefits are calculated on the project at hand, rather than on the cumulative effects of all related development. In many instances, for example, a proposed industrial plant will attract new workers, who will have to be housed. By examining the industrial project in isolation from the housing, however, the plant appears to be fiscally sound. Factories require fewer social services than do people, and are therefore evaluated more favorably. When the housing is later evaluated, also separately, it appears to be costly because the tax-generating employment is absent from the analysis. The logical result is that each locality seeks employment-generating uses within its own borders but tries to force workers' residences into other areas. When this cannot be done, as in large cities, officials accept industrial projects on misleading fiscal grounds. The system favors projects that build the basic economy, trapping certain localities into paying for development patterns in which the elements do not balance.

EIRs also go astray in the *kinds* of costs and benefits they record. Most of the putative benefits of projects can be easily expressed in "hard" terms (for example, dollar additions to the tax base, or number of new jobs), but liabilities are not as easy to quantify. Extra service costs like police, fire protection, and road repair are difficult to estimate. Still more problematic are aesthetic losses and the effects of congestion, which often can only be "discussed" as "other factors." Even some costs that can be quantified (such as increased health and maintenance expenses caused by pollution) are not usually specified, given the complexity of dealing with such indirect effects among many individual victims. Some risks cannot be meaningfully evaluated at all, like those of nuclear power plants, which, based on past experience, appear to pose little threat. The difficulty, of course, is the unprecedented nature of the catastrophe that could occur in any given plant, and in the growing probability of disaster that comes with additional plant approvals. Manageability of the risk assessment task requires the analyst to project on the basis of a past record rather than speculate on a plausible future (see Perrow, 1984). Lack of a past catastrophe makes it difficult to discuss a prospective one.

EIRs do sometimes result in negative findings, which by law either must be mitigated or must result in denial of the project. The resulting mitigations can bring use value gains for large numbers. Governments may require developers to provide "in lieu" funding for open space they eliminate or for low-income housing they remove from the market (Popper, 1981). But other efforts to mitigate may be less benign. Even a decision so common and uncontroversial as creating one-way streets to relieve congestion has environmental effects that are seldom noticed in the EIR process. If a two-way street in a residential area is changed to a one-way street, it may become a thoroughfare for people passing through. Problems of noise, danger, and tension are the cost of increasing the rate of flow of vehicles. The costs that would have been paid by "outsiders" in extra travel time are instead shifted to residents in the form of environmental decline. The decisions behind these transfers of costs are not socially neutral: low-income people are more likely to live adjacent to intensified uses and are therefore the ones who more often pay the costs. Mitigation, in effect, can redistribute penalties geographically and socially, but cannot eliminate them. The process of mitigating the effects of development does not necessarily minimize total public costs; instead it may shift the burden of development from a visible to a less visible form or from social groups capable of combating the costs to groups with less political clout. Public hearings grind on until the professionals and politicians find the right social fix.

When an EIR concludes that a development has impacts so severe that there can be no possible mitigation, government approval can still be given if there is a finding of "overriding considerations"—that is, the total benefits of the project outweigh its costs.[6] There are several kinds of overriding considerations in the repertoire of growth-oriented city councils and planning commissions, and they are cited so often that they have become a litany

6. Much of our analysis rests on California law, specifically, the California Environmental Quality Act; comparable federal and state legislation, we believe, makes our observations generally relevant.

of local decision making. Decision makers can claim that any industrial or commercial project "brings jobs"; however misleading, this view will be widely accepted by the media and much of the public. They can also override with the pronouncement that a project will "increase the tax base," another claim that will ordinarily be uncritically received. Finally, any project that involves the construction of housing can be welcomed for the relief it will bring to the "housing crisis." To bring up one extreme case, environmentally damaging projects have been approved in Santa Barbara partly on the grounds that the housing (at over $300,000 per unit) will help lower housing costs. Given the pervasiveness of a marketplace ideology that says housing prices will inevitably decline with increases in supply, local officials easily cite the "housing crisis" as an overriding consideration. With jobs, housing, and taxes perennial problems on the local agendas, any project has its "overriding consideration" waiting in the wings.

Sometimes, EIRs fall victim to growth machine pressures between drafts when the findings of the professional staff are subject to outside scrutiny. The Westway superhighway project proposed for Manhattan's West Side floundered in 1984 when the draft environmental review reported that the associated landfilling would endanger striped bass in the Hudson River. Under law, this finding would have required a road design without the landfill—and without the projected 169 acres of high-density development that was also scheduled for that new land. The final environmental report, therefore, redefined the Westway scheme as an economic redevelopment project, for which alternative highway designs had no bearing. Initial court judgments rejected this redefinition (*Schenectady Gazette,* August 8, 1985), and the project appears at this writing to be dead. Nevertheless, the case stands as an example of the outrageous tinkering with documentation that growth activists will engage in.

The main virtue of the EIR for those trying to preserve use values is perhaps its capacity to *delay* projects, helping to buy time, to discourage investors, to mount political opposition. It is not unusual for the preparation of such reports to take many months, and lengthy public hearings can be necessary before the EIR is certified as complete. Even after that, the claim can be made in court (by opponents as well as proponents) that the EIR omitted information required by the law, an easy claim to make, since it is impossible for any document to fully respond to the vague and comprehensive demands contained in the legal requirements. If project opponents have the time, money, and skill to read through the lengthy materials, just the *fact* of the EIR requirement for a project can be put to significant use. Indeed, linked with other environmentalist strategies (outlined in chapter 6), the EIR seems to have helped eliminate certain major projects, such as the construction in the United States of supersonic airplanes, the Clinch River Breeder Reactor (at Oak Ridge, Tenn.), the California Peripheral Canal and—it seems—Westway.

Federal Incentives

In contrast to regulations traditionally imposed by cities and counties, many of the federal government's land-use programs are based on positive incentives. Given the U.S. tradition of home rule on land-use issues, the national government is inhibited from issuing restrictions. Instead, it subsidizes entrepreneurs or local governments to pursue a given development pattern. Although politicians and planners almost always justify this use of federal funds in the name of use values, once again exchange goals are much in evidence. When use values are a part of a program's founding formulation, they tend to be displaced over time either through amending legislation or in the administrative process. On occasions when programs are later reformed to favor use value outcomes, the programs themselves seem then to be phased out, rendering the progressive changes moot.

In recent years, the rhetoric of federal policy has stressed the need for urban programs, if they are to exist at all, to come "closer to the people," which means that even if the federal government supplies the money, it should exert no control over how state and local governments spend it. By implication, just moving the *level* of decision making into the hands of cities, counties, or the states will enhance people's use values. There is thus no need to make sure that social goals are being reached; this can be assumed. We question this assumption as well as other premises of federal policies' use value benefits by examining how various federal programs have, over time, aided local growth elites at the expense of urban residents—particularly those residents whose interests the programs were originally supposed to serve.

Public Housing and Urban Renewal.   The major break-through in generating explicit federal commitment to planning for urban use values was the National Housing Act of 1949. The act was passed in a postwar enthusiasm to reward returning veterans with adequate housing, with lobbying from a building and banking industry eager to construct and finance the authorized projects. The wording in the legislation called for "the realization as soon as feasible of the goal of a decent home and a suitable living environment for every American" (United States President's Committee on Urban Housing, 1969:1). Companion legislation authorized construction of 135,000 units of public housing annually (Douglas, 1968:110, as cited in Friedland, 1982:80), and there were great hopes of using good housing to bring hope and accomplishment into the lives of the urban poor. Only about 200,000 units were, in fact, built over the six-year life of the legislation, but the program did deliver gains to at least some of those in need. Distressed cities received the largest share (Cho and Puryear, 1980:201–202). Although the long waiting lists for the units perhaps attest to their superiority over the slum alternatives, the "projects" were stigmatized with mean-spirited architectural designs and authoritarian administrations. Despite some planners' energetic efforts to have the projects built outside existing slum areas as a way to increase class and racial integration, the political realities meant that the projects would be constructed outside the good neighborhoods and away from zones slated for higher-rent developments. Neither the quantitative nor qualitative goals of the public-housing agenda were closely approximated (Meyerson and Banfield, 1955; Rainwater, 1970).

Ironically, the real impact of the Housing Act (and successive modifications) was its potential for raising exchange values through the vehicle of urban renewal. Over time, an increasing percentage of a city's federal aid for slum clearance could be used for projects other than housing. To gain urban renewal money, a locality had to put up one-third of the funding required for a project, but there was an increasing liberalization of what localities could use to make up the one-third. After the 1954 legislative amendments, private expenditures, like those made by hospitals and universities on their own facilities, could be considered part of the city share. Wed to purposes like expanding inner-city institutions and enhancing the prosperity of downtown areas, the urban renewal program became a device for protecting central city business and property investments (a massive rent redistribution) and the careers of white politicians (Mollenkopf, 1983).

The first example of the forces involved in urban renewal was a group organized by the Mellon banking family in Pittsburgh, who brought together downtown elites as the Allegheny Conference; this led to similar organizations in other major cities, and these groups pledged themselves to the common fight against "urban blight" and to the need to "save the city" (Keith, 1973). Domhoff (1978, 1983) has traced how the elites of New Haven, Connecticut (including officials and trustees of Yale University), sponsored the vast New Haven program (Dahl [1961] portrays them as passive). These downtown-oriented actors then worked with (or created) sympathetic politicians and public planning officials to transform the central core in ways that would intensify land use and increase rents. In his description of the urban renewal process in Atlanta, Georgia, Stone (1976) reports that even when neighborhood activists came up with alternative renewal proposals, they seldom could reach official agendas even for discussion. Business groups, on the other hand, had a direct line to policy makers in pursuing their growth strategy (see also Phelan and Pozen [1973] on renewal in Wilmington, Del.). The same picture of dominance by business elites emerges from Mollenkopf's general urban renewal history (1983:118)—even as he argues, incorrectly we think, that it was "political entrepreneurs" who were (as Dahl had proposed) the real movers and shakers.

There seems to be little disagreement about the devastating effects of urban renewal on the poor and minorities (Gans, 1962; Rossi and Dentler, 1961). Although improving the housing of the poor was ostensibly the program's key goal, less than 20 percent of all urban renewal land went for housing; over 80 percent went for developing commercial, industrial, and public infrastructures (Friedland, 1982:81). In reality, urban renewal destroyed more housing (especially poor people's housing) than it created (Fried, 1971:88–89; Greer, 1965). As Friedland (1982:85) calculated,

"90 per cent of the low income housing destroyed by urban renewal was not replaced." It now also appears that even the alleged fiscal benefits, never based on any real evidence, were an illusion. At least that is what is suggested by the results of Friedland's (1982:195) survey of 130 central cities; net of other effects, higher levels of participation in urban renewal were followed by increased city tax burdens in later periods. Even with the great bulk of the bill paid by the federal government, urban renewal was most likely a fiscal loser.

After the urban disorders of the 1960s, the urban renewal program underwent reform. Beginning with the 1965 Housing and Urban Development Act and more dramatically continued in 1968 legislation, subsidies for low-income housing were greatly expanded, and increased restrictions were placed on displacing people. Rentiers and other elites remained key beneficiaries of urban renewal, but the poor were affected less than in the past (Keith, 1973; Mollenkopf, 1983). But soon after the reforms took hold, and coincident with the election of Richard Nixon, the reforms were undermined by piecemeal cutbacks and the elimination of urban renewal and related programs. "Just as neighborhoods had won some influence . . . the Nixon administration began its onslaught against them" (Mollenkopf, 1983:209).

The most recent federal initiative in housing is the Reagan-backed housing voucher, which would subsidize individual tenants, but leave them to find housing on the unchanged private market. In the guiding economistic theory, the resulting increased demand for housing would stimulate new construction (and lower rents), with a relatively small immediate direct outlay of federal funds. In fact, after experimenting with voucher programs, the Department of Housing and Urban Development (HUD) concluded that rent subsidies had negligible impact on private construction, much less on market prices (U.S. Dept. of HUD, 1978). As with longstanding federal programs that pay landlords directly to house the poor in existing structures, government does not compete with the private sector. The government does not build low-cost housing that could potentially lower overall rent structures; indeed by putting more money into the private market through current programs, the government could conceivably inflate total rent collections. The broader implications are also clear:

use value goals like racial integration, energy conservation, or environmental amenity cannot be shaped by a national housing policy in which government passively writes checks to be spent in the marketplace.

Urban Development Action Grants.   On the heels of the demise of urban renewal came new federal initiatives oriented toward serving local growth goals, but at lower costs. Under the Carter administration, the government introduced urban development action grants (UDAGs) to "revitalize" U.S. cities. The strategy was to use federal money to leverage still greater investments from the private sector. By subsidizing a hotel "anchor" here, a trendy shopping promenade there, the federal grant would stimulate entrepreneurs to invest in projects they would otherwise avoid. Still other entrepreneurs would make additional investments nearby to benefit from the positive neighborhood effects of the subsidized project, and a cycle of revitalization would be in motion. The use value benefits would be indirect as new growth brought jobs and a higher tax base.

These grants were plagued by their own special problems. The most glaring difficulty was that "success" could most easily be demonstrated if grants were made for the most advantageously situated projects, which meant avoiding areas where they might have had the most benign effects. Distressed neighborhoods in declining cities are most likely to benefit from federally subsidized growth, but such places had the least to offer either bureaucrats or entrepreneurs involved with the program. Thus the grants, essentially blind to need and social consequences, could subsidize factories and company offices moving from central cities to the suburbs, or help firms build modern, capital-intensive facilities that, in effect, replaced jobs with government-financed robots. On some occasions, grants were given for projects that would have been built anyway; sometimes the grant even *followed* a developer's announcement of the intention to build (Gist, 1980:243), turning the subsidies into simple "taxpayer's gifts" (Tabb, 1984b:259).

In the end, it is doubtful that many of the projects did much for use values. Only 15 percent of UDAG money was spent under the classification "neighborhood facilities," and even this was accomplished only after officials began to place projects like shopping malls in the "neighborhood" rather than "commercial" category (Gist, 1980:245). Even with adjustments in the categories, the majority of the funding went to commercial developments, especially to downtown hotel and hotel-related projects (Gist, 1980; Tabb, 1984b). One of the few victories of big city mayors under Reagan's first term was winning presidential support for UDAG funds (Herbers, 1982), on the grounds that severe cutbacks in such programs would endanger the vitality of urban downtowns.

Some states have had their own urban development grant programs. The biggest was the New York State Urban Development Corporation (UDC), established in 1968 "as a tool for creating housing and jobs for minority group members and the poor" (Gottlieb, 1983). The agency was given the power to build housing and economic development projects and, briefly but quite remarkably, to bypass local zoning and building codes as it deemed appropriate. Once again there is the familiar pattern of idealistic intention with eventual adjustment to practical constraints. In its early history, the UDC made efforts to construct low and moderate income housing at dispersed sites in New York City and its suburbs—efforts for the most part blocked by well-organized local opposition. After this initial "do-good" period, the agency, hampered by charges of mismanagement and corruption, was saved from bankruptcy in 1975 only through private bank loans. Perhaps as a result of the new creditors' demands, the focus of the corporation changed, and investments in the next period shifted toward growth projects. In the 1978–1983 period, the $4 billion invested in "jobs" provided $3.6 billion for the New York City Convention Center and the high-rise office buildings of the controversial Times Square Renewal Project (Gottlieb, 1983). Both of these projects, which will displace thousands of residents and businesses, are high on the agendas of the local growth machine.

Block Grants and Revenue Sharing.   The federal block grant and revenue sharing programs, developed in 1972 and 1974, respectively, were alike in their embrace of the "new federalism" sponsored by the Nixon administration. According to Gerald Ford, who signed the Community Development Block Grant program into law in 1974, the goal was to move "power from the banks of the Potomac to the people in their own communities" (Rosenfeld, 1980:213). In effect, these programs merged numerous grants with specific targets into a very few "pots"; each state and locality received a predetermined share, which each then allocated on its own. Many of the canceled programs dated from the 1960s and the War on Poverty, and included grants for Head Start, job training, and model cities. Although some of these programs had been oriented toward growth infrastructure (like urban renewal), most—especially after they were reformed—were direct efforts at improving the life chances of the poor and working class (Rosenfeld, 1980:212).

By statute, the new programs also contained language that stressed use value goals; block grants were explicitly aimed at "providing decent housing [and] expanding economic opportunities principally for persons of low and moderate income" (U.S. Congress, 1974:Sec. 101c). But the discretion given to localities provided opportunity for growth machine governments to deflect the grants to other purposes. Thus, for example, although cities were at times required to invest the bulk of their block grant money in low or moderate income neighborhoods, there was no requirement that low or moderate income *people* benefit from the expenditures. Indeed, the largest percentage of money spent in poor neighborhoods went for clearance projects and renewal of infrastructure (like highways that passed through them); other sizable expenditures for "housing rehabilitation" primarily served to improve life for new, higher-class residents (Rosenfeld, 1980:230). Over time, even controls on *where* the money was spent were weakened and grant money was spent on everything from landscaping marinas to building tennis courts in affluent suburbs.

The revenue sharing legislation contained priorities for how the money should be spent—public safety, environmental protection, transportation, and any capital construction whatever—and forbade expenditures on aid to education or welfare of any sort. Although there was a definite tilt against use values, especially those of the poor, the program was not supposed to replace federal programs that were directly aimed at the distressed (Nathan et al., 1975:19). But once revenue sharing was adopted, deep cuts in welfare spending were increasingly justified by pointing to the new programs (Terrell, 1976:6).

Based on interviews with over two thousand state and local officials throughout the country, as well as direct analysis of a subset of local budgets, Juster and his colleagues (1977) concluded that revenue sharing grants tended to be used for capital expenditures (primarily roads and sewers), as well as police and fire protection services; these services were especially favored in cities most pressed for operating funds.[7] Although Juster considers the distributive effects of these expenditures difficult to trace because they "affect the well-being of rich and poor alike" (1977:11), the expenditures were clearly less oriented to the use values of the poor than were the programs they replaced. Juster thus concludes (surely in understatement) that "perhaps the principal message that comes from the study is that a program [such as revenue sharing] is simply not a good vehicle for focusing on disadvantaged population segments" (1977:11).

Because the block grant and revenue sharing dispersal formulas allowed a much larger number of cities to qualify for aid, the poorer places (as well as poorer individuals) began to lose the relative advantage they had enjoyed under the more closely targeted War on Poverty programs. By 1977, with Carter in the White House, urban aid benefits were now directed toward the suburbs and growing sunbelt cities; Dallas's receipts alone had grown tenfold in four years (Mollenkopf, 1983:135; Nathan et al., 1975). This finally led to court action, which resulted in reforms requiring suburbs to construct low-income housing as a condition of revenue sharing support.[8] After fighting such restrictions con-

7. In reviewing the "actual use reports" filed by jurisdictions on how they spent their money, Nathan et al. (1975:232) came up with a similar portrayal, but with a stronger tendency for localities to have folded their grant aid into existing budgets to stave off tax increases.

8. In 1975 Hartford, Connecticut, attempted to block seven of its surrounding suburbs from receiving grant money that would not conceivably be used to benefit the poor. In response, the U.S. district court enjoined HUD from disbursing $4.5 million in community development funds until the Hartford suburbs developed plans for low-income housing within their boundaries (New York Times, January 29, 1976, p. 1). On appeal, a higher court ruled against Hartford but HUD began pressuring specific suburbs to build low-income housing as a condition for receiving funds (New York Times, August 16, 1977, p. 36).

tinuously, the Reagan administration finally ended the program completely in 1985.

Tax Increment Redevelopment.   A more enduring way to promote urban intervention is the tax increment redevelopment (TIR) program, which, unlike its predecessors, requires no direct federal subsidy. The "theory" behind TIR is that since renewal ends up paying for itself in higher property tax revenues, cities should be able to use part of this anticipated tax "increment" to fund renewal in advance. Cities can do this by following a simple plan. First, officials declare part of the city a blighted redevelopment area. Next, all gains in property taxes that this area produces after the date of official designation are earmarked for spending by the city's redevelopment agency (including even increments from general inflation on preexisting structures). The city then acquires land, clears buildings as it chooses, and subsidizes development, with costs paid either by current incremental tax revenues or, more commonly, by bonds floated for the purpose. If bonds are used, they are retired with future tax increment revenues. The premise is that the whole process will be so lucrative that there will be money left over to build low-income housing or "do something about poverty" in some other way (Weickert, as cited in Wolinsky, 1984:30). Despite the rhetoric of local self-sufficiency, the bonds that finance much of the redevelopment are tax exempt, making the federal government again a source of subsidy.

Cities in California have made the most extensive use of the TIR mechanism; in 1985, over 250 municipalities spent $1 billion on redevelopment, in part to pay off $2.6 billion in bond debts. Although disadvantaged communities might have most need for the program's putative benefits, these places have been least able to offer subsidies, to attract investors even with subsidies, or to sell their bonds on the marketplace. Thus, in this "subsidy derby" (Wolinsky, 1984:3), prosperous towns and suburbs have been the heaviest users. Cities like Palm Springs, Santa Barbara, and Belmont have designated their most valuable and booming areas as redevelopment zones; the city of Indian Wells, with one of the highest per capita incomes in the world, made *all* land within its city limits (even wilderness) an official redevelopment area. The city that went deepest into redevelopment debt was tiny City of Industry, which began the process with the largest tax base per capita of any city in the state.

There are three main incentives for this profligate use of redevelopment. First, local growth elites can, in effect, use tax-free and hence low-interest loans for subsidizing projects, without the awkward requirement of applying for a federal grant. Second, redevelopment agencies can use eminent domain to redistribute property from one owner to another, thereby helping to generate more synergistic rent arrangements. Finally, all of this occurs beyond the oppositional reach of other taxing jurisdictions like school districts and county governments, which, while losing their share of all the incremental taxes, have to provide the public services that the projects will require.

Thus subsidies for renewal projects that were probably never cost effective, even when most of the money was coming from the federal government, are now supplied in much larger degree by the localities themselves. Tax revenues that might, at least in part, have offset the costs of development are instead used primarily to subsidize still more development. And since, unlike urban renewal, such "self-financing" schemes are perpetual, they may easily lead to an unending spiral of decline in fiscal health and services in the urban areas that use them, particularly in the poorer places, which have to subsidize more in order to participate. The scheme is a circle difficult to break because of the insulation of redevelopment agencies from the usual scrutiny that confronts government bureaucrats, who must fight one another publicly for a share of the urban budget (see Friedland, Piven, and Alford, 1978). The redevelopment process "pays its own way" only by making the tax-paying public (at federal and local levels) absorb its losses. The redistribution of rents and the transfer of benefits is massive.

Historic Preservation.   Sometimes a part of redevelopment schemes, particularly in central city areas, are programs of historic preservation. Rather than preserve buildings by simply forbidding their demolition (a "stick" method), governments *pay* owners to let their structures survive. Developers who rehabilitate buildings within the boundaries of historic districts (which may also be redevelopment zones) are eligible for a federal tax credit equal to 25 percent of their expenses.[9] Another program permits entrepreneurs to redevelop the *interior* of a historic building and to take a tax deduction for donating the exterior to a preservationist organization (Ryon, 1984). The dollar value of this gift of a "façade easement" is based on the appraised worth of the site should it be developed to its full commercial value, less the value of the structure operating under its preserved configuration—potentially a very large sum.

Sometimes public agencies participate in this scheme. To raise money for its own operations, the Los Angeles Public Library "sold" its historically important central building to a private developer, who then, as part of the deal, turned the building back to the library for its perpetual use. Then, as its legal owner, the developer was able to claim a donation equal to the development potential of the site, yielding a $38 million tax break as well as a beautiful focal point for the adjacent office towers he was building. As part of the agreement, the library received a portion of his tax savings, as a sort of kickback, to remodel and beautify the old structure and its gardens. The external benefits of the preserved structure are thereby caught as extra rents ("spillover" gains) for the adjacent parcels, and the library gets money without having to go through the normal budget process. The library is saved only by increasing the overall density of the city and providing a good tax deal for the entrepreneur.

Still another historic preservation program, one operating in a number of areas (for example, Collier County, Fla., New York City, Boulder, Colo., and Suffolk County, N.Y.), permits the owner of a historic property to sell development rights to another entrepreneur, who then uses the development "credits" to build beyond allowable densities elsewhere (see James and Gale, 1977). Historic structures, increasingly appreciated by rentiers as centerpieces for surrounding growth projects, can be preserved with no sacrifice by the affected owner or in aggregate growth. This type of historic preservation (called transferable development rights programs) makes sense in the logic of the growth machine.

9. Homeowners who occupy their own buildings in historic districts (and thus gain only use values) are not eligible for this tax relief.

Much historic preservation occurs with gentrification. Whole neighborhoods can be given special benefits to create a particular ambiance and the hoped-for rents and fiscal benefits that might follow. Such schemes may indeed be making cities more charming, but they involve far more costs than are ordinarily recognized. Recent evidence suggests that the much heralded tax benefits of gentrification may be greatly exaggerated, particularly given the size of subsidies offered to developers. Even without special deals, however, a city's gains are held back by its reluctance to reassess improved property; city officials don't want to discourage others from making similar investments. In his study of 152 private rehabilitation projects in ten different cities, Peterson (1973:110–12) found that after four years only 19 parcels had been reassessed and these at a fraction of their actual market value (see also DeGiovanni et al., 1981:293; Schill and Nathan, 1983:38–40). Given the high demands such places make for services and amenities—cobblestone walks, street trees, parkland (Weiler, 1978:11)—the preciously gentrified districts may be net fiscal losers, regardless of the social costs paid by those displaced. Although they may be artistically successful, many of these districts are, in social and fiscal terms, the work of philistines.

Industrial Bonds. As still another development incentive, local governments can offer private corporations cheap factories and low-interest plant financing by floating bonds to construct industrial facilities. Industrial development agencies (IDAs) may acquire land and build structures, which are then sold or leased to private firms at below-market prices. The use of bonds for commercial projects rose sharply from $6.2 billion in 1975 to $44 billion in 1982. Since the bonds are tax exempt, the federal government is again the source of subsidy. The 1983 federal tax loss was $7.4 billion (*Public Administration Times,* 1984).[10] Sometimes the plants themselves are put under the ownership of a nonprofit organization as a ploy to spare their corporate occupants local property taxes as well (Bernard, 1983:219).

In the Albany, New York, metropolitan area, one law firm has

10. This tax loss led Congress during 1985 to enact restrictions on the private use of such bonds, over the strong opposition of state and local officials.

become a specialist in promoting development bonds, actively recruiting clients who have planned construction of any kind. Their own law offices, for example, were financed in this manner (Cipriano, 1984).[11] In another Albany case, Pyramid Construction Company, after deciding to build a major regional shopping mall and defeating intense neighborhood opposition to its plans, applied for millions of dollars in IDA financing *after construction had begun*. Turned down by the IDA of the suburban town in which the mall is located, the firm succeeded in obtaining development bonds from Albany County's IDA. As these incidents indicate, many urban policies not only fail to serve use values but also can be cynically manipulated, like the UDAG grants, to subsidize projects that would have been built anyway.

A Summary Note

Given the ebb and flow of specific programs and their modifications, the most durable feature in U.S. urban planning is the manipulation of government resources to serve the exchange interests of local elites, sometimes at the expense of one another and often at the expense of local citizens. For all the commotion of the civil rights movement and community activism of the 1960s, there was little disruption of this way of doing business. Although increasingly packaged as programs for the public good, resources that were supposed to help "the cities" had little positive impact on use values, because of their design, their administration, or their elimination just at the point when they might have done some good. Land-use-oriented urban programs, in service to the place entrepreneurs, inhibited progressive change in the stratification of either classes or places.

Ironically, many of the programs used to promote local growth may not even have stimulated the investments attributed to them. With so many levels of government giving deals to capital inves-

11. Generating public subsidies for developers has become an important legal specialty. Lawyer John Zuccotti, a former deputy mayor and chair of the New York City Planning Commission, "has played the city's Industrial and Commercial Incentive Board like a pinball machine" (Guttenplan, 1985:23), resulting in $58 million in tax abatements for his clients over an eight-year period.

tors, local growth programs often neutralize one another (Vaughn, 1979). And other things do matter to capital investors besides local taxes and plant financing; investors traditionally consider access to markets, materials, and a docile labor supply when choosing a location. For example, in 1985 General Motors decided to locate its $5 billion Saturn automotive plant at a nonsubsidized Tennessee location, rejecting all the special offers from dozens of competing states. This and other examples will probably not discourage the subsidy system; from the local elites' perspective, an inducement to capital investors can't really hurt growth, and there is always the possibility that the growth project stupidly underwritten may turn out to be one's own.

Throughout the period we have been discussing, while the wide array of explicitly "urban policies" were often going wrong, whether local or federal, land-use oriented or social, there were other, vastly larger interventions hitting their mark: the unbroken exploitation of national resources to develop the suburban freeways and the great infrastructural projects and defense procurements that led to vast regional shifts in population, production, and rent collection. While reformers were contesting for essentially minor resources in the name of use values, rentiers had been *continuously* well served through their ongoing coalitions with political actors at all levels. Although national initiatives on issues like abortion reform, educational policies, or welfare rights may lead to conflict with local governments and parochial elites, any national scheme that facilitates growth in a given locality "will be executed with a good deal of cooperation and mutual accommodation" through all levels of government (Peterson, 1981:82). That has been the real basis of U.S. urban policy.

Planning to Win

Instead of being antithetical to this growth machine patterning of local and national policy, the highly decentralized U.S. government system only increases the number of actors competing for growth and the intensity of the contest. The dispersal of land-use authority in the United States is often treated either as an irrational residue of the English home-rule tradition or as a reflection of the antiurban American yearning for a simpler, smaller-scale agrarian past (White and White, 1962; Wood, 1958). These explanations overlook the manner in which land-use authority is exercised. The mere existence of multiple units of decision making itself promotes certain kinds of land-use policies, policies that in turn affect the hierarchy of people and places. Granting planning authority to suburbs allows the residents and entrepreneurs attached to each suburb to wage their own separate battle to maximize use or exchange values. The real consequence of governmental fragmentation is, not the realization of place-based democracy, but the ability of self-interested elites (either business groups or affluent residents) to control governments in order to pursue their own goals (Newton, 1976). Political incorporation itself is, in Hill's (1974) words, "an important institutional mechanism for creating and perpetuating inequality . . . a decentralized, fragmented metropolitan government facilitates the maintenance and perpetuation of class and status group privilege." Such fragmentation, we repeat, does not imply urban chaos (Wood, 1961); rather, it is the key ingredient of a certain kind of planning and administrative apparatus.

The suburban towns are important on a number of grounds. First, by 1970, the suburban residential population was greater than the population of the central cities (Ashton, 1984). Even blue-collar workers (in fact, especially blue-collar workers) were more likely to be living in suburbs than in central cities (Mollenkopf, 1983:38). Second, the small-scale government potentially creates at once another sense of community—a cultural *sui generis* brought forth by legal fact (Firey, 1945)—and the means to enhance and perpetuate that particular sense of community through public policy (Wood, 1958). Although it is true that political wards also help to create community and organize the power resources of neighborhoods in some central cities, there is a difference between the ability to negotiate within a party machine and the formal power to zone, tax, and budget. Political autonomy thus expands the governmental resources that can be used to advance (or retard) the interests of one's place and can reveal the ways in which governmental authority can matter. Finally, by looking at policies in the suburbs, we can gain a sense of how, in microcosm, competitive relations within and between legally distinct places work themselves out and affect individual lives.

The Development of Suburban Autonomy

At one time, the growth of the metropolis was accomplished by a city annexing adjacent areas. This was virtually the only way property owners could secure utilities, transportation, and basic urban services that would make urban development possible (Ashton, 1984). In the middle of the nineteenth century, annexation was also a way to dilute the growing political power of the urban ethnic machines beginning to take hold of the central cities. Only by retaining the suburban Protestants as members of the same polity could the city elites mitigate the effects of rising numbers of foreign-born, largely Catholic and Jewish voters (Kotler, 1969:14–20; Markusen, 1984:89).

The extension of the metropolis through annexation did not fundamentally alter the social or political ordering of urban life. Even as population and industrial development spread into an outlying district, they were still within city boundaries. Physical distance merely helped to insulate wealthy people from the working classes and the noxious industrial plants that employed them. Moreover, although rich and poor were residents of the same political jurisdiction, rich neighborhoods were often provided superior services and amenities. That the rich had to pay their taxes to the city as a whole was not, in such a situation, a deprivation.

But when "corrupt" machines used favoritism to channel public resources to their own kind, or when demands for equality deprived the privileged of their special treatment, annexation to the central city was less advantageous for the affluent. Thus one of the early motives behind the suburban "home-rule movement" in the latter decades of the nineteenth century was the desire by the affluent for fiscal segregation (Markusen, 1984). Residents used incorporation to control metropolitan expansion well before the urban growth booms of the post–World War II period (Warner, 1973). By 1930, the great majority of state legislatures had ended the period of annexation by creating laws that "put the decision to join or not to join the central city in the hands of the residents of the annexable area" (Markusen, 1984:92). In some states, such as California, the crucial power was given, not to residents, but to *property owners* in the outlying areas. Thus, property owners were made the key group in generating proposals for incorporation and were the key actors in obtaining approval by regional and state agencies (Hoch, 1984; Miller, 1982).

Incorporation was facilitated by the development of new ways of gaining urban services without annexation. For example, one way was to create special assessment districts that allowed property owners to "go it on their own" by taxing themselves and owners of neighboring property to pay for growth infrastructures. Or, towns could contract with larger municipalities (or county governments) for services not economical on a small scale, such as police, water, and sewage treatment. Relieved of carrying out basic services, town elites were left with little to manage except land-use issues—the last responsibility they would ever turn over to another jurisdiction. Towns could have their cake and eat it too—land-use autonomy with the benefits of scale economies when it suited them (Warren, 1966). Infrastructural costs were lowered further with the increased participation of state and federal governments in the development of highways, water supplies, and sewage facilities. Without the state and federal governments, suburban towns would have had to provide these facilities alone. In still later stages (beginning in the mid-1960s) incorporation gave suburban towns greater access to the expanded urban aid programs. Taken together, these factors made it easier for advocates to demonstrate, as they were often legally required to do, the fiscal viability of incorporation.

The role of elite residents notwithstanding, the more critical figures in suburban incorporation have been business groups. Local rentiers—builders, real estate investors, farmer-developers, and their small business allies—have been an active force on behalf of incorporation. Often forming suburban Chambers of Commerce (Dinerman, 1958), they sniff out the advantages and disadvantages of incorporation for rent revenues and profits. Overall, their goal is not simply to lure a particular developer here or an entrepreneur there, but to facilitate—with the right infrastructure and social climate—the complete transformation of the hinterland into a dynamic region of industrial and residential expansion.

In his study of the nation's "first suburbs," Binford (1985) found that the elites of Boston's early satellite settlements (Cambridge and Somerville) were simultaneously land entrepreneurs and manipulators of government and infrastructure. They invested heavily prior to 1820 in private bridges and roads that would channel traffic into Boston, and bought up the developable land surrounding the transportation bottlenecks they created. Entrepreneurs tried to guarantee that the major traffic arteries would go through their towns and, at the same time, that their road and bridge projects (not another speculator's) would be approved by the state legislature. Thus, they had two kinds of investment to protect: transportation infrastructure and real estate. As Binford notes, the contest among the entrepreneurs was intense: "Vigorous competition and jealous promotion surrounded every bridge, every turnpike, every scrap of road. Fighting for interests that seem trivial today, rival entrepreneurs spent years pursuing partners with capital, strategic bits of land, and the patronage of town meeting, county court, or state legislature." This struggle "created suburban villages and made them different from each other. [It] passed on a legacy of competitive localism to the next generation, and beyond" (Binford, 1985:21). Even the earliest suburbs seem to owe their existence to the machinations of place entrepreneurs as much as to the desire of residential populations to live outside central city zones.

Though commonly believed to have been created as bedroom communities, Boston's early suburbs were primarily commercial and trade centers—an early indication of what later suburbanization was going to be like. According to Binford, the early nineteenth-century towns provided nearby Boston with vegetable and dairy products, brokering and processing of agricultural products, and taverns and other services to Boston travelers. The more intense and general industrialization of the suburbs occurred at the turn of the century as factory-based "satellite cities" developed (Taylor, 1915; see also Berger, 1960). The movement of industry into the suburbs continued throughout the following decades, making the suburbs the heart of U.S. industrial growth in the postwar era (Logan, 1976a; see also Douglas Commission, 1969:413–14). Between 1963 and 1977, in the country's twenty-five largest metropolitan areas, total employment in manufacturing dropped by 700,000 (– 19%) in the central cities, but grew by 1.1 million in the suburban areas (+ 36%). Wholesale and retail employment dropped slightly in central cities, but more than doubled in the suburbs. Thus, urban work, like urban residence, had become suburban (see also Ashton, 1985; Masotti and Hadden, 1973).

Researchers conventionally cite a number of ecological and technological factors to explain this new distribution of industry and workers. Shifts in the economy from heavy manufacture toward light industry and service sector activities erode the advantage of central city locations, with their once-prized proximity to rail crossings, deep water ports, and dense concentrations of suppliers. New forms of continuous feed production require large-scale open sites ("green fields") rather than the multistory buildings found in dense central cities. Complementary changes in transport (favoring cars, trucks, and planes) alter the nature of space efficiencies. Because urban airports tend to be located in suburban regions (by dint of sheer acreage requirements), an increase in the importance of air transport draws the focus away from downtowns. Freeways mean that large parts of the urban region are proximate to some form of fast transportation: the number of critical points of access (on-off interchanges) is large and continuous compared to, say, ocean shipping technologies. In this "auto-air-amenity epoch," these factors make the suburbs the obvious arena for industrial expansion (Borchert, 1967:117; for a more detailed review, see Berry and Kasarda, 1977, chap. 13).

But these so-called technological determinants did not appear by accident; they were made possible in part by manipulating institutions. As many have noted (see Whitt, 1982; Yago, 1983), federal subsidies of interstate highways, oil production, and air transport sharply lowered the costs of transportation systems dependent on them. Federal Home Administration loan guarantees and the mortgage interest tax deduction enabled many to be housed in the hinterlands. In addition, employers were attracted to the suburban work force because it was thought to be more tractable than its heavily unionized central city counterpart (Storper and Walker, 1983; Walker, 1981). Suburbia contained, among other groups, large numbers of "housewives" who could be drawn into low-paying, routine jobs, but who had the nonunion, consensual-oriented work habits associated with their respectable middle-class life styles (Saxenian, 1984; see also Massey, 1984). Incorporation of the suburban town, therefore, was a useful governmental mechanism for generating these favorable industrial conditions. As in the early history of Cambridge and Somerville, armies of suburban place entrepreneurs did all within their power to use these small-scale governments to provide the needed infrastructures and business climates. These organizational factors along with the public subsidies of the suburban technologies strongly suggest that institutional forces behind the "natural" process of suburbanization were crucial to the massive suburban shift.

Not just rentiers, but industrialists also appear to have played a significant role in the incorporation movement. Gordon (1977:77) has gone so far as to assert that it was only "after industrialists joined the movement against central city extension . . .[that] political fragmentation became the natural consequence." Industrialists and their rentier allies turned to the incorporation process with specific preferences. If suburban town boundaries can be drawn to minimize residential population, there will be little pressure for pollution abatement or for high taxes to support social services. Nor will there be effective resistance to using public budgets to serve industrial infrastructure needs. If the boundary lines can be drawn in a certain manner, the act of incorporation can also help seal out particular kinds of residents whose very presence might upset good labor relations. Workers spatially removed from city vices might lead more diligent, wholesome, and hardworking lives. Such reasoning has long been one of the motivations behind the formation of suburban company towns, at least since the creation of Pullman near Chicago in the late nineteenth century (Buder, 1967).

We know of no national study on which interest groups (residents, rentiers, or industrialists) prevailed in conflicts among incorporation contenders. We do have, however, Hoch's (1984) report on the forty-six incorporation attempts in the San Gabriel region (Los Angeles County) between 1950 and 1963. Of the four efforts by industrial organizations to incorporate given areas, all succeeded. Of the twenty-one attempts by Chambers of Commerce (a rough proxy for rentiers and retailers), all but one met with success (although half needed more than one try). Of the twenty-one efforts sponsored by homeowners' associations, only one was eventually implemented. These findings suggest that the incorporation movement, although joined by many diverse groups, has not been an effective tool for those seeking to enhance use values for existing populations. Instead of reflecting a sentiment for "smallness," or the desire to maintain exclusivity or low residential tax rates, incorporation was more frequently the result of the search for exchange value by business groups. That residents did not sponsor many successful incorporation efforts does not mean they never derived any benefits from them. But the boundaries of those towns, as well as the administrative and fiscal forms they took (and even their names), were most often somebody else's doing—providing at least a clue to whose primary interests they would end up serving.

Autonomy alters the fiscal and social structure of metropolitan areas, and this in turn changes the nature of how capital investors can benefit from a locality. Incorporation allows town officials to choose a set of policies that makes their town distinct from others, and, in the Tiebout style, capital settlers can pick and choose among the entire group of towns. For example, suburbs can manipulate taxes and although differential tax rates may not be important to industries choosing among *regions* (McMillan, 1965; Nishioka and Krumme, 1973; Weinstein and Firestine, 1978), taxation is significant *within* a given metropolitan region—where there is similar access to markets, work force, and transport facilities. Under such conditions, the choice of location will be influenced, according to surveys of corporate executives, by fiscal differences between suburbs and central cities and among suburbs (Advisory Commission, 1967; Burns and Pang, 1977:541; Fox, 1981; Mueller, 1961; Netzer, 1966:124–36; Schneider and Logan, 1984; Wayslenko, 1980, 1981; Wood, 1958:206–25).

In social terms, suburban autonomy also probably helps sustain differentiation; large-lot zoning (see chapter 4) helps provide, for example, a reliable homogenous affluence that may attract certain firms seeking good surroundings for their professional employees. An autonomous police force may be more willing to help local employers guard their property or harass union organizers than a constabulary responsive to more heterogeneous constituencies. Indeed, some suburbs are attractive precisely because their autonomous political structures can be easily manipulated to serve business needs. One of the inducements to locate in a suburb is the adaptability of the fiscal, geographical, and social structure of relatively undeveloped and small-scale fringe areas (Logan, 1976a:337) and "the political stability offered by a local city government dedicated to industrial needs" (Hoch, 1984:112).

Despite the cries about "big government on the back of business," fragmentation of the outer city in the United States means that the increase in scale of both the corporate firm and the metropolis during the last half-century has not been paralleled by an increase in scale of the jurisdictional units with which capital ordinarily deals. Instead, the pattern of suburban growth has provided capital investors with new opportunities for playing one small unit against another, thereby maximizing their options and further straining the resources of weak places. In contrast to culture-bound individuals, capital has great mobility and can be compared to a consumer choosing among products. Instead of a force to protect residential use values, incorporation has been a complement to the industrialization of the U.S. hinterland and the extraordinary rent booms created in its wake. Where use values have been enhanced, it has been because of the capacity of privileged residents to insulate their towns from growth machine dominance.

Types of Modern Suburbs

Each local government strives for a "desirable" pattern of development. But what is or is not "desirable" depends on the interests that control local authority, and these certainly do not necessarily reflect—as has often been assumed—the interests of either current or future residents. In city-planning operations, the dominant formal goal is maximizing benefits and minimizing costs. One expert on the planning process claims that "in the case of the residential suburb, the usual analysis is to estimate the city government's costs and revenues arising from each possible land use and then to use zoning ordinances and capital improvement programs to encourage the fiscally most 'profitable' uses" (Margolis, 1957:225–27). Researchers have discussed two kinds of "fiscal zoning" growth strategies (Coke and Gargan, 1969; Danielson, 1972). The first is to restrict residential growth to units with high assessed value (Stuart and Teska, 1971); the second is to attract new industry and commerce. Suburbs may combine these strategies, aspiring to the ideal of an affluent residential community supported by a strong industrial and commercial tax base.

In fact, suburbs have followed a variety of strategies, from the promotion of extensive residential tract development to the prohibition of industry altogether. Because growth machines are active at the suburban level, fiscally irrational projects can often be approved. And because use value activism is strong in some places, there are residential towns that willingly sacrifice fiscal gains to preserve their amenities (Eulau and Prewitt, 1973:542; Williams et al., 1965). These different strategies stem from the varied opportunities available to places according to their location in the place stratification system: how rich they are and who wins the battles between entrepreneurs and residents. A similar pattern of competition and conflict exists among central city neighborhoods, but political autonomy introduces some new wrinkles. Let us look at three types of U.S. suburbs as a means of catching the essential differences among modern suburban towns that are created by political structure: the affluent employing suburb, the working-class residential suburb, and the exclusive residential town. These are by no means "pure types," but they are based on empirically relevant and analytically useful distinctions.

The Affluent Employing Suburb.   The modern successful suburban town combines substantial industrial-commercial development with an affluent residential population. Logan (1976a) has shown in his study of suburbs in Silicon Valley (Santa Clara County, Calif.) that the major centers of employment in this newly developing zone are unlike the working-class factory towns outside central cities prior to the Second World War. Rather than housing the poorest suburbanites, these towns have residents who tend to be well-off (while those who work in their industries are more varied in social class). In 1970, in a comparison with suburbs in this region that had only minor industrial-commercial development, "employing" suburbs had a higher median income ($13,300 versus $11,667), higher median home value ($30,667 versus $25,200), a much stronger tax base per capita ($3,542 versus $2,172), a significantly lower tax rate ($1.13 versus $1.53 per $100 assessed valuation), and far higher public service expenditures per capita ($161 versus $93). These patterns have more recently been confirmed on a national scale by the 1980 census data (Logan and Golden, 1986).[12]

The affluent employing suburb "makes sense" because of two factors. First, modern suburban employment facilities (high-tech plants, regional shopping malls) are relatively compatible with affluent residence. Clean industry and attractive residences can go together. Second, suburban fragmentation allows the social costs of production in one jurisdiction, such as servicing low-income employees, to be transferred to another. In certain instances, the fiscal segregation can be so extreme that towns become, literally, "cities of industry" with only a handful of privileged residents. This was the consequence for the L.A. area's City of Industry, which was deliberately created in 1958 to have boundaries that limited its population to 624 people (including 169 sanitarium residents). Local employment, however, was over 3,000 and there were parcels of land that would serve, little more than a decade later, as work place sites for a total of 50,000 employees—with virtually no growth in residential numbers (Hoch, 1984; Stanford Research Institute, 1964).[13] Despite the larger irrationalities involved, a successful suburb can thus achieve a privileged position, with gains for its industrial employers, its residents, and the property entrepreneurs who collected the rents accompanying the transformation.

12. Retail and wholesale trade employment centers, often the communities with regional shopping malls, are the most favored. Older manufacturing suburbs have relatively low socioeconomic status, and face growing fiscal problems. But newly developing suburban manufacturing centers are more affluent and more fiscally secure than residential suburbs (Logan and Golden, 1984).

13. The ideal of a "company town," realized a century ago through corporate construction of entire communities (e.g., Pullman, near Chicago), can be approximated through such business domination of a small place, although with more explicit concern for fiscal benefits than ensuring docile workers. Indeed, this was the expressed plan of those managing the successful incorporation of a suburban town in California, whose spokesperson summarized the objectives of the industrial landowners: "Our sole aim is to attract additional industry and it is hoped that we can maintain complete freedom from the tax burdens which confront other cities. By the creation of this new industrial entity, we hope that in due time we can reduce extensively, if not eliminate entirely the personal property tax" (*La-Puente Journal,* May 1956, as quoted in Hoch, 1984:111).

The experiences of residents in affluent employing suburbs vary according to social class and their exact physical location. To the degree that local business is, in fact, clean, residents bear relatively few degrading spillover costs. But even under comparatively benign conditions, costs and benefits depend on residents' social class and tenure: lower-income residents tend to be situated closest to industrial development, paying whatever (inevitable) external costs are involved. Renters (again, more likely to be poor people) carry the increased housing costs generally found in economically growing areas (Appelbaum, 1978). Homeowners, who tend to live farther from the congestion, benefit as serendipitous entrepreneurs from growth in land values. Sometimes the potential can be so great that residents offer their houses as a single package to industrial developers and thereby transform the neighborhood (see chapter 4).

The employing suburbs are not without tensions and conflict. Those with a direct stake in exchange values—rentiers, developers, and local business leaders—will tend to pursue development for its own sake, with little regard to environmental or other costs. Residents, even homeowners located far from industrial sites, may join (or lead) coalitions to oppose developments. Often growth is not challenged at the outset; instead, residential opposition grows steadily as the social costs of intensive development begin to outweigh increments in fiscal wealth (Baldasarre and Protash, 1982; Rudel, 1983). Again, in the Atlanta, Georgia, area (Schmidt, 1984), even as some residents happily sold their homes to high-paying industrial developers, other homeowners (not quite so squarely in the path of development) intensely fought their neighbors' collusion in the rent intensification process.

Working-class Residential Suburbs. Because their local government must supply services to people who live in a town but are employed elsewhere, residents of low or middle income bedroom towns subsidize the employing suburbs, contributing to their affluence. The resulting chronic fiscal difficulties, exacerbated by the towns' otherwise valued political independence, make them especially vulnerable to projects promoted as "helping the tax base." Similarly, their high unemployment rates make it especially difficult for the towns to turn down any project that promises to bring jobs. Regardless of the speciousness of the evidence that either budget problems or unemployment will be eased through such projects, the financially pressed working-class towns are apt to settle for what they can get. Sometimes facilitated by their own internal growth machine of small-scale entrepreneurs (and abetted by corrupt local politicians), towns make deals that can only undermine their long-term fiscal and environmental health.

The absence of the sort of close (and often expert) citizen scrutiny common in the more affluent places makes unwise outcomes even more likely. Several working-class residential suburbs of Dallas, Texas, have adopted a "freeway" zoning strategy: on land parcels adjacent to major arteries, freeway zoning allows unrestricted development. As a result, one team of developers in the early 1980s built or obtained permits for thousands of residential condominiums in these strips, undermining any effort at a fiscally rational zoning policy (Harlan and Pusey, 1983). Millions of dollars in low-interest revenue bonds were offered by suburban politicians to entice such development into their localities, with virtually no opposition from residents. Pressed by the need to make ends meet "on their own," towns are using their autonomous authority to ruin themselves.

Exclusive Residential Towns.   Some suburban cities exclude both industry and working-class housing, utilizing such tools as large-lot zoning, open space preserves, and restrictions on utility access.[14] These strategies reflect not only community tastes but also the nature of community resources. Expensive houses yield high tax revenues, and owners of such houses create effective organizations to protect their property. Political autonomy in this context thus becomes a useful tool for restricting de-

14. Sometimes the utility limitations can affect much larger and distant jurisdictions. Bucks County, Pennsylvania, is trying to take over regional water supplies in order to block new supplies from spurring additional growth in the county. The new facility was needed to service a wider area of Philadelphia suburbs as well as the newly constructed Limerick nuclear power station ("Delaware River Project Is Denounced at Hearing," *New York Times,* December 4, 1983). In another instance, several Santa Barbara County communities have been able to eliminate the entire county's participation in the California State Water Project because of its "growth-inducing" effects. In order for these communities to keep the state water project from stimulating local growth, they had to block it for all communities in the county.

velopment. This deviation from the normal chase after growth can be tolerated because, by its nature, it is reserved for a small minority of places. Aggregate growth of the metropolitan area is unaffected by "spot" restrictions that enhance the use values of people who manage the capital and rentier apparatus. Indeed, exclusionary zoning in the showplace neighborhoods may stimulate overall growth and raise regional land values (Cox, 1981:443; see also chapter 4). Despite periodic court assaults on exclusionary zoning, the practice remains common and largely sustained by judicial decisions.[15]

Fiscal Disparities

The formation of different types of suburbs has created sharply varied fiscal conditions among places. The extent of the disparities, and the responses of suburbs to them, are by now amply documented. In their study of a national sample of suburban towns, Schneider and Logan (1981) compared the fiscal resources and levels of service demands found in suburbs of different household-income levels. They found that, consistent with the Silicon Valley pattern, towns with a disproportionate population of lower-income families have a substantially lower property tax base than suburbs generally, and only two-thirds that of exclusive residential towns. Surprisingly, these working-class residential towns raise more revenues and spend more money than other communities. They impose higher tax rates and receive more outside financial help. Poor suburbs must pay for higher levels of social welfare services, such as special education programs, income supplements, public hospitals, and housing. They spend two to four times as much as other communities on these functions. In con-

15. Courts have ruled against exclusionary zoning in California (*Associated Home Builders v. Livermore*, in 1976), Pennsylvania (*Surrick v. Providence Township*, in 1977), and New York (*Berenson v. Town of New Castle*, in 1975). The New Jersey Supreme Court ruled in 1975 that zoning that fails to take into account regional (not just local) needs for low-income housing is unconstitutional (Rose and Rothman, 1977) and in 1983 that cities have an affirmative obligation to ensure that such housing is actually constructed (Zax and Kayden, 1983). But U.S. Supreme Court decisions have sustained exclusion (Danielson, 1976). In a 1977 race-related case, the Supreme Court ruled (*Village of Arlington Heights v. Metropolitan Housing Development Corporation*) that discriminatory *intent* was necessary rather than just outcome in order to overturn local land-use authority. Intent is hard to prove.

trast, rich suburbs spend considerably more, and at a lower tax rate, on more common municipal services, such as fire and police protection. Suburbanization creates, ipso facto, a regressive tax structure.

The combination of a weak tax base, high service demands, and high indebtedness leads to the fiscal crises that are common among poor suburbs. In the early 1970s, aid from state and federal governments helped many towns cover basic costs of services, thus postponing inevitable fiscal collapse. By 1983, however, a report by the Joint Economic Committee of Congress found that medium-size cities and towns, many of them presumably suburbs, had the highest proportion of operating deficits—47 percent for the 1982 fiscal year, an increase of 36 percent over the previous year (Boyd, 1983; see also Wiesenthal, 1984b). In 1984 the older New York suburb of Yonkers, near default and facing a $50 million deficit, was forced to accept a state-imposed emergency financial control board in return for an advance on state aid payments (Oreskes, 1984). Although none has reached, in absolute terms, the scale of New York City's well-publicized problems, the suburban cases repeat both the causes and the control mechanisms that operated in the New York City bail-out (David and Kantor, 1979; Tabb, 1984b).

The fiscal situation of middle-class residential suburbs is only marginally better than that of poor suburbs. With comparable tax rates and slightly lower debt, but with less extralocal aid, these suburbs were able to provide the lowest level in public services during the 1972–1977 period. On the other hand, these towns are less damaged by federal and state cutbacks when they do occur; indeed such cutbacks increase their *relative* standing compared to poorer towns. Perhaps this gives such cutbacks (and the politicians advocating them) a special appeal in middle-class suburban circles. But here, too, the conditions exist for a desperate search for capital investment that discourages skepticism about the touted fiscal benefits or the distributional consequences of growth.

Racial Segregation and the Black Suburban City

Like the central city black neighborhood, the black suburb is a special case, involving problems not only of class and fiscal stress but also of stigma and caste. The first evidence of its specialness is its very existence: despite generations of urban experience and substantial geographical distance from the urban core, blacks in the suburban fringe still live in ghettos, albeit sometimes with the distinction of having autonomous black-controlled governments. The pattern of racial segregation found in suburbs closely resembles that found in central cities, along with a degree of racial isolation that cannot be explained by different income levels of blacks and whites (Bianchi, Farley, and Spain, 1982; Farley, 1977; Hermalin and Farley, 1973; Taeuber and Taeuber, 1965). The vast majority of whites living in suburbs reside in places that are "lily white"; 86 percent of whites live in suburbs with a black population of less than one percent. These data, based on our reanalysis of figures reported in Logan and Schneider (1984), indicate an *increasing* level of racial segregation over time in the suburbs.

In addition to the routine discrimination by realtors and property owners that confronts them in the central city, blacks searching for suburban housing must deal with the special tactics that exclusionary suburban towns can use to forestall racial change. One tool is the process of granting zoning, building, and business permits, which can be informally managed to harass black applicants as well as whites suspected of opening up neighborhoods to blacks. Further, a local police force can be encouraged to ignore criminal acts in which blacks are victims. Finally, white-dominated suburban governments can consciously manipulate housing and welfare programs to avoid black beneficiaries. They can refuse to participate in them altogether if integration is a feared result. Reminiscent of big city public-housing controversies in the early post–World War II era (Meyerson and Banfield, 1955), suburban towns are free to reject housing programs that either require racial integration or insist on the scattered site development that could lead to the greater integration of blacks already present. Thus in a federal lawsuit brought in 1980, a former Yonkers, New York, city councilman has testified that the city council rejected scattered sites for public housing in order to discourage neighborhood racial integration.[16]

16. The suit was settled in 1984 with the city's agreement to build two hundred units of new public housing in a predominantly white area (Williams, 1984).

The result of all this is segregation in the suburbs; even in comparison with other working-class suburbs, black residential suburbs have the least favorable social and physical conditions. According to Schneider and Logan's data (1982b), black suburbs face a still tighter fiscal squeeze than their white counterparts: a combination of high service needs and an exceptionally low tax base has resulted in high taxes, high debt levels, and heavy dependence on intergovernmental transfer payments. These findings are derived from an analysis of the racial composition of suburbs, independent of any effects of different levels of household income between whites and blacks (Schneider and Logan, 1984).

Given the tendency of black neighborhoods not to be organized as self-sufficient economic enclaves (see chapter 4), black suburbs probably also do not provide advantages of social mobility for their residents. Indeed, the exclusion of blacks from the employing suburbs intensifies their isolation from mobility networks. Perhaps the only gain blacks derive from the suburbs is that while deprived compared to white suburbanites, they, like suburbanites in general, report better public services than their counterparts in the central city (Ostrom, 1983). The point is not that suburbanization creates absolute deprivations, but that suburbanization replicates the class and racial disparities found within cities.

Fateful Differences: Suburban Stratification

The disparities among governments in the metropolis reinforce the advantages of fiscally stronger communities in their competition for high-income residential development and desirable forms of industrial-commercial growth. Privileged places able to provide more advantages at lower costs influence the decisions of industry and people of different social classes, generating different levels of benefit for the area and its residents. Rich places get richer as the well-off seek places that will make them still better off. Research on population changes in individual suburbs reveals that, apart from any other community characteristics, whites and wealthy families are significantly more likely to move into communities with a strong property tax base, whereas blacks and the poor tend to go elsewhere (Schneider and Logan, 1982a,

1982b). And as we previously indicated, business firms in both manufacturing and trade take into account the local tax base (and social milieu) in a similar way in evaluating alternative suburban locations. It is a self-reinforcing system in which the presence of a well-off population base acts as an attraction for capital investment; the industrial presence then induces more affluent residence.

Suburbanization thus operates as a stratifying process. The well-to-do harness the resource of government autonomy to work on their behalf, and the dynamics of the competitive system cause the already weak to grow weaker through their relative inability to use autonomy in the same way. Whereas in the past urban administrations may have used class elitism, ethnic favoritism, or racism as a basis for discriminatory taxation and service delivery, political ecology now accomplishes the same end in a postreform era. Excluded as always from the residential enclaves of the wealthy, the marginal groups are now also jurisdictionally segregated from the richest tax bases and job settings as well. The poor are left to support public services in their communities from their own meager tax revenues, and to rely on their own group's political and economic resources for individual mobility. Small government is best exploited region-wide either by rentiers (serving the needs of capital) or by the most affluent residents (because they have the power to keep the system from intruding in their own lives). For those without resources, location and its autonomy become still another hindrance to use value goals. In short, growth politics, coupled with small-scale government independence, favors exchange over use values: but even when use values are by chance or by design enhanced, they are the use values of the well-off. Suburbanization fuels the growth machine and reinforces place and social inequality.

These patterns of inequality are not a consequence of government autonomy by itself. Instead, the decisive issue is the fiscal and economic context of this autonomy. In the pre-1950 period, before modern suburban industrialization, autonomous suburbs did exist, but with less tendency to engage in fiscal zoning. There were fewer fiscal plums to capture and bigger environmental costs to pay if successful. Hoch (1984) found in his study of Southern California suburbs that differences between towns in social class, wealth, and revenue were far greater among suburbs incorporated after 1960 than among the older suburbs incorporated before 1950. Similarly, Logan and Schneider (1982) report that the household-income gap between central cities and suburbs is significantly greater in those parts of the United States in which local property taxes support a larger share of municipal services, implying again that the fiscal context influences the geography of privilege. It is the particular conditions of modern suburbanization that shape the patterns of place stratification.

Fiscal disparities among suburbs, and between central cities and suburbs, are both a continuing cause and a result of class and racial segregation in the metropolis. Together, segregation and home rule prevent the equal application of governmental resources to the needs of the metropolitan black and poor population. When coupled with the other structures for opportunity that community provides, city incorporation patterns become part of the basis for the "cycle of poverty" often attributed to cultural or personality traits. At the same time, the typical suburban land development process allows business and industry—at least those sectors of business and industry that are geographically mobile or sufficiently large-scale to dominate a local community—to be insulated from the costs of maintaining groups most disadvantaged by their own hiring and wage patterns. In the active, dynamic process that creates and sustains the suburbs, the actors with the greatest impact are the rentiers and the industrialists. Just as they managed the timing, boundaries, and administrative structure of towns to maximize private advantage, so they continue to dominate the planning and fiscal policies of these places. Working-class towns and unincorporated residential areas remain *residual* phenomena, containing the people and land that nobody else wanted. This, in brief, is the heart of their problem.

The meaning of suburban differences, like all differentiation of territory, depends on the overarching political structure. In Britain, France, the Netherlands, and Scandinavia, the advent of suburbanization has not meant fiscal fragmentation and service inequalities. Hence, the growth of the metropolis does not inherently carry with it a new form of social stratification. The federal role in local growth in the United States has been primarily to subsidize it; the federal government does not even go so far as to coordinate the sometimes contradictory directions of these subsidies. Federal sponsorship of local advisory "councils of government" (the 1968 "A-95" program), which were supposed to encourage towns and cities to coordinate their development, were effective only on matters that would help regional growth as a whole, such as water supply and transportation (Hallman, 1977; Horan and Taylor, 1977). Otherwise, the councils, representing little more than local growth machine interests, accomplished little and were eliminated under the first Reagan term.

The unequal development of American suburbs replicates, on a small scale, the patterns of inequality that have long been noticed throughout world regions between rich and poor zones (see chapter 7). In the suburban milieu, as in the larger world system, the advantages adhere to the places of the rich and the disadvantages to the places of the poor (Frank, 1967; Hymer, 1972, 1979a; Wallerstein, 1979). The affluent employing suburbs and the exclusive residential towns are privileged because they can attract residents and migratory capital as a place of first resort. Corporations, if they can get into such places at all, are less often there because of inertia or special subsidy, which is more often the case with working-class suburbs or distressed central cities. Corporations in privileged places are likely to be part of the core economy, which makes them better able to respond to demands to provide amenities and be a "good corporate citizen." All this helps make the privileged "core towns" fiscally sound and insulated from the changes of federal aid policies. Their residents have access to the "good life" not only because of relatively high incomes but also because of the superior public services and premium (and higher value) shopping opportunities in their areas (see Caplovitz, 1963). Economically peripheral places (whether older cities or poor suburbs) have the opposite set of characteristics: high fiscal vulnerability, inability to independently attract capital, and residents who are left out of the favored life style and economic mainstream. As is generally true with geographically uneven development, people's location at the low end of the stratification of places compounds their individual disadvantages. For someone trapped behind political boundaries, geography becomes destiny.

In the United States today, communities are encouraged, even by national urban policy, to compete like business enterprises, to attract business enterprises, and to externalize the costs of their success. Making the city into a business displaces other values and concerns, such as the role of the polity in helping people find greater satisfaction in life, the role of government in building a strong community, or the role of government in caring for the disadvantaged. The business style of local politics and of urban planning is often couched in a technocratic argot that allows "bottom lines," like growth of the tax base, to be the only public goals. Moral issues disappear because most of the people who need empathetic attention end up segregated behind boundary lines, deployed into jurisdictions where the least help is available (see Newton, 1975). Not only are the poorer citizens out of sight and out of mind, they lack even legal standing to demand wealth and service redistribution. The Great Depression and postwar gains wrested by the poor and minorities in spheres such as welfare, education, and civil rights are being undermined by locational strategies that change the meaning of citizenship.

Both planning and home rule have been used to benefit affluent communities, and to benefit especially the local elites—of any community—who can manipulate municipal policy to their entrepreneurial advantage. In the following chapter, we consider the consequences of these local manipulations in an era in which the scale of capital and of politics is fast outgrowing all local bounds.

6

Overcoming Resistance to Value-free Development

Despite its long history, the organization of land use through a system of competing growth machines is not necessarily a permanent feature of U.S. cities. The growth machine apparatus has provided only one possible way for coordinating the place needs of capital investors with the material interests of land-based parochials. Rentiers and their allies mediated between capital investors and the other social classes by dominating local governments and by exerting ideological leadership on matters of land use and production. But fundamental tensions have emerged. In this chapter, we examine how new modes of capital organization have decreased the utility of growth for local elites while at the same time inducing broad-based citizen opposition, primarily in the form of environmentalist groups. In part as a means of dealing with the resulting decline in the efficiency of the growth machine system, certain counterforces have appeared to make localities again safe for capital. We examine how the basic class configurations underlying the growth machine are being altered (particularly relations between cosmopolitan capital and parochial rentiers), how opponents to value-free development have moved to

exploit these changes, and how recent trends, in investment maneuvers and political policy making, may overcome these impediments.

Changing Utilities of Local Growth

The most important factor affecting the growth machine
system is the increasing international concentration of productive
activities in the hands of fewer firms. Stephens and Holly (1980:
162) describe the trend:

> Between 1954 and 1974, the share of the total industrial sales of
> the 500 largest industrial corporations rose from one-half to two-
> thirds. In terms of jobs controlled, between 1960 and 1973, the
> number of domestic and foreign jobs accounted for by the 500
> largest industrials grew from 9.2 million to over 15.5 million, a
> growth rate twice that of U.S. nonagricultural employment over
> the same period. [See also Borchert, 1978; Martin, 1975; Pred,
> 1977:99.]

Similarly, Ross (1982) has traced changes in the number of production facilities controlled by metropolitan-based multilocational
firms over the period 1955–1975. He found that although the
number of firms in his study increased by only 14.3 percent, the
number of production facilities controlled by those firms rose by
68.4 percent (from 3,814 to 6,420). This implies a relative increase in control activity at the headquarters locations of the country's largest firms. Given the wave of merger and conglomeration
that swept U.S. industry in the late 1970s and early 1980s, we can
safely assume that the same pattern has only intensified since
these data were gathered.

Concentration among firms implies the concentration of economic "control points" (Borchert, 1978:214) in fewer urban
areas. Although some cities of the Northeast are losing their lead
in the numbers of headquarters they contain, top managements
and related activities are still very much centered in the traditional
corporate cities. Because of the overall increase in corporate concentration, cities in the Northeast had modest growth in the number of their "control linkages" to other places, despite an absolute

loss in the number of headquarters located in them. All in all, the concentration of economic activity into fewer corporations has meant a concentration of decision making in fewer cities (with crucial consequences, which we will elaborate in the next chapter, for the role of various kinds of cities in the larger stratification of places).

Concentration of control results from a number of business dynamics. As firms grow in size, they are better able to separate control functions, often located in big city skyscrapers, from production activities in the "field." Other organizational developments have also been at work, such as the tendency for large firms in big cities to swallow up smaller ones in small cities. This concentrates executive decision making at the site of the acquiring firm, even when the local plant continues to produce. Certain critical economic functions also tend to "stick" in the old headquarters cities even when parts of the corporate headquarters are dispersed. Thus, among the corporations headquartered outside New York, "nearly all" (Cohen, 1977:223) operate through investment bankers in New York City. Similar locational patterns (although less pronounced) exist among pension fund administrators, law firms, and accounting firms (Cohen, 1977). The result is that the events in any given place are made dependent on decisions executed elsewhere; we call this process delocalization.

In one sense, delocalization has been going on for many generations, at least in the governmental sphere. Increasing federal and state participation in welfare and urban infrastructure development has preempted local governments in a number of realms and affected local life accordingly (Vidich and Bensman, 1960; Warren, 1963). Similarly, many observers have pointed to the effectiveness of technology (including media) in homogenizing life throughout a region or the country. Here we are concerned with delocalization resulting from changes in the organization of the private firm, rather than technological change and government transformations.

The movement of business control activity into fewer places has important effects not only upon the way places are used but also upon the relations among rentier and capitalist groups. The movement disrupts old patterns of achieving harmony among the classes through land-use decisions, and this, in turn, makes siting more difficult than in the past. Our goal in this chapter is to identify the implications of the new organization of capital for the way places are integrated into the production system, how places are linked with one another, and how those seeking both use and exchange values have come to deal with this reordering.

Declining Multipliers

Local branch operations of large corporations are less useful to the local growth machines than indigenous firms used to be. In large corporations, executive posts are less accessible to the local management class: recruitment is from within the firm or the occupational pool, not from the community (Kroll, 1981). Even ordinary labor is more likely to come from outside the community and all workers are more prone to be replaced by the automated production techniques favored by well-financed cosmopolitan firms (Birch and MacCracken, 1981; Brue, 1975; Stern and Aldrich, 1980). With raw materials and support/producer services often provided by other branches of the firm or by other companies specified by headquarters (Britton, 1974), there are fewer spinoff benefits for local entrepreneurs. In other words, the growth multiplier effects of branch operations are less than those of locally owned establishments (Cross, 1981; Erickson, 1980, 1981; Storey, 1981). Just as they have been tried and found wanting as "growth poles" in underdeveloped regions (Mingione, 1981:155), these branch operations tend to function as economically isolated business activities, failing to stimulate growth in other local economic sectors.[1]

Branch operations are not entirely useless to local growth machines, for something may be better than nothing. But these limitations may narrow the range of local people and institutions that can anticipate direct advantages of the arrival of new branch plants, and therefore reduce the local elites' ardor for pleasing the outsiders.

1. There is an absence of local agglomeration effects because spatial propinquity now has less significance in determining patterns of "interindustry linkages" than in the past (Pred, 1976). This upsets, Pred argues, the basic assumptions of location theory.

Absentee Ownership and Control

Owners of branch plants, which may be important local enterprises, live and work elsewhere. Branch and division managers do not participate as widely in local politics and civic affairs as did the families who used to control local firms (French, 1970; Galaskiewicz, 1979a, 1979b; Mills and Ulmer, 1970; Noland, 1962; Schulze, 1961). Under the old order, local industrial figures were prominent civic leaders (Dahl, 1961), whose presence was felt in all civic realms (Boorstin, 1965). Hence, the industrial leaders were linked in many ways to the rentier groups; indeed they sometimes owned speculative properties themselves (Boorstin, 1965). They likely belonged to the same churches and clubs, cutting one another in on the same deals. When rentiers prepared the ground for capital, this capital was—to a large degree—represented by local friends and neighbors whose needs the rentiers personally understood. Limited by their own horizons and economic power (see Friedland and Palmer, 1984:411), the industrialists were themselves locals, tied to a social world that their conglomerate successors would consider narrow.

Under the old order, the local industrial elite also may have had closer ties, at least in symbolic terms, with the less affluent classes. Especially before the Depression, when welfare was largely left to private charities, the do-good enterprises of the rich were among the few noticeable sources of beneficence around. Conspicuous constructions of hospitals and schools, such as those of Eastman (cameras) in Rochester, New York, the Ball family (jars) in Muncie, Indiana, and the Motts (General Motors) in Flint, Michigan, helped reinforce the vision that all residents had a common stake in a company's success.

At a later stage, when government took over more welfare functions, capital's relative inability to relocate elsewhere ("exit power" as Friedland and Palmer [1984:407] term it) still meant that a firm's wealth could be trapped through local taxation and hence redistributed as welfare. Local corporations' profits could devolve to the locality, through either the tax system or charity. Beyond their actual material significance, these small good works and minor wealth redistributions had important benefits for growth ideology. Today's branch managers, with fewer resources and higher rates of geographical mobility, do not ordinarily bring about, either through noblesse oblige or the local tax structure, the kinds of personal and symbolic class linkages achieved by their predecessors.

As the outlying regions lose business headquarters, the capitalist families move their investments, residences, and allegiances to the more cosmopolitan centers. The Rockefellers are an early example of elite delocalization. The family's wealth was created in the nineteenth century in Cleveland, but Rockefeller enterprises became national and then world oriented as one multilocational firm after another was either formed or taken over by Rockefeller interests. Cleveland was the focal point of John D. Rockefeller's earliest civic interests; he tithed to his local church even while working for $3.50 a week as a clerk, with his local giving climbing to $65,000 in 1882 (Collier and Horowitz, 1976:48). But by the time of his decision to engage in "wholesale philanthropy" (his adviser's term) at the end of the century, his commitments were moving toward the greater metropolises: the University of Chicago was reestablished under his sponsorship and the seeds were also planted for what was to become New York's Rockefeller University. By his mature years, he had three residences, in New York, Maine, and Florida, with his main corporate headquarters in Manhattan and industrial activities spread across the world. The Rockefeller offspring have further diffused both their moneymaking routines and the objects of their charitable donations. Although their investments are far-flung (and their residences include places like Arkansas and West Virginia), the drift—financially, residentially, and culturally—has been to New York City. The present sources of the family's wealth are headquartered there, and the Rockefellers have become major benefactors of elite institutions on the East Coast: the Metropolitan Museum of Art, New York Museum of Modern Art, Princeton Institute for Advanced Studies, and Rockefeller University, to name a few.

The overall result is a philanthropic trend toward disinvestment in the "old" areas, a process that amounts to a cultural redlining of the abandoned cities. This loss further weakens, in the economic periphery, the visible ties between local corporate activity and civic benefits. And the social power and national connections of those in control of the local economic system become less available to aid the local growth machine. The loss is crucial because today, as in the past, locally headquartered firms are the ones "more central in local networks and more influential in local politics than absentee controlled firms" (Friedland and Palmer, 1984:404; see Galaskiewicz, 1979a, 1979b).

Even those institutions at the very heart of the growth machine have been affected. Urban media, traditionally critical for growth coalitions, are being absorbed into ever-larger corporate structures. By 1983, twenty companies controlled more than half of all the newspapers sold in the United States (Bagdikian, 1983). Local publishers and editors are becoming branch managers, weakening the daily newspaper as a force for integrating diverse elite groups and selling growth to the public.

The major local financial institutions, active in city boosting during earlier eras, have joined—or perhaps even lead—the delocalization process. Decreasingly satisfied with an investment role of providing mortgages for local home buyers, financiers look more widely for loan targets.[2] As repositories of wealth from diverse sources (rents, corporate profits, wages), financial institutions coordinate and reallocate investment opportunities among people and places (Mintz and Schwartz, 1985). It is nothing new for these institutions to find distant boom areas attractive for investment (Horowitz, 1978),[3] but it matters whether this is an adjunct to local investing or a replacement for it. Particularly as town financial institutions become part of state or national firms, they have less interest in loaning to Main Street than in boosting aggregate activity and net returns, regardless of the local effects (Lehmann, 1985). Even financial institutions that formally remain local have become more cosmopolitan. According to Ratcliff (1979, 1980), banks in old cities like St. Louis, Missouri, have been

2. The home-buyer loan market may also be declining. There has been a recent drop in the percentage of Americans owning homes, particularly single-family, detached houses—the first decline since the 1930s (Rivera, 1983b). This may also decrease citizens' interest in sacrificing on behalf of growth and the higher "property values" growth may bring.

3. Horowitz (1978) says that the eastern colonists' investments in land in the western territories led to their support for British participation in the French and Indian Wars. After the British victory, the founding fathers found the British a hindrance to exploitation of the new territories, a hindrance eliminated by the War of Independence.

shifting their investments to more opportune locations elsewhere in the United States and the world. The largest and best connected of these institutions lead the way in exporting locally generated wealth; the smaller institutions, with fewer cosmopolitan connections and resources, are relegated to the declining function of fulfilling the investment needs of the faltering locality. The big banks' disinvestment represents a covering of geographical bets; and the fortunes of some of the most crucial local actors are thus less tied to their old home base.

City as Module

The erosion of a clearly visible and locally committed capitalist elite has its counterpart in the loss of visibility for local products. Increasingly, branch plants produce only a particular part (or carry out part of a process) rather than a complete product (Bluestone and Harrison, 1982; Hill, 1982). Items produced today are more frequently either parts of other items or products sold to make other products. Further, whereas firms once had branch operations in order to make either different products or the same product for *different markets* (Noyelle, 1983:115), the trend today is for firms to use their branch plants to make different parts of the same product—with enough duplication to ensure that no one factory has a monopoly in the production of a single element. Finished goods, in other words, are made up of components "sourced" from different places, produced in "parallel" operations. This is the organizational analogue of the "deskilling" of workers, by which various craft activities were broken down into simpler worker movements earlier in this century (Braverman, 1974, but see Form, 1983). From this, the factory—or the city— has become a deskilled module that is plugged into an international production apparatus and can be replaced by another module as necessary (see Hill, 1982). The local product can no longer be a symbol for the fusion of civic pride and corporate needs.

In more concrete terms, communities may be less willing to sacrifice their welfare to the parent industry if all it produces is a component rather than a visible product. A "motor city" may no longer produce cars but, quite literally, only motors. Prosperity for the Ford or Honda corporations, for example, may mean little for a given community if the transmission it manufactures happens not to be the one used in the best-selling models. Communities in the United States are not simply being given different, or even more specialized, roles in production. Many are being fitted and retrofitted for new roles at the tail end of the "product cycle," roles ordinarily associated with the Third World. The theory of the product cycle holds that production processes are perfected in places with highly skilled and professionalized innovators and are then sloughed off to more ordinary places lacking special human and organizational resources. Each innovation thus moves down the hierarchy of places over time, with places at the bottom specializing, more or less permanently, in routine production. This tendency for activities in a given place to be controlled by executives and technical innovators located elsewhere may undermine the bases of civic pride and commitment to value-free development.

Growth in the Scale of Infrastructure

Most previous types of urban infrastructure (railheads, ports, airfields) generated growth in immediate areas and thus directly benefited local elites. Because of the limited scale of such developments, local rentiers captured the benefits while avoiding the liabilities (congestion, pollution) by locating their residences at a safe but convenient distance. The benefits of the newer types of infrastructures, however, are delocalized, but their costs are increasingly inescapable. The wealth that such projects generate escapes local elites, unless they happen to be shareholders in the corporations involved. Southern California's offshore oil will be refined in Texas and consumed anywhere in the country; electricity generated by nuclear power plants can be fed into vast energy grids serving remote locations. Yet all residents of a given locality are potential victims of toxic wastes, a nuclear meltdown, or an oil spill; these effects cannot be confined to poor neighborhoods. This collective liability produces a new potential for cross-class coalitions within the locality to oppose such installations. At the same time, the large scale and complexity of modern infrastructure projects requires explicit government participation and this, in turn, has led to regulatory safeguards requiring public participation. Various public constituencies may become part of the development process, and their acquiescence, if not active support, becomes a necessity.

Local Resistance to Growth

These structural changes in the organization of enterprises and their infrastructural needs have spawned efforts at the local level to oppose particular investments, efforts led by either rentiers or residents, or a combination of the two. Opposition has appeared in several realms, but can be examined according to two broad categories: rentier opposition to growth that threatens exchange values and citizen opposition to projects endangering use values.

Defense of Exchange Values

Certain kinds of growth-related enterprises (for example, a toxic dump) can obviously destroy the income-producing potential of adjacent properties. More generally, particular types of development may inhibit the success of an alternative, and preferred, growth strategy. In places that are attracting many forms of capital, even local growth elites may choose to oppose certain forms of development as dangerous to long-term goals.

Unlike cities and towns in the late nineteenth and early twentieth century, seemingly characterized by a uniform interest in manufacturing or commodities processing (see Belcher, 1947; Boorstin, 1965; Scheiber, 1962), contemporary places have more diverse growth goals. Many sunbelt cities discourage (or at least do not seek) heavy industry; even some towns and cities in the Northeast have consciously embraced alternative growth schemes. Boston emphasizes higher education and the "clean" research and development that it spawns, in contrast to Detroit, which remains wedded, out of adaptive necessity, to an updated version of the "foundry" economy (Hill, 1984). Some large U.S. cities are dependent on tourism: it is number one in San Francisco, number two in Phoenix, and a major part of the economies of New Orleans and Miami (Corso, 1983:330; Hirsch, 1983; Luckingham, 1983:

314). In part this is, again, the result of scale factors: a given form of industrial activity may preclude alternatives, especially ones that are environmentally sensitive. The result can be resistance to new industrial projects that might interfere with more favored economic functions. Rentiers, in such cases, become unwilling to prepare the ground for just *any* form of capital, and respond only to those consistent with the chosen development strategy. Three examples will indicate how local groups not ordinarily opposed to development per se can, for one reason or another, be prompted to oppose particular forms of growth.

    Oil Drilling off Santa Barbara, California.   Tourism accounts for one-third of the economic base of Santa Barbara, a city of 75,000 people one hundred miles north of Los Angeles on the California coast. Retirement, education, and research and development account for most of the rest. Malecki (1980:230) has classified the area as one of the country's twenty-three "innovation centers," with its activities on the cutting edge of technology (aerospace, instrumentation, and electronics). In the late 1960s, oil drilling began in offshore federal waters, resulting in a major oil spill that created strident local denunciation of the oil companies (Molotch, 1970). Several issues are at the heart of this confrontation. Oil drilling is capital intensive (not labor intensive), with most equipment and supplies furnished by sources outside the area (indeed outside the country). As a result, the oil industry generates little wealth for local rentiers or other elite groups. Moreover, because oil drilling occurs in federal waters, beyond local tax jurisdictions, there are fewer fiscal benefits for adjacent localities. On the other hand, drilling operations generate both air and water pollution—both well publicized after the 1969 oil spill, which inundated twenty miles of coastal beaches, sharply reducing tourist revenues for several months (Dye, 1971; Molotch, 1970). For virtually all social groups in the area, the costs of drilling outweighed any benefits, given the viable economic alternatives. As the local newspaper was still (albeit, more moderately) editorializing fifteen years later, oil development must not be allowed to threaten the "capacity for diverse economic development" ("Lowering the Boom," *Santa Barbara News Press,* June 21, 1984, p. E12). This attitude contrasts with that of other coastal

cities in nearby Ventura County, which have less economic dependence on tourism (and other amenity-dependent activities) and
have called for *increased* oil development (Sollen, 1983a).

But in Santa Barbara local outrage, crucially including the
growth elites, was sufficiently powerful to delay additional drilling
for a decade. In addition, the federal government has tightened
safety standards and has extended the terms of corporate liability
for future spills. The Santa Barbara oil spill "is considered by
many to be a watershed for the national environmental movement,
and an even more irrevocable turning point for California"
(Brownstein and Easton, 1982:5). As a result, certainly in Santa
Barbara and probably in other parts of the country as well, the
freedom of capital to move where and when it chooses has been
compromised.

The MX Missile in Nevada and Utah.   Localities in the
United States have traditionally welcomed defense industries and
military installations. A military presence may have enhanced
feelings of security during the time when a foreign attack could
be repulsed by local tanks and antiaircraft guns. Changes in technology and scale, however, mean that the defense apparatus now
serves a much more diffuse "national interest"—certainly not the
protection of a specific community in which it is located. Military
installations can still be accepted on general patriotic grounds by
those believing that one's locality should "do its part," but no one
any longer thinks any *special* protection is gained in the process.
Indeed, there may be an increased vulnerability from living near
an enemy's strategic target.

Apart from reasons of patriotism and security, war facilities are
accepted because they generate growth; indeed they have been a
critical factor in the historic development of many western and
sunbelt regions (Bernard, 1983:214; Bernard and Rice, 1983;
Mollenkopf, 1983; Soja, Morales, and Wolff, 1983). The Nevada-
Utah area has a record of enthusiastic support for such activities,
going back at least to the early period of nuclear arms testing and
development. When nerve gas leaked from the Army Proving
Grounds near Salt Lake City in 1966 killing 7,600 sheep, the
city's press and civic establishment continued to support the military's presence. Local authorities accepted and perpetuated the

U.S. Defense Department's claim—later admitted to be false—that the sheep had died from "natural causes" (Hirsch, 1969; Lester, 1971). The role of defense activities in the economic life of the region helps explain this support for the military; Defense Department per capita payroll expenditures in Utah are double the national average.[4] Only a severe threat to other goals could bring into question continued support for military activity.

This threat appeared in 1982 in the form of the proposed MX missile system. The original MX proposal would have created a tunnel system in which nuclear-armed "erector-launchers" would continuously move under a ten-thousand-square-mile territory of Nevada and Utah. The military rationale for the scheme was that it would provide an impregnable defense by depriving the enemy of precise warhead locations. Much of the regional opposition to the MX represented neither a shift from militaristic patriotism nor a new-found concern for protecting the environment. Both elements may have played a role, but another factor was certainly as critical: the system's heavy land and water demands were a threat to ranching, mining, and other major regional economic activities. Ranchers feared the land taken for the project would mean a loss to them of their bargain basement rental rights to federal grazing lands. Access to these lands has no real equity value, and the ranchers could not be certain they would receive any compensation for what was the private use of a public good (Culhane, 1981).

Even more critical was the expected demand on water supplies (Glasmeier and Markusen, 1981).[5] By a conservative estimate, the project would use more water than is currently consumed by Nevada's capital (Carson City) in a region where existing water supplies were already overcommitted. Locals feared that developing the MX would preclude other types of industrial projects and additional growth. In the words of one Nevada state official, the material requirements of the project "could stop all [other]

4. Defense-spending calculations are based on federal expenditure reports (U.S. Bureau of the Census, 1984).

5. Many of our observations on MX are based on the descriptions presented in Glasmeier and Markusen (1981) and Schoenberger and Glasmeier (1980). We are also grateful to Amy Glasmeier for a lengthy telephone discussion with Molotch on her research on the MX issue.

construction in the entire state of Nevada" (Schoenberger and Glasmeier, 1980:19). Growth would be concentrated in a highly capital intensive industry that, given the short-lived utility of weapons systems, would probably last no longer than twenty years. In a pattern typical of boom town growth and decay (Markusen, 1978), the region might be left with a useless hodgepodge of roadways, tunnels, and hardware.

These concerns led regional elites to oppose the MX, adding to the more publicized opposition based on "states' rights" or the Mormon church elders' desire to make their home region "a base from which to carry the gospel of peace" ("Mormons Reject . . .", *New York Times,* May 10, 1981, p. 4:4). The local elites' preferred development scenario for the region conflicted with the goals of the federal government and the arms industry, which had billions at stake in the outcome. The considerable economic and political power of the region's elites prevailed at the national level. The MX compromise approved in 1983 limits the nuclear hardware to existing stationary, hardened shelters. Even though the enemy will know just where to aim, the impact on the region's land and water supplies will be mitigated. Although this scheme contradicts the entire military rationale for the project (Drew, 1983), it ensures that the project is not incompatible with regional growth strategies. Different hardware will be built, with lower government costs and corporate profits. In more abstract terms, redistributional rents will be enhanced at the expense of government transfers to the arms industry.

Nuclear Power in Midland, Michigan.   Nuclear power has generated more difficulties for capital mobility than any other kind of infrastructural investment. Midland, Michigan, a city of 70,000 people one hundred miles northwest of Detroit, was the site of one battle. In 1967, plans were announced for a nuclear power plant that would lock into the power grid serving much of Michigan (Yoo, 1981).[6] Dow Chemical, a multinational firm with headquarters in Midland and by far the area's largest employer, contracted with Consumers Power Company (the regional source

6. Our discussion of the Midland case relies on extensive fieldwork by Kisook Yoo (see Yoo, 1981).

of electricity) to construct the plant. The projected low cost of the energy would "help keep Dow's Midland complex competitive" (Simison, 1980:12). Although Dow and Consumers gained the backing of the Midland Chamber of Commerce and the city government, a locally organized antinuclear movement won a series of important victories, beginning with the delay of the initial construction until 1972. Although the partially built project may one day be completed despite growing local opposition (and characteristically steep cost overruns), the delays have already been a burden to Dow, which must temporarily upgrade other power sources. For the utility, the delays mean higher interest payments, additional safety studies, and added costs for public relations and litigation. In the end, and quite critically, support for the nuclear power plant declined even among local business groups as estimates of the plant's price for delivered energy were continuously revised upward. Increasingly, residents and elites considered alternative energy strategies more favorable to Midland's growth prospects. By 1977, Dow itself no longer regarded the plant as cost effective and attempted, with partial success, to back out of its contractual agreements to purchase a share of the plant's output (Simison, 1980).

Midland's opposition to a nuclear plant is symptomatic of the general collapse of the U.S. nuclear industry, which has already seen the abandonment of 102 projects after $9 billion had been spent in design and construction.[7] Another $11 billion in investment is about to be lost in other projects (Wald, 1983). The success of the locally based antinuclear movements is unique in the history of U.S. infrastructure. In numerous instances, local protests have "significantly delayed" (Campbell, n.d.:30) construction of plants or increased their overall costs (Bupp and Derian, 1978:157, as cited in Campbell, n.d.:30; Lewis, 1972:111; Wald, 1983). The demise of the industry cannot be explained simply in terms of its own diseconomies; the canal-building spree of the nineteenth century was just as ridiculous, but ran its course with little local opposition. The Midland case is particularly striking

7. The approximate tenfold increase in the projected cost of the Midland plant is not unusual by nuclear industry standards. The Nine Mile Point 2 reactor at Scriba, New York, will come on line at a cost of about $5 billion, after initial estimates of $382 million (Wald, 1983).

because all of the components needed to support an effective growth machine were clearly present: the region was suffering from decline; a small city was dependent on a single powerful corporation for its prosperity; Dow had been around Midland since Herbert Dow founded the firm in 1897; and the family and the firms' executives had a long tradition of participation in local philanthropies and public works.

But these elements were not enough. A concern about electricity too costly to sustain a strong economic future and the fear of nuclear pollution affecting people of all social classes helped thwart the plans of capital to invest where and how it wanted. Most of this occurred, it should be noted, before the 1979 accident at Three Mile Island, which had the effect of increasing opposition to nuclear plants, particularly in host communities (Freudenburg and Baxter, 1984).

The Midland case is also a good example of how government procedural controls provide local citizens with many avenues of resistance—agencies and jurisdictional levels whose approvals are necessary to move a plant into operation (see Campbell, 1983). The unimpeded success of nuclear energy in Europe may, by comparison, be related in part to the lack of autonomous local decision making on land-use matters—although higher levels of technical competence and more expensive oil costs may be other explanations (Lewis, 1984).

Defense of Use Values

Those with only use values at stake in a locality are always structurally available to oppose development. But whereas neighborhood preservation movements may have once been the best tool for protecting use values, the new threats to life routines (air pollution, nuclear meltdown) require a broader response. The shrinking overlap of industrial interests with those of local elites, combined with the increased scale of potential damage, opens the way for broader alliances, between local entrepreneurs and environmental activists.

Environmental movements are efforts to preserve use values at the expense, if need be, of rents and profits. These attempts at collective control over common place resources are a key dynamic of activism in American communities in the present day, and are at least equal to class and ethnic conflict as a basis for grass-roots organizing. Once again, however, we distinguish these oppositional groups from Castells's "urban social movements," whose orientation is toward quality of local services and other forms of "collective consumption," bureaucratically produced and distributed (Castells, 1983). Environmentalists' complaints are directed equally to private and public production, although it is the inherently collective nature of their experience that gives rise to the oppositional activity.[8]

In its most profound form, environmentalism reflects a simple vision that humanity itself will cease to exist should the earth continue to be exploited as a simple series of commodities. In the formulations of a generation of visionaries, scientists, and activists (see, for example, Bookchin, 1971; Commoner, 1971; Ehrlich, 1977; Schnaiberg, 1980), the simplification of the species mix of the earth, combined with practically irreversible pollution of the atmosphere and oceans, will mean the end of all use values for the human community. Polanyi long ago observed that without some kind of institutional "protective covering," physical resources would cease to support settlement. "Nature would be reduced to its elements, neighborhoods and landscapes defiled, rivers polluted . . . the power to produce food and raw materials destroyed" (Polanyi, 1944:33). We don't know how many people who vote for bottle bills have this world view, but some do and others sense the larger ideas in the air. This vision has helped sustain the environmental movement over the past decade.

Popular Base.   Environmentalism can appeal to a wide array of people in numerous areas. Use values in frostbelt regions are threatened, in particular, by residues of old industrial processes, such as the toxic wastes that are only now surfacing in gardens and playgrounds. Among the best known cases are the toxic leakage at Love Canal, New York, and the radioactive residues discovered at Times Beach, Missouri. In both instances, community anxiety over environmental safety led the government

8. Castells's category is too specific and too structurally disconnected from exchange processes to aptly catch the most dynamic centers of opposition in the United States (see Molotch, 1984; Domhoff, forthcoming).

to condemn the homes and land, on the grounds that pollution had possibly rendered them permanently unfit for human habitation (Fowlkes and Miller, 1985; Levine, 1982). Other crises have received less attention: for example, in Richmond, Kentucky, forty-five people were hospitalized as a result of escaping gases from an army nerve gas storage depot (Barron, 1985). Most recently, Union Carbide's toxic gas leaks at Institute, West Virginia, have raised general concern about the environmental safety of chemical manufacturing plants all over the country (Diamond, 1984). We are only now beginning to discover the extent of industrial and military pollution of America's "old" communities (Fowlkes and Miller, 1985:9); these cases, and the reactions to them, are an indicator of what lies ahead. Thus, contrary to the notion that environmental regulation is a specialty of the sunbelt zones, the Northeast and Midwest states have been at least as active as other regions in enacting controlling legislation (Duerksen, 1982).

The regulations that exist in the old areas consist heavily of efforts to deal with damage that has already occurred, such as toxic waste cleanup. In the newly developing regions, environmentalism takes the form of regulating investment that is trying to come in (Frieden, 1979a; Miller, 1981). In particular, the sunbelt regions catering to retirement, tourism, and high-tech industries are also places with strong resistance to development. Although the country's growth zones are not limited to areas with specific climatic or industrial conditions (the villages of Vermont share development pressure with sunnier locales), our focus is on the economically advanced sunbelt regions as the locus of this conflict between development and conservation. Nevertheless, much of our discussion is relevant to other places with profiles of strong growth.

In addition to certain unique natural characteristics, the advanced sunbelt growth regions have distinctive populations and social structures that give broad support to environmentalism. Migrants to these zones (often a majority of the local populations) are not a cross section of the American people. Although economic expansion may be responsible for the direction and size of most streams of migration, other factors, including cultural preferences, help determine *which* people decide to migrate and *where* they choose to go. We thus suspect that part of the flow to a number of the new areas consists of people seeking a better living environment. In the case of retirees, this is obvious enough. But even people who migrate in their working years are likely to do so for environmental (and related "life style") reasons. They therefore resist sacrificing the amenities they have gained for additional growth.

Compared to past migration streams, these people are skilled and educated (Kasarda, 1983; Mollenkopf, 1983:232–42). Indeed, some of the high-tech colonies of California, Texas, and North Carolina are now concentrations of the most highly educated workers in the country. These people have strong organizational skills and high rates of political participation, which they put to use in resisting the fiscal and social costs of development. Indeed, even a casual observer discovers that within the sunbelt, the cities with the largest numbers of high-tech migrants (Palo Alto, Santa Barbara, Austin) also have the strongest environmental movements. By contrast, the sunbelt areas with more traditional industrial bases (Houston, Texas, and southeastern textile towns) have growth machines that operate without much challenge.[9] In certain zones, amenity-oriented citizens are now numerous enough to produce political consequences.

Gender Differences.   Women's increased participation in the labor force over the past several decades has a number of implications for the struggle between use and exchange values. The participation of women in the work force could arguably make them more "like men," generating greater concern for exchange issues at the sacrifice of more traditional female concern with neighborhood use values. The problem with this assumption is that women do not lose their household and child-rearing re-

9. In contrast to our position, Peter Pashigian of the University of Chicago Business School has argued that federal environmental restrictions were created by frostbelt interests to frustrate the development of the West and Southeast (Pashigian, 1982). But since sunbelt areas tend to have the strictest *locally enacted* controls, it is more reasonable to see federal controls as consistent with local interests and demands. The state of California, for example, has had to work hard, using its congressional delegation, to create automobile emission limits that are stricter than those in force for the rest of the country. But perhaps frostbelt interests *should* try to protect sunbelt environments as a means to frustrate development in the growth zones. Pashigian's conspiracy theory would be a good basis for policy advice.

sponsibilities when they enter the labor force. Even when they are living with male partners, they continue to carry the major share of household and child-rearing burdens (Berk and Shih, 1980). This means that the dilemmas of managing the daily round are compounded by outside work, rather than ameliorated through major shifts of home responsibilities to husbands. Women thus have a stronger reason to be concerned about certain issues of the environment, particularly those that affect their ability to manage these multiple responsibilities. In neighborhoods that are secure from dangerous traffic, for example, children can be left home alone at an earlier age and in good conscience; similarly, high levels of traffic complicate all the maneuvers that busy people must manage as they move from child-care centers, wash-and-fold laundries, school events, and work.

Just as there is a gender gap in attitudes toward war and military spending, so there is one toward the significance of the home environment, nuclear plants, and development in general. Across the board, women tend to give higher priority to home values than to those stressing hardware, production, and economic growth (Boulding, 1981; Freudenburg, 1981; Markusen, 1980; Stout-Wiegand and Trent, 1983; Trent and Stout-Wiegand, 1984). At the same time, the participation of women in the work force seems to give them greater power in the family (Baca Zinn, 1980) and, we presume, in society generally. The continued salience of the home combined with the increasing social power of women will, we anticipate, help sustain environmentalism in the United States rather than enervate it.

Class and Ethnic Cleavages.   The less precise racial, ethnic, and class divisions in the newly developing areas, particularly in the West, are also a factor in sustaining environmentalist energies. There are lower degrees of traditional class consciousness (workers versus the boss), evidenced by a weaker union movement and less tendency to vote according to class. Certainly among non-Hispanic whites, ethnic solidarities are less pronounced than in the old areas, lessening the degree to which social commitments form around specific neighborhoods and immediate residential daily rounds. This opens up the opportunity for use values to be more connected to the "environment," allowing people to develop a large-scale concern for places beyond (but not excluding) the immediate milieu. Similarly, a lack of traditional class consciousness permits conflict to be posed in terms of rentier versus resident, not capitalist versus worker. Taken together, these factors mean that the grounds for cross-class and cross-ethnic solidarity are more fertile, and protection of the environment (both the proximate neighborhood and a rather distant wilderness) can rise to the top of the agenda. Organizing around problems of health, aesthetics, endangered species, traffic, and life style has heavily influenced the politics of sunbelt regions.

Working-class Environmentalism.   Our emphasis on consensus in the sunbelt runs counter to a commonly held view that environmentalism represents the selfish desires of the privileged at the expense of the working class. Some claim that the poor oppose these policies that threaten their jobs, raise the cost of their housing, and eat up the tax monies that might otherwise be used for more direct public benefits (see Chrisman, 1970; Deacon and Shapiro, 1975; Frieden, 1979a; Krieger, 1970; Sills, 1975). We disagree with this assessment of the distributive effects of environmental policy and the assessment of working-class opposition. Although we have already touched upon working-class interests in opposing the growth machine (chapter 3), we consider this issue so important to our analysis that we give it closer attention here.

Environmental protection directly and immediately benefits the poor. The poor live adjacent to the worst sources of industrial pollution (Berry, 1977; Buttel and Flinn, 1978; Lake, 1983; Love, 1972; McCaull, 1976). When hillside houses are built for the rich without adequate drainage, working-class people's homes are flooded on the flatlands below (Johnson, 1983:247). It is the working class whose occupational environments are most likely to involve toxins. Preservation of open spaces and laws controlling access to them (for example, the California Coastal Act) enable the less affluent to experience environments that otherwise would be available only to the wealthy.

Critics offer several challenges to the assertion that the working class participates in and benefits from the environmental movement. First, the well-off provide most of the leadership of the environmental movements (Dunlap, 1975; Lauber, 1978); this is true, but their rate of political participation in movements is higher than that of other groups generally (Milbrath, 1965; Verba and Nie, 1972; Warren, 1963). Second, higher-status communities have been the most likely to institute growth controls (Dowall, 1980; Protash and Baldasarre, 1983), to be more mobilized on environmental issues generally (Bridgeland and Sofranko, 1975; Eulau and Prewitt, 1973), and to be less interested in promoting further development (Krannich and Humphrey, 1983; Maurer and Christenson, 1982). We consider these observations accurate, but in our view, they simply reflect the greater ability of affluent residents, based on the resources at their command, to exercise control over their communities.

None of these challenges means that the working class does not support environmental reforms. An authoritative survey of over a dozen studies of the social correlates of environmentalism (Van Liere and Dunlap, 1980) concludes that there is little evidence that education, income, or occupation, taken together, correlate with environmentalist attitudes or voting behavior, although the literature has more than its share of mixed findings.

There are a number of ways to explain the empirical inconsistencies within and between studies. First, researchers often group diverse issues together as "environmental." Thus in one research project (Calvert, 1979), a bottle bill (found to be relatively unattractive to the working class) is lumped together with a coal severance tax and wildlife preservation (both more highly favored by the working class). Combining such different kinds of items in the same study mutes any significant class differences on *types* of environmental controls. Workers would favor regulation costly to rentiers or capitalists like an oil severance tax, compared to a regulation inconvenient for wage earners, like a bottle bill. More subtly, as Neiman and Loveridge (1981) point out, researchers have drawn on individuals' responses to survey items and ballot propositions that vary greatly in their direct relevance to people's lives, ranging from vague abstractions about "support for the environment" to cleaning up a nearby toxic dump. Again, this means that researchers are using noncomparable items, sometimes even within the same study.

Still another problem arises when researchers deal with populations experiencing different political and economic stimuli. More so than with most other social issues (war, abortion), environmental problems are local and timely in their nature. People recently threatened by toxic waste are going to be more environmentally sensitive than those who have never been so threatened; residents in an area with a nuclear plant become more opposed after a publicized nuclear accident than residents in other locales (Freudenburg and Baxter, 1984). Sometimes, in the context of a given political campaign, antienvironmentalist rentier interests may overwhelm local media with a pro-working-class pitch. Neiman and Loveridge (1981) report this behavior in a Riverside, California, growth control election; working-class voters tended to vote for growth, but only because (Neiman and Loveridge imply) there had been a well-funded campaign aimed at working-class concerns about jobs.

Further, some of the inconsistencies among the findings reflect the usual statistical problems encountered in most literatures: some studies fail to use any statistical controls (for example, Calvert, 1979) and a number rely on ecological correlations. In her analysis of California voting data, for example, Lake (1983) concludes that there is a positive association between class and environmentalism because high-income *places* tended to show greater support for environmentalist ballot propositions. But because Lake used entire counties as her data units (which vary in population size by a factor of 100) there is an inescapable risk of the ecological fallacy leading to false interpretations.

Finally, even studies showing the working class to have a *tendency* to be less environmentalist than other classes also show strong working-class environmentalist support, making any notion of sharp class division untenable. Indeed, the greatest cleavage seems to be between public opinion of all social classes, on the one hand, and urban growth machine elites on the other. Chambers of Commerce and other growth machine organizations take positions diametrically opposed to the viewpoints of most citizens; similarly, the voting records of politicians tend to be consistently less environmentalist than the opinions of their constituents (Calvert, 1979).

Environmental groups are, like any other movement organizations, made up of coalitions with overlapping and sometimes not-identical goals (Zald and Ash, 1966; Zald and McCarthy, 1979). Indeed, the ability of the environmental movements to break the unanimity of groups ordinarily in strong support of exchange values is one of their key strengths. Particularly effective are instances in which coalitions include either rich and powerful residential neighborhood groups or rentiers seeking to preserve a particular development strategy. The presence of these elite elements, and the consistent participation of the affluent generally, should not obscure the usual thrust of these movements: to enhance use values of the public at large, particularly of the less affluent populations. The strength of environmentalism clearly lies in the structural conditions that give it strong cross-class appeal.

The Fragility of New Places.   The physical reality of the new areas enhances the potential for coalitions of different classes. Ecological protection is not a new idea, but now that developers have covered the North American continent, people have begun to look back on the utterly extravagant waste of resources characteristic of prior eras and to appreciate the limits of nature, particularly in obviously fragile regions. The newly developing sunbelt zones were too resource poor (in water, power, and riverways) to have easily supported heavy industrial development. They can be developed today largely because contemporary forms of economic growth are less dependent on the traditional natural resources.

Nevertheless, even the so-called clean industries have consequences for the environment and these are cumulatively substantial. Effluents from high-tech manufacture endanger water supplies; modern factory exhausts are sometimes more dangerous, if less visible, than the smoke of nineteenth-century factories. Artificial infrastructures (irrigation, freeways, dredged harbors) have their own ecological backlash. Low-density and high-mileage commuting work forces drain resources in a way that tenement-living proletarians did not. This results in extremely high environmental costs for areas on the country's economic cutting edge. We list some of the major effects of development in these regions to suggest why the current residents of these areas often resist additional land-use intensification.

1. Water. Southern California and the Southwest are semiarid regions in which natural rainfall is insufficient to replace ground water supplies needed to sustain growth. Typically this becomes known to a community only after local growth machines use local water agencies to divert water from nearby rivers and lakes or to overdraft the natural underground basins (Walker and Williams, 1982). These tactics are cheap and easy, but wells dry up and surface soils sink into the vacuum created below. Modern-day Houston, Feagin reports (1983b), is sinking faster than Venice, which is also sinking because of the efforts of its modern rentier class to industrialize the region (Montanelli, 1970). San Antonio's water supplies are continuously threatened by overdevelopment; a referendum to stop a vast tract development from being constructed over the city's major aquifer (which might have led to underground pollution) resulted in the local growth machine's first significant political reversal (Fleischmann, 1977:165). A similar story unfolded in growth-oriented Dallas-Fort Worth when voters rejected, in 1973, funding for a canal that would have linked their city to the Gulf of Mexico, thereby challenging Houston as the great port of the Southwest. Besides the high cost of the project, concern for drinking water quality was an important part of the campaign (Melosi, 1983:186).

After exhausting local supplies, water must be imported from other places or generated through costly and complex schemes like reclamation, desalting ocean water, or cloud seeding. Distant water sources also eventually run dry; California's majestic Mono Lake has almost completely dried up. Resorting to dams (temporary because of silting) will destroy substantial acreage, and the taming of wild rivers will eliminate habitats and lessen recreational and aesthetic benefits. Fiscal costs rise along with the ecological penalties as the scale of construction escalates.

The tightening squeeze on resources inevitably leads to intraclass conflicts by growth machines competing for the same water. It was growth elites interested in developing more central parts of San Antonio who joined the environmentalists in protecting that city's aquifer (Johnson, 1983:245). The rancorous disagreements among the powerful make water a more prominent public issue, increasing the visibility of each project's destructiveness. Inconveniently for growth machine goals, public controversies develop on distributional issues (see Molotch and Lester, 1974).

In large-scale contests over water rights, intraelite conflict makes federal government financial and administrative support less likely because competition among jurisdictions (and public response) puts federal decision makers in a no-win situation. Such difficulties have played havoc with efforts to locate a source of water for the growth of Southern California. The efforts of Los Angeles to divert supplies from the Colorado River have intensified legal and political battles with adjoining states. Efforts to import Northern California water (perhaps with the Peripheral Canal) have disturbed the carefully coordinated unity of Northern and Southern California growth elites (Whitt, 1982) as well as sparked major battles with environmentalists in both regions. When residents find that financing must be provided with local funds, as it increasingly must be, environmentalists are joined by conservative "taxpayers" in their opposition to these projects.

2. Air. The very sunshine that beckons migrants to the "good life" cooks pollutants into smog. Just as the western sunbelt lacks adequate water resources, so it also lacks healthy air. The detrimental effects of smog, for personal health, aesthetic values, and physical damage, have been clearly documented and well publicized (see, for example, Downing, 1972; Lave and Seskin, 1977; Waldbott, 1978). Indeed the pervasive impacts of smog sometimes facilitate broad coalitions between environmentalists and business groups who fear that poor air will hinder prosperity in tourism, retirement, and agriculture.

3. Farm Lands. Especially in the Southwest, farm lands have been developed only at high costs (given irrigation needs), but the long growing season and high soil fertility make some of this land the most productive in the world. Whenever urbanization threatens farms, publics become disturbed at the loss of open space. But whereas much of the loss of farm land in the Northeast and Midwest has been in areas of marginally productive soils, losses in places like coastal California are more significant.

Although the amount of productive crop land in the United States has actually declined by only a small fraction of the total (just one-tenth of one percent of the base during the 1967–1975 period), these *net* changes obscure important absolute losses (Price, 1984). At least in California, the crop land sacrificed to urbanization is fertile, proximate to markets, and already served by irrigation. The crop land gained is more distant and marginal, thus requiring chemical treatment and extended irrigation to sustain productivity (Crosson and Brubaker, 1982; Worster, 1982). The capital-intensive quality of such "hard-path" (and less efficient) farming penalizes small-acreage agriculture (Villarejo, 1982); these newly generated farms tend to be vast enterprises, often owned and managed by large oil companies originally in the land business for mineral exploitation (Villarejo, 1982).

Relatively small-scale farming near cities gives way to urban expansion, whereas larger-scale agribusiness develops on the far periphery. This means considerable inefficiencies in both zones. The dynamic is identical to that underlying the urban growth machine, but in a rural context: entrepreneurs strive to intensify uses on both types of "open" lands, with redistributive rents made possible through public subsidy of new infrastructures in both zones.

Support for this type of rural development is not appealing to voting publics, who are not as sympathetic to subsidizing water supplies for "agribusiness" as they might be to helping out family farmers.[10] Even if people are not completely aware of the ecological costs,[11] they have little reason to support the extraordinary financial expenditures involved. Hence the defeat in California of the Peripheral Canal Project and growing resistance to other ambitious water schemes.

4. Wildlife Habitats. Because of the historic development of many frostbelt regions into either urban or agricultural uses, the pristine wilderness areas of the country are primarily within the

10. Molotch has found, in administering survey questionnaires in the Santa Barbara area, that replacing the word *agriculture* by the word *farming* substantially increases local sympathy for government support to this sector.

11. The destruction of agricultural lands through overintensive use poses anew the classic Malthusian dilemma (properly understood as a needless failure in social organization). The soil of seventeenth-century Spain was never restored after the overexpansion of sheep farming, which, after turning "sand into gold," eventually ruined the earth completely (Polanyi, 1944:34). The same dynamic has been at work in more recent times. Irrigation transformed North African grazing lands into crop farms, but then destroyed even the potential for grazing as salinization eliminated all productivity. Irrigation always entails this possible consequence.

western and sunbelt zones. Some residents seem to appreciate these habitats for their recreational and aesthetic values, integrating these assets into their leisure activities. A minority may even sense the profound need to maintain these habitats as precious biosphere resources.

The same land that is particularly valuable as habitat has high development potential. It would seem, for example, that the entire ecological structure of the Florida peninsula (which is, in significant part, the Everglades) is inconsistent with any further development in the rapidly growing southern half of the state (Carter, 1974; Mohl, 1984). Coastal estuaries and barrier islands are particularly popular as recreation and home sites; Atlantic coastal barrier islands like Miami Beach were, until the 1980s, being converted at a rate of six thousand acres per year. But development was possible only after bridges were built, water supplies provided, and erosion and flood control systems put in place. This cost the federal government $800 million between 1975 and 1982 (Rice, 1982), which means per acre federal subsidies of $25,000. After including repairs for repeated storm damage, total federal costs for these lands were $53,000 per acre.[12] Again, such expenses can help make development unpopular.

5. Climate. At least in the semiarid Southwest, development alters the climate. Imported water, used to irrigate landscapes and fill artificial lakes, swimming pools, and reservoirs, raises humidity levels. Local flora are altered; some allergy sufferers lose the very rationale for their migration. One historian estimated that one-fourth of prewar migrants to Southern California came for reasons of health (Baur, 1959:176), and we presume large numbers still migrate for this reason.

The nature of the new areas, combined with the types of people who live in them, promotes a durable concern for environmental use values. Along with an ecological sensitivity in the older regions, there is a sturdy national constituency for land-use regulation. Indeed, even as public commitment to the other reforms of the late 1960s and 1970s waned (civil rights, welfare), sympathy for environmentalist goals persisted. Data gathered by the Roper

12. The Coastal Barrier Resources Act (1982), passed by Congress under pressure from environmentalists, now cuts back federal subsidies of such development.

organization indicate that from 1973 to 1981 there was little change in the proportion of the public who thought the country had not gone "far enough" (34 percent versus 31 percent) in regulating the environment. Although the proportion who thought environmental controls have "gone too far" increased over the period (13 percent versus 21 percent), the percentage saying that government either has not gone far enough or has "struck about [the] right balance" actually rose over the period (66 percent versus 69 percent) (*Public Opinion,* 1982:32). Perhaps even more impressive, the proportions who say they would pay higher prices to protect the environment have been consistently high—62 percent in 1978 (Mitchell, 1979:18).

Environmentalism brought Ronald Reagan his only important first-term defeat: the forced resignation of Secretary of the Interior James Watt and related personnel, and policy reversals at the Environmental Protection Agency. Even during the Reagan reign, environmental leaders remain influential. Unlike the approach to other issues on the conservative agenda (abortion, Central America, taxation), there could be no frontal attack on environmental use values.

New Mechanisms for Generating Sites

None of these reversals means that the U.S. profit-generating system is on the verge of collapse for lack of appropriate sites. Capital, whether through cunning strategy or awkward stumblings, has means of responding to the challenge. No longer able to reliably depend on local rentiers, capital must depend on its own substantial resources. In some instances, this is because the rentiers have alternative growth strategies in mind, or because a prospective development (for example, a branch plant) will have too few benefits to generate their enthusiastic backing. Or, parochial growth activists may simply lack enough sophistication, money, or cosmopolitan connections to control their highly motivated use-value-oriented opposition.

The solution for corporate actors is, in one way or another, to penetrate the local scene. The goal may be to gain sites for their own particular firm or, playing the role of land entrepreneurs themselves, provide sites for others' activities. Although big capital is not always popular and operates under burdens that rentier entrepreneurs do not share, it nonetheless has special resources. We now examine how capital keeps localities open for cosmopolitan investment.

Activating Local Managers

Corporations can have their branch plant officers play more active roles in local affairs. In areas where the environmentalist challenge has been strong, levels of corporate participation appear to be increasing.

Again we turn to Santa Barbara as an instructive case. By the 1970s the region had become what the *Wall Street Journal* called "a major proving ground for various measures that have held back residential, commercial and industrial development" (Hill, 1978). In all ten Santa Barbara referenda involving environment and growth issues between 1967 and 1983, the environmentalist position prevailed (Sollen, 1983b). In response, corporate executives in Santa Barbara adopted more visible roles in local political affairs, helping to elect enough growth-oriented politicians at the county level to keep the most important legislative decisions favoring investment and population increase. Until the early 1970s, local managers of national firms in Santa Barbara were visible only on the volunteer boards of organizations like the zoo, museum, and symphony. The only exception was a middle-level professional of a research and development firm who won a city council seat on an environmentalist platform. But by 1980, a top official of the largest corporation with a Santa Barbara branch (Raytheon) had become leader of the most active progrowth organization (Santa Barbara Futures Foundation), and helped found the Chamber of Commerce political action committee (Rankin, 1981). His firm was to request, three years later, approval for the largest industrial expansion ever submitted for a local industrial operation. The research and development corporations formed their own association to lobby local governments, support political candidates, and publicize their views on zoning, land use, and the free enterprise system (McKown, 1980).[13] Members of this organization appeared regularly on campaign contribution lists and as members of support groups for prodevelopment political candidates. Without systematic studies of recent national trends in executive participation in parochial politics, we can only observe that corporate muscle is always a potential resource at the local level. Its invisibility at other times and places may simply be a sign that it has not been needed.

Disciplining Deviant Politicians

Campaign contributions are a useful tool for electing politicians sympathetic to development. Politicians need money and in increasingly large amounts. Spending on state and local elections doubled between 1978 and 1982 in California and other regions (Gillam, 1983; Rankin, 1982). In Los Angeles, races for the city council involve expenditures of well over $250,000 for a single seat (Clifford, 1985c:II,1).

The impact of campaign contributions and "the aphrodisiacal potency of corporate treasuries" (Kempton, 1985:4) on politicians' behavior has been amply demonstrated by numerous studies.[14] In his analysis of initiative campaigns over the 1978–1980 period, Lydenberg (1980:1) concluded that campaigns that affect business interests "provoke very expensive campaigns." Almost always, the business interest side generates the largest war chest,

13. Speaking of the political job ahead, an executive of another local firm, Computer Communications Technology, said:

> We hope to involve all of the chief executive officers . . . in analyzing issues and presenting an industry point of view. . . . We expect to take a very active role in those issues that have an impact on the industrial climate in Santa Barbara. There has been a lack of a voice in the community. We want to make sure our side is heard in some sort of unified way. [McKown, 1980:4.]

14. See, especially, Edsall (1984) for a telling analysis. On the other hand, some pluralist scholars make much of the fact that a good share of business money goes to Democratic candidates. But this is misleading for a number of reasons: these candidates tend to be the most conservative of Democrats, or incumbents so entrenched that the "smart money" must work through their quasi-permanent presence (it doesn't really elect them). It appears that corporate actors, making increasing use of PACs, are more consistently ideological than independent contributors (Clawson and Clawson, 1985).

often by ratios of two to one. Of the fourteen campaigns in which this was the case, the business side won in eleven instances. Similarly, Ashford (1985) reports a positive link between contributions from business groups and candidate success in the 1980 congressional elections. Ashford also found that business-sponsored candidates, once elected, tended to vote the general conservative "line" favored by their sponsors (see also Clawson and Clawson, 1985; Daws and Cooper, 1984). A comprehensive analysis of the five-person Los Angeles County Board of Supervisors (Curran and MacAdams, 1985) found that the top twenty contributing developers (who gave candidates a total of nearly $1 million over a five-year period) put over 90 percent of their money into the three supervisors who consistently voted to support their projects. In all twenty-four instances in which one of the top twenty appealed a planning commission rejection or restriction of a project, the board majority overturned the decision of its own appointed (and notoriously prodevelopment) planning commission.

Sometimes all major candidates in local elections receive their largest contributions from property entrepreneurs, often from those operating at state and national levels (Boyarsky and Gillam, 1982). In New York City, in 1985, over half of the major campaign contributors to the mayor, borough presidents, and other members of the city's powerful Board of Estimate were developers. Financiers made up a good portion of the rest. Together, these actors contributed a total of $4.2 million of the $8.5 million raised by the officeholders (Barbanel, 1985:16). Developers provided the largest block of contributions to San Francisco supervisor candidates in the 1984 election (Hsu, 1984:1). In Los Angeles, the two 1985 mayoral candidates were similarly dependent on real estate interests. Of the 1,573 contributors of over $100 to either Tom Bradley or John Ferraro over the previous two-year period (which covered the vast bulk of all campaign money), 25 percent of the contributors identified their profession as real estate—by far the largest single block of contributors. Even this understates growth machine participation, for the next largest contributing groups were finance, miscellaneous service providers, political action committees, and attorneys. Many within these categories are also involved in real estate, either as investors or in more indirect roles (such as financing property and representing developer-clients). Together, these groups represented 71 percent of all contributors and probably about the same percentage of all contributions (Clifford, 1985a).

In the California state legislature, the pattern appears to be the same; even in the liberal state assembly, Speaker Willie Brown received many of his largest contributions from development interests: Southern Pacific, Irvine Company, Consolidated Capital, and Shapell Industries, to name a few (see Bancroft, 1984:1). As Walter Zelman, executive director of Common Cause, said in 1982, referring to the heightened involvement of large development firms in California campaigns, "There is a great deal of money involved and—unlike many other public policy areas—it all seems to be on one side of the issue" (*Los Angeles Times,* 1982, sec. I, p. 26). Among the increasingly significant political action committees at the national level, the National Association of Realtors spends the most, with the American Bankers Association and Associated General Contractors holding eighth and tenth place, respectively (Foley, 1982).

Thus, even for use-value-oriented candidates running on Democratic party tickets, especially if they have state or national ambitions, getting around the growth machine is a vexing problem. Republicans can perhaps do without growth elites' contributions (though they certainly do not), being able to rely directly on corporate contributions (Alexander, 1972, 1980, 1983; Gillam, 1982). But for Democrats, who have few other places to go, tapping growth entrepreneurs, some of whom are liberal on social issues, is a difficult habit to break.[15] And these entrepreneurs, like their more ideologically conservative economic peers, do require policies that foster exchange value interests.

The careers of three politicians illustrate the harsh consequences when government leaders fail to find a niche with either corporate or rentier elites.

1. Dennis Kucinich. The case of Dennis Kucinich, for a brief period (1978–1980) the upstart populist mayor of Cleveland, shows what happens when a politician ignores the needs of

---

15. Walter Mondale's largest fund-raiser in the 1984 election campaign was Nathan Landau, a Washington-based real estate developer (Jackson, 1984:1). Another of the "nation's ranking 'checkbook' Democrats" (Maita, 1985:21) is Walter Shorenstein, San Francisco's largest high-rise landlord.

both capital and rentier groups. Kucinich was not merely offensive to local elites with his brash demeanor (Swanstrom, 1985); his policies threatened their concrete interests. At a time when cities were vigorously competing for federal aid to boost downtown development, Kucinich turned down a $41 million federal grant for a transit project designed to enhance downtown property development. With reasoning similar to academic analyses on the same subject (Mollenkopf, 1976), he argued that the citizens of Cleveland would not gain from a transit system designed essentially for the well-to-do and laid out in a manner that would disrupt poor people's neighborhoods. He also undermined the local tax abatement program, which had been subsidizing national corporate expansion in downtown Cleveland, expansion that, the evidence suggests, would probably have occurred anyway (Swanstrom, 1985). And when a consortium of local banks tried to force the city to sell its municipally owned electric utility to the competing private utility corporation, in which the banks had heavy investments, Kucinich's response was to revive a $325 million antitrust suit against the private utility.

On these and other issues Kucinich was challenged by a well-funded and outspoken coalition of corporate capital and development interests. They not only financed opponents' campaigns but also undermined the city's solvency by refusing to refinance the city's debt, thus publicly embarrassing the mayor. Swanstrom (1981:385) calls it "fiscal blackmail." Others have called it, in other contexts, a "capital strike." As Kucinich said in a 1978 public statement, his demise "became the civic project of the city's power brokers, the business elite, both political parties, three local television stations, five radio stations and three major newspapers" (Kucinich, 1978:9). Kucinich won his initial election in 1977, then successfully defeated a referendum to sell the municipal utility in 1978, and then survived a recall election later the same year. But he finally lost in his reelection effort of 1979. He fought four election battles in a bit more than two years. The active intervention of leading corporate actors and financial institutions, coupled with omnipresent rentier opposition, set up a gauntlet that few other politicians have ever had to run.

2. Jerry Brown.   Although hardly based in populism, California governor Jerry Brown's political career again shows the price paid for deviating even slightly from the growth machine agenda. Although Brown backed many growth projects and supported tax breaks to bring more business to California, his sympathy for environmental regulation was too much for growth interests. In 1974, Standard Oil of Ohio (Sohio) proposed a $1 billion oil terminal and pipeline to carry Alaskan oil from the port of Long Beach, California, to eastern markets. The Brown administration successfully negotiated compromises with Sohio under which new pollution generated by the Long Beach facility would be offset by decreases in pollutants from the firm's other plants in the area (a standard practice in many states). But in a sudden 1979 reversal, Sohio abandoned the project, blaming the "endless government permit procedures" of the Brown administration for making the project economically unfeasible (Redburn and Blakeslee, 1979:1). Although a combination of a drop in projected energy demand and falling oil prices was the more likely reason for Sohio's loss of interest, Brown could not counter a wave of negative publicity throughout California and much of the United States. He was ridiculed as "Governor Moonbeam." Within California, the reaction was particularly negative, with the project's demise provoking well-publicized "bitterness and chagrin" among other officials (Gore, 1979:3). The result was, as the *Los Angeles Times* said in a headline, a "black-eye" (Skelton, 1979:3) for Brown's presidential hopes and a boost to then presidential aspirant Ronald Reagan, who said for all to hear:

> It's another example of where we've gone overboard in regulation without really assessing the overall effect on the economy and on employment—let alone our dependence on foreign oil. It's about time someone in office started using some common sense. [Skelton, 1979:3.]

On oil pipelines, coastal protection, and air pollution, Brown was continuously castigated for—in the words of the president of the California Business-Industry Political Action Committee— "an unreasonable approach to regulatory policies" (Zacchino and Boyarsky, 1982:1). In an action considered by two *Los Angeles Times* reporters to be business "revenge" (Zacchino and Boyarsky, 1982:3), record sums were raised for Brown's 1982 senatorial election opponent. Brown lost the election to lackluster Pete Wilson, a man who won his first electoral contests in San Diego on an environmentalist platform but who subsequently "emerged as the darling of the speculator-contractor set" for his support of "inevitable" growth (Corso, 1983:341). Although there is no way to know the "real reason" for any one politician's demise, Brown's career is certainly an example to other politicians as they weigh decisions that might affect corporate investments in their bailiwicks.

   3. Jan Cartwright.   Much less well known nationally than either Kucinich or Brown is Jan Cartwright, attorney general of the state of Oklahoma until 1982. According to historian Richard Bernard's (1983) account, which we follow closely, Cartwright went wrong when he upset a key part of the region's growth strategy and directly intervened in the mechanism of providing corporations with plant sites. To attract more industry to Oklahoma, the state provided for a public Industrial Trust, which leased space to corporate developers. Besides the subsidies of low-interest construction loans, the firms were also spared property taxes, since their plants were technically owned by the nonprofit trust.

Attorney General Cartwright ruled the scheme was illegal and eliminated the tax-exempt status of the properties. The growth machine's defenses were activated on a number of fronts. The one television station that had provided most coverage of the charges of impropriety lost considerable amounts of advertising from various firms, including $100,000 from the major local bank (whose head was also a director of the Trust). Although the Trust's general manager admitted, "I can't stand on a stack of Bibles and say everything has been white" (*Wall Street Journal,* June 29, 1982, cited in Bernard, 1983:220), Cartwright was accused of "downright slanderous statements" for his legalistic opposition to the Trust's operations. The other local media incessantly attacked Cartwright, particularly the major city daily and a local radio station that were owned by E. K. Gaylord, also chairman of the Trust's board of directors. Cartwright lost his 1982 bid for reelection and was replaced by a Gaylord-backed candidate, who also had the support of corporate actors and traditional rentiers. We presume that examples of such defeats are so common in the

United States, in both high offices and low ones, that they are usually not even noticed.[16] Capital joins rentiers in defeating those who seriously threaten the siting system.

Merging with Rentiers

Coordinating the activities of capital investors and rentiers ceases being a problem when the two become identical. Corporate capital has been changing "circuit" (Lefebvre, 1970:13; Marx, 1967:3:770), moving away from manufacturing and entering large real estate operations on a worldwide scale (Mingione, 1981:38). Corporations such as Ford and Alcoa, along with newer conglomerates like Gulf and Western and Transamerica, now have significant property development operations that bear little or no relation to their other corporate activities. Foreign corporations (some devoted primarily to international land investment) similarly play a major role in U.S. real estate schemes. Their investments have increased significantly since 1975, especially in California and New York City (Jackson, 1980; Ricks and Racster, 1980).[17] This is still another aspect of the trend toward capitalist penetration in all spheres, in which "all branches of the economy are fully industrialized for the first time" (Mandel, 1975:191). At the same time, real estate entrepreneurs have made such vast fortunes that some of them now approach corporate actors in the scale of the economic resources under their control. In 1985, 20 percent of the richest one hundred living Americans (as listed in the *Forbes* 400) had real estate as one of the main bases of their fortunes. Compared to others among the superrich, these fortunes were not inherited (Broom and Shay, 1985). This means that "the distinction between capitalist and landlord has blurred concomi-

16. A still more recent case is the defeat of the eleven-term congressman Joseph Minish (D-N.J.), who lost his 1984 bid for reelection after a bitter campaign in which his opponent received substantial financing from military and development interests. Minish said developers opposed him "because of . . . efforts to curtail development in southern New Jersey to protect the water supply there" (Narvaex, 1984:40). Along with military defense interests, the developers, according to Minish, "made me a target . . . they finally got even."

17. Because there are no meaningful reporting requirements of such foreign investments in most states, there are no reliable aggregate data on the subject.

tantly with the blurring of the distinctions between land and capital and rent and profit" (Harvey, 1983:254).[18] Parvenu rentiers move into the ranks of the cosmopolitan capitalists while corporate interests happily deign to invest in local turf.

Cosmopolitan investors have particular advantages in real estate manipulations that, given the right circumstances, allow them to overcome impediments that might thwart smaller, less sophisticated operators. We turn now to the ways that capital uses its special resources to pursue extraordinary rent returns from local place.

Synergistic Rents. Both active entrepreneurs and structural speculators strive to capture differential rents, increments produced by the relative locational advantage of one site as opposed to another. But if projects are large and internally diverse, they *contain* in themselves a set of spatial relations that can be manipulated to push up the total rent. We call the rent gain made possible by this internal management of spatial relations synergistic rent.[19] The American shopping mall is the prototypical case: the department stores "anchored" at both ends lure customers to the shops between them; people drifting out of the shoe store grab lunch or a snack at the restaurant strategically located in the high-traffic path adjacent to the on-site cineplex. Maintaining the proper "tenant mix" is an important part of the management art. The positive effects of each function are caught by the other businesses, all operating on the same owner's site. External costs, such as noise, pollution, or garbage, generated by each particular use are minimized—at least within the project itself.

The most ambitious effort of this sort in the United States is the new town of Columbia, Maryland, a commercial-industrial-housing complex that provides residences for 55,000 people and employs 34,000 (Columbia Marketing Department, 1983). It was

18. Mingione (1981:38) probably overstates the case when he says that "concentrated capital (i.e. large financial-industrial corporations) has become fully integrated with urban building speculation."

19. Building upon the Marxian rent typology, Lamarche (1976:101–104) refers to this as "Differential Rent II." We prefer the substitute term, *synergistic rent,* as more descriptive.

a joint project of a large building firm (Rouse Company) and a giant insurance-based conglomerate (CIGNA). Its commercial success, despite enormous initial expenses, is made possible by the juxtaposition of complementary land uses, all within a context of carefully controlled, high-amenity landscapes and structures. The regional costs of traffic and air quality degradation are not, of course, paid by the project developers. New town development has gone much further in other countries but under public ownership. In the United States, private capital manages large-scale environments to produce maximum returns, and only sophisticated, expert, and well-financed property corporations can do it.

Monopolistic Rents.   Compared to parochial rentiers, capital also has better capacity to create rental contexts that are unique in order to generate monopoly rents. In the past, a given shopping street, even in the hands of many different owners, may have gained a monopoly status through symbolic connotation. Retailers pay extra rents to be on Beverly Hills's Rodeo Drive or London's Bond Street. Parcels on adjacent streets have sharply lower rents, which cannot be fully explained by any locational theory based on gradual changes in distance. Sophisticated place entrepreneurs can create these extraordinary rent magnets by design.

The regional shopping mall again is the obvious example of the effort to establish a qualitative distinction from other commercial settings, however proximate. Besides its tenant mix (which itself may be unique), the regional mall uses architecture, advertising self-promotion, and often a unique transportation access pattern. A city may have only one commercial spot where its two freeways cross or only one parcel of land between the downtown business district and its tourist-centered harbor. Development and management of these projects are guided by a three-part principle: enclosure, which separates them from their environment; protection, which ensures security for merchants and customers; and control, which synergistically maximizes returns from internal spatial and social relations (Kowinski, 1985:312). It is no coincidence that such large shopping centers were one of the first property development arenas in which cosmopolitan capital became involved. These centers tend to be owned and managed by nonlocal real estate corporations, and to have as the majority of their tenants chain store outlets.[20]

Not only is the ownership, management, and tenancy nonlocal, sometimes the customers are as well. The success of one shopping center, a downtown San Diego project developed by Ernest Hahn (one of the country's largest retail center developers), became contingent on enough Mexican visitors crossing the border to shop in San Diego. Partly for this reason, $100 million was spent to build a transit line to the border (the "Tijuana trolley") to satisfy the developer's condition for participating in the project (Trillin, 1981).

With experience, various development firms have become adept at producing these special environments and are now able to apply "cookie cutter" designs and tenants to diverse settings: old factories in San Francisco (Ghirardelli Square), a historic market in Boston (Faneuil Hall), new waterfront buildings in downtown Baltimore (Harbor Place). The same or similar tenants, known for their reliability and merchandising skills, reappear in project after project. The result is a standardized mix of premium ice cream and cookie stands, stuffed animal shops, and various trendy clothing and bric-a-brac emporia—some with fashionably foreign nameplates. The same principle, in other words, that generates extra profits for chains like McDonald's or Radio Shack provides chain store efficiencies for these masters of urban quality control and place packaging. Again, this translates into extra financial returns through synergistic and monopoly rent effects not available to provincial landlords.

Extraordinary resources are needed to acquire large and expensive sites, to hire consultants, and to develop "up-front" infrastructures. Complex projects must be maneuvered through government agencies, public hearings, and environmental report procedures. At least lip service must be paid to problems of natural environment, urban architecture, and historic significance of sites. Skilled hands must be available to pull in maximum subsi-

20. Molotch and his colleagues compared occupant characteristics in the retail core in Santa Barbara with that in the area's single regional shopping center (operated by Ernest Hahn Company). Whereas 48 percent of downtown retailers were local, only 12 percent of those in the shopping center were local. (See Appelbaum et al., 1974:6.11.)

dies from various governments and to make local publics feel good about them. A track record of past accomplishments helps convince local authorities of the investors' ability to complete the project, and to deliver the promised financial results—especially if tax abatements or other special incentives are part of the deal. Only large corporate development firms have all these resources.

Finally, capital brings to the property business a marketing strategy that, taking advantage of the peculiar conditions of real estate markets (see chapter 2), leads to the pricing of rental space at maximum rates. Smaller operators (the proverbial "ma and pa" landlord) tend to underprice, either out of ignorance of what markets can bear or in response to personal considerations. Often, since they are residents of the same community in which they are entrepreneurs, their exchange value greed is tempered by their use value interests, allowing such considerations as appreciation for good neighbors and ethnic solidarity to intervene in the pricing decision. Capital does not do this, creating further returns through its constant, unsentimental efforts to push prices up (Appelbaum and Gilderbloom, 1983; Krohn, Fleming, and Manzer, 1977). In the terms of the property business, corporate operators "lead" the price structure in their market areas.

Capital Mergers: The Fox Case.   The outcome of capital investors' efforts to create various special rents are so crucial that prospects of such success can alter the market value even of corporations that appear to operate with little connection to the land development business. Such an instance is Twentieth Century-Fox, a corporation created for the production of entertainment films, later to acquire such enterprises as a Minnesota Coca-Cola bottling company, ski resorts in Colorado, and subsidiaries in video cassettes and phonograph records.[21] In a recent corporate transformation, Fox found its market value dependent on how much its land was worth: that is, what could be done with the Los Angeles movie acreage that still remained under its control. Like

21. These details are drawn from the highly useful, alas somewhat dated, "irreverent guide to corporate America" produced by Moskowitz, Katz, and Levering (1980).

the other studios, Fox held ownership of large tracts of land used for film making in earlier days when "location shooting" was relatively infrequent. Eventually, large tracts of land became less necessary, just as adjacent land areas became intensely developed as the heartland of the diversified Los Angeles economy. This is how the old Warner Brothers Studio had given way to the office high rises of what is now Warner Center. Much of MGM's property has been developed as Studio City, and other Fox holdings had earlier been turned into the upscale hotel-office-shopping complex known as Century City. The remaining Fox property has now similarly become more valuable as a site for intensified development than for making movies.

The issue became timely when Marvin Davis, the Denver-based oil magnate (listed in the *Forbes* 400 as the twelfth-richest American in 1985), made his moves to take over the Fox Corporation. The wisdom of the Davis investment turned on the question of the zoning for the acreage in question. One appraisal put the worth of the land at about $300 million, but its realizable values were calculated to be as low as $100 million or as high as $1 billion, according to a prominent securities analyst (Anthony Hoffman of A. G. Becker, New York). Since Davis finally paid $800 million for Fox, he probably presumed that zoning would permit development at the higher end of the range. Similar gaps in appraisals were involved in another Fox property, this one at Pebble Beach, California, and acquired as part of the Fox assets. According to the same securities analyst, the development of the Fox land "is going to require tremendous political clout. . . . It appears that one of the motivations for Marvin Davis to build his blue ribbon board of directors is to put in politically powerful people who will lend their weight . . . to the effort to get the zoning regulations changed."[22] Indeed, his first board of directors was to include Gerald Ford and Henry Kissinger, neither of whom had much movie business expertise.

The large scale of the Fox holdings in Los Angeles, their centrality, and the financial resources of the new owners contain obvious potential for unlocking every sort of rent, from the serendip-

22. *Los Angeles Times,* August 2, 1981, sec. VI, pp. 1–10.

itous advantage of the land having been kept off the market for so long,[23] to the monopolistic potential for creatively organized new uses near the heart of Los Angeles. That the Fox deal went through is evidence that the new out-of-town owners were confident they could utilize their cosmopolitan advantages to gain the preferred local decisions. Through the right board of directors and appropriate local maneuvers, the higher rents may be brought into existence, and through social manipulations, the rents will be set at a level that would have been beyond the reach of smaller-scale, more parochial rentier groups.[24]

Manipulating the Boundaries of Home Rule

Another advantage corporate place investors enjoy over local rentiers is access to state and federal government. This means that corporations that encounter difficulty at a local level, either in generating sites for plants or in preparing parcels for speculative developments, can use their influence with nonlocal jurisdictions to get their way. A powerful method to overcome local resistance to land-use change is to weaken localities' ability to determine land-use outcomes.

The federalist system of home rule, which sanctifies local control of land use, was not a challenge to the needs of capital so long as value-free development was a virtually unanimous ethos and government units could be administratively organized to serve capital's needs. But under different conditions, home rule can become a liability, and new conceptions of local boundary lines become attractive. We agree with Walker and Heiman (1981:82) that as a general rule of thumb, "the level of government is chiefly a tactical and technical question . . . depending on the issue and the interests at stake." In California, ironically, a major turn away from home rule was the Coastal Protection Act, an environmen-

23. This is a case in which forgoing rent over time leads eventually to still-higher rents. For a discussion of "absolute rent" see Harvey (1982:181, 182); Lamarche (1976:107–109); Marx (1967:3:760–762); or Walker (1974:53–55).

24. In a subsequent buy-out, Davis was able to sell his Fox holdings to media baron Rupert Murdoch, netting $300 million in the deal even though the Fox movie business suffered severe losses and the properties remained undeveloped during his stewardship.

talist reform created through popular referendum in 1972. But since that time, state legislation has moved consistently toward favoring development, imposing restrictions on localities' capacities to restrict land use, including state efforts (partly successful) to undermine the Coastal Act itself.

Of course, any attempts to eliminate home rule risk the opposition of local officials, who have a vested bureaucratic interest in maintaining their own authority, leading them to resist intrusions from above even when inspired by their political allies. Thus, when the California legislature recently considered bills that would have prevented localities from restricting condominium conversions, the developer pushing the measure found that even though he had contributed $16,500 to the campaign chest of Willie Brown (the liberal Speaker of the House), who supported this bill, it was not possible to overcome the opposition of the less liberal mayor of San Francisco, Dianne Feinstein (see Endicott and Gillam, 1983).

Sometimes, however, the opposition of local political actors is not enough. One telling incident was the California state legislature's passage of a bill that removed local governments' authority to affect the location of liquefied natural gas (LNG) plants in the state. LNG installations convert tankered liquid gas (to be shipped in this case from Indonesia) back into more usable gaseous form. There were few options in choosing a location for this project given its size and site requirements. It was easy to anticipate that the local governments with jurisdiction over the chosen coastal site, in Santa Barbara County, would not approve the project. Besides its physical ugliness, the project was considered horribly dangerous; the potential of a firestorm with a twenty-mile diameter was widely publicized. The legislation that took away from localities the authority to site LNG plants contained other land-use and site restrictions that virtually guaranteed that the only possible location would be the one already chosen. There were only three votes in the state legislature against the bill, including one from the affected county's own environmentalist state assemblyman.

Similar initiatives have been taken in other states to eliminate local authority over siting decisions affecting the location of power plants (particularly nuclear) and other large-scale infrastructural facilities. Particularly since the Love Canal incident, toxic waste disposal has become a critical issue between local and nonlocal authorities. In at least one important case, the state of Maryland, in order to overcome local resistance to hazardous dumping, has passed legislation that gives the Maryland Environmental Service the authority to override county zoning laws in its search for new toxic landfill sites (Benesch, 1982).

The federal government has also been used as an instrument to overcome local resistance. Federal legislation has substantially altered local authority over the route and environmental conditions of the Alaska pipeline just as federal actions (primarily in the courts) have greatly reduced the states' ability to control offshore oil development. Sometimes the request for federal control can come from a local leader. In 1983 Mayor Koch of New York urged that federal legislation be used to stop local agencies' ability to further delay the Manhattan Westway project.[25]

In the Sohio pipeline case so costly to Governor Brown, there was enough fuss on the national level to begin the process of limiting the authority of local governments over such developments. It caused the late Senator Henry Jackson (chair of the Senate Energy Committee and among the most powerful politicians in the country) to argue that "federal action is essential to speed up approval of key energy projects."[26] These trends are the result of efforts by cosmopolitan capital, and their specific regional allies, to defeat offending local arenas by moving the decision making to a higher level where capital has more clout.

A "New Federalism"

Any national policy may enhance or frustrate the U.S. system of value-free development and thus vary in its impact on capital's ease in finding sites. As we indicated in the previous chapter, federal support for use values was eroding well before Ronald Reagan's election. But Reagan's "New Federalism" or "New Beginning" was a clear effort to rearrange jurisdictional au-

25. *New York Times,* December 6, 1983, sec. I, p. 1.
26. *Los Angeles Times,* March 28, 1979, sec. I, pp. 3, 6.

thority and funding responsibilities to help overcome local resistance to capital investment. Some of these policies were never billed as "urban programs" but they have more consequences for the urban system than the vast majority of federal interventions that have carried that label over the years.

Of course, increased expenditure in other realms (for example, defense) that draws spending from urban use values is, just as the guns versus butter metaphor implies, an urban policy. But much of Reagan's program was not a simple result of preferring guns over butter; federal programs were manipulated to alter the balance in local struggles between use and exchange goals. For example, substituting block grants and revenue sharing for entitlement programs shifts money to state and rural governments, which, unlike big city halls, do not have to contend with neighborhood demands and minority coalitions. This means the money will end up (as we now know it has) supporting growth infrastructures, the only form of urban spending acceptable to Reagan. Indeed, the single major increase in directed domestic funding favored by Reagan was in highway construction. Here he also supported his only tax increase, that on gasoline, earmarked for roads.

The Reagan administration tried cutting back federal *standards* on local programs in welfare, building codes, occupational safety, and environmental protection. Combined with lower federal funding levels, elimination of federal standards makes use-value-oriented programs a double burden for localities. Not only must expenditures come from local revenue; city "generosity" becomes a liability that may scare off capital investors. Local fears increase that employers will be chased away by the higher taxes needed to support such programs as well as by the indolent, welfare-coddled work force that supposedly results. This sets the stage for the familiar competition of meanness in which each locality, if the process works correctly, underbids the next in what it will do to keep its underclasses alive, its workers functioning, and its environment viable.

More than any single legislative scheme, the Reagan-backed enterprise zone program combines all these elements into a single government program. Under the enterprise zone concept, firms investing in designated distressed areas would receive expanded federal tax credits and additional financial incentives to hire the unemployed, including a relaxation of minimum wage laws. Localities, for their part, would compete for federal enterprise zone designations by offering favorable packages with such inducements as property tax abatements, exemption from pollution rules, assistance with land and plant financing, employee-training programs, and easier zoning and building permit procedures. In other words, the federal government would officially encourage and streamline the sort of competitive bidding for capital that has been going on more informally for many decades.

Besides the direct impacts on the cities participating, virtually all places would be affected by this lowering of acceptable operating standards. Across the whole system of competing growth machines, the ante for attracting capital would be raised. Although no national enterprise zone legislation has yet been approved, some version of the program had become law in twenty-one states by mid-1984 (Wiesenthal, 1984c).

Contrary to the purported goals of the enterprise zone of helping the economies of distressed central cities, the first-term Reagan tax reforms all worked in the opposite direction. Accelerated capital depreciation and more generous investment tax credits encouraged abandonment of still useful physical plants in favor of constructing new facilities. Since the vacant land and the most favorable social and political conditions tend to be outside the old central cities, Reagan tax policies encouraged disinvestment from the traditional manufacturing heartland (see Bluestone and Harrison, 1982; Peterson, 1976; Vaughn, 1979). As Vaughn (1979) observes, "Tax credits, applied without regional targeting, generally represent a subsidy to growth areas . . . at the expense of those areas that are growing more slowly" (quoted in Luger, 1984:225). Instead of the city being able to hold the corporation hostage (demanding tax, wage, and service "ransom"), lower moving costs help the corporation hold the city hostage (demanding subsidies, tax breaks) as the price for staying. The competition for capital intensifies as the federal government's role is restricted to subsidizing the choices made by private enterprise within a context that, given other policies, was designed to increase the range of those choices.

If all these policies are carried out in their various spheres, the result is an aggregate decline in welfare, wages, environmental protection, and amenities of urban life as capital optimizes local conditions. But the effort to achieve these goals under Reagan was not smooth sailing; there were particular difficulties, as we have indicated, on the environmental issues. Similarly at state and local levels, there has been no wholesale capitulation to development interests. The most significant case we know of is that of the state of Rhode Island, whose voters defeated by a 4 to 1 majority the Greenhouse Compact program, a comprehensive plan for subsidies and inducements to capital that had been approved by both the state legislature and the governor (Lewis, 1984). So lopsided a loss on an issue that rentiers, capital, and politicians strongly favored is surely evidence of enduring public skepticism toward government-subsidized value-free development.

We are in no position to predict final outcomes of the continuing struggle to determine the distribution and conditions of siting. We certainly do not wish to overemphasize the significance of Reagan's coming to power; many of the critical trends were on course before Reagan's presidency and are destined to persist after Reagan retires (Edsall, 1984). These are the larger dynamics of corporate concentration and the emerging international place stratification system (Logan, 1978). No longer part of the only important capitalist society on the earth, U.S. cities are being pushed, by dint of internationalization, to be competitive—not just with one another—but with places all over the world. This development increases the tension between exchange and use values in the United States. The role of international corporate organization and its implications for the future use of place are the subject of our next chapter.

7

The Dependent Future

Social scientists can't tell fortunes. If they are good at anything, it is telling how fortunes are made. We cannot predict from either natural laws of development or the logic of accumulation. Nevertheless, we shall here try to outline the forms that the struggle for use and exchange values will take in the ongoing competition for growth in and between cities. Because of organizational changes in the international political economy, a city's search for capital is leading to new sorts of urban roles for people and places. But there are also certain political strategies, which we shall describe, through which citizens can overcome the urban futures that otherwise appear ahead.

Although we have emphasized the role of rentier groups in managing the place-oriented conflicts between capital and residents, any analysis of city growth, and of the struggles that underlie growth, must take into account the organization of the larger structures in which cities are embedded. Here we focus directly on the emergence of a "new international division of labor" (Frobel, Heinrichs, and Kreyo, 1979; Cohen, 1981; Moulaert and Salinas, 1983) and how it changes relations within and between places.

In the earlier, spatial division of labor (a relatively simple one), people in rich countries, under the aegis of "their own" capitalist firms, processed into finished products the raw materials imported from poor regions. In the new order, the products themselves are being made outside the rich countries; the dichotomy between the raw material and finished product no longer defines what people in various countries do. The domicile of the coordinating firm, we would add, also becomes a matter of ambiguity. Transnationalization of production as well as of corporate organization pressures places within all countries to adopt new roles. These roles entail specific consequences for the exchange and use values of local people and institutions. In short, to a degree never known before, local interests in place are being shaped by the changing ordering of international spatial relations. This high degree of regional dependence on "foreign" events has long been true for cities in the Third World; it is now becoming true for the industrial societies as well—even for the United States.

The "Foreign" Firm and U.S. Cities

Changes in trade patterns are clear evidence of new kinds of linkages between the United States and places abroad (Glickman, 1983a). The share of the U.S. economy comprising foreign trade more than doubled betweeen 1950 and 1984, rising from 3.8 percent to 9.4 percent of the gross national product (U.S. Dept. of Commerce, 1985:7). With perhaps more direct implications for the future of particular American cities and regions, the content of foreign trade has also changed.

Agricultural exports have increased rapidly at the expense of manufactured goods. A broad range of products, whose manufacture used to define a "core" country in the international system, is now imported, with particularly great losses for firms in the traditional industrial heartland. Although there has been a shift of new manufacturing investment toward the South and West of the United States, there have also been high rates of manufacturing plant closings in these areas, particularly in the Southeast (Glickman, 1983a). Consumer goods manufacturers, previously attracted to low-wage areas in the United States, are finding areas with even lower wages abroad.

The United States has remained relatively successful in high-technology fields based on investments in research and development. Exports of computers, military hardware, and other complex systems have been substantial. Nevertheless mass production of even some high-technology products, such as circuit boards and silicon chips, has tended to move abroad. By 1984, the United States was running an annual deficit in merchandise trade of more than $100 billion (*Business Conditions Digest,* 1985).

Rapid expansion of international trade has resulted in growth of the white-collar service and financial sectors of some major cities, particularly New York, Los Angeles, and San Francisco. This economic expansion is not, however, exclusively American. For example, foreign banks have heavily entered the U.S. market, with 96 percent of their American assets in New York, Chicago, San Francisco, and Los Angeles in 1978 (Glickman, 1983a:216; Soja, Morales, and Wolff, 1983:224). But service exports from these centers—data processing, insurance, advertising, medicine—helped provide a net annual U.S. *services* trade surplus of $30 to $40 billion in the 1979–1983 period (Kristof, 1984).

This complex pattern of importing and exporting both services and goods implies that after decades in which the United States influenced and sometimes controlled the economies and cultures of peoples abroad, now the United States is being penetrated from outside. Foreign firms and foreign subsidiaries of U.S. firms are taking larger and larger shares of consumer markets in sectors in which U.S. producers once enjoyed a worldwide commanding lead. In an important twist, much of this "foreign competition" comes from U.S. corporations operating abroad; this block accounts for a third of U.S. imports (Tabb, 1984a: 404).

A central feature in the transnationalization process is the changing nature of potentially all firms, including "our own." Transnational firms are becoming less "American," and that change carries profound implications for the relation between people and their place. Industrial U.S. society was created more or less as a series of parochial events; local families managed and supplied capital for industries in their region (Davis, 1969:89; Jung, 1985; Navin and Sears, 1955). Prosperity from industrial production in a given region translated into wealth for land developers, merchants, and service producers. There was a rising standard of living, strikingly among the blue-collar work force that labored on behalf of the national prosperity (Wolfe, 1981). It was tempting to take this connection between private and general prosperity for granted: to presume, in the U.S. context, that corporate wealth inevitably benefits all and touches even the local working class.

The trickle-down imagery was always misleading; labor *exacted* its gains from capital through militant organization and political struggle. The role of the State (local or national) is critical here. Traditionally the state has played the role of maintaining a balance between the dominant controlling class, on the one hand, and popular pressures on the other. Especially in moments of crisis, the State in its "relative autonomy" from direct capitalist control (Poulantzas, 1973) has served to channel and absorb popular demands, thus preserving overall legitimacy for the existing order. State action to secure legitimacy results not merely in symbolic gestures toward democratic forms such as civil liberties and populist rhetoric; it also results in concrete change that can make reforms in wealth distribution, including levels of local use value (see Esping-Andersen, 1985; Hibbs, 1977; Hicks, Friedland, and Johnson, 1978; Offe, 1982).

The rise of the transnational corporation makes this role of the State increasingly problematic. These firms are not just larger versions of previous forms, although they do have the extraordinary political and economic potency that size alone implies (Domhoff, 1970, 1983; Herman, 1981:180; Vernon, 1975). They are *qualitatively* distinct (Amin, 1974; Hymer, 1979a). As we mentioned earlier, their multilocationality means that not all production, distribution, and administrative activities need occur at the same site. The local effects of a firm depend on what specific functions, along with what relations to employees, outside suppliers, and consumers, are being located in a given area. The resultant kind of place specialization has existed for a long time, producing a hierarchy of cities. It was always especially noticeable in Third World countries, given their cities' obviously subsidiary role in the international production system. But now transnationalization opens up North American cities to similar possibilities.

Multinational scale means that the range of a firm's operation straddles the sovereignty levels of *all* units of government. Most of the headquarters activities of a firm may take place in a New York building, with the bulk of its product assembly in Latin America, but its legal status may put it in the Bahamas. As with the yachts that crowd luxury marinas all over the East Coast with Delaware as the state of registration painted on their stern, "everybody knows" that location is an act of legal convenience, not a place that is "home."

If a government attempts to tax one of its "own" firms, the multinational operation can present a stiff challenge.[1] Corporations can engage in numerous tactics to protect themselves, such as "transfer pricing." If a firm produces its own raw materials in one country and then processes those materials in another, it "buys" supplies from itself. It can, in effect, set the cost of raw materials at a high level in the country of origin in order to show a low profit in the country of destination (or the other way round). It can launder income receipts through banks in Switzerland or the Bahamas; it can transship goods through duty-free ports and it can overevaluate or underevaluate imports and exports (Barnet and Muller, 1974; Rugman and Eden, 1985). Capital becomes difficult to trap because it dissolves, moves, redefines its internal relations, transforms itself into something else. Unlike the experience for people, "homelessness" serves capital well. Homeless money is liquidity, and liquidity is an advantage, not a tragedy.

Foreign firms have lobbied hard to maintain these advantages, fighting "unitary taxation," for example, the method still used in 1985 by six states to determine corporations' income taxes (Kershner, 1985:9). Under unitary taxation, firms are taxed, not on their reported profits made in the state, but on the proportion of their total worldwide economic activity carried on within state borders. Thus, for example, if 10 percent of a given firm's worldwide payroll is dispensed in state X, 10 percent of total corporate earnings would be the basis of state X taxation. During legislative consideration of a proposal to weaken unitary taxation in California in 1984, the board chairman of Sony Corporation released a study showing that Japanese businessmen would invest $1.4 billion in the state if the tax were repealed (*New York Times,* September 18, 1984, p. D4). The Japanese similarly paid for a multipage advertising insert in the August 1984 issue of *Fortune,* pressing

1. The contrasting view holds that the large size of the multinational firm makes it increasingly visible, thus making attention to the details of its operations more feasible (see, for example, B. Warren, 1975). For reasons we state, size is not the critical issue.

their attack on unitary taxation and threatening to invest only in states that provided a more favorable tax environment. Much of this talk, of course, is mere rhetoric. In Florida, where a unitary taxation law was modified under pressure from businesses in December 1984, none of the promised investments has so far come about (Schmedel, 1985), although other taxes had to be raised in order to make up for the lost revenue. The abolishing of unitary taxation goes on anyway, even in the face of opposition from indigenous capitalists, who like the idea that outside firms pay at least their fair share and who gain nothing from the "almost guaranteed" tax increases that follow for themselves (Huff, 1985:5).

Without options like unitary taxation, governments become dependent on international firms' own reports of their internal activities and costs. This represents an extreme end point in the continuing evolution of the placelessness of wealth. The dawn of the capitalist age released the rich from their fiefdoms and manors; these were no longer the exclusive arena through which people could make fortunes. The small capital enterprises of handicraft and early machine production were still, however, tied to localities that possessed the resources necessary for production (water power, raw materials). Production was typically sited in places near the residential location of the entrepreneurs themselves. With mass industrialization, the boundaries of production became wider; firms established in one place found they could simultaneously produce in many others as well.

With each of these increases in range of movement, there was a similar shift in the government unit that could stand as the "last hope" for safeguarding residents' use values. Under the medieval order, local lords and bishops demanded and received their rents and tithes; whatever redistribution of bounties there was going to be came through their action. We don't argue that the system was just, only that the area of the struggle was small and clear. Wealth was at the manor house and the church. To seize power or to demand reform one knew where the leverage had to be applied; there was a clear site for an "appeal for the use of public power" (Vernon, 1975:IX, as cited in Cohen et al., 1979:10). Under the age of iron and steel, firms could bid one locality against another, but still under the strict limits imposed by physical resources, knowledge of alternative geographical possibilities, and primitive institutions of international trade and finance. These limits on capital movement meant that even governments of cities and states could exact some of the surplus to benefit local residents. As firms increased their ability to locate in other parts of the country (for example, "runaway shops" in the Deep South), the power of localities to pursue policies of redistribution weakened and the federal government became the control instrument of last resort. At least when the political climate was right, the State could still regulate firms that could not easily move investments beyond the national boundaries.

But this is no longer the case. The emerging nature of capital means that however willing the State may be to tax corporations and impose restrictions, it will be increasingly unable to do so (Hymer and Rowthorn, 1979). That, at least, is the prospect. When the State becomes unable to serve as a vehicle for trapping capital (and perhaps redistributing it), it places more than its legitimacy at risk; it loses some of its very meaning. Being inside or outside borders has less bearing on human fortunes. The remaining autonomy of the State is used, not to gain the public a larger share, but to package better deals for migratory capital in the hope (sincere or contrived) that this will translate into higher standards of living. The State, reduced to a locality, can perhaps continue to serve those collecting rent, but it cannot serve workers by responding to their demands.

U.S. Cities as Examples of Dependency

The issue of the effects of "foreign" investment is relevant now for Americans, and we may now speculate on what lies ahead for the United States, particularly for those American cities and communities that will play subsidiary roles in the new international division of labor.

Neoclassical economics teaches that cross-national investments maximize productive efficiencies and thus inevitably devolve to the benefit of the receiving country and virtually all groups within it. The "foreignness" of the firm making the investment is essentially irrelevant. Foreign investment means more people are put to work, indigenous growth infrastructures are built, and, finally, coherent economies "take off" on their own. New industrial cities thus recapitulate development patterns in the West as birthrates fall, rural to urban migration declines, and city amenities increase. Quality of life rises as productive efficiency grows.

Marxian critics, that is, "dependency" theorists, oppose this benign interpretation of foreign investment. First, foreign investing is driven, not necessarily by efficiency considerations, but by the desire to *control* (Hymer, 1976:25, 1979a). Movement into a foreign market may, for example, be designed to kill off an incipient foreign competitor precisely because it may be introducing a better product to the market. As for the consequences on most residents in the foreign country, the classic Marxian position holds that such investments inevitably impoverish the masses, exacting more wealth from the receiving societies than they generate within (Magdoff, 1966). The local economies are "misdeveloped" or "deformed" (Portes and Walton, 1981; see also Amin, 1976; Frank, 1967, 1972) as the indigenous elites squander their cut of the local production on superfluous imported luxury goods. In addition, foreign cultural domination eliminates traditional systems of coping through ecologically sound production techniques, kinship support systems, and pride in one's people and place (Brewer, 1980; Caufield, 1985; Peet, 1980, 1982; Perez, 1975). Rather than reaching economic takeoff, such countries become permanently *dependent*.

Researchers have investigated the relationships between levels of foreign investment and economic well-being in a large sample of poor countries. Chase-Dunn (1975) found that higher rates of outside corporate investment lead to weaker, not stronger, national economies. Other reports show similar results (see Altschuler, 1976; Stoneman, 1975). But such studies have been criticized because they lump together all Third World societies regardless of their levels of wealth or their specific roles in the international system. Bullock and Firebaugh (1984) have responded with more refined measurements of both foreign penetration and dependency; their findings suggest strong agreement with the dependency perspective, but also show that there are indeed variations within the Third World in the effects of outside investment. The poorest countries seem to be most hurt by penetration; those better-off (like the oil-producing states) seem to show gains. In still another refinement, it appears that much of this gain may be transitory. Initial increases in the gross national product, where they occur, are often followed by decline (Bornschier and Chase-Dunn, 1985).

The Third World cities that have developed in this distorted context, often referred to as "primate cities" (Davis and Golden, 1954), are frequently caricatures of the cities in rich countries. Such cities (for example, Cairo, New Delhi, and Caracas) have an infrastructure and job base adequate for only a fraction of their huge populations, with the majority living in sprawling squatter settlements and eking out a marginal livelihood. Portes and Walton (1976:28) have summarized the Latin American case.

> First, a scarcity of capital, investment resources, and trained personnel leads to concentration of the little that is available in a few centers . . . [and leads] foreign-sponsored industrial ventures to center in the same areas. . . . Second, chronic inflation and control of major industrial development by large, usually foreign-owned corporations have led a large portion of domestic capital to be invested in the urban land market . . . and the pattern of rapid urban growth has resulted in sharp increases in the real value of land.

In this situation, local elites become "more adept at the role of *rentiers* than that of competing entrepreneurs" (1976:69).

Although this development pattern is often considered a problem of "overurbanization" (Davis and Golden, 1954) in which population "explosions" have overtaken industrial growth, more critical observers point to Third World countries' colonial heritage and continuing export-oriented dependence (Linsky, 1965). Specialized production for export thwarts the development of a balanced internal economic structure (Linsky, 1965). Tied to the vicissitudes of the dominant world system (McGee, 1967; Sovani, 1964), the Third World nation confronts every international downturn as a potential catastrophe.

The ecologists Berry and Kasarda (1977:397–99) accept the thesis that international dependency and unequal external trade relations are at the root of "massive inward flows of rural migrants" to primate cities. Yet they conclude simply that migrants "confounded the trickle-down process." In our view this interpretation stretches neoclassical theory of regional development in a context that ought to shake it to its foundations. For us, there are two important lessons to be learned from the Third World experience. First, the neoclassical assumptions are false: like capital investment moving among places *within* the United States, international movement of capital does not *necessarily* improve the quality of life either by bettering employment conditions or by enhancing place-related use values in the receiving societies. Second, given the empirical variation of the effects of foreign investment, we remain skeptical of any analytical scheme, whether ecological or Marxian, that might hold urban development consequences to be the same across time and place. Finally, the levels of rents, wealth production, and standards of living can diverge widely *within* cities that are the destination of foreign investment.

We certainly do not favor any direct or simplistic application of the primate city model to U.S. places, but repeat that American cities, like those in the Third World, must increasingly deal with transnational economic organizations. We look for further clues as to what this will mean.[2]

The New U.S. Cities

Ecologists build typologies of places based on population size, on centrality, or on the products or services that places provide in a national urban system. In these schemes, each place performs a useful role for the national system as a whole; there is little acknowledgment that actors or organizations in these places manipulate place to gain special advantages or that the entire system has links to the rest of the world. Places are "dominant" only in the sense that their specialized task may happen to be the coordination of tasks that occur in a large number of other areas.

In our view, U.S. cities are tied to a transnational system whose integration is accomplished through networks of purposive individuals and organizations. We have gone to great lengths to reject

2. As John Berger (1974) has said in a different context, "It is space, not time, that hides consequences from us" (Berger, 1974, as cited in Soja, 1985); we look across space to detect consequences.

the notion of natural laws of urban development, of an unfolding of spatial relationships dictated by a free market that is driven by efficiency. Domination and control, achieved by interested parties, can leave different sorts of people and social groups in permanent states of advantage and disadvantage. Given the increased mobility of capital and the lower capacity of the State to enforce development conformity among localities, the future conditions of urbanization will be diverse, and so too the fates of specific groups within each type of city. The uneven capacity of areas to deal effectively with capital will make metropolitan economies "uneven" and "distorted" in and among places in ways that contradict the neoclassical theories. An uneven capacity to attract growth is the key element in our typology of cities.

In the future urban places will likely play one of five roles: (1) headquarters, (2) innovation center, (3) module production and processing, (4) Third World entrepôt, and (5) retirement site. These types are not perfect reflections of real cities or an exhaustive typology of all possibilities, but are useful categories for suggesting how use and exchange values are beginning to cluster. For each urban setting, we demarcate the underlying economic organization at work and then describe the particular rewards from use and exchange values that lie ahead for different sorts of people within them.

1. Headquarters

The decline of the United States as the dominant world economy does not make its cities unimportant to transnational capitalism. Many of the great corporations of the world are headquartered in this country and the cities that house their key activities (alternatively referred to as "headquarter," "world," "global," or "capital" cities) will remain significant. Although we here emphasize the economic role of these places, we think of their dominance as multidimensional, one that includes a cultural leadership and, as the ecologists would also assert, a centrality in transportation and communication networks (see Abrahamson and Du-Bick, 1977).

Although the precise measurement that is used can yield different results, there is wide agreement on which city is at the top.

New York, by virtually any indicator, is number one. In 1979, 132 of the country's largest firms (including industrials, banking, insurance, retailing, transportation, and utilities) were located within the New York SMSA (Ward, 1984). This was double the number in the runner-up metropolis (Chicago) and four times that of the next leading place (Los Angeles). Even this description understates New York's position, given the large scale and international penetration of its firms compared to those in other metropolitan areas. New York is also the location of a host of other leading institutions in the arts, education, and commerce.

The most rapidly developing national center is Los Angeles; it surpasses strong San Francisco (and is gaining on Chicago) in number of headquarters and is especially important because many of its headquarters are of firms in growing sectors. Looking only at industrial firms in the years between 1971 and 1982, the number of *Fortune* 500 headquarters within the L.A. central city increased from 14 to 21.[3] Chicago and San Francisco were modest losers of big industrial headquarters over a similar period (Cohen, 1981:305; Soja, Morales, and Wolff, 1983:224).

Notwithstanding the rise of Los Angeles and some well-publicized moves to the sunbelt (for example, American Airlines relocated to Dallas in 1978), there has been an overall pattern of sustained corporate concentration in certain major metropolitan areas. Assertions of widespread "flight" from the old regions are exaggerations. Numerous studies have shown net gains or only trivial losses of firm headquarters in the frostbelt areas in the years from 1960 to 1979 (Birch, 1979; Burns and Pang, 1977; Palmer and Friedland, forthcoming; Schmenner, 1982; Ward, 1984). Using a different indicator of "dominance," Ross (1982) found that over the 1955–1975 period, metropolitan areas in most of the frostbelt regions experienced net gains in the national labor force controlled by firms located within them (although several other regions increased employment control at a faster rate).

There has indeed been a net outflow in number of corporate headquarters from old central cities like New York (Quante,

3. Los Angeles is also emerging as a center of international banking, primarily through the purchase of California banks by foreign interests (Crocker and Union banks are British owned) and through foreign banks locating their U.S. center of operations in Los Angeles (Soja, Morales, and Wolff, 1983:224).

1976), but these have primarily been relocations to the surrounding suburbs, where firms still have access to the major business centers (albeit less immediate) as well as to the surrounding transport networks. Certain types of firms have been responsible for this modest headquarter dispersal to the suburbs: industrials, retailers, and transportation companies, rather than those in banking and insurance (Ward, 1984). When firms have moved to another national region, it has again been transportation and retailing (along with utilities) that led the way (Ward, 1984). But overall, in the years 1969 to 1979, the Northeast states still lost virtually none of their dominance in industrial, banking, and insurance headquarter activities. This seems to imply that the most cosmopolitan and ecologically dominant types of firms have dispersed the least, whereas companies that more directly service specific populations have, quite reasonably, tended to spread out along with their clientele.

Part of the reason for the continuing dominance of many old headquarter cities is the geographical pattern of acquisitions and mergers. In 1983, New York firms led the country in the number of firms they acquired; California was second in acquisition activity. Just as significant, however, was that California led the country in the number of its firms that were acquired by firms located elsewhere (heavily in New York City). The major hinterland cities apparently play a role in propagating new firms that are then scooped up by other corporations (see Schmenner, 1982); some of the acquiring firms are in the headquarter cities of the sunbelt (like Los Angeles), but more are in New York (Vartabedian, 1984:1). The hierarchy of urban dominance seems to be reflected in a hierarchy of acquisition. Thus once again, declines in absolute or relative numbers of headquarters in a given city may obscure real growth in the level of headquarters activity of a place when its existing firms grow larger through acquisitions.

Regardless of the specifics used to project *which* of the large cities will be dominant, there can be no doubt that headquarters will continue to be concentrated in certain major places, rather than dispersed to small ones. This pattern supporting the continued significance of the big cities (even of the same big cities) suggests that there is a particular quality of such places that makes them appropriate for this dominant role. The difficult question is what this quality might be.

Headquarter cities are a well-known type (although not called by that name) within ecological models of the urban hierarchy. Ecologists have argued that the large size of such places not only results from their functional superiority but also reinforces that superiority. After a city first develops because of an initial physical advantage (for example, centrality), size alone becomes a dynamic factor. Large size generates a self-sufficient market for the goods that are produced, leading to a rich internal division of labor that creates economies of its own, further sustaining growth and development (Duncan et al., 1960). Thus, for example, New York may owe its origins to an excellent natural harbor, but urban greatness was facilitated by the efficient agglomerations that took over after threshold size and density had been achieved. When technological change in production causes new places to reach threshold levels of growth, which is occurring today in the West and South, cities generate their own internal markets and hence a basis for sustaining additional growth and semiautonomous development (Berry and Kasarda, 1977:276).

In a break with ecological reasoning, other scholars have recently interpreted the great metropolis as a response to the *organizational* needs of the modern corporation (see Palmer and Friedland, forthcoming), and are therefore directing attention away from physical factors, demographic dynamics, and technology. The ongoing trend toward monopolistic and oligopolistic control of product markets, for example, ipso facto feeds the administrative growth of the cities where major corporations are already established. As firms grow larger, increasing amounts of economic activity involve transactions *within* them as goods and services are moved from one plant or office to another of the same firm (Noyelle, 1983; Pred, 1977). The market mechanism (less geographically specific) is replaced by intrafirm bureaucracies, which are located at the major headquarter cities.

Concentrations of services important to modern firms thus build up in these corporate centers. Firm headquarters typically carry out tasks with an "orientation" nature (Thorngren, 1970; see also Stephens and Holly, 1980), relying on supportive services from certain other business enterprises. Compared to marketing in the past, the marketing of a particular product now uses a much larger array of specialized activities "up front." Accounting and law firms advise management on finance, personnel practices, licensing, and international contracting; engineering consultants and graphic design studios assist in product development and packaging; advertising agencies stimulate consumer demand; specialized catalog and media merchandisers produce materials that will generate orders (see Stanback et al., 1981). The American economy's much heralded shift toward "services" is actually a shift toward *producer* services that facilitate the development, manufacture, importation, and distribution of products. Producer services grew from 29 to 36 percent of the gross national product from 1947 to 1977, while retail and consumer services either remained stable or declined during the same period (Noyelle, 1983:118).

It is the producer services that cluster in the largest places and seem to have had the least tendency toward dispersal. As Stephens and Holly (1980:164) put it, "Orientation processes are extremely contact dependent; therefore, the geographical environment best suited to meeting the firm's needs for face-to-face contacts is that of the large, economically diversified urban center." Even though New York City lost over 100,000 manufacturing jobs between 1977 and 1984, it gained 192,000 jobs in business services and finance (Greer, 1984). Banking, law, advertising, and accounting, found in the largest centers (primarily Manhattan), dominate on a national and international scale.

This locational pattern is significant because it suggests *specific* kinds of advantages of cities to *specific* kinds of firms. Palmer, Friedland, and Roussell (1985) report that the presence of large corporate headquarters activities is associated less with SMSA size than with the degree of local business service specialization. Not all cities (even large ones) offer the broad range of producer services, financial institutions, and international connections that modern multinational firms require. Conversely, not all large firms require presence in a "headquarter" city. It is the changing nature of the firm, then, that affects the city and its size, not the other way around (Palmer and Friedland, forthcoming).

The importance of the organization of a firm for the nature of the urban system means we must take a closer look at exactly what benefits are being delivered by these agglomerations of "orientation" and "support" services. If these spatial arrangements increase the efficiencies of firms, then the new organizationally oriented spatial theories are compatible, albeit modified, elaborations of the older ecological models. Places grow large because they contain organizational agglomerations that serve the efficiency-maximizing goals of component firms and hence of the whole system of cities. The organizational differentiation of cities replaces the ecologists' natural bases of differentiation, but an impersonal efficiency maximization drives the urban system in both perspectives.

But if the real specialty of headquarter places is the *control* they facilitate over a firm's own operations and those of other firms, both locally and nonlocally (see Friedmann and Wolff, 1982), then we must reexamine the given theories. The difference between control and efficiency is critical. Arrangements that facilitate control can be present merely because of the advantage they provide for one group of actors *in opposition to* the interests of others. Neo-Marxians analyzing the labor process (for example, Braverman, 1974; Gintis, 1976) have made a similar distinction regarding the work process; managers may tolerate less efficiency rather than create work arrangements that might, for example, risk worker insurgency. This is a difference between "quantitative" and "qualitative" efficiency or between what Gordon (1976:31) calls "technical efficiency" and "capitalist efficiency" (see also Marglin, 1974). If capitalist efficiency is efficiency at all, it is a "crackpot efficiency"[4] in which maximization of control at the expense of production serves only a narrow, proximate rationality and not the productive system as a whole.

There are a number of reasons to suppose that the headquarter cities' control advantages (or capitalist efficiencies) are certainly as important as technical efficiencies in maintaining the role of these cities in the urban system. One evidence is that not all large firms seem to need them; big and regularly profitable corporations can exist in small cities off the beaten track. Procter and Gamble thrives in Cincinnati, Ohio (Peters and Waterman, 1982), John-

---

4. The term is adapted from Mills's (1959) "crackpot realism."

son's Wax in Racine, Wisconsin, and John Deere in Moline, Illinois. Although we have not undertaken a systematic study of firms in the "boondocks," we observe that these companies are devoted to production of kindred product lines, and are conservative in their borrowing and financial manipulations. They do well in the corporate hinterland perhaps because they are oriented toward actual production.

We thus suspect that the energy behind the growing headquarter city is something other than coordinating efficient production, in the technical sense. Instead, the real advantage of such places may be in their ability to support corporate financial assets, only loosely tied to production results. According to Fligstein (1985), corporations' finance departments have become the most powerful component of the large modern firm, replacing first the production experts and then the marketing departments that were prominent in two previous eras (see Perrow, 1970). This is symptomatic of the rise of a "paper entrepreneurialism" (Reich, 1983), which can take a number of different forms. Finance managers can use a firm's assets to merge one firm with another or, in cases of "unfriendly takeover" threats, to discourage such mergers. Observers have long been aware that this merging and conglomeration activity has no necessary connection to technical efficiency (Herman, 1981:101; Nelson, 1959:7). In some instances, an acquisition is prompted by the need of one firm to gain the tax credits of a failing firm or to depreciate (for tax purposes) the assets of a profitable one. Sometimes the aim is to get control of a "cash cow" that can then be milked for still other financial maneuvers. Increasingly, the acquiring firm or investment group uses borrowed cash to tender its offer, and then pays back the loan out of the earnings or assets of the conquered company, which it may badly weaken in the process (this is the "junk bond" phenomenon).

"Opportunism" (Williamson, 1975) is always a force in structuring markets, and the current process of mergers and acquisitions is rife with opportunities for skulduggery by those within or outside the firms. Speculators can set up a merger to earn profits on their stock, which will rise with just the *appearance* of growth and vitality (Jung, 1984). Even if an attempted takeover is unsuccessful, the stock value of a firm that is being courted by another company often rises quickly, providing payoffs to the insiders who made it happen. In another variant, those who threaten a takeover are handsomely paid off by the courted company to "go away" ("greenmail" as it is called), thereby receiving enormous profits from activities that have nothing whatever to do with enhancing productive efficiency.

Sometimes a merger is used by managers of one firm (who may fear being ousted from their jobs) to ward off a takeover from still another company (see Herman, 1981:101). The consumer products company Chesebrough-Ponds borrowed $1.25 billion to acquire Stauffer Chemicals (an unprofitable company) just to make itself less attractive to investor Carl Icahn's takeover bid. Maneuvers in which, in the words of a Wall Street analyst of the Stauffer deal, there is "little, if any, synergism between the two companies" (Hughes and Gilman, 1985:3) have become an almost everyday experience in the corporate world. Indeed, acquisitions of firms that engage in businesses unrelated to a corporation's existing products have risen continuously since the end of World War II (Fligstein, 1986).

Regardless of their wastefulness, these forms of manipulation build the existing headquarter centers because they contain the dominant firms that acquire the less dominant ones (Dicken, 1976; Smith, 1982; Vartabedian, 1984) and because of the local activity generated by the manipulations. Such maneuvers yield large fees to the supporting firms in law, banking, and accounting. The local resources that help this process along (the no doubt useful agglomeration of lawyers, financiers, and brokers) do not make production more efficient; they make control more efficient. The reported growth in the producer-service sector may be one reflection in the labor force of this increase in control activity.

Whatever the mix of control and coordinating functions, the role of headquarters places will probably continue to grow for several reasons. First, large-scale and multinational corporations are only increasing in their levels of activity. The internationalization of production is still on the rise; the multinational corporations' share of the gross world product is expected to grow from its 1971 level of 20 percent to 40 percent by 1988 (Jazairy, Kuin, and Somavia, 1977, as cited in Blackbourn, 1982:147). Unlike smaller businesses, large multinational firms can seek a government bail-out to prevent bankruptcy, whether the firm is located in the United States or abroad, as the histories of Chrysler, Lockheed, Citroen, Lancia, Leyland, and Rolls Royce indicate (Blackbourn, 1982:155). Mergers and acquisitions among firms from different countries (increasing rapidly) are also likely to increase geographical concentration. When foreign firms start up new operations in another country, they tend to be dispersed; but when they acquire control over an existing foreign company, they inject capital into the centers where the acquired firms are already located (Smith, 1982). Similarly, the continuing decline in the number of family-owned firms, which tend to be single-location operations in secondary cities (Burt, Christman, and Kilburn, 1980; Zeitlin, 1974), and the least likely to expand through acquisition (Palmer et al., 1984), will also feed geographical concentration.

A second reason to anticipate increasing concentration is the continuing trend toward ever-larger trading zones. Either through formal institutions like the European Economic Community or more ad hoc trade agreements, free trade eases the way for large firms to invest wherever they wish. Free trade gives the multinationals an advantage by limiting regulation and other "artificial" barriers to their manipulations of resources across political borders. The deregulatory climate sweeping the United States in the 1980s will also contribute to the growth of headquarter cities. Weakening of antitrust controls enhances concentration regardless of its social or productive consequences. Deregulation in areas such as banking and securities trading similarly inhibits the imposition of criteria for technical efficiency on mergers and acquisitions. Many of the results will not be easily reversed, if only because of inertia, should reform regulation eventually follow. Locational efficiencies and habits will have been established, optimizing both productive and control capacities, further entrenching the role of the headquarter cities.

Finally, the most powerful local growth machines in the country are probably those of the corporate centers and are a force in themselves; their rentier classes have the greatest resources and their corporate tenants (who are increasingly themselves local property owners) have clout at the national level. This means that a group of highly motivated and powerful people will monitor and influence national decisions, with an eye toward maintaining locational advantage for headquarter cities.

The dynamic role of these headquarter places is at present obscured by their sloughing off the activities that once marked them as major manufacturing centers. This is a process of "restructuring" (Soja, Morales, and Wolff, 1983), in which the number of jobs declines in the heavy manufacture sector as new development occurs in finance, information processing, and other producer services. Cities like New York generate growth in office and service jobs as they lose jobs in other sectors. Boston and San Francisco, both "old cities" with crumbling manufacturing plants, have experienced robust growth in the office economy (Mollenkopf, 1983). In still another variant, Los Angeles is expanding in headquarters activities while simultaneously growing in certain goods manufacture sectors (electronics, clothing) and declining in others (automobiles, tires). Whatever the rest of the mix, the headquarter cities will have as a growing part of their economic base the activities endemic to corporate control and coordination.

2. Innovation Centers

Research and development (R & D) carried out by private firms, government, and nonprofit institutions are at the top of the product cycle. Their innovations in technology and organization are then applied in other settings to specific and more routine purposes. Innovation activities, although in one sense "producer services," are not necessarily to be found in headquarter locations—or at production sites.

Malecki (1980) has outlined a number of different patterns of R & D location. Some R & D activities directly support corporate decision making and these tend to be located adjacent to other orienting functions within the headquarters city. In still other cases, each plant operating under a corporate wing must have its own R & D facility nearby (for example, a testing lab for raw materials for a steel factory). In low-level R & D, there is wide dispersal of facilities, but they are near corporate production units. Finally, some R & D activities are free of these constraints, and tend to be located near pools of professional labor and other research-related assets, like big universities (see Jobert, 1975). This is the "pure" type of R & D, in which the special agglomeration benefits peculiar to innovation can come into existence. Examples of innovation centers are Austin, Texas, Cambridge, Massachusetts, the Silicon Valley towns of Northern California, and the Research Triangle area of North Carolina.[5]

Like their headquarter city counterparts, these agglomerations are themselves by no means "natural." They are at least helped along by the capitalists and growth elites who have a use for them. We have already discussed the development of many university campuses as intrinsic parts of local growth schemes as well as the recent intense competition to attract the Microelectronics and Computer Technology Corporation's high-tech installation (see chapter 3). But certainly as common as the recourse to centers of higher education (and often linked with them) is the use of military contracting as a means of stimulating growth and development. What we have been calling innovation centers are, to a significant degree, war preparation centers. In the post–World War II era, according to Robert Reich, "the Defense Department . . . has been the center of high-technology industrial policy in this country" (quoted in Schrage, 1984:3). The Defense Department's $35 billion annual R & D budget is about one-third of all R & D activity in the United States.

The military has long had distinct effects on the distribution of urban growth—a fact not lost on local elites. Deep South growth leaders whose areas depended on World War I and World War II military facilties always favored high defense expenditures. More profoundly, "World War II [government] investments . . . provided the basic, private capital stock for the postwar growth of Sunbelt cities" (Mollenkopf, 1983:105; see also Fleischmann, 1977; Soja, Morales, and Wolff, 1983:207). More than is the case for nonmilitary R & D, which is located predominantly outside the sunbelt (Cohen, 1977:219), the defense installations and government-financed high-tech complexes, such as those of Southern

5. Using three industrial sectors (aerospace, electrical and electronics, and instruments), Malecki has isolated twenty-three "innovation centers." But by using SIC codes as the basis for his typology, Malecki ends up lumping together diverse activities into a single urban type; this makes it impossible to isolate the more basic and important research functions. See Hodson and Kaufman (1982) and Baron and Bielby (1984) on the issue of sector typologies. Thus Malecki's method leads to some anomalous results; Dayton, Miami, and Baltimore become innovation centers along with Boston, San Diego, and Phoenix.

California, depend on the war machine for their survival.[6] Unlike design and production for consumer goods, security considerations preclude going abroad, making defense one of the few secure domestic industries (Keller, 1983:350; Taplin, 1984:3).

Even minor changes in defense strategy can have an immense impact on given areas. A nuclear-testing moratorium would knock eight thousand workers off the payroll at the Nevada test site alone, a prospect that was headlined in a local Nevada news report of the 1985 Soviet moratorium proposal.[7] This "vast addiction," as George Kennan (1984:78) has recently called the dependence of so many localities on war industries, prompts many growth activists to prefer a national agenda that gives high priority to defense expenditures and to the specific military strategies that will bring development to their locale. Such addiction to U.S. defense spending is even spreading to European countries. Britain has demanded a share of the "Star Wars" development budget for its own engineering firms in return for its political backing of the Reagan administration project (*New York Times*, 1985). Within the United States and perhaps throughout the world, value-free R & D may be the growth machine system's most profoundly dangerous manifestation.

3. Module Production Places

The urban areas that are becoming the sites for routine economic tasks have in common two disturbing qualities: they are dependent on control centers located elsewhere and they are expendable in the system of places. Whether the enterprises of an urban area are engaged in assembling car parts shipped in from various parts of the world, processing magazine subscriptions arriving from remote parts of the country, or distributing secret sauce to fast-food franchises in their surrounding region, they are

6. Hill and Negrey (1985) point out that federal expenditures generally short-change the frostbelt region, or at least the Great Lakes states.

7. The story's lead sentence was "The Soviet Union proposed a moratorium on nuclear testing that, if adopted, would affect jobs of 8,000 Nevada Test Site workers." "Nuclear Testing Moratorium Would Affect 8000 at NTS," *Pahrump Valley (Nev.) Times Star,* April 26, 1985, p. 4.

not sustained by any of the unique organizational constellations that make up control or innovation centers. Each place will be chosen because it meets certain minimum criteria that ecological theory would imply it must: distribution centers need reasonable proximity to markets and naval stations must have water. But many places will satisfy these requirements, leaving the chosen area in a poor position to drive a hard bargain.

Some module cities achieve their utility through proximity to a natural resource (for example, mining centers) or a government function that local promoters have been able to attract (Social Security headquarters is in Baltimore). Cheap property and cheap labor are among the reasons that Omaha, Nebraska, has become the "800" telephone exchange center of the country (also helping Omaha was excess phone line capacity and operators whose Midwest diction is unproblematic for the rest of the country). Citicorp has put its credit-processing center in Sioux Falls, South Dakota, again to take advantage of inexpensive land and labor (Sassen-Koob, 1984:143). Small cities on the periphery of the large metropolitan areas as well as semirural towns are also favored, as we indicated in our discussion of suburban industrialization (chapter 5), for their tractable, low-cost labor (Storper and Walker, 1983) and the open land favored for building sites by contemporary mass manufacture (Beale and Fuguitt, 1978:157–80; Sassen-Koob, 1984:146).

The military can also make or break module centers by how it deploys its own routine activities, such as troop bases and maintenance sites. The Reagan administration's commitment to expansion of the country's battleship fleet is doubling defense spending in Connecticut, making that small state "the richest beneficiary of increased military spending" (Lueck, 1984:1). Simultaneously, the navy's decision to disperse its operational bases set off intense competition among potential sites. In 1984, at least seventeen Gulf Coast ports were bidding for a new base for thirty-five hundred sailors that would bring an annual payroll of $50 to $60 million, $100 million for port construction projects, and up to thirty-five hundred civilian jobs (*Schenectady Gazette,* 1984a:7).

Instead of becoming the destination for new innovations, the old factory cities of the Northeast and Midwest, struggling for a viable role under the changing economic order, are likely to become module cities. But success in achieving even this future depends on the presence of obedient and cheap labor, as well as inexpensive open land for new factory construction. The efforts of elites in these old manufacturing cities to physically and socially retrofit their turf for new investment sharply illustrate the requirements for module development. Detroit is the classic case of urban decline and struggle.[8] As one of many efforts to subsidize development, $200 million in public funds was spent to clear land for a new automated General Motors factory (the Poletown project). In addition, the car companies succeeded, with local political support, in holding back auto workers' wages.

Ironically in light of the cutbacks, Detroit remains strong in some aspects of its corporate influence over the world. As measured by sales volume, assets, and the number of worldwide employees controlled by the firms headquartered within it, Detroit (in 1975) ranked second only to New York among U.S. cities in international dominance (Stephens and Holly, 1980:176). But Detroit is not now and never has been a headquarter city, even though a number of the world's largest corporations have their head offices in or adjacent to it. The auto companies are not headquartered in Detroit because of any *general* headquarters agglomeration benefits, but rather because of the circumstances that enabled the car industry to develop there—that is, access to raw materials and markets and the growth elite machinations that were effective at the time (Ewen, 1978). Suppliers dependent on one industry clustered together at the center of the "automotive realm" (see Hill, 1984:314). But these firms are in Detroit *despite* the deficiency of its headquarters support structure, not because of it.

Symptomatic of this weakness is the current dispersal of some of the auto companies' orientation activities to other places—either headquarter cities or innovation centers. Although other corporate headquarters often *absorb* such functions from the outside, Detroit seems to export them. General Motors, for example, is establishing an automobile design center in Southern California to "inject new perspective" (Boyle, 1983:1) into the building of its cars. Having a California studio, GM hopes, will help "stem

8. Much of our discussion of Detroit is based on the work of Richard Child Hill, whose important papers are cited frequently in this book.

the exodus of talented designers," who have gone to work in the U.S. studios of Japanese car manufacturers, all of which are in California (Boyle, 1983:2).

Similarly, in the increasingly common joint production between American and foreign firms, the most sophisticated design and development work is allocated to the foreigners—particularly the Japanese. This means that headquarters is less of a headquarters. GM's new Saturn cars, although made in the United States, are based on Japanese design and production methods, not Detroit's. Similarly GM's recent multibillion-dollar acquisition of Dallas-based Electronic Data Systems and California's Hughes Electronics will shift GM innovation activity to Texas and Los Angeles, and away from Michigan. The role of the module city thus shifts more to assemblage and coordinating local markets. For localities such as Detroit, this means that they have even less potential for developing diverse support systems for control and orientation activities.

It is not likely that a headquarter city can be created through physically rebuilding downtown. Detroit learned this lesson when it built the Renaissance Center, a downtown complex of round office towers, complete with a dramatic Portman-designed, atrium-centered, convention hotel. It is a copy of installations that have succeeded easily in San Francisco and Los Angeles. But the results have been disastrous in Detroit; the complex sits amid acres of undeveloped rubble, teetering close to insolvency (Dentzer and Manning, 1983). And too many of the tenants who were attracted to the towers merely moved in from other Detroit buildings, leaving the downtown with little discernible gain.

The future of the module cities cannot be remade by mimicking the physical structures of headquarter cities. Moreover, the glitter of rising sunbelt cities should not necessarily be taken as a sign that they are on their way to enduring dominance as major control centers. A number of these places have also had their growth tied to specific regional resources. Houston's corporate growth essentially recapitulates Detroit's development; the Texan city does not sustain corporate headquarters functions in the manner of New York City (Hill and Feagin, 1984). Instead, Houston's headquarters are wedded to the historic development of regionally based industries (oil and shipping). The implication is that as these industries decline, as they will (Texas oil will be depleted by the early 1990s), much of the local economy will be undermined. Houston will then have to join places like Detroit in searching for a routine function in the system of places.

At least Houston (and Detroit) have had their day in the sun. The lowest tier among the module places will be occupied by places serving as a social or physical dumping ground for production carried out elsewhere. Leaders of three California towns (Avenal, Adelanto, and Blythe) are courting state prison authorities, who "usually . . . don't run into this kind of reception" (Hurst, 1983), to locate a new penitentiary in their town because of the jobs and money it would bring. One rural town in South Dakota has proposed itself as a site for the disposal of low-level radioactive wastes as a strategy to develop the local economy (Daniel, 1984). Hanford, Washington, "the city that loves nukes" (Licht, 1983:5), welcomes nuclear waste as its development strategy. Although these results are extreme, the phenomenon is the same wherever places accept growth without scrutiny.

4. Third World Entrepôt

Another type of city, even more transparently tied to the emerging internationalization of American life, is the border metropolis. In the United States, these places are linked primarily to Latin American countries, specifically to those for whom the United States remains a neocolonial center. These cities typically have substantial immigrant populations and many social and organizational ties with cities on the other side of the border (Bloomberg and Martinez-Sandoval, 1982). Sensing a good growth machine strategy, but not located near a Third World country, Mayor Andrew Young of Atlanta offered to have his city play this role for the African continent (*New York Times,* January 12, 1982). Such visionary efforts aside, the important border cities are those near Central America. These cities have substantial numbers of Hispanic residents: Miami with its large Cuban population; El Paso and Brownsville, Texas (60 percent and 70 percent Hispanic in 1980, respectively); and San Antonio (now the tenth-largest American city, with half of its population Spanish-speaking). In various ways, San Diego and even Los Angeles (in addition to its other important roles) have entrepôt city attributes.

Border cities are major labor centers because of their large numbers of low-paid foreign workers, who either migrate for the day or week ("border people") or take up permanent residence (Bloomberg and Martinez-Sandoval, 1982). The aggregate potential is not trivial; the numbers of foreign-born people, primarily Latinos and Asians, who took up permanent residence in the United States during the 1970s rose sharply over previous decades (see the census report in the *New York Times,* October 21, 1984). The United States has again become the destination of more foreign migrants than all other countries of the world combined. Many of these workers, primarily the Latinos, are undocumented; their uncertain legal status makes them especially willing to accept both low wages and poor working conditions. According to some estimates, about 15 percent of the U.S. work force consists of "illegals" (Portes and Walton, 1981:178).

This labor supply is important in a number of sectors. Some of the Southern border cities are major tourist centers requiring service workers at the lowest occupational rungs (busboys, dishwashers, maids). These cities also need cheap labor for sweatshop manufacturing, particularly in those industries that do best when designers and marketing experts can have their production apparatus nearby. About 80 percent of the employees in the burgeoning L.A. area apparel industry are undocumented immigrants from Central America. Most of these are women (Soja, Morales, and Wolff, 1983:221), and about 90 percent of the firms employing them are in violation of major sections of the state labor code (Clark, 1983:282). Even in the so-called high-tech field, many small U.S. firms (of which there are a good number) require low-wage assemblers. Only the large firms can easily move abroad and thereby lower wage costs (Musgrave, 1975:13; Portes and Walton, 1981:143; see also Soja, Morales, and Wolff, 1983:226; Yago et al., 1984). Those that remain provide high-tech settings for low-tech workers. In another variant, the border cities enable high-tech firms to solve some of their problems by putting routine manufacture on the Mexican side and headquarters and innovation activity on the U.S. side. Probably no location better provides capital with this best-of-both-worlds option than San Diego-

Tijuana, where the electronics industry (for example, Infomag Corporation) increasingly distributes itself this way.

The border cities also function as trade and financial centers for importing, marketing, and distributing imported goods, including illicit materials like drugs and counterfeit brand-name products (for example, pirated music recordings or shirts with alligator logos).[9] They are also export platforms; Miami is the location for the Latin American regional offices of fifty-five U.S. multinationals (Cohen, 1977:218). Money can be laundered or otherwise dispersed in the growing Miami banking industry. Although profits fluctuate with the strength of the dollar, San Diego is a major shopping destination for Mexican nationals living on the other side of the border. The elites of Latin America use these places as centers of expertise, harbors for safe investment, and personal recreation and culture.[10] All of this is made possible, of course, by U.S. laws and administrative procedures in immigration policy, foreign trade, banking, and product copyright, which funnel a massive stream of goods and people through these specialized gates of regulation and evasion.

The border metropolises are control centers for a substantial range of hemisphere activities; though perhaps not world-class cities, they are at least Third World class cities.

5. Retirement Centers

The aging of the country's indigenous population, as well as the changing pattern of that aging, leads to a different sort of migration. People retire earlier with fewer children, and with weaker ties to grown-up sons and daughters. This has led to an increasing geographical concentration of large numbers of elderly people—especially in places with good climates in the South and West. The migrations of retired people in the 60 to 70 age bracket

9. The counterfeit production of name-brand merchandise is now big business worldwide, estimated by the International Chamber of Commerce to constitute between 3 and 9 percent of total world trade (James, 1985:D-4).

10. The significance of Latin America for Miami is reflected in the prices of Miami condominiums, which dropped by 25 percent in the year after Latin American governments imposed restrictions on the movement of dollars out of Latin America by indigenous nationals.

are an important component of the growth boom of many sunbelt cities; some specialize in it. Elderly migration has also been part of the growth in states like Vermont and New Jersey, where retired people can find a pleasant semirural environment, often within easy reach of kin elsewhere in the Northeast (Biggar, 1980).

Growth strategies vary among retirement cities. Elites in some places press for more of the same; elites in others, like Tampa and St. Petersburg, Florida, seek to augment retirement with other types of industry (Mormino, 1983). The ability of the growth interests of Atlantic City to make their city a gambling resort disrupted the lives of many of the retired elderly, as well as other low-income residents (Sternlieb and Hughes, 1983a). Officials and entrepreneurs in South Miami Beach, Florida, are priming their "art deco" architectural district for a conversion from old people's rooming houses to high-rent hotels and apartments (O'Connor, 1984).

Like the exclusive suburbs of the middle aged, affluent old people's towns maximize life-style benefits and services. Their residents' high private incomes substitute for some of the support that ties to kin and more youthful neighbors would otherwise provide. But we know that the typical older persons' suburb has relatively low average incomes, poor housing, and high taxes (Fitzpatrick and Logan, 1985). In these less affluent settings, whole cities are becoming dependent on pensions, social security payments, and other federal and state programs to support the local economy. Fortunes are closely linked to the future of the Social Security Administration and private pension plans. As the proportions of the very old increase, these parts of the country will face the problem of supporting medical care, home nursing, and social services at levels far exceeding local resources. If the federal government manages to make medical care and old-age social service assistance a private or local government affair, these areas (and their populations) are headed for a crisis.

With their longer life expectancy, women will make up a large part of the elderly urban population. There will also be a tendency for more of these women to have been low-wage workers with poor benefits on which to draw. Higher rates of divorce, combined with the drastically lower earning power of women in their post-divorce years (Weitzman, 1981), will also contribute to the problem. As "prisoners of space" (Rowles, 1980), the old will be penalized by local support networks that likely will be both socially and fiscally weak. There may lie ahead old people's slum cities, disproportionately female, dependent, and empty of resources.

Emerging Patterns of Use and Exchange

The different urban roles we have described will all have place-specific consequences. Let us now review these outcomes in terms of (1) rents, (2) wages and wealth, (3) taxes and services, and (4) daily life. As always, we seek to discover the manner in which exchange and use values will work themselves out in each setting.

Rents

Rentiers in all the growth areas—headquarter cities, innovation centers, border metropolises, and the more affluent retirement areas—are the place entrepreneurs who will gain most from the transformation of the industrial order. In the headquarter cities, booming high-rise construction is a symptom of the enormous press upon space by investors. In the early 1980s, New York City construction rates were far ahead of the rest of the country, with new office construction amounting to more than $700 million annually (Sassen-Koob, 1984:150). In Los Angeles, a city that had to invent its modern downtown through renewal and redevelopment programs, high-rise office space increased by over 50 percent in the decade after 1972 (Soja, Morales, and Wolff, 1983:224).

Cosmopolitan investors increasingly replace local rentiers in these corporate centers. Although it is impossible to systematically trace nonlocal purchasing of local property, one recent estimate for Los Angeles (Byron, 1982) is that 21 of the 75 most valuable properties in the downtown area are foreign owned. The rest of the major projects are obviously not restricted to local interests either.

The residential market follows the same pattern. In the growing headquarter cities and innovation centers, cosmopolitan capital, local investors, and affluent residents have combined to produce the country's highest rates of housing price inflation. San Francisco, Los Angeles, and New York are the three most costly cities on the continental United States in which to live (Eaton, 1980). Other large cities with weaker headquarters economies (Detroit, Baltimore) have much cheaper housing costs (with Chicago in between). The other high-cost areas are in the affluent resort regions (for example, Hawaii) and the important innovation centers (for example, California coastal counties and, to a lesser extent, the Boston area). Again, in whatever setting, a disproportionate amount of the gain goes to the active and structural speculators, particularly to the corporate property entrepreneurs whose cosmopolitan stance enables them to direct their investments toward those areas and project formats that yield the highest returns. As we indicated in the previous chapter, these cosmopolitan operators are most able to create synergistic and monopolistic land-use patterns, often involving large-scale mixed-use projects. They thus play a role in raising rent levels, exerting their price leadership in the favored areas.

For those without financial stakes in land and buildings in the developing zones, these triumphs for exchange values do not imply benefits; they mean costs. Even the high-wage earners of the headquarter cities—the "professional-managerial class" (Ehrenreich and Ehrenreich, 1979)—are penalized by the higher housing prices they must endure. For those fulfilling the less remunerative roles, a more severe penalty is paid.

Although housing costs in the United States, as a whole, rose at only a moderate rate from 1970 to 1980 (Howenstine, 1982:10), certain places experienced sharp increases. In cities like Phoenix, Boulder, Palo Alto, and San Diego, for example, the annual average rent inflation was double or triple the rates in places like Kansas City, Indianapolis, or Cleveland (Miller, 1981:17). Urban coastal California, which was at parity with the rest of the United States in 1974, had residential prices 60 percent above the national average by the end of 1980 (Dodson, Fox, and Harshbarger, 1980).

The most common explanation for these housing price differences has been the "excess" environmental regulation putatively found in the higher-cost areas. Scholars on the conservative right

(Frieden, 1979a, 1979b), the liberal middle (Downs, 1984), and even on the left (Saxenian, 1984:182) have argued, in effect, that land-use regulation on behalf of use values actually backfires, raising costs and thus lowering the quality of housing that citizens can afford to buy in the marketplace. We have already presented a good deal of evidence (in chapter 5) that environmental regulation has had little impact on local housing markets. There is an extensive literature on the subject,[11] but there is one telling piece of evidence bearing on the controversial overregulation hypothesis. The prices have been inflated in the western sunbelt zones not just for finished houses and prepared lots but also for raw land (Black and Dunau, 1981; Miller, 1981). If it were true, as the regulation critics say, that owners "can't do anything" with their land (Adams et al., 1968; Frech, 1982:261), then land prices should actually have gone *down*. In fact, the inflation of raw land substantially surpassed the inflation of improved lots *only* in the areas (western sunbelt cities) where prices of all property increased the most.

This general upward price trend of all forms of real estate in the growth areas, regardless of the price direction regulation should cause, implies that speculation, not regulation, has been driving prices up. Active speculators invest in the probability that even more capital investment will come to the growth zones—or at least that enough other speculators think this will be the case to make future prices go even higher. More ambitiously, structural speculators bet that they can guarantee that higher prices do lie ahead, and they protect their bet by helping, in the example of Southern California, to accelerate rates of military spending, promote government subsidies for new water supplies, and encourage free trade with the Pacific Rim countries. For the leading market areas as a whole, there can be no price disciplining through directly observable sales of "comparable properties." Investors can

11. Studies that support the overregulation thesis tend to be based on developers' reports of the extra costs regulation imposed (see Case and Gale, 1981; Frieden, 1979a; Nicholas, 1981; Peiser, 1981; Richardson, 1976; Seidel, 1978). In other instances, the analysis is of suburban towns or neighborhoods, not whole market areas (Danielson, 1976; Sagalyn and Sternlieb, 1973; White, 1978; see also Dowall, 1980, 1984; Dowall and Landis, 1980; Wolf, 1981). For contrary results, see Appelbaum (1985), Davies (1977), Elliot (1981), Franklin and Muller (1977), Metropolitan Council (1976), Molotch and Kasof (1981), Muth and Wetzler (1976), Richardson (1976), Rick (1978).

easily believe, for example, that in places like Manhattan or San Francisco or Carmel-by-the-Sea, city uniqueness makes only the sky the limit on ultimate rent levels. Analysis of the components of housing inflation reveals that land cost increases, not construction cost increases, account for the major portion of the housing price rise (Howenstine, 1982:18).

The federal government, for its part, does nothing to stem this price-inflating speculation; indeed, it helps fuel it. Speculative profits are usually taxed as long-term capital gains, making the effective rate of taxation lower than that on profits resulting from investments in actual production of goods and services. In addition, some of the entrepreneurs' major business expenses, like property taxes and mortgage interest payments, can be deducted from income. And finally, owners can treat their property as depreciating in value annually, thus permitting still another tax break, one based on the fiction that real estate loses value as it is "used up." Taken together, these tax incentives encourage fairly rapid turnover (or "bail-out" as it is called in the business) because these advantages decline over time as owners run out of depreciation and interest write-offs on each given property. The entrepreneurs thus sell each other the same stock of properties (on approximately five-year cycles), in what is still another upward pressure on rents, as each new owner looks for ways to pay off higher mortgages of newly financed projects. One estimate attributes 25 percent of recent commercial property inflation in the United States to the draw of these tax subsidies on speculative investment (Meyer, 1984, 1985).

From the standpoint of improving use values, of course, mutually reinforcing tax policies and patterns of speculation are major problems. Once again we find exchange pressures working against the ability of people to make their lives in the city. This is the true nature of the so-called housing crisis in the growth areas, and not the modest regulations that have provided a small measure of use value gains for urban residents.

Wages and Wealth

The same trends in the political economy that are changing the economic base and physical arrangements of cities also have implications for how much money ordinary people will be making and how much local inequality there will be. We might ask, at the outset, whether those working in growth regions of the country (often in growth sectors of the economy as well) will at least do well enough to meet the higher housing costs.

In general, despite the growth in numbers of U.S. jobs over the past decade—breathlessly termed America's "astounding job machine" (Wayne, 1984:III–1)—the future does not appear to hold either high wages or egalitarian urban occupational structures, particularly for those in the growth zones. The decline of the Northeast cities is evidence of workers' deteriorating position relative to other groups; less obviously, the "rise of the sunbelt" is not evidence to the contrary. States like Michigan, Illinois, Indiana, and Ohio still had higher average factory wages in 1983 than California or Texas (Hill and Negrey, 1985). Although official unemployment rates have been higher in the old industrial areas, sunbelt cities are prone to certain types of "subemployment" (Perry and Watkins, 1977:293–98). Thus the sunbelt leads in the proportion of part-time workers who would rather have full-time jobs; similarly, the sunbelt has proportionately larger numbers of full-time workers making wages that put them below the poverty line. In terms of discouraged workers (people who have given up the search for work), the Northeast does poorly compared to the sunbelt. But when all the indicators are combined, Perry and Watkins (1977:296) conclude, "The rising levels of sunbelt affluence have done little for the poor."

Sunbelt cities may have considerably harsher employment problems than even appear in the data. Particularly in the entrepôt cities, the illegal status of large numbers of immigrants makes even counting their numbers a dubious task, much less assessing their income or employment rates. The phenomenon of this miscounted labor force may hide a substantial low-wage component in the sunbelt job structure as well as higher rates of real unemployment among the people who are there.

One reason the growth regions have failed to provide good jobs for those not well-off may be simply the nature of new job creation in our society. Fifty-four percent of new U.S. jobs created between 1960 and 1975 were in the lower earning segments; 35 percent were in the upper segments; but the "relative number of workers in the medium earning segment decreased dramatically, from about 36 to less than 28 per cent" (Noyelle, 1983:122; see also Stanback and Noyelle, 1982). Thus, although federal welfare cutbacks are also involved, the changing job structure may be a cause of rising income inequality, which began in the 1970s (Thurow, 1980:156–57) and continues in the 1980s (Sawhill and Palmer, 1984, as reported in Silver, 1984:1).

The bifurcation of the labor force is evident in almost all of the high-growth settings.[12] Service sector growth in headquarter cities does provide jobs for women and blacks, but primarily in low-wage fields like hotel, restaurant, and office services. The proportion of New York workers engaged in marginal, nonunionized, nonsecure employment has been rising, not falling (Ross and Trachte, 1983). A similar labor force split exists in innovation centers, where "high-technology industries . . . tend to have two levels of income distributions—high and low—as opposed to the smokestack industries, like machine tools, with their high wage, skilled blue-collar workers" (Thurow, 1984:3; see also Harrison and Hill, 1979). The manufacturing labor force in high-tech Silicon Valley is, for example, 80 percent low-wage, primarily female, and predominately from Third World countries (Katz and Kemnitzer, 1983, as cited in Taplin, 1984).

Worthington (1984) presents occupational and wage data for Binghamton, New York, where, between 1960 and 1980, lost jobs in the shoe and leather industry have been more than offset by job growth in such high-technology firms as IBM and Singer. During this period there was indeed some growth in male employment in managerial, professional, and technical positions that paid over $20,000. But female employment in these categories, which gained equally in absolute numbers, provided average earnings of only about $11,000. Male employment in skilled and semiskilled jobs, with average earnings of $13,000 to $15,000, declined, and female employment in these categories increased, but with earnings of only $7,000 to $9,000. Finally, there were large increases

12. Uneven development thus exists not only among distant places but within regions as well, including the high-growth and affluent areas. The precise nature of this "segmented labor market," more complex than originally outlined (Edwards, Reich, and Gordon, 1975; O'Connor, 1973; Piore, 1970), still needs to be defined (see Baron and Bielby, 1984).

in sales, services, and female unskilled labor, in the $4,000 to $9,000 bracket. The net result, clearly, was increasing wage disparities in the region, resulting from a sharp decline of jobs in the "middle" earnings categories and the low earnings of newly employed women. Worthington's Binghamton results are consistent with Greenberg's North Carolina findings (see chapter 3) that transition into service economies does little, in itself, to boost wages of those on lower occupational rungs.

Workers who lose high-paying manufacturing jobs thus have few alternatives at the same wage levels. Instead, they must take less well paid jobs in the service sector, like retail clerking—a "K-Marting" of the labor force (Soja, Morales, and Wolff, 1983). Evidence from case studies and cross-city comparisions indicates that the restructuring of manufacturing activity has hit hardest the better-off blue-collar workers, particularly the black men among them (Remy and Sawers, 1984; Squires, 1984). Silver (1984:24) reports that in the 1970s "the greater the deindustrialization of an SMSA [standard metropolitan statistical area], the greater the proportional rise in both general and racial income inequality." Although beginning with a more egalitarian wage pattern, frostbelt manufacturing cities that are losing good jobs have an increase in inequality that is about twice the rate of increase in the sunbelt (Silver, 1984:19). A relatively egalitarian past is being lost through the restructuring process, a dynamic confirmed by the finding that places now growing as manufacturing centers (albeit a relatively smaller number than in the past) "still appear to temper inequality, especially for blacks" (Silver, 1984:27).

Nevertheless, regardless of region or urban type, virtually every SMSA with over half a million people experienced an increase in inequality over that in the 1970s (Silver, 1984; see also Eberts, 1979).

There are few signs that these trends toward inequality are being reversed through political or union intervention. Whereas militant labor organization in past eras was the tool through which lower-skilled, poorly paying jobs were converted into middle-income occupations (Thurow, 1980), this is unlikely in the present day, given the weakness of unions in the sunbelt and in the service and high-technology sectors (Thackray, 1984). The growing investment of U.S. capital abroad similarly bodes ill for working-class futures. Whatever may be the *net* flows back into the hands of capitalists in this country,[13] foreign investment apparently decreases labor's *share* of national income (Musgrave, 1975; Frank and Freeman, 1978, as cited in Portes and Walton, 1981:161).

It is very unlikely, in other words, that the new international division of labor in which U.S. manufacturing jobs are being transferred abroad is going to benefit American workers as a whole, or any geographical subset of them. We are often told that this capital migration represents a natural event in the product cycle; the jobs lost to South Korea in routine manufacture come back, like karma, in the form of even better jobs in the headquarters, services, and advanced product development sectors. This is a myth. Instead, the evidence suggests that investment abroad causes U.S. labor to lose wages and inequality to grow—just as longstanding research indicates that inequality and deprivation often increase in the Third World as a result of their *receipt* of such investment. The mere *circulation* of wealth between cities and countries does nothing in itself to benefit disadvantaged people and places; appropriate *institutional* forces are always necessary to direct the flow toward the disadvantaged. But such arrangements are not now in evidence, and without them the trickle won't be down.

Taxes and Services

Local taxation and public services are a conceivable means to better the lives of ordinary people. But module production centers and most retirement cities are likely to be unable to provide income redistribution through taxes, and regions experiencing the most robust economic development are not inclined to tax at a high level or in a progressive way (Friedland and Palmer, 1984:408). Modern-day Houston, for example, has a rich industrial base (at least for now), but low taxes and poor public services (Feagin, 1983b, 1985; Kaplan, 1983). Like many other growing areas, Houston uses the taxes collected to fuel expansion of the

---

13. The methodological difficulties in measuring such net flows are substantial, but evidence suggests the net consequences are negative. For a summary of a number of relevant studies, see Portes and Walton (1981, chap. 6).

tax base, always "investing in the future" (and incurring huge debts) but never providing for use values in the present. Unlike the old frostbelt areas, which in their heyday led the nation in welfare, education, and health expenditures (New York is still near the top), the booming sunbelt regions eschew "doles" that might compensate the poor for living in the midst of so much wealth production.

Indeed, we see in the "tax revolt" movements of the 1970s (such as California's Proposition 13 and Massachusetts's Proposition 2½, and similar limits in Nevada and Idaho) an effort to roll back the amounts that otherwise might be spent for public betterment. The history of Proposition 13 shows what can result when rentiers seeking higher investment returns team up with resentful but well-off homeowners (Lo, 1984). For property owners on record before 1974, Proposition 13 reduced property taxes to their 1974 level, and restricted further tax increases, for them and all others, to an annual 2 percent. Businesses got the majority of the savings.[14] Among residents the wealthy (more likely to be homeowners and the owners of expensive property) received the greatest benefits. Further, the gains were limited to those who bought before the high inflation of California property, people who already had reaped the windfall of home price inflation.[15]

In order to compensate for Proposition 13 losses, local governments received temporary "bail-out" funds from state government. More enduringly, localities decreased social service spending and instituted a wide range of users' fees to make city services pay for themselves, hence removing use value benefits from those most in need.[16] These methods of raising revenue increase inequality within cities as equal access to public goods declines fur-

14. The gains to business will grow over time because business properties are sold (and thus reassessed) less often than residential properties (Hogan, 1980).

15. Besides their regressive nature, reforms like Proposition 13 *misallocate* housing because they provide a powerful disincentive to move. The owner of a modest $117,000 house would pay in 1984 $457 annual taxes with Proposition 13 benefits, but $1,221 without (Council, 1984). Elderly owners of large houses are discouraged from selling to young families, who thus face a truncated housing supply.

16. Localities with the weakest tax resources are, we presume, driven to impose users' fees, whereas the affluent towns and cities can offer free more of their public goods.

ther. But cleansing locality of its welfare function, through the vehicle of tax reform, does help streamline the city as a competitive player in the international growth machine system.

Although there have been signs of resistance (Hogan, 1980; Lo, 1984), construction of growth infrastructures goes on, facilitated by, among other things, tax increment redevelopment money (see chapter 5), increased federal highway taxes, and the diversion of other grants and resources to support the growth agenda. And when special fees have been placed on new developments (for example, for new schools), they seem most often levied on housing projects, not on the industrial expansions that create the housing demand in the first place.[17]

Daily Life

As always, changes in production and rent collection affect the way people carry on their daily lives. The elites and affluent residents of the innovation centers have much of the best of all worlds. Their places are in demand by capital; local governments can exact amenities from developers to mitigate life-style threats. But the growth of innovation centers intensifies land use in previously small-scale cities and semirural settings. The more parochial life styles of "native" residents are overwhelmed by the new social order. Rents rise, congestion develops, families must live with less space.

In a different process, the coming of large concentrations of retired people transforms more varied local communities into homogeneous social settings for the elderly. Depending on the social class of the new residents, specific political and social consequences can follow. Among the nonaffluent elderly in places like Santa Monica and West Hollywood, California, for example, the result has been strong backing for rent control and a "let live" attitude toward others with contrasting life styles (for example, gays). Diverse groups make common cause against the local real estate investors. In more affluent, often walled and guarded retire-

17. This special impact on housing is consistent with most other forms of growth regulation (see chapter 5). Court rulings (e.g., *Candid Enterprises v. Grossmont Union High School District*) sustain development fees on new housing construction because of the direct consequences for school enrollments.

ment places like Sun City, Arizona (Fitzgerald, 1983), residents maintain a narrow range of acceptable ways to carry on.

Life in the headquarter cities is permeated by its underlying economic dynamics. Control functions require large numbers of white-collar professionals whose daily round makes access to work and cultural opportunities the spatial prizes. This urbane professional life style emerges as an alternative American ideal; low-fat cuisine and BMW replace the dour gothic imagery of knitting needle and pitchfork. Gentrification introduces into the central city a specific version of the good life, resembling suburbia in its whiteness and the innovation centers in educational levels. Even so, these changes are only a modest urban demographic blip. In almost all of the restructuring cities, affluent movers continued to choose suburbs rather than central cities during the 1970–1980 period; only New York, Los Angeles, Washington, and San Francisco gained or held their own in this regard (Nelson, 1984). But this vision of urban "rebirth" helps justify, both in headquarter cities where it might work and in module places where chances are very slim, the subsidized destruction of old neighborhoods for the sake of the rent-rich uses that will replace them.

Poor people's neighborhoods probably will not disappear from even the thriving metropolises. Instead, as in the primate cities of the Third World, wealth and poverty are increasingly found side by side but functionally isolated from one another (Ross and Trachte, 1983).[18] Because these cities are not defined by their ability to produce for and service a large *internal* market (but instead by their locus as a center of control and coordination), they càn thrive even if a majority of the surrounding population lives in deprivation. They become "bipolar" places of the rich and poor (Sternlieb and Hughes, 1983b:462). By 1984, the proportion of city residents below the poverty line had reached 20 percent in Los Angeles, and nearly 25 percent in New York City (Purnick, 1984). In the module cities, large numbers will obviously continue to live in poverty-stricken neighborhoods, places whose

18. It is always necessary, as Ross and Trachte (1983:401) urge, not only to classify places but also to disaggregate them "into different types of relations between capital and labor."

fragile use values will be under threat less from boutiques than from schemes to reindustrialize under automation (as in Detroit's Poletown development).

The continuing decline of poor people's neighborhoods may foster social adaptations appropriate to the growing economic marginality of their populations, in what has been aptly termed a "peripheralization at the core" (Sassen-Koob, 1984:140). There may develop even further elaboration of reciprocity among kin and neighbors and informal exchange of goods (Portes and Walton, 1981; Stack, 1974). There may even be new sorts of formal organizations created. This is the sort of thing that social workers like to celebrate as "self-help," visionaries as "backyard revolution" (Boyte, 1980), sociologists as "urban social movements" (Castells, 1983). But it is not necessarily self-help that makes possible upward mobility or transforming rebellion; it is more likely the necessity for sheer survival found among destitute people all over the world.

Low-income city neighborhoods seem certain to continue to have a colored complexion. Without an economic miracle in Central America, the press of migrants will continue to increase the numbers of Hispanic workers, as well as to invigorate the culture of barrio life (Alvarez, 1971). For the entrepôt cities especially, this means a break with past assimilation models and implies an enduring pluralism. In the case of module and headquarter cities that began their restructuring with heavy minority populations, the slum-dwelling underclass is and seems likely to remain disproportionately black, both because of the concentration of blacks at the bottom of the occupational hierarchy and because of the slow rate of change in residential segregation patterns (Denowitz, 1980; Farley, 1977; Taeuber, 1983). Levels of segregation remain high and are present in all types of cities and all national regions, lending support to the assertion that "ghettos will continue to be the primary housing providers for blacks of the rest of this century and early into the next" (Rose, 1982:147; see also Berry, 1976, 1980).

Although less extreme than racial segregation, class segregation remains equally prevalent in both central cities and suburbs (Farley, 1977), restricting those at the bottom to the social and physical shadow of the city. Some make a living in crime, drugs, and prostitution; others work through their day as beggars and petty thieves. New occupations emerge on the margin such as "watching" cars for a small fee (long common in Mexico) or waiting in lines (for tickets or other goods) and then selling one's place to a more affluent newcomer (this job has been around for a long time in Naples, Italy). These livelihoods are not a "vestigial" form of urban life (Walton, 1982:122). They grew as an intrinsic part of the development of Third World cities and we anticipate they will increase with the current development of U.S. cities. Such ways of life require proximity to a vibrant city center where marks and lines are plentiful. Unfortunately, these are also places where housing is especially dear and where gentrification and renewal systematically eliminate the physical refuge of those at the bottom. The result is a pathetic "Tom and Jerry" chase between the authorities eager to socially sanitize the urban center and the underclass needing access to it. This is what gives the center of headquarter cities their particular social ambiance: splendor and destitution, side by side but always fluctuating in the spatial details.

The lack of compensatory wage benefits or public services puts those at the bottom in a special predicament. Unable to pay the going rents and without government housing aid, the ultimate alternative is homelessness—a way of coping that seems at least as prevalent amid the prosperities of the great headquarters and sunbelt innovation centers as in the declining zones of the Midwest and East. Those who track the homeless think Los Angeles leads the country in numbers without shelter; New York City supposedly follows next. Estimates of the 1984 total of homeless in the United States range as high as two million (Appelbaum, 1984; Schanberg, 1984). The confluence of capital and the manipulations of rentiers results in the *displacement* of these people, modern-day vagabonds, unable to command enough money for a place to be.

Cities even withhold the resource of a public toilet because of a concern, as expressed by downtown Atlanta interests, that such amenities might attract "undesirables to the very area we are trying to get business to move back into" (Schmidt, 1984:14). In order to discourage homeless people from remaining in town, prosperous Ft. Lauderdale, Florida, passed a law that prohibits taking food from garbage cans. Without a permanent address to give, a routine way to stay clean and presentable, people face a formidable challenge in just trying to prepare for a job interview. The plight of the homeless is an extreme case of an inability to use place-related use values to advance in the status hierarchy.

Summary: The Next Cities

We have gone to great lengths to show that places will not be performing just *different* roles, but stratified ones. Metropolitan areas, national regions, and nation-states are driven, by those who seek exchange values from places, to make their deals for growth. Success or failure in these endeavors helps shape the status of place in the system—and helps determine how various indigenous subgroups will fare.

The world's cities today are engaged in a self-defeating struggle for advantage. As Mayor Coleman Young of Detroit has put it (with some bravado), "This suicidal competition among the states has got to stop but until it does, I mean to compete. It's too bad we have a system where dog eats dog and the devil takes the hindmost. But I'm tired of taking the hindmost" (cited in Swanstrom, 1985:3a). This is, at best, a zero-sum game in which victories for some limit the possibilities for others. Those places at the bottom of the hierarchy compete for waste dumps, and on the poorest terms, because otherwise they will not get even waste dumps. The growth dynamic in this system of cities informally puts into practice the philosophy of the enterprise zone: to reduce to a bare minimum the place constraints on the organization of capital. This philosophy drives all places down.

The changing nature of corporate organization is lessening the connection between profits and the well-being of people in the places where wealth is generated. This unhinging of the locus of wealth production from the locus of wealth distribution creates the possibility of completely new systems of uneven development. Increasingly, use values will come, not from citizenship per se, but from one's particular location in the two systems of hierarchy: the hierarchy of specific places, including one's country, and one's social location within that place.

Rentiers in Tokyo will do well, just as will their counterparts in Los Angeles or London. Owners of capital or manipulators of finance will survive at high levels of life whether they purchased their shares on the exchanges of New York or Singapore,[19] whether they live in a headquarter city or no city at all. And for those less well placed, living without capital and without rents, whether in Detroit or Istanbul, the differences will also decrease. The lowest prevailing international wage pushes down the domestic wage standard, especially for the low-skilled jobs directly comparable to analogous tasks performed abroad. And capital will try to use this lower wage as a standard for all routine work, whether in internationally competitive industries or in purely domestic ones. While U.S. auto companies were demanding "give-backs" to deal with Japanese competition, California's Disneyland—hardly subject to direct foreign competition—took the same position in bargaining with its U.S. work force (Zeitlin, 1984b).

The new international division of labor implies a dispersing of similar productive activities across the globe. The redundance in sourcing of components for products will encourage a redundance in economic conditions of populations. This implies, for the United States, a regression to the international mean of wages and community conditions. All places are being pressured into this "mosaic of unevenness" (Walker, 1978), and specific social groups are headed for fortunes understandable only in terms of the roles they and their places will play. Location in a rich country, or in a country with an important headquarter city, will not guarantee anything. Great Britain declines to the role of a semiperiphery State even as London remains a world-class financial control point with the earth's highest rents in its center.[20] The weakening of national boundaries as a limiting force in capital flows, along with technological advances that continue minimizing physical distance, means that mileage and legal boundaries

19. "City-states" like Singapore have emerged as major financial centers. Singapore houses 123 commercial banks; 10 percent of its GNP is derived from financial services (Lohr, 1984:33). The commodities exchange in Singapore completes a trading net that gives brokers and traders a worldwide, virtually twenty-four-hour marketing capability.

20. At $91.50 per square foot, London prices for office space were the highest in the world in 1981. ("Four Walls Dear, Two Legs Cheap," *Economist,* August 7, 1982). London executives, rather than receiving higher wages to compensate for higher property costs, actually received lower wages than those found among their counterparts in the other headquarters cities.

less insulate one place from the economic and social conditions in another. Wealth streams move laterally among elites wherever they may be.

Making the Future

Current urban arrangements, we now know, are not there simply because they maximize efficiency, or because they follow a uniform pattern of capitalist exploitation. Instead, they represent the physical and social consequences of cumulative strivings by capitalists bent on profit, rentiers seeking property returns, and neighborhood groups striving for use values from place. Each group, within its limits, has left no stone unturned in the attempt to mobilize and manipulate every political, cultural, and economic institution on its behalf. The city, the meeting ground of these activities, is the result of all this work and will be modified, transformed, or undone through similar efforts in the future.

Based on our repeated statements that the markets in capitalist societies do not work as they are "supposed" to, and that the markets in urban property are especially fictitious, we can see that whatever good and goods the present system delivers are not coming through a free market. Nor could they be. This means that the issue of whether or not to intervene, as a principle, can be dispensed with. The only issue is the form intervention might take and the goal it might serve.

Any program of serious reform must wind down the growth machine system through which places (towns, regions, and nations) contort their cultural, physical, and social agendas in order to attract capital. In essence, U.S. cities must stop competing among themselves for capital and use their relatively high levels of legal autonomy to compete as a collective force against the growth machine system that has captured them all. Is this possible to do? It is often said, by both politicians and academic analysts (for example, Peterson, 1981), that attracting capital is the only mechanism through which places can sustain themselves. If so, is reform possible only through transformation at the national level with local politics largely irrelevant to the future of use values?

As the blunted careers of uncooperative politicians and the frustrations of thwarted environmentalists make clear, the opposition will be formidable, but we think there is room for maneuver. We have argued repeatedly that development damages localities, hurting their poor, their middle classes, sometimes even their rentiers and elites. It frequently also undermines the fiscal well-being of urban governments. Many localities, we are saying, can afford to "toughen up" in their dealings with capital. There is no logic that drives these growth policies foward; it is a political situation.

The Beginning: Upping the Ante for Growth

While all places can, in principle, change the conditions they impose on capital for the right to a site, citizens in certain cities are more strategically placed than others to begin this process. These are the locations to which we look for the vanguard actions that might change the urban system.

The places that need to make the first and most strident moves are those whose politics tend to receive the least attention from urban analysts: the privileged zones most attractive to capital. Some of these areas are often considered almost problem free, despite the high rates of poverty, environmental destruction, and severe labor exploitation within them. Attention to these problems can help mobilize people against value-free development. Affluent professionals, especially in the lower-density innovation centers, recognize the life-style damage of the continuing press for intensified land use. Wage earners are squeezed by the increasing rents that speculation exacts from their paychecks.

Just as the sweatshops of Asia tend to set the world standard for conditions of routine assembly, the most privileged U.S. places set the terms for how much capital is going to have to pay to operate at the top of the product cycle. Some California cities— San Francisco, Santa Barbara, Santa Monica—are beginning to require industrial developers to offset increasing housing demand with subsidies for low or middle income housing. Such policies create, in effect, a development tax—a tax that, if high enough, may deflect development to other zones. In 1985, San Francisco imposed five separate development fees on high-rise office construction, to support child care, transit, housing, open space, and public arts (Smith, 1985:16). The city also imposed an annual growth limit in high-rise office construction of 950,000 square feet.[21] The city did not overlook the role of the military. During the same year, San Francisco formally opposed basing the battleship Missouri in San Francisco Bay, rejecting its $50 to $60 million annual contribution to the local economy on social and cultural grounds (Harnet, 1985).

Only when they test their options can places, like people, discover what the real possibilities may be; otherwise they cannot overcome the "anticipatory anxiety" (Garfinkel, 1967:70) that keeps them ignorant of the range of their freedom. For all its publicized "overregulation" during the intense 1972–1977 reform period, California added more manufacturing jobs to its economy in those years than any other state (Duerksen, 1982). Localities not only can often "get away" with controls over the physical environment, they also can sometimes make stipulations regarding labor conditions. Thus, for example, to settle a citizens-labor group court case, the town of Vacaville, California, imposed new labor conditions upon a firm relocating to its redevelopment zone from another city. Vacaville agreed to insist that such firms provide a year's notice of plant closure to current employees, comply with high affirmative action standards in choosing new employees, and negotiate with the same union that had represented workers at the old plant (Wiesenthal, 1984a). Similarly, Clarke (n.d.) reports that localities as low in the hierarchy as Schenectady, New York, and Newark, New Jersey, have successfully demanded concessions from developers, like employment guarantees and partial city ownership of new private projects. There are no doubt limits to how far places on the lower levels in the place hierarchy can go and still win their plants; we also don't know what Schenectady and Newark had to give in order to win their concessions. But these examples indicate that governments in many sorts of places may be able to make gains, albeit of different sorts, that they routinely fail to seek. They fall victim to the local growth machines, which eagerly sustain the anxiety that locality will fall apart if capital is for any reason displeased.

The best way for the hands of the weak to gain strength is for

21. The city exempted buildings with less than fifty thousand square feet, a policy that may merely lead to an increase in low-rise buildings rather than blocking new construction.

the privileged places to get tougher. By squeezing capital's locational options from the top, residents can force firms to move down the place hierarchy in their search for satisfactory sites. This will strengthen the bargaining position at each place below, and each place, by imposing its own tougher criteria, will have the same effect on places still lower. All places will gain through this process, even places at the bottom of the hierarchy that must make the most deleterious deals. This is a trickle-down we can believe in. This general strategy of getting tough with capital does not, we reemphasize, require bluffing. It only demands that localities do in fact act in their own fiscal and social interests. That simple move would be sufficient to set off a dramatic reverberation throughout the urban system.

Dealing with the Third World

The strategy outlined above could flounder on the dilemmas arising from internationalization: the capacities of firms to escape even national boundaries and to play places in one nation against places in others. How can localities increase use values if they are locked in competition with other localities across the world? Isn't there a long-term prospect that so much production assigned to the Third World will spell disaster for the entire U.S. economy?

The good deals that Detroit and Atlantic City give to corporate investors are nothing compared to the deals offered in Seoul, Ankara, or Bhopal. One reason for this is the historic subjugation of these places by the powerful States and corporations of Europe and the United States. The Third World rentier and commercial classes, to a substantial degree *created* by this cross-world penetration, join in the subjugation process providing for easy capital access (Hymer, 1979a, 1979b). Ruling through their derived legitimacy (or brutal dictatorships), they keep the costs of development low. U.S. policy, in particular, has been assiduously devoted over the last century to lowering the costs of capital investment abroad even to the point of undermining the governments of those countries that might thwart investment (Tanzer, 1968). Value-free development was *imposed* on the Third World; an army of anthropologists and historians can testify to the brutal, deceitful, and totalitarian methods that were used to establish it as ideology and material fact. If capital had to pay for proper wages and social programs in Third World places, "proper" as defined by indigenous progressive social elements as opposed to rentiers, generals, and commercial elites, the results would likely be higher use values for people both at home and abroad.

The upshot for our purposes is clear: anything that can be done to cause other governments to raise the costs of foreign investment will perforce limit the degree of capital flight from the United States. Such limits will diminish the capacity of capital to threaten the paychecks and social wages of American workers and to demand subsidies from local U.S. governments as the price of their investments. In other words, American workers and their union representatives should, following this analysis, support progressive movements in the Third World, not only out of common decency but also to protect their own jobs and communities.

The organization of capital beyond the scale even of nations means that the futures of individual places cannot be decided solely by the struggles within their own borders. The choices that are made in cities at the top of the hierarchy will affect the terms of conflict in the module production centers in the United States and around the world. Conversely the deals that are made in Brazil and South Korea will have ramifications back up the ladder. People have to recognize, as all true ecologists have long known, that we live in a profoundly interdependent system.

Appelbaum (1977:49) has aptly warned, "The future is made, not predicted." Fortunes are always up for grabs. In this book we have tried to show how the running trends, if left more or less on their present course, will work themselves out. But people *can* capture control over the places in which they live and critically judge the value of what they make and the community conditions under which they produce it. By doing this consistently over time and place, diverse urban peoples can together build better lives.

References

Abraham, Nabeel. 1983. "Political Conflict and Factionalism among Yemeni Immigrants: Some Theoretical Considerations on the Role of Ideology in Factional Disputes." Paper presented at the 78th annual meeting of the American Sociological Association, Detroit, Michigan, August 31–September 4.

Abraham, Sameer Y., and Nabeel Abraham (eds.). 1983. *Arabs in a New World: Studies on Arab-American Communities*. Detroit, Mich.: Wayne State University, Center for Urban Studies.

Abrahamson, Julia. 1959. *A Neighborhood Finds Itself*. New York: Harper.

Abrahamson, Mark, and Michael A. DuBick. 1977. "Patterns of Urban Dominance." *American Sociological Review* 42(5):756–768.

Adams, F. Gerald, Grace Milgran, Edward Green, and Christine Mansfield. 1968. "Undeveloped Land Prices during Urbanization: A Micro-Empirical Case Study over Time." *Review of Economics and Statistics* 50(May):248–258.

Advisory Commission on Intergovernmental Relations. 1965. *Metropolitan Social and Economic Disparities: Implications for Intergovernmental Relations in Central Cities and Suburbs*. Washington, D.C.: Government Printing Office.

Advisory Commission on Intergovernmental Relations. 1967. *State-Local Taxation and Industrial Location*. Washington, D.C.: Government Printing Office.

Agger, Robert, Daniel Goldrich, and Bert E. Swanson. 1964. *The Rulers and the Ruled: Political Power and Impotence in American Communities*. New York: Wiley.

Agnew, John A. 1978. "Market Relations and Locational Conflict in Cross-National Perspective." Pp. 128–143 in Kevin R. Cox (ed.), *Urbanization and Conflict in Market Societies*. Chicago: Maaroufa Press.

Ahlers, D. M. 1977. "A New Look at U.S. Commercial Banking." *Executive* 3(2):8–22.

Aiken, Michael. 1983. "Comments on Kasarda's 'Entry Level Jobs, Mobility, and Minority Unemployment.'" Albany Conference on Urban Theory and National Urban Policy for the 1980s, Albany, New York, April 8–9. Photocopy.

Albrecht, Don, Gordon Bultena, and Eric O. Hoiberg. Forthcoming. "Constituency of the Antigrowth Movement: A Comparison of the Growth Orientations of Urban Status Groups." *Urban Affairs Quarterly*.

Alexander, Herbert E. 1972. *Money in Politics*. Washington D.C.: Public Affairs Press.

Alexander, Herbert. 1980. *Financing Politics: Money, Elections and Political Reform*. 2d ed. Washington, D.C.: Congressional Quarterly Press.

Alexander, Herbert. 1983. *Financing the 1980 Election*. Lexington, Mass.: D. C. Heath.

Alexander, Rodney, and Elisabeth Sapery. 1973. *The Shortchanged: Women and Minorities in Banking*. New York: Dunellen.

Alford, Robert, and Roger Friedland. 1975. "Political Participation and Public Policy." *Annual Review of Sociology* 1:429–479.

Alford, Robert, and Eugene Lee. 1968. "Voting Turnout in American Cities." *American Political Science Review* 67:796–813.

Alihan, Milla A. 1938. *Social Ecology*. New York: Columbia University Press.

Alinsky, Saul D. 1969. *Reveille for Radicals*. New York: Vintage.

Allen, Robert L. 1970. *Black Awakening in Capitalist America*. Garden City, N.Y.: Anchor.

Allen, Robert L. 1974. *Reluctant Reformers: Racism and Social Reform Movements in the United States*. Washington, D.C.: Howard University Press.

Alonso, William. 1960. "A Theory of the Urban Land Market." *Papers and Proceedings of the Regional Science Association* 6:149–157.

Alonso, William. 1964. *Location and Land Use*. Cambridge, Mass.: Harvard University Press.

Alonso, William. 1973. "Urban Zero Population Growth." *Daedalus* 102(4):191–206.

Altschuler, Lawrence R. 1976. "Satellization and Stagnation in Latin America." *International Studies Quarterly* 20:39–82.

Alvarez, Rodolfo. 1971. "The Unique Psycho-Historical Experience of the Mexican People." *Social Science Quarterly* 52(1):15–29.

Amin, Samir. 1974. *Accumulation on a World Scale,* vol. 1. New York: Monthly Review Press.

Amin, Samir. 1976. *Unequal Development: An Essay on the Social Formations of Peripheral Capitalism,* trans. B. Pearce. New York: Monthly Review Press.

Anderson, Elijah. 1976. *A Place on the Corner.* Chicago: University of Chicago Press.

Ann Arbor, Michigan, Planning Department. 1972. *The Ann Arbor Growth Study.* Ann Arbor, Mich.: City Planning Department.

Anton, Thomas. 1975. *Governing Greater Stockholm: A Study of Policy Development and System Change.* Berkeley and Los Angeles: University of California Press.

Apilado, Vincent P. 1971. "Corporate-Government Interplay: The Era of Industrial Aid Finance." *Urban Affairs Quarterly* 7(2):219–241.

Appelbaum, Richard P. 1977. "The Future Is Made, Not Predicted—Technocratic Planners vs. Public Interests." *Society* 14(4):45–53.

Appelbaum, Richard P. 1978. *Size, Growth and U.S. Cities.* New York: Praeger.

Appelbaum, Richard P. 1984. "Analysis of HUD Report on Homelessness in America. Testimony in Hearings before House Subcommittee on Banking and Finance." May 24. Washington, D.C.: Government Printing Office.

Appelbaum, Richard P. 1985. "Regulation and the Santa Barbara Housing Market." Report to the California Policy Seminar, Department of Sociology, University of California, Santa Barbara.

Appelbaum, Richard P. Forthcoming. "Swedish Housing in the Postwar Period." *Urban Affairs Quarterly.*

Appelbaum, Richard P., Jennifer Bigelow, Henry Kramer, Harvey Molotch, and Paul Relis. 1974. *Santa Barbara: The Impacts of Growth.* Santa Barbara, Calif.: Office of the City Clerk.

Appelbaum, Richard P., Jennifer Bigelow, Henry Kramer, Harvey Molotch, and Paul Relis. 1976. *The Effects of Urban Growth.* New York: Praeger.

Appelbaum, Richard P., and John Gilderbloom. 1983. "Housing Supply and Regulation: A Study of the Rental Housing Market." *Journal of Applied Behavioral Science* 19(1):1–18.

Aronson, J. Richard, and Eli Schwartz. 1973. "Financing Public Goods and Their Distribution in a System of Local Government." *National Tax Journal* 26(2):137–160.

Ashford, Kathryn L. 1985. "The Role of Corporations in the 1980 U.S. Congressional Elections." Paper presented at the 80th annual meeting of the American Sociological Association, Washington, D.C., August 26–30.

Ashton, Patrick. 1984. "Urbanization and the Dynamics of Suburban Development under Capitalism." Pp. 54–81 in William Tabb and Larry Sawers (eds.), *Marxism and the Metropolis*. New York: Oxford University Press.

Averitt, Robert T. 1968. *The Dual Economy*. New York: Norton.

Babcock, Richard F. 1969. *The Zoning Game*. Madison: University of Wisconsin Press.

Babcock, Richard F. 1982. "Houston: Unzoned, Unfettered, and Mostly Unrepentant." *Planning* 48(3):21–23.

Baca Zinn, Maxine. 1980. "Employment and Education of Mexican American Women: The Interplay of Modernity and Ethnicity in Eight Families." *Harvard Educational Review* 50(1):47–62.

Bachrach, Peter, and Morton Baratz. 1962. "The Two Faces of Power." *American Political Science Review* 56:947–952.

Bagdikian, Ben. 1983. *The Media Monopoly*. Boston: Beacon Press.

Baldasarre, Mark, and William Protash. 1982. "Growth Controls, Population Growth and Community Satisfaction." *American Sociological Review* 47(June):339–346.

Balk, Alfred. 1966. "Invitation to Bribery." *Harper's* 233(October): 18–24.

Bancroft, Ann. 1984. "Willie Brown Raises $2.5 Million War Chest." *San Francisco Chronicle*, October 25, p. 1.

Banfield, Edward C. 1961. *Political Influence*. New York: Macmillan.

Banfield, Edward C., and James Q. Wilson. 1963. *City Politics*. Cambridge, Mass.: Harvard University Press.

Barbanel, Josh. 1985. "Abundant Political Gifts by Developers Faulted." *New York Times*, November 27, p. 16.

Barnet, Richard J., and Ronald E. Muller. 1974. *Global Reach: The Power of the Multinational Corporations*. New York: Simon and Schuster.

Baron, James N., and William T. Bielby. 1980. "Bringing the Firms Back In: Stratification, Segmentation, and the Organization of Work." *American Sociological Review* 45(5):737–765.

Baron, James N., and William T. Bielby. 1984. "The Organization of Work in a Segmented Economy." *American Sociological Review* 49(4):454–473.

Barron, James. 1985. "Kentuckians Unsettled by Nerve Gas Disposal." *New York Times,* March 13, sec. A, p. 12.

Baur, John. 1959. *The Health Seekers of Southern California.* San Marino, Calif.: Huntington Library.

Beale, C. L., and Glen Fuguitt. 1978. "Population Trends in Nonmetropolitan Cities and Villages in Subregions of the United States." *Demography* 15(4):605–620.

Becker, Howard. 1967. "Whose Side Are We On?" *Social Problems* 14(Winter):239–247.

Belcher, Wyatt W. 1947. *The Economic Rivalry between St. Louis and Chicago, 1850–1880.* New York: Columbia University Press.

Bell, Daniel. 1961. "Crime as an American Way of Life." Pp. 127–150 in Daniel Bell, *The End of Ideology: On the Exhaustion of Political Ideas in the Fifties.* New York: Collier Books.

Bender, Thomas. 1983. "The End of the City?" *Democracy* 3(1):8–20.

Benesch, Jane. 1982. "Marylanders Battle Landfill Siting." *Re:Sources* 4(4):4.

Benveniste, Guy. 1981. *Regulations and Planning: The Case of Environmental Politics.* San Francisco: Boyd and Fraser.

Berger, Bennett. 1960. *Working Class Suburb.* Berkeley and Los Angeles: University of California Press.

Berger, John. 1974. *The Look of Things.* New York: Viking Press.

Berk, Sarah F. 1985. *The Gender Factory.* New York: Plenum.

Berk, Sarah F., and Anthony Shih. 1980. "Contribution to Household Labor: Comparing Wives' and Husbands' Reports." Pp. 191–228 in Sarah Fenstermaker Berk (ed.), *Women and Household Labor.* Beverly Hills, Calif.: Sage.

Berkenbosch, Jan. 1985. "Senior Fellow Compares Regional Planning Practices in the Netherlands and the U.S." *Metroline* (Center for Metropolitan Planning and Research at Johns Hopkins University) 13(7):1, 3.

Bernard, Richard M. 1983. "Oklahoma City: Booming Schooner." Pp. 213–234 in Richard M. Bernard and Bradley R. Rice (eds.), *Sunbelt Cities: Politics and Growth since World War II.* Austin: University of Texas Press.

Bernard, Richard M., and Bradley R. Rice (eds.). 1983. *Sunbelt Cities: Politics and Growth since World War II.* Austin: University of Texas Press.

Berry, Brian J. L. 1976. "Ghetto Expansion and Single-Family Housing Prices: Chicago 1968–1972." *Journal of Urban Economics* 3:397–423.

Berry, Brian J. L. (ed.). 1977. *The Social Burdens of Environmental*

Pollution: A Comparative Metropolitan Data Source. Cambridge, Mass.: Ballinger.

Berry, Brian J. L. 1980. "Inner City Futures: An American Dilemma Revisited." *Transactions of the Institute of British Geographers* 5: 1–30.

Berry, Brian J. L., and John Kasarda. 1977. *Contemporary Urban Ecology.* New York: Macmillan.

Betz, D. Michael. 1972. "The City as a System Generating Income Inequality." *Social Forces* 51(2):192–198.

Bianchi, Suzanne, Reynolds Farley, and D. Spain. 1982. "Racial Inequalities in Housing: An Examination of Recent Trends." *Demography* 19(1):37–51.

Biggar, Jeanne C. 1980. "Reassessing Elderly Sunbelt Migration." *Research on Aging* 2:177–190.

Binford, Henry C. 1985. *The First Suburbs: Residential Communities on the Boston Periphery 1815–1860.* Chicago: University of Chicago Press.

Birch, David L. 1979. *The Job Generation Process.* Cambridge, Mass.: MIT Program on Neighborhood and Regional Change.

Birch, David L., and S. MacCracken. 1981. *Corporate Evolution: A Micro-Based Analysis.* Cambridge, Mass.: MIT Program on Neighborhood and Regional Change.

Bish, Robert L. 1971. *The Public Economy of Metropolitan Areas.* Chicago: Markham.

Black, J. Thomas, and Frank Dunau. 1981. *The Effect of Regulations on Residential Land Prices.* Washington, D.C.: Urban Land Institute.

Blackbourn, A. 1982. "The Impact of Multinational Corporations on the Spatial Organization of Developed Nations: A Review." Pp. 147–157 in Michael Taylor and Nigel Thrift (eds.), *The Geography of Multinationals: Studies in the Spatial Development and Economic Consequences of Multinational Corporations.* London: Croom Helm.

Blauner, Robert. 1972. *Racial Oppression in America.* New York: Harper and Row.

Bloom, Gordon F., F. Marion Fletcher, and Charles R. Perry. 1972. *Negro Employment in Retail Trade.* Philadelphia: University of Pennsylvania Press.

Bloomberg, Warner, and Rodrigo Martinez-Sandoval. 1982. "The Hispanic-American Urban Order: A Border Perspective." Pp. 112–132 in Gary Gappert and Richard V. Knight (eds.), *Cities in the Twenty-first Century.* Beverly Hills, Calif.: Sage.

Bluestone, Barry, and Bennett Harrison. 1982. *The Deindustrialization of America.* New York: Basic Books.

Boast, T. 1977. "Federal Programs, Urban Resources and the American Capital Market." Paper presented at the Conference on Urban Resources and State Power, Center for International Studies, Cornell University, New York, June.

Bogue, Donald J. 1951. *State Economic Areas: A Description of the Procedure Used in Making a Functional Grouping of the Cities of the United States*. Washington, D.C.: U.S. Government Printing Office.

Bogue, Donald J. 1971. *The Structure of the Metropolitan Community: A Study in Dominance and Subdominance*. New York: Russell and Russell.

Bonacich, Edna. 1973. "A Theory of Middleman Minorities." *American Sociological Review* 38(October):583–594.

Bonacich, Edna. 1980. "Class Approaches to Ethnicity and Race." *Insurgent Sociologist* 10(2):9–23.

Bonacich, Edna, Ivan H. Light, and Charles W. Wong. 1977. "Koreans in Business." *Society* 14(September–October):54–59.

Bookchin, Murray. 1971. *Post-Scarcity Anarchism*. Berkeley, Calif.: Ramparts Press.

Boorstin, Daniel. 1965. *The Americans: The National Experience*. New York: Random House.

Borchert, John R. 1967. "American Metropolitan Evolution." *Geographical Review* 57(3):301–332.

Borchert, John R. 1978. "Major Control Points in American Economic Geography." *Annals of the Association of American Geographers* 68:214–232.

Bornschier, Volker, and Christopher Chase-Dunn. 1985. *Multinational Corporations and Underdevelopment*. New York: Praeger.

Boulding, Elise. 1981. "Women as Integrators and Stabilizers." Pp. 119–149 in Elizabeth Moen et al. (eds.), *Women and the Social Costs of Economic Development: Two Colorado Case Studies*. Boulder: Westview Press.

Bouma, Donald. 1962. "Analysis of the Social Power Position of a Real Estate Board." *Social Problems* 10(Fall):121–132.

Boyarsky, Bill, and Jerry Gillam. 1982. "Hard Times Don't Stem Flow of Campaign Gifts." *Los Angeles Times,* April 4, sec. I, pp. 1,3,22,23.

Boyd, Gerald M. 1983. "Congress Study Finds More Middle-Size Cities Face Budget Deficits." *New York Times,* November 28, sec. B, p. 12.

Boyle, Patrick. 1983. "GM Will Open Southland Automotive Design Center." *Los Angeles Times,* March 30, sec. I, pp. 1,2.

Boyte, Harry. 1980. *The Backyard Revolution: Understanding the New Citizen Movement*. Philadelphia: Temple University Press.

Bradburn, Norman M., and David Caplovitz. 1965. *Reports on Happiness: A Pilot Study of Behavior Related to Mental Health*. Chicago: Aldine.

Bradbury, Katherine L., Anthony Downs, and Kenneth A. Small. 1982. *Urban Decline and the Future of American Cities*. Washington, D.C.: Brookings Institute.

Bradford, David F., and Harry H. Kelejian. 1973. "An Econometric Model of Flight to the Suburbs." *Journal of Political Economy* 81(3):566–589.

Branfman, Eric, Benjamin Cohen, and David Trubek. 1974. "Measuring the Invisible Wall: Land Use Controls and Residential Patterns of the Poor." Pp. 57–82 in David Listokin (ed.), *Land Use Controls: Present Problems and Future Reform*. New Brunswick, N.J.: Center for Urban Policy Research.

Braun, Stephen. 1984. "Zoning Laws Being Used in War on Bondage Clubs." *Los Angeles Times,* August 4, pp. 1,13.

Braverman, Harry. 1974. *Labor and Monopoly Capital*. New York: Monthly Review Press.

Breines, Simon. 1984. "As New York Keeps Losing Light and Open Space." *New York Times,* July 25, p. 22.

Breton, Raymond. 1964. "Institutional Completeness of Ethnic Communities and the Personal Relations of Immigrants." *American Journal of Sociology* 70(September):193–205.

Brewer, Anthony. 1980. *Marxist Theories of Imperialism: A Critical Survey*. London: Routledge and Kegan Paul.

Brewer, H. Peers. 1976. "Eastern Money and Western Mortgages in the 1870's." *Business History Review* 50(Autumn):356–380.

Bridgeland, William M., and Andrew J. Sofranko. 1975. "Community Structure and Issue-Specific Influences: Community Mobilization over Environmental Quality." *Urban Affairs Quarterly* 11(December):186–214.

Brilliant, Eleanor L. 1975. *The Urban Development Corporation*. Lexington, Mass.: D. C. Heath.

Britton, J. 1974. "Environmental Adaptation of Industrial Plants: Service Linkages, Locational Environment and Organization." Pp. 363–390 in F. E. Ian Hamilton (ed.), *Spatial Perspectives on Industrial Organization and Decision-Making*. London: Wiley.

Brooks, Joseph. 1984. "The Extinction of the Black Farmer." *Freedomways,* 3d quarter. Reprinted in *Utne Reader* 9(April):102–107.

Broom, Leonard, and Ruth Riemer. 1973. *Renewal and Return: The Socio-Economic Effects of the War on Japanese Americans*. Berkeley and Los Angeles: University of California Press.

Broom, Leonard, and William Shay. 1985. "The Social Structure of Great Wealth." Unpublished ms., Department of Sociology, University of California, Santa Barbara.

Brower, John. 1972. *The Black Side of Football*. Ph.D. dissertation, Department of Sociology, University of California, Santa Barbara.

Brown, Kelly L. 1984. "Black Capitalism: Problems Without Solutions." Unpublished ms., Department of Sociology, University of California, Santa Barbara.

Brown, Mike. 1979. *Laying Waste: The Poisoning of America by Toxic Chemicals*. New York: Pantheon.

Brownstein, Ron, and Nina Easton. 1982. "How California Beat Watt." *Re:Sources* 4(2):5.

Brue, Stanley L. 1975. "Local Employment and Payroll Impacts of Corporate Mergers." *Growth and Change* 6(4):8–13.

Buder, Stanley. 1967. *Pullman: An Experiment in Industrial Order and Community Planning, 1880–1930*. New York: Oxford University Press.

Bullard, Robert D. 1983. "Solid Waste Sites and the Black Houston Community." *Sociological Inquiry* 53(Spring):273–288.

Bullock, Brad, and Glenn Firebaugh. 1984. "Richer versus Poorer LDCs: Do World System Characteristics Matter?" Paper presented at the 79th annual meeting of the American Sociological Association, San Antonio, Texas, August 27–31.

Bupp, Irwin, and Jean-Claude Derian. 1978. *Light-Water: How the Nuclear Dream Dissolved*. New York: Basic Books.

Burawoy, Michael. 1974. "Race, Class and Colonialism." *Social and Economic Studies* 23(4):521–550.

Burd, Gene. 1977. "The Selling of the Sunbelt: Civic Boosterism in the Media." Pp. 129–150 in David Perry and Alfred Watkins (eds.), *The Rise of the Sunbelt Cities*. Beverly Hills, Calif.: Sage.

Burgess, Ernest W. 1925. "The Growth of the City." Pp. 1–46 in Robert Ezra Park, Ernest W. Burgess, and Roderick D. McKenzie (eds.), *The City*. Chicago: University of Chicago Press.

Burnett, Alan. 1983. "Neighborhood Participation, Political Demand Making, and Local Outputs in British and North American Cities." Pp. 316–362 in Andrew Kirby, Paul Knox, and Steven Pinch (eds.), *Public Service Provision and Urban Development*. New York: St. Martin's Press.

Burns, Leland S., and Wing Ning Pang. 1977. "Big Business in the Big City." *Urban Affairs Quarterly* 12(4):533–544.

Burt, Ronald, Kenneth P. Christman, and Harold C. Kilburn. 1980. "Testing a Structural Theory of Corporate Cooptation." *American Sociological Review* 45:821–841.

Burton, Dudley, and M. Brian Murphy. 1980. "Planning, Austerity, and the Democratic Prospect." *Kapitalistate* 8:67–98.

Business Conditions Digest. 1985. "U.S. International Transactions," 25(5):93.

Butler, John S. 1976. "Inequality in the Military: An Examination of Promotion Time for Black and White Enlisted Men." *American Sociological Review* 41(October):817.

Buttel, Frederick, and William L. Flinn. 1978. "Social Class and Mass Environmental Beliefs: A Reconsideration." *Environmental Behavior* 10:433–450.

Byron, Doris A. 1982. "High-Priced Boom Molds New Skyline." *Los Angeles Times,* April 25, sec. I, pp. 1,3,30,32.

California Governor's Office, Office of Planning and Research. 1979. "New Housing: Paying Its Way." Sacramento.

Calvert, Jerry W. 1979. "Social and Ideological Bases of Support for Environmental Legislation: An Examination of Public Attitudes and Legislative Action." *Western Political Quarterly* 33(September):327–337.

Camarillo, Albert. 1979. *Chicanos in a Changing Society.* Cambridge, Mass.: Harvard University Press.

Campbell, John L. 1983. "Nuclear Waste and the Political Economy of Indecision." Paper presented at the 78th annual meeting of the American Sociological Association, Detroit, Michigan, August 31–September 4.

Campbell, John L. n.d. "The Antinuclear Movement in the United States: A Case Study." Unpublished ms., Department of Sociology, University of Wisconsin, Madison.

Caplovitz, David. 1963. *The Poor Pay More.* New York: Free Press.

Carnoy, Martin, and Derek Shearer. 1980. *Economic Democracy: The Challenge of the 1980s.* White Plains, N.Y.: M. E. Sharpe.

Caro, Robert A. 1974. *The Power Broker: Robert Moses and the Fall of New York.* New York: Knopf.

Carter, Luther. 1974. *The Florida Experience: Land and Water Policy in a Growth State.* Baltimore: Johns Hopkins University Press.

Carter, Steven, Lyle Sumek, and Murray Frost. 1974. "Local Environmental Management." Pp. 255–664 in *Municipal Year Book.* Washington, D.C.: International City Management Association.

Case, Fred E., and Jeffrey Gale. 1981. "Impact of Housing Costs from the California Coastal Zone Act." *Journal of the American Real Es-*

tate and Urban Economics Association 9(4):345–366.

Castells, Manuel. 1976. "Theory and Ideology in Urban Sociology." Pp. 60–84 in C. G. Pickvance (ed.), *Urban Sociology: Critical Essays*. New York: St. Martin's Press.

Castells, Manuel. 1979. *The Urban Question*. Cambridge, Mass.: MIT Press.

Castells, Manuel. 1983. *The City and the Grassroots: A Cross-Cultural Theory of Urban Social Movements*. Berkeley and Los Angeles: University of California Press.

Caufield, Catherine. 1985. *In the Rainforest*. New York: Knopf.

Changing Times. 1985. "When Neighbors Sell as a Group." August, pp. 45–48.

Chase-Dunn, Christopher. 1975. "The Effects of International Economic Dependence on Development and Inequality: A Cross-National Study." *American Sociological Review* 40:720–738.

Cho, Yong Hyo, and David Puryear. 1980. "Distressed Cities: Targeting HUD Programs." Pp. 191–210 in Donald B. Rosenthal (ed.), *Urban Revitalization* (Urban Affairs Annual Reviews, vol. 18). Beverly Hills, Calif.: Sage.

Chrisman, Robert. 1970. "Ecology Is a Racist Shuck." Pp. 72–78 in Robert Buckhout and 81 concerned Berkeley students (eds.), *Toward Social Change: A Handbook for Those Who Will*. New York: Harper and Row.

Christaller, Walter. 1933. *Die Zentrale Orte in Süddeutschland* [Central Places in South Germany]. Stuttgart: Fischer.

Cipriano, Ralph. 1984. "Interest Soars for Bond Firm." *Albany Times-Union*, April 22, sec. A, pp. 1,10.

Clark, David L. 1983. "Improbable Los Angeles." Pp. 268–308 in Richard M. Bernard and Bradley R. Rice (eds.), *Sunbelt Cities: Politics and Growth since World War II*. Austin: University of Texas Press.

Clark, Terry. 1968. "Community Structure, Decision-Making, Budget Expenditures, and Urban Renewal in Fifty-one American Cities." *American Sociological Review* 33(August):576–593.

Clark, Thomas A. 1979. *Blacks in Suburbs: A National Perspective*. New Brunswick, N.J.: Rutgers University, Center for Urban Policy Research.

Clarke, Susan E. n.d. *The Local State and Alternative Economic Development Strategies: Gaining Public Benefits from Private Investment*. Boulder, Colo.: Center for Public Policy Research, University of Colorado.

Clawson, Marion. 1972. *America's Land and Its Uses*. Washington, D.C.: Resources for the Future.

Clawson, Dan, and Mary Ann Clawson. 1985. "The Logic of Business Unity: Corporate Contributions in the 1980 Election." Paper presented at the 80th annual meeting of the American Sociological Association, Washington, D.C., August 26–30.

Clayton, Janet. 1984. "South-Central L.A. Fears Olympics to Disrupt Lives." *Los Angeles Times,* February 5, sec. II, p. 1.

Clifford, Frank. 1985a. "Stevenson and Picus Face Toughest Tests in Council Elections." *Los Angeles Times,* February 19, sec. II, pp. 1,6.

Clifford, Frank. 1985b. "Contributors to Mayoral Race Seek a Friendly Ear." *Los Angeles Times,* March 25, sec II, pp. 1,3,14.

Clifford, Frank. 1985c. "L.A. to Enforce Building Limits." *Los Angeles Times,* April 3, sec. II, pp. 1,6.

Clifford, Frank. 1985d. "Ouster of City Planner Sought." *Los Angeles Times,* July 15, sec. I, pp. 1,13.

Cohen, Robert B. 1977. "Multinational Corporations, International Finances and the Sunbelt." Pp. 211–226 in David C. Perry and Alfred J. Watkins (eds.), *The Rise of the Sunbelt Cities.* Beverly Hills, Calif.: Sage.

Cohen, Robert B. 1981. "The New International Division of Labor: Multinational Corporations and Urban Hierarchy." Pp. 287–315 in Michael Dear and Allen J. Scott (eds.), *Urbanization and Urban Planning in Capitalist Society.* New York: Methuen.

Cohen, Robert B., Nadine Felton, Morley Nkosi, and Jaap van Liere (eds.). 1979. "General Introduction." Pp. 1–40 in Stephen Hymer, *The Multinational Corporation: A Radical Approach: Papers.* Cambridge: Cambridge University Press.

Cohn, D'vera. 1979. "Big Is No Longer Beautiful for Many U.S. Communities." *Santa Barbara News-Press,* March 4, sec. A, p. 18.

Coke, James G., and John J. Gargan. 1969. *Fragmentation in Land-Use Planning and Control.* National Commission on Urban Problems, research report no. 18. Washington, D.C.: Government Printing Office.

Collier, Peter, and David Horowitz. 1976. *The Rockefellers.* New York: Holt, Rinehart and Winston.

Columbia Marketing Department. 1983. *Columbia, Maryland, Quarterly,* March 31, 1983.

Commoner, Barry. 1971. *The Closing Circle.* New York: Knopf.

Conzen, Kathleen N. 1976. *Immigrant Milwaukee, 1836–1860.* Cambridge, Mass.: Harvard University Press.

Copetas, A. Craig. 1984. "How the Barbarians Do Business." *Harper's,* January, pp. 37–43.

Cornwall, Elmer. 1969. "Bosses, Machines and Ethnic Politics." Pp.

190–206 in Harry Bailey and Ellis Katz (eds.), *Ethnic Group Politics*. Columbus, Ohio: Merrill.

Corso, Anthony. 1983. "San Diego: The Anti-City." Pp. 328–344 in Richard M. Bernard and Bradley R. Rice (eds.), *Sunbelt Cities: Politics and Growth since World War II*. Austin: University of Texas Press.

Council of the University of California Faculty Associations. 1984. *Faculty Association Newsletter,* October. Berkeley, Calif.

Cox, Harvey, and David Morgan. 1973. *City Politics and the Press: Journalists and the Governing of Merseyside*. Cambridge: Cambridge University Press.

Cox, Kevin R. 1978. "Local Interests and Urban Political Processes in Market Societies." Pp. 94–108 in Kevin R. Cox (ed.), *Urbanization and Conflict in Market Societies*. Chicago: Maaroufa Press.

Cox, Kevin R. 1981. "Capitalism and Conflict around the Communal Living Space." Pp. 431–456 in Michael Dear and Allen J. Scott (eds.), *Urbanization and Urban Planning in Capitalist Society*. New York: Methuen.

Cox, Kevin R. 1984. "Social Change, Turf Politics, and Concepts of Turf Politics." Pp. 283–315 in Andrew Kirby, Paul Knox, and Steven Pinch (eds.), *Public Service Provision and Urban Development*. New York: St. Martin's Press.

Cox, Kevin R., and Jeffrey M. McCarthy. 1980. "Neighborhood Activism in the American City." *Urban Geography* 1:22–28.

Cox, Oliver Cromwell. 1948. *Caste, Class and Race: A Study in Social Dynamics*. New York: Doubleday.

Crain, Robert L., and Donald B. Rosenthal. 1967. "Community Status as a Dimension of Local Decision Making." *American Sociological Review* 32(6):970–984.

Crenson, Matthew. 1983. *Neighborhood Politics*. Cambridge, Mass.: Harvard University Press.

Cross, Michael. 1981. *New Firm Formation and Regional Development*. Farnborough, Hants, England: Gower.

Crosson, Pierex R., and Sterling Brubaker. 1982. *Resource and Environmental Effects of U.S. Agriculture*. Washington, D.C.: Resources for the Future.

Culhane, Paul J. 1981. *Public Lands Politics: Interest Group Influence on the Forest Service and the Bureau of Land Management*. Baltimore: Johns Hopkins University Press.

Curran, Ron, and Lewis MacAdams. 1985. "The Selling of L.A. County." *L.A. Weekly,* November 22–28, pp. 24–49.

Czamanski, Daniel Z., and Stan Czamanski. 1977. "Industrial Complexes." *Papers of the Regional Science Association* 38:93–111.

Dagenais, Julie. 1967. "Newspaper Language as an Active Agent in the Building of a Frontier Town." *American Speech* 42(2):114–121.

Dahl, Robert Alan. 1961. *Who Governs?* New Haven: Yale University Press.

Dahmann, Donald C. 1982. "Housing Opportunities for Black and White Households: Three Decades of Change in the Supply of Housing." *Special Demographic Analyses* (CDS-80-6). Bureau of the Census, Washington D.C.: Government Printing Office.

D'Ambrosio, Mary. 1985. "Coyne Slates Talks on Hockey Franchise." *Albany Times Union,* February 14, sec. B, p. 1.

Daniel, Leon. 1984. "S.D. Town Wants Nuke Waste Dump." *Schenectady Gazette,* January 16, p. 44.

Daniels, Arlene Kaplan. 1986. *Invisible Careers: Women Community Leaders in the Voluntary World.* Chicago: University of Chicago Press.

Danielson, Michael. 1972. "Differentiation, Segregation, and Political Fragmentation in the American Metropolis." Pp. 143–176 in A. E. Keir Nash (ed.), *Research Reports of the Commission on Population Growth and the American Future.* Washington, D.C.: Government Printing Office.

Danielson, Michael. 1976. *The Politics of Exclusion.* New York: Columbia University Press.

D'Antonio, William V., and Eugene C. Erickson. 1970. "The Reputational Technique as a Measure of Community Power: An Evaluation Based on Comparative and Longitudinal Studies." Pp. 251–265 in Michael Aiken and Paul E. Mott (eds.), *The Structure of Community Power.* New York: Random House.

Darden, Joe T. 1980. "Lending Practices and Policies Affecting the American Metropolitan System." Pp. 91–110 in Stanley D. Brunn and James Wheeler (eds.), *The American Metropolitan System: Present and Future.* New York: Wiley.

David, Stephen M., and Paul Kantor. 1979. "Political Theory and Transformation in Urban Budgetary Areas: The Case of New York City." Pp. 183–220 in Dale Rogers Marshall (ed.), *Urban Policy Making.* Beverly Hills, Calif.: Sage.

Davidson, Chandler, and George Korbel. 1981. "At Large Elections and Minority Group Representation: A Re-Examination of Historical and Contemporary Evidence." *Journal of Politics* 43:982–1005.

Davidson, Jeffrey L. 1981. "Location of Community-based Treatment Centers." *Social Service Review* 55(2):221–241.

Davies, Gordon W. 1977. "A Model of the Urban Residential Land and Housing Markets." *Canadian Journal of Economics.* 10(3):393–410.

Davis, Lance. 1969. "Financial Immobilities and Finance Capitalism." *Explorations in Entrepreneurial History,* Second Series, 1(1):88–105.

Davis, Kingsley, and Hilda Golden. 1954. "Urbanization and the Development of Preindustrial Areas." *Economic Development and Cultural Change* 3:6–24.

Davis, Kingsley, and Wilbert E. Moore. 1945. "Some Principles of Stratification." *American Sociological Review* 10(2):242–249.

Daws, Gavan, and George Cooper. 1984. *Land and Power in Hawaii: The Democratic Years.* Honolulu: Benchmark Press.

Deacon, Robert, and Perry Shapiro. 1975. "Private Preference for Collective Goods Revealed through Voting on Referenda." *American Economic Review* 65:943–955.

Dear, Michael. 1981. "Social and Spatial Reproduction of the Mentally Ill." Pp. 481–497 in Michael Dear and Allen J. Scott (eds.), *Urbanization and Urban Planning in Capitalist Society.* New York: Methuen.

DeGiovanni, Frank F., et al. 1981. "Private Market Revitalization." Report prepared for Office of Policy Development. Research Triangle Park, N.C.: Research Triangle Institute.

Delafons, John. 1969. *Land-Use Controls in the United States.* New York: Cambridge University Press.

Denowitz, Ronald M. 1980. "Racial Succession in New York City, 1960–1970." *Social Forces* 59(2):440–455.

Dentzer, Susan, and Richard Manning. 1983. "Renaissance Center." *Newsweek,* January 24, p. 58.

DeVault, Marge. 1984. "Women and Food: Household Work and the Construction of Family Life." Ph.D. dissertation, Department of Sociology, Northwestern University.

Devereux, Sean. 1976. "Boosters in the Newsroom: The Jacksonville Case." *Columbia Journalism Review* 14:38–47.

DeZutter, Hank. 1981. "Race Ways: On Blacks, Whites, and the Failure to Communicate." *Chicago Reader,* June 19, pp. 3,37.

Diamond, Douglas. 1980. "Taxes, Inflation, Speculation, and the Cost of Homeownership." *Journal of the American Real Estate and Urban Economic Association* 8(3):281–298.

Diamond, Stuart. 1984. "Jobs and Risks Are Linked in a U.S. Chemical Valley." *New York Times,* December 5, sec. A, pp. 1,12.

Dicken, Peter. 1976. "The Multiplant Business Enterprise and Geographical Space: Some Issues in the Study of External Control and

Regional Development." *Regional Studies* 10(4):401–412.

Dinerman, Beatrice. 1958. "Chambers of Commerce in the Modern Metropolis." University of California, Los Angeles, Bureau of Government Research.

Dodson, E. N., Harry Fox, and W. C. Harshbarger. 1980. "Growth Impact Study for the South Coast Area of Santa Barbara County." Santa Barbara, Calif.: General Research Corporation.

Domhoff, G. William. 1967. *Who Rules America?* Englewood Cliffs, N.J.: Prentice-Hall.

Domhoff, G. William. 1971. *The Higher Circles: The Governing Class in America.* New York: Random House.

Domhoff, G. William. 1978. *Who Really Rules: New Haven Community Power Re-Examined.* Santa Monica, Calif.: Goodyear.

Domhoff, G. William. 1983. *Who Rules America Now? A View for the 80's.* Englewood Cliffs, N.J.: Prentice-Hall.

Domhoff, G. William. Forthcoming. "The Growth Machine and the Power Elite: A Challenge to Pluralists and Marxists Alike." In Robert Waste (ed.), *Community Power: Directions for Future Research.* Beverly Hills, Calif.: Sage.

Douglas, Paul. 1968. *Report of the National Commission on Urban Problems.* Washington, D.C.: Government Printing Office.

Douglas Commission. 1969. *Building the American City.* Washington, D.C.: Government Printing Office.

Dowall, David E. 1980. "An Examination of Population-Growth-Managing Communities." *Policy Studies Journal* 9:414–427.

Dowall, David E. 1984. *The Suburban Squeeze.* Berkeley: University of California Press.

Dowall, David E., and John Landis. 1980. "Land-Use Controls and Housing Costs: An Examination of San Francisco Bay Area Communities." Center for Real Estate and Urban Economics Working Paper No. 81–24. Berkeley: University of California.

Downie, Leonard, Jr. 1974. *Mortgage on America.* New York: Praeger.

Downing, Paul B. (ed.). 1972. *Air Pollution and the Social Sciences.* New York: Praeger.

Downs, Anthony. 1970. "Uncompensated Nonconstruction Costs Which Urban Highways and Urban Renewal Impose upon Residential Households." Pp. 69–106 in Julius Margolis (ed.), *The Analysis of Public Output: A Conference of the Universities—National Bureau Committee for Economic Research.* New York: Columbia University Press.

Downs, Anthony. 1984. "Blueprint for a Fairer Housing Policy." *Los*

Angeles Times, September 16, sec. IV, p. 5.

Drake, St. Clair, and Horace R. Cayton. 1945. *Black Metropolis.* New York: Harcourt Brace.

Drew, Elizabeth. 1983. "A Political Journal." *New Yorker* 59(18):39–75.

Drewett, Roy. 1973. "Land Values and the Suburban Land Market." Pp. 197–245 in Peter Hall et al., *The Containment of Urban England,* vol. 2. London: George Allen and Unwin.

Due, John F. 1961. "Studies of State-Local Tax Influences on Location of Industry." *National Tax Journal* 14:164–165.

Duerksen, Christopher. 1982. *Siting New Industry: An Empirical Perspective.* Washington, D.C.: Conservation Foundation.

Duncan, Otis Dudley. 1957. "Optimum Size of Cities." Pp. 759–773 in Paul K. Hatt and Albert J. Reiss, Jr. (eds.), *Readings in Urban Sociology,* 2d ed. Glencoe, Ill.: Free Press.

Duncan, Otis Dudley. 1961. "From Social System to Eco-System." *Sociological Inquiry* 31:140–149.

Duncan, Otis Dudley, and Beverly Duncan. 1957. *The Negro Population of Chicago.* Chicago: University of Chicago Press.

Duncan, Otis Dudley, W. R. Scott, Stanley Lieberson, Beverly Duncan, and Hal Winsborough. 1960. *Metropolis and Region.* Baltimore: Johns Hopkins University Press.

Dunlap, Riley E. 1975. "The Socioeconomic Basis of the Environmental Movement: Old Data, New Data, and Implications for the Movement's Future." Paper presented at the annual meeting of the American Sociological Association, San Francisco, August.

Dunlap, Riley E., and Michael Patrick Allen. 1976. "Partisan Differences on Environmental Issues: A Congressional Roll-Call Analysis." *Western Political Quarterly* 29(3):384–397.

Dye, Lee. 1971. *Blowout at Platform A: The Crisis That Awakened a Nation.* Garden City, N.Y.: Doubleday.

Eaton, Michael. 1977. "Safety Risks of Liquefied Gas." *Los Angeles Times,* March 13, sec. VII, p. 3.

Eaton, William. 1980. "Survey Finds S.F. Has Highest Housing Costs in Nation; L.A. in Second Place." *Los Angeles Times,* June 5, sec. I, p. 9.

Eberts, Paul R. 1979. "Growth and the Quality of Life: Some Logical and Methodological Issues." Pp. 159–184 in Gene F. Summers and Arne Selvik (eds.), *Nonmetropolitan Industrial Growth and Community Change.* Lexington, Mass.: Lexington Books.

Edelman, Murray. 1964. *The Symbolic Uses of Politics.* Urbana: University of Illinois Press.

Edelman, Murray. 1977. *Political Language: Words That Succeed and Policies That Fail*. New York: Academic Press.

Editors. 1975. "Where America Runs Out of Continent: A Survey of the West Coast." *The Economist* 257(December 13):66–94.

Editors. 1981. "Roundtable on Rouse." *Progressive Architecture* 62(7):100–106.

Edsall, Thomas B. 1984. *The New Politics of Inequality: How Political Power Shapes Economic Policy*. New York: Norton.

Edwards, Richard C., Michael Reich, and David M. Gordon. 1975. *Labor Market Segmentation*. Lexington, Mass.: D. C. Heath.

Ehrenreich, Barbara, and John Ehrenreich. 1979. "The Professional-Managerial Class." Pp. 5–45 in Pat Walker (ed.), *Between Labor and Capital*. London: Harvester Press.

Ehrlich, Paul R. 1977. *Ecoscience: Population, Resources, Environment*. San Francisco: W. H. Freeman.

Eidson, Bettye K. 1971. "Institutional Racism: Minority Group Manpower Policies of Major Urban Employers." Ph.D. dissertation, Johns Hopkins University.

Eitzen, D. Stanley, and George H. Sage. 1978. *Sociology of American Sport*. Dubuque, Iowa: William C. Brown.

Ellickson, Robert C. 1977. "Suburban Growth Controls: An Economic and Legal Analysis." *Yale Law Journal* 86(3):385–511.

Elliott, Michael. 1981. "The Impact of Growth Control Regulation on Housing Prices in California." *Journal of the American Real Estate and Urban Economics Association* 9(2):115–133.

Endicott, William, and Jerry Gillam. 1983. "Developer, Senator Push Bill to Beat Local Condo Law." *Los Angeles Times,* March 22, sec. I, pp. 3,12.

Erickson, Rodney A. 1980. "Corporate Organization and Manufacturing Branch Plant Closures in Nonmetropolitan Areas." *Regional Studies* 14(6):491–501.

Erickson, Rodney A. 1981. "Corporations, Branch Plants and Employment Stability in Nonmetropolitan Areas." Pp. 135–153 in John M. A. Rees, Geoffrey J. D. Hewings, and Howard A. Stafford (eds.), *Industrial Location and Regional Systems: Spatial Organization in the Economic Sector*. New York: Bergin.

Ervin, David, James Fitch, R. Kenneth Godwin, W. Bruce Shepard, and Herbert Stoevener. 1977. *Land Use Control: Evaluating Economic and Political Effects*. Cambridge, Mass.: Ballinger.

Esping-Andersen, Gosta. 1985. *Politics against Markets*. Princeton, N.J.: Princeton University Press.

Euclid v. *Ambler Realty Co.* 1926. 272 U.S. 365.

Eulau, Heinz, and Kenneth Prewitt. 1973. *Labyrinths of Democracy.* Indianapolis: Bobbs-Merrill.

Evers, Adalbert. 1976. "Urban Structure and State Interventionism." *Kapitalistate* 4–5(Summer):141–157.

Ewen, Stuart. 1976. *Captains of Consciousness: Advertising and the Social Roots of the Consumer Culture.* New York: McGraw-Hill.

Ewen, Lynda Ann. 1978. *Corporate Power and Urban Crisis in Detroit.* Princeton, N.J.: Princeton University Press.

Fainstein, Susan, and Norman Fainstein. 1984. "Governing Regimes and the Political Economy of Redevelopment in New York City." Paper presented at the 79th annual meeting of the American Sociological Association, San Antonio, Texas, August 27–31.

Fainstein, Susan, Norman Fainstein, and P. Jefferson Armistead. 1983. "San Francisco: Urban Transformation and the Local State." Pp. 202–244 in Susan Fainstein (ed.), *Restructuring the City.* New York: Longman.

Farley, Reynolds. 1977. "Residential Segregation in Urbanized Areas of the United States in 1970." *Demography* 14(4):497–518.

Feagin, Joe R. 1982. *Social Problems: A Critical Power-Conflict Perspective.* Englewood Cliffs, N.J.: Prentice-Hall.

Feagin, Joe R. 1983a. "The Capital of the Sunbelt: Houston's Growth and the Oil Industry." Unpublished manuscript, Department of Sociology, University of Texas, Austin.

Feagin, Joe R. 1983b. "The Seamy Side of Boomtown: A Closer Look at Houston." Paper presented at meetings of the Society for the Study of Social Problems, Detroit, Michigan, August 30.

Feagin, Joe R. 1985. "The Socioeconomic Base of Urban Growth: The Case of Houston and the Oil Industry." *American Journal of Sociology* 90(6):1204–1230.

Fellows, Lawrence. 1976. "Hartford Blocks Aid for Suburbs." *New York Times,* January 29, p. 1.

Finkler, Earl. 1972. "No-Growth as a Planning Alternative." Planning Advisory Report No. 283. Chicago: American Society of Planning Officials.

Firey, Walter. 1945. "Sentiment and Symbolism as Ecological Variables." *American Sociological Review* 10(April):140–148.

Fischel, William A. 1975. "Fiscal and Environmental Considerations in the Location of Firms in Suburban Communities." Pp. 119–174 in Edwin S. Mills and Wallace E. Oates (eds.), *Fiscal Zoning and Land Use Controls: The Economic Issues.* Lexington, Mass.: Lexington Books.

Fischer, Claude S. 1982. *To Dwell among Friends*. Chicago: University of Chicago Press.

Fischer, Claude S. 1984. *The Urban Experience*. San Diego: Harcourt Brace Jovanovich.

Fischer, Claude S., Mark Baldasarre, and R. J. Ofshe. 1975. "Crowding Studies and Urban Life—A Critical Review." *Journal of the American Institute of Planners* 41(6):406–418.

Fish, John, Gordon Nelson, Walter Stuhr, and Lawrence Witmer. 1966. *The Edge of the Ghetto: A Study of Church Involvement in Community Organization*. Chicago: Church Federation of Greater Chicago.

Fishman, Mark. 1978. "Crime Waves as Ideology." *Social Problems* 25(5):532–543.

FitzGerald, Frances. 1983. "A Reporter at Large—Interlude." *New Yorker* 59(10):54–109.

Fitzpatrick, Kevin, and John R. Logan. 1985. "The Aging of the Suburbs, 1960–1980." *American Sociological Review* 50(February):106–117.

Flacks, Richard. 1976. "Making History vs. Making Life: Dilemmas of an American Left." *Sociological Inquiry* 46(3–4):263–280.

Flacks, Richard. Forthcoming. *Making History vs. Making Life: Dilemmas of Political Consciousness in America*. New York: Columbia University Press.

Fleischmann, Arnold. 1977. "Sunbelt Boosterism: The Politics of Postwar Growth and Annexation in San Antonio." Pp. 151–168 in David Perry and Alfred Watkins (eds.), *The Rise of the Sunbelt*. Beverly Hills, Calif.: Sage.

Fliegel, Frederick C., Andrew J. Sofranko, and Nina Glasgow. 1981. "Population Growth in Rural Areas and Sentiments of the New Migrants toward Further Growth." *Rural Sociology* 46(3):411–429.

Fligstein, Neil. 1985. "The Interorganizational Power Struggle: The Rise of Finance Presidents in Large Firms, 1919–1979." Paper presented at the 80th annual meeting of the American Sociological Association, Washington, D.C., August 26–30.

Fligstein, Neil. 1986. "Anti-trust Law and the Growth of Large Firms: 1860–1985." Colloquium presentation. Dept. of Sociology, University of California, Santa Barbara. March 12.

Fogelson, Robert M. 1967. *The Fragmented Metropolis: Los Angeles, 1850–1930*. Cambridge, Mass.: Harvard University Press.

Foley, Donald L. 1950. "The Use of Local Facilities in a Metropolis." *American Journal of Sociology* 56:238–246.

Foley, Thomas. 1982. "Biggest Givers among Political Committees." *U.S. News and World Report*, December 20, p. 28.

Follett, Ross. 1976. "Social Consequences of Urban Size and Growth:

An Analysis of U.S. Urban Areas." Ph.D. dissertation, Department of Sociology, University of California, Santa Barbara.

Form, William. 1954. "The Place of Social Structure in the Determination of Land Use." *Social Forces* 32(May):317–323.

Form, William. 1983. "Sociological Research and the American Working Class." *Sociological Quarterly* 24(Spring):163–184.

Form, William H., and William V. D'Antonio. 1970. "Integration and Cleavage among Comunity Influentials in Two Border Cities." Pp. 431–442 in Michael Aiken and Paul E. Mott (eds.), *The Structure of Community Power*. New York: Random House.

Fowlkes, Martha R., and Patricia Miller. 1985. "Toward a Sociology of Unnatural Disaster." Paper presented at the 80th annual meeting of the American Sociological Association, Washington, D.C., August 31.

Fox, W. 1981. "Fiscal Differentials and Industrial Locations." *Urban Studies* 18:105–111.

Frank, Andre Gunder. 1967. *Capitalism and Underdevelopment in Latin America*. New York: Monthly Review Press.

Frank, Andre Gunder. 1972. "Economic Dependence, Class Structure and Underdevelopment." Pp. 19–45 in James D. Cockcroft (ed.), *Dependence and Underdevelopment: Latin America's Political Economy*. New York: Doubleday.

Frank, Robert H., and Richard T. Freeman. 1978. "The Distributional Consequences of Direct Foreign Investment." Pp. 153–176 in William G. Dewald (ed.), *The Impact of International Trade and Investment on Employment: A Conference on the Department of Labor Research Results*. Washington, D.C.: Government Printing Office.

Franklin, James J., and Thomas Muller. 1977. "Environmental Impact Evaluation, Land Use Planning and the Housing Consumer." *Journal of the American Real Estate and Urban Economics Association* 5(3):279–301.

Frazier, E. Franklin. 1957. *Race and Culture Contacts in the Modern World*. Boston: Beacon Press.

Frazier, E. Franklin. 1962. *Black Bourgeoisie*. New York: Free Press.

Frazier, E. Franklin, and Eric C. Lincoln. 1973. *The Negro Church in America*. New York: Schocken.

Frech, H. E., III. 1982. "The California Coastal Commission's Economic Impacts." Pp. 259–274 in M. Bruce Johnson (ed.), *Resolving the Housing Crisis: Government Policy, Decontrol and the Public Interest*. San Francisco: Pacific Institute for Public Policy Research.

Freidel, Frank. 1963. "Boosters, Intellectuals and the American City." Pp. 115–120 in Oscar Handlin and John Burchard (eds.), *The Historian and the City*. Cambridge, Mass.: MIT Press.

ian and the City. Cambridge, Mass.: MIT Press.

Freitas, Gregory. 1980. Personal communication from the Petaluma planning director, December 7.

French, Robert Mills. 1970. "Economic Change and Community Power Structure: Transition in Cornucopia." Pp. 181–189 in Michael T. Aiken and Paul E. Mott (eds.), *The Structure of Community Power.* New York: Random House.

Freudenburg, William R. 1981. "Women and Men in an Energy Boomtown: Adjustment, Alienation and Adaptation." *Rural Sociology* 46(2):200–244.

Freudenburg, William R., and Rodney Baxter. 1984. "Public Attitudes toward Local Nuclear Power Plants: A Reassessment." Paper presented at the 79th annual meeting of the American Sociological Association, San Antonio, Texas, August 27–31.

Fried, Joseph P. 1971. *Housing Crisis U.S.A.* New York: Praeger.

Fried, Marc. 1963. "Grieving for a Lost Home." Pp. 151–171 in Leonard S. Duhl (ed.), *The Urban Condition.* New York: Basic Books.

Fried, Mark, and Peggy Gleicher. 1961. "Some Sources of Residential Satisfaction in an Urban Slum." *Journal of the American Institute of Planners* 27:305–315.

Frieden, Bernard J. 1979a. *The Environmental Protection Hustle.* Cambridge, Mass.: MIT Press.

Frieden, Bernard J. 1979b. "New Regulation Comes to Suburbia." *Public Interest* 55(Spring):15–27.

Friedland, Roger. 1982. *Power and Crisis in the City.* London: Macmillan.

Friedland, Roger. 1983. "The Politics of Profit and the Geography of Growth." *Urban Affairs Quarterly* 19(1):41–54.

Friedland, Roger, and Carole Gardner. 1983. "Department Store Socialism." Testimony before the City of Santa Barbara Redevelopment Agency. Photocopy.

Friedland, Roger, and Donald Palmer. 1984. "Park Place and Main Street: Business and the Urban Power Structure." Pp. 393–416 in Ralph Turner (ed.), *Annual Review of Sociology,* vol. 10. Beverly Hills, Calif.: Sage.

Friedland, Roger, Donald Palmer, and Mary DuMont. 1983. "The Relocation of Corporate Headquarters, 1960–1975." Unpublished ms., Department of Sociology, University of California, Santa Barbara.

Friedland, Roger, Frances Piven, and Robert Alford. 1978. "Political Conflict, Urban Structure, and the Fiscal Crisis." Pp. 175–225 in Douglas Ashford (ed.), *Comparing Urban Policies.* Beverly Hills, Calif.: Sage.

Friedman, Milton. 1962. *Capitalism and Freedom*. Chicago: University of Chicago Press.

Friedmann, John, and Goetz Wolff. 1982. "World City Formation: An Agenda for Research and Action." *International Journal of Urban and Regional Research* 6(3):309–344.

Frobel, Volker, Jurgen Heinrichs, and Otto Kreyo. 1979. *The New International Division of Labor*. Cambridge: Cambridge University Press.

Fuchs, Victor. 1967. "Differentials in Hourly Earnings by Region and City Size, 1959." Paper 101. New York: National Bureau of Economic Research.

Fuguitt, Glenn V., and Calvin L. Beale. 1978. "Population Trends in Nonmetropolitan Cities and Villages in Subregions of the United States." *Demography* 15(4):605–620.

Fuller, Justin. 1976. "Boomtowns and Blast Furnaces: Town Promotion in Alabama, 1885–1893." *Alabama Review* 29(January):37–48.

Fullinwider, John. 1980. "Dallas: The City with No Limits?" *In These Times* 5(6):12–13.

Gaffney, M. Mason. 1961. "Land and Rent in Welfare Economics." Pp. 141–167 in *Land Economics Research* (papers presented at a symposium on land economics research, Lincoln, Nebraska, June 16–23). Washington, D.C.: Resources for the Future. Distributed by Johns Hopkins University Press, Baltimore.

Galaskiewicz, Joseph. 1979a. *Exchange Networks and Community Politics*. Beverly Hills, Calif.: Sage.

Galaskiewicz, Joseph. 1979b. "The Structure of Community Organizational Networks." *Social Forces* 57(4):1346–1364.

Galaskiewicz, Joseph. 1985. *The Social Organization of an Urban Grants Economy*. New York: Academic Press.

Gallup, George H. (ed.). 1979. *The Gallup Poll: Public Opinion, 1978*. Wilmington, Del.: Scholarly Resources.

Gamson, William. 1968. *Power and Discontent*. Homewood, Ill.: Dorsey Press.

Gans, Herbert. 1962. *The Urban Villagers*. New York: Free Press.

Gans, Herbert. 1967. *The Levittowners: Ways of Life and Politics in a New Suburban Community*. New York: Pantheon.

Gans, Herbert. 1968. *People and Plans*. New York: Basic Books.

Gans, Herbert, John D. Kasarda, and Harvey Molotch. 1982. "Symposium: The State of the Nation's Cities." *Urban Affairs Quarterly* 18(2):163–186.

Garfinkel, Harold. 1967. *Studies in Ethnomethodology*. Englewood Cliffs, N.J.: Prentice-Hall.

Gargan, Edward A. 1983. "Koch Would Limit Project Reviews." *New*

York Times, December 6, sec. I, p. 12.

Garrison, Charles B. 1971. "New Industry in Small Towns: The Impact on Local Government." *National Tax Journal* 21(4):493–500.

Geertz, Clifford. 1963. "The Integrative Revolution: Primordial Sentiments and Civil Politics in New States." Pp. 105–157 in Clifford Geertz (ed.), *Old Societies and New States: The Quest for Modernity in Asia and Africa.* New York: Free Press.

George Schermer Associates. 1968. "Report on Five Cities" (an interim report to the National Commission on Urban Problems). Washington, D.C. Paul H. Douglas, chairman.

Giddens, Anthony. 1973. *The Class Structure of the Advanced Societies.* New York: Harper and Row.

Giddens, Anthony. 1984a. "New Developments in Social Theory and Their Empirical Application." Colloquium talk, Department of Sociology, University of California, Santa Barbara, January 13.

Giddens, Anthony. 1984b. *The Constitution of Society: Outline of the Theory of Structuration.* Berkeley: University of California Press.

Gilderbloom, John I. 1981. "Moderate Rent Control: Its Impact on the Quality and Quantity of the Housing Stock." *Urban Affairs Quarterly* 17(2):123–142.

Gilderbloom, John I. 1983. "The Impact of Moderate Rent Control in New Jersey: An Empirical Study of Twenty-six Rent Controlled Cities." *Journal of Urban Analysis* 7(2):135–154.

Gilderbloom, John I. 1984. "The Impact of Rent Control on Apartment Valuation and Rents in New Jersey." Paper presented at the 79th annual meeting of the American Sociological Association, San Antonio, Texas, August 27–31.

Gillam, Jerry. 1982. "Interest Groups Gave Candidates $8.5 Million." *Los Angeles Times,* November 10, p. 3.

Gillam, Jerry. 1983. "1982 Election Campaigns Cost a Record $83 Million." *Los Angeles Times,* February 26, sec. II, p. 1.

Gintis, Herbert. 1976. "The Nature of the Labor Exchange and the Theory of Capitalist Production." *Review of Radical Political Economics* 8(2):36–56.

Gist, John R. 1980. "Urban Development Action Grants." Pp. 237–252 in Donald B. Rosenthal (ed.), *Urban Revitalization.* Beverly Hills, Calif.: Sage.

Glaab, Charles N. 1962. *Kansas City and the Railroads.* Madison: State Historical Society of Wisconsin.

Glasmeier, Amy K., and Ann R. Markusen. 1981. "The Socio-Economic Impacts of the Proposed MX Missile Project." Working Paper No. 346, March. Berkeley: Institute of Urban and Regional Development, University of California.

Glazer, Nathan. 1971. "Blacks and Ethnic Groups: The Difference and the Political Difference It Makes." Pp. 193–211 in N. I. Huggins, M. Kilson, and D. M. Fox (eds.), *Key Issues in the Afro-American Experience*. New York: Harcourt Brace Jovanovich.

Glickman, Norman J. 1983a. "International Trade, Capital Mobility, and Economic Growth: Some Implications for American Cities and Regions in the 1980s." Pp. 205–239 in Donald Hicks and Norman J. Glickman (eds.), *Transition to the Twenty-first Century: Prospects and Policies for Economic and Urban-Regional Transformation*. Greenwich, Conn.: JAI Press.

Glickman, Norman J. 1983b. "National Urban Policy in an Age of Economic Austerity." Pp. 301–343 in Donald Hicks and Norman J. Glickman (eds.), *Transition to the Twenty-first Century: Prospects for Economic and Urban-Regional Transformation*. Greenwich, Conn.: JAI Press.

Goering, John M. 1978. "Marx and the City: Are There Any New Directions for Urban Theory?" *Comparative Urban Research* 6(2):3.

Goldstein, Joan. 1983. *The Political Economy of Offshore Oil*. New York: Praeger.

Goodall, Leonard E. 1968. *The American Metropolis*. Columbus, Ohio: Merrill.

Goodman, George J. 1968. *The Money Game by Adam Smith*. New York: Random House.

Goodman, Paul, and Percival Goodman. 1947. *Communitas: Means of Livelihood and Ways of Life*. New York: Random House.

Goodman, Robert. 1971. *After the Planners*. New York: Simon and Schuster.

Goodman, Robert F., and Bruce B. Clary. 1976. "Community Attitudes and Action in Response to Airport Noise." *Environment and Behavior* 8(3):441–470.

Goodrich, Carter. 1950. "The Revulsion against Internal Improvements." *Journal of Economic History* 10:145–151.

Gordon, David. 1976. "Capitalist Efficiency and Socialist Efficiency." *Monthly Review* 28(3):19–39.

Gordon, David. 1977. "Class Struggle and the States of American Urban Development." Pp. 55–82 in David C. Perry and Alfred J. Watkins (eds.), *The Rise of the Sunbelt Cities*. Beverly Hills, Calif.: Sage.

Gordon, David. 1978. "Capitalist Development and the History of American Cities." Pp. 25–63 in William K. Tabb and Larry Sawers (eds.), *Marxism and the Metropolis*. New York: Oxford University Press.

Gordon, Margaret T., Linda Heath, and Robert leBailly. 1979. "Some Costs of Easy News: Crime Reports and Fear." Paper presented at the annual meeting of the American Psychological Association, New York.

Gore, Robert J. 1979. "Harbor Officials React Bitterly to Sohio Pullout." *Los Angeles Times,* March 14, sec. I, pp. 3,31.

Gottdiener, Mark. 1977. *Planned Sprawl: Private and Public Interests in Suburbia.* Beverly Hills, Calif.: Sage.

Gottdiener, Mark, and Max Neiman. 1981. "Characteristics of Support for Local Growth Control." *Urban Affairs Quarterly* 17(1):55–73.

Gottlieb, Martin. 1983. "U.D.C. Looking to Suburbs and Rural Areas." *New York Times,* November 27, p. 40.

Graber, Edith. 1974. "Newcomers and Oldtimers: Growth and Change in a Mountain Town." *Rural Sociology* 39(4):504–513.

Granovetter, Mark. 1973. "The Strength of Weak Ties." *American Journal of Sociology* 78(May):1360–1380.

Greenberg, Stephanie. n.d. "Rapid Growth in a Southern Area: Consequences for Social Inequality." Unpublished manuscript, Denver Research Institute, University of Denver, Denver, Colorado.

Greer, Scott. 1962. *The Emerging City: Myth and Reality.* New York: Free Press.

Greer, Scott. 1965. *Urban Renewal and American Cities.* Indianapolis: Bobbs-Merrill.

Greer, William R. 1984. "Businesses That Serve Businesses Are Pacing Growth in Jobs in City." *New York Times,* December 3, sec. B, p. 4.

Grier, George, and Eunice Grier. 1980. "Urban Displacement: A Reconnaissance." Pp. 252–268 in Shirley Laska and Daphne Spain (eds.), *Back to the City: Issues in Neighborhood Renovation.* New York: Pergamon.

Guest, Avery M. 1985. "The Mediate Community: The Nature of Local and Extra-Local Ties within the Metropolis." Paper presented at the 80th annual meeting of the American Sociological Association, Washington, D.C., August.

Guest, Avery M., and Barrett A. Lee. 1983. "The Social Organization of Local Areas." *Urban Affairs Quarterly* 19(2):217–240.

Guest, Avery M., and R. S. Oropesa. 1984. "Problem-Solving Strategies of Local Areas in the Metropolis." *American Sociological Review* 49(December):828–840.

Gutman, Herbert. 1976. *Work, Culture, and Society in Industrializing America.* New York: Knopf.

Guttenplan, D. D. 1985. "Concrete Solutions: Why Developers Build on John Zuccotti's Reputation." *Manhattan, Inc.,* August, pp. 23–29.

Hadden, Jeffrey K., and Edgar Borgatta. 1965. *American Cities: Their Social Characteristics.* Chicago: Rand McNally.

Haeger, John. 1981. *The Investment Frontier.* Albany: State University of New York Press.

Halberstam, David. 1979. *The Powers That Be.* New York: Knopf.

Hall, Peter. 1973. "The Urban Growth Process." Pp. 613–629 in Peter Hall et al. (eds.), *The Containment of Urban England,* vol. 1. London: George Allen and Unwin.

Hallman, Howard W. 1977. *Small and Large Together: Governing the Metropolis.* Beverly Hills, Calif.: Sage.

Handlin, Oscar. 1951. *The Uprooted.* Boston: Little, Brown.

Haney, Richard, Jr. 1980. "Real Estate Heavyweights in the Eighties." *Real Estate Review* 10(2):35–43.

Harlan, Christi, and Allen Pusey. 1983. "Homeowners Organize against Condo Boom." *Dallas Morning News,* December 25, sec. A, p. 16.

Harnet, Richard M. 1985. "San Francisco Split over Battleship Group." *Schenectady Gazette,* February 25, p. 5.

Harris, Chauncey D. 1943. "A Functional Classification of Cities in the United States." *Geographical Review* 33:86–99.

Harris, Chauncey D., and Edward L. Ullman. 1945. "The Nature of Cities." *Annals of the American Academy of Political and Social Science* 242(November):7–17.

Harrison, Bennett, and Edward Hill. 1979. "Changing Structure of Jobs in Older and Younger Cities." Pp. 15–45 in Benjamin Chinitz (ed.), *Central City Economic Development.* Cambridge, Mass.: Abt Books.

Harrison, Bennett, and Sandra Kanter. 1976. "The Great State Robbery." *Working Papers for a New Society* 4(1):57–66.

Hartman, Chester, and Rob Kessler. 1978. "The Illusion and Reality of Urban Renewal: San Francisco's Yerba Buena Center." Pp. 153–178 in William K. Tabb and Larry Sawers (eds.), *Marxism and the Metropolis.* New York: Oxford University Press.

Harvey, David. 1973. *Social Justice and the City.* Baltimore: Johns Hopkins University Press.

Harvey, David. 1976. "Labor, Capital and Class Struggle around the Built Environment in Advanced Capitalist Societies." *Politics and Society* 6(3):265–295.

Harvey, David. 1980. "The Space-Economy of Capitalist Production: A Marxian Interpretation." Paper presented at a conference on new perspectives on the urban political economy, American University, Washington, D.C., May 22–24.

Harvey, David. 1982. *The Limits to Capital.* Chicago: University of Chicago Press.

Harvey, David. 1983. "Class-Monopoly Rent, Finance Capital and the Urban Revolution." Pp. 250–277 in Robert W. Lake (ed.), *Readings in Urban Analysis: Perspectives on Urban Form and Structure*. New Brunswick, N.J.: Center for Urban Policy Research, Rutgers University.

Hauser, Philip. 1967. "Observations on the Urban-Folk and Urban-Rural Dichotomies as Forms of Western Ethnocentrism." Pp. 503–519 in Philip M. Hauser and Leo F. Schnore (eds.), *The Study of Urbanization*. New York: Wiley.

Hawley, Amos. 1950. *Human Ecology: A Theory of Community Structure*. New York: Ronald Press.

Haworth, Charles T., James E. Long, and David W. Rasmussen. 1978. "Income Distribution, City Size, and Urban Growth." *Urban Studies* 15(1):1–7.

Hayden, Dolores. 1981. *The Grand Domestic Revolution*. Cambridge, Mass.: MIT Press.

Hayes, Thomas C. 1984. "Shortfall Likely in Olympic Income." *New York Times,* May 9, p. 5.

Hays, Samuel P. 1964. "The Politics of Reform in Municipal Government in the Progressive Era." *Pacific Northwest Quarterly* 55(4):157–169.

Hechter, Michael. 1975. *Internal Colonialism: The Celtic Fringe in British National Development, 1536–1966*. Berkeley and Los Angeles: University of California Press.

Henig, Jeffrey R. 1982. *Neighborhood Mobilization: Redevelopment and Response*. New Brunswick, N.J.: Rutgers University Press.

Herbers, John. 1982. "Administration Seeks to Cut Aid to Cities, Charging It's Harmful." *New York Times,* June 20, sec. A, pp. 1,25.

Herbers, John. 1983. "Industrial Flight in Minnesota." *New York Times,* April 12, sec. D, pp. 1,19.

Herbers, John. 1984. "Cities Spurning Washington in Bid to Reassert Authority." *New York Times,* February 19, sec. A, pp. 1,22.

Hermalin, Albert I., and Reynolds Farley. 1973. "The Potential for Residential Integration in Cities and Suburbs: Implications for the Busing Controversy." *American Sociological Review* 38:595–610.

Herman, Edward S. 1981. *Corporate Control, Corporate Power*. New York: Cambridge University Press.

Hibbs, Douglas A., Jr. 1977. "Political Parties and Macroeconomic Policy." *American Political Science Review* 71(4):1467–1487.

Hicks, Alexander, and Duane Swank. 1983. "Civil Disorder, Relief Mobilization, and AFDC Caseloads: A Reexamination of the Piven and Cloward Thesis." *American Journal of Political Science* 27(4):695–716.

Hicks, Alexander, Roger Friedland, and Edwin Johnson. 1978. "Class Power and State Policy: The Case of Large Business Corporations,

Labor Unions and Governmental Redistribution in the U.S." *American Sociological Review* 43(3):302–315.

Higham, John. 1975. *Send These to Me: Jews and Other Immigrants in Urban America*. New York: Atheneum.

Hill, Christian. 1978. "Keeping the Lid On." *Wall Street Journal,* February 8, pp. 1,27.

Hill, Richard Child. 1974. "Separate and Unequal: Governmental Inequality in the Metropolis." *American Political Science Review* 68(December):1557–1568.

Hill, Richard Child. 1982. "Transnational Capitalism and the Crisis of Industrial Cities." *Journal of Intergroup Relations* 10(3):30–41.

Hill, Richard Child. 1983. "Market, State and Community: National Urban Policy in the 1980s." *Urban Affairs Quarterly* 19(1):5–20.

Hill, Richard Child. 1984. "Economic Crisis and Political Response in the Motor City." Pp. 313–338 in Larry Sawers and William K. Tabb (eds.), *Sunbelt/Snowbelt: Urban Development and Regional Restructuring*. New York: Oxford University Press.

Hill, Richard Child, and Joe R. Feagin. 1984. "Detroit and Houston: Two Cities in Global Perspective." Paper presented at the 79th annual meeting of the American Sociological Association, San Antonio, Texas, August 27–31.

Hill, Richard, and Cynthia Negrey. 1985. "The Politics of Industrial Policy in Michigan." Pp. 119–138 in Sharon Zukin (ed.), *Industrial Policy: Business and Politics in the United States and France*. New York: Praeger.

Hirsch, Arnold R. 1983. "New Orleans: Sunbelt in the Swamp." Pp. 100–137 in Richard Bernard and Bradley Rice (eds.), *Sunbelt Cities*. Austin: University of Texas Press.

Hirsch, Seymour. 1969. "On Uncovering the Great Nerve Gas Coverup." *Ramparts* 3(July):12–18.

Hoch, Charles. 1984. "City Limits: Municipal Boundary Formation and Class Segregation." Pp. 101–119 in William K. Tabb and Larry Sawers (eds.), *Marxism and the Metropolis*. 2d ed. New York: Oxford University Press.

Hoch, Irving. 1972. "Urban Scale and Environmental Quality." Pp. 231–286 in U.S. Commission on Population Growth and the American Future, Ronald G. Ridker (ed.), *Population, Resources, and the Environment*, vol. 3 of Commission Research Reports. Washington, D.C.: Government Printing Office.

Hochschild, Arlie R. 1983. *The Managed Heart: The Commercialization of Human Feeling*. Berkeley and Los Angeles: University of California Press.

Hodson, Randy, and Robert L. Kaufman. 1982. "Economic Dualism: A

Critical Review." *American Sociological Review* 47(6):727–739.

Hogan, Mike. 1980. "Newport Beach: A Storm Rages over Development." *California Business,* June, pp. 65–68.

Holland, Stuart. 1975. *Capital vs. the Regions.* New York: St. Martin's Press.

Holli, Melvin G. 1969. *Reform in Detroit: Hazen S. Pingree and Urban Politics.* New York: Oxford University Press.

Hollingshead, A. B. 1947. "A Re-Examination of Ecological Theory." *Sociology and Social Research* 31(January-February):194–204.

Horan, James F., and G. Thomas Taylor, Jr. 1977. *Experiments in Metropolitan Government.* New York: Praeger.

Horowitz, David. 1978. *The First Frontier: The Indian Wars and America's Origins: 1607–1776.* New York: Simon and Schuster.

Howe, Irving, and Kenneth Libo. 1979. *How We Lived: A Documentary History of Immigrant Jews in America.* New York: Richard Marek.

Howenstine, E. Jay. 1982. *Attacking Housing Costs: Foreign Policies and Strategies.* New Brunswick, N.J.: Rutgers University, Center for Urban Policy Research.

Hsu, Evelyn. 1984. "S.F. Political Gifts—Developers Lead." *San Francisco Chronicle,* October 25, p. 1.

Huff, Martin. 1985. "Axing the Unitary Method Would Open Tax Loopholes." *Los Angeles Times,* June 17, sec. II, p. 5.

Hughes, Kathleen, and Hank Gilman. 1985. "Chesebrough to Buy Stauffer for $1.5 Billion." *Wall Street Journal,* February 20, p. 3.

Humberger, Edward. 1983. *Business Location: Decisions and Cities.* Washington, D.C.: Public Technology.

Humphrey, Craig, and Richard Krannich. 1980. "The Promotion of Growth in Small Urban Places and Its Impact on Population Change, 1975–78." *Social Science Quarterly* 61(December):581–594.

Hunter, Albert. 1974. *Symbolic Communities: The Persistence and Change of Chicago's Local Communities.* Chicago: University of Chicago Press.

Hunter, Albert, and Gerald Suttles. 1972. "The Expanding Community of Limited Liability." Pp. 44–81 in Gerald Suttles, *The Social Construction of Communities.* Chicago: University of Chicago Press.

Hunter, Floyd. 1953. *Community Power Structure: A Study of Decision Makers.* Chapel Hill: University of North Carolina Press.

Hunter, Floyd. 1980. *Community Power Succession.* Chapel Hill: University of North Carolina Press.

Hurst, John. 1983. "Two Small Towns Believe That Crime Pays, After All." *Los Angeles Times,* July 31, sec. I, p. 1.

Hymer, Stephen. 1972. "The Internationalization of Capital." *Journal of Economic Issues* 6(1):91–111.

Hymer, Stephen. 1976. *The International Operations of National Firms*. Cambridge, Mass.: MIT Press.

Hymer, Stephen. 1979a. *The Multinational Corporations: A Radical Approach*. London: Cambridge University Press.

Hymer, Stephen. 1979b. "The Multinational Corporation and the Law of Uneven Development." Pp. 386–403 in George Modelski (ed.), *Transnational Corporations and World Order: Readings in International Political Economy*. San Francisco: W. H. Freeman.

Hymer, Stephen, and Robert Rowthorn. 1979. "Multinational Corporations and International Oligopoly: The Non-American Challenge." Pp. 183–208 in Stephen Hymer, *The Multinational Corporation: A Radical Approach*. Cambridge: Cambridge University Press.

Jackson, Brooks. 1984. "Election Laws Change Campaign Role of Rich But Don't Diminish It." *Wall Street Journal,* October 24, sec. I, p. 1.

Jackson, Robert. 1980. "Foreign Investors Love New York." *Real Estate Review* 10(3):55–61.

Jackson, Robert. 1984. "Pay 42% Higher for Aerospace Executives." *Los Angeles Times,* October 28, sec. I, p. 5.

Jacobs, Jane. 1961. *The Death and Life of Great American Cities*. New York: Random House.

Jacobs, Jerry. 1979. *Bidding for Business: Corporate Questions and the Fifty Disunited States*. Washington, D.C.: Public Interest Research Group.

James, Barry. 1985. "Fakes Are Big Business." *Santa Barbara News Press,* February 3, pp. D1, 4.

James, Franklin J., Jr., and Dennis Gale. 1977. *Zoning for Sale: A Critical Analysis of Transferable Development Rights Programs*. Washington, D.C.: Urban Institute.

James, Franklin J., Jr., and Oliver Windsor. 1976. "Fiscal Zoning, Fiscal Reform and Exclusionary Land Use Controls." *Journal of the American Institute of Planners* 42:130–141.

Janelle, Donald G. 1977. "Structural Dimensions in the Geography of Locational Conflicts." *Canadian Geographer* 21(4):311–328.

Janowitz, Morris. 1951. *The Community Press in an Urban Setting*. Glencoe, Ill.: Free Press.

Jazairy, Idriss, Pieter Kuin, and Juan Somavia. 1977. "Transnational Enterprises." Pp. 157–160 in Jan Tinbergen, *Reshaping the International Order: A Report to the Club of Rome*. New York: Dutton.

Jencks, Christopher. 1983. "Discrimination and Thomas Sowell." *New York Review of Books* 30(5):33–38.

Jobert, Bruno. 1975. "Planning and Social Production of Needs." *Sociologie et Sociétés* 6(2):35–51.

Johnson, David R. 1983. "San Antonio: The Vicissitudes of Boosterism." Pp. 235–254 in Richard M. Bernard and Bradley R. Rice (eds.), *Sunbelt Cities: Politics and Growth since World War II*. Austin: University of Texas Press.

Johnson, Michael, and James L. Roark. 1984a. *Black Masters: A Free Family of Color*. New York: Norton.

Johnson, Michael, and James L. Roark. 1984b. *No Chariot Let Down: Charleston's Free People of Color on the Eve of the Civil War*. Chapel Hill: University of North Carolina Press.

Johnston, Robert. 1980. "The Politics of Local Growth Control." *Policy Studies Journal* 9(Winter):427–439.

Jones, Bryan D., Saasia R. Greenberg, Clifford Kaufman, and Joseph Drew. 1978. "Service Delivery Rules and the Distribution of Local Services: Three District Bureaucracies." *Journal of Politics* 40(2):332–368.

Jordon, Winthrop D. 1974. *The White Man's Burden: Historical Origins of Racism in the United States*. New York: Oxford University Press.

Judd, Dennis. 1983. "From Cowtown to Sunbelt City." Pp. 167–201 in Susan Fainstein (ed.), *Restructuring the City*. New York: Longman.

Jung, Maureen A. 1983. "Influences of Durkheim and the Political Economists on the Sociological Theory of Robert E. Park and Ernest E. Burgess." Unpublished paper, Department of Sociology, University of California, Santa Barbara.

Jung, Maureen A. 1984. "Formal and Substantive Views of the Economy: A Sociological Study of Stock Market Speculation of the 1920s." Paper presented at the 79th annual meeting of the American Sociological Association, San Antonio, Texas, August 27–31.

Jung, Maureen A. 1985. "Organizational Perspectives on Firm Formation and Transformation." Unpublished paper, Department of Sociology, University of California, Santa Barbara.

Juster, Francis Thomas (ed.). 1977. *The Economic and Political Impact of Revenue Sharing*. Ann Arbor: Survey Research Center, Institute for Social Research, University of Michigan.

Kanter, Rosabeth. 1977. *Men and Women of the Corporation*. New York: Basic Books.

Kaplan, Barry J. 1983. "Houston: The Golden Buckle of the Sunbelt." Pp. 196–212 in Richard M. Bernard and Bradley R. Rice (eds.), *Sunbelt Cities: Politics and Growth since World War II*. Austin: University of Texas Press.

Kaplan, Sam Hall. 1984. "Will Times Square Plan Destroy It?" *Los Angeles Times*, October 3, sec. I, p. 1.

Kasarda, John. 1983. "Entry Level Jobs, Mobility, and Minority Unemployment." *Urban Affairs Quarterly* 19(1):21–40.

Kasarda, John, and Morris Janowitz. 1974. "Community Attachment in

Mass Society." *American Sociological Review* 39(3):328–339.

Katz, Naomi, and D. Kemnitzer. 1983. "Fast Forward: The Internationalization of Silicon Valley." Pp. 332–345 in June Nash and Maria P. F. Kelley (eds.), *Women, Men and the International Division of Labor*. Albany: State University of New York Press.

Katz, Steven, and Margit Mayer. 1985. "Gimme Shelter: Self-Help Housing Struggles within and against the State in New York City and West Berlin." *International Journal of Urban and Regional Research* 9(1):15–46.

Katznelson, Ira. 1981. *City Trenches: Urban Politics and the Patterning of Class in the United States*. New York: Pantheon.

Katznelson, Ira, Kathleen Gille, and Margaret Weir. 1982. "Race and Schooling: Reflections on the Social Bases of Urban Movements." Pp. 215–235 in Norman Fainstein and Susan Fainstein (eds.), *Urban Policy under Capitalism*. Beverly Hills, Calif.: Sage.

Keith, Nathaniel. 1973. *Politics and the Housing Crisis since 1930*. New York: Universe Books.

Keller, John. 1983. "The Division of Labor in Electronics." Pp. 346–373 in June Nash and Maria P. F. Kelley (eds.), *Women, Men and the International Division of Labor*. Albany: State University of New York Press.

Keller, Suzanne I. 1968. *The Urban Neighborhood: A Sociological Perspective*. New York: Random House.

Kemp, Jack. 1980. Testimony before U.S. House of Representatives, Committee on Banking, Finance and Urban Affairs, Subcommittee on the City, hearing on urban revitalization and economic policy. Washington, D.C.: Government Printing Office.

Kempton, Murray. 1985. "The Wind That Blew in Reagan." *New York Review of Books* 32(3):3–7.

Kennan, George. 1984. "Two Letters." *New Yorker* 60(32):55–80.

Kershner, Vale. 1985. "Questions, Answers on the Unitary Tax." *San Francisco Chronicle,* August 21, sec. A, p. 9.

Keyfitz, Nathan. 1965. "Political-Economic Aspects of Urbanization in South and Southeast Asia." Pp. 265–310 in Philip Hauser and Leo F. Schnore (eds.), *The Study of Urbanization*. New York: Wiley.

Kieschnick, Michael. 1981. *Taxes and Growth: Business Incentives and Economic Development*. Washington, D.C.: Council of State Planning Agencies.

King, Wayne. 1983. "Houston Spawns a Thriving Underground Market in Sewer Rights." *New York Times,* November 28, sec. I, p. 18.

King, Wayne. 1985. "U. of Texas Facing Cuts in Its Budget." *New York Times,* March 17, p. 12.

Klein, Maury. 1970. *The Great Richmond Terminal: A Study of Busi-*

nessmen and Business Strategy. Charlottesville: University Press of Virginia.

Kochman, Thomas. 1981. *Black and White: Styles in Conflict.* Chicago: University of Chicago Press.

Koenig, Thomas, and Robert Gogel. 1981. "Interlocking Directorates as a Social Network." *American Journal of Economics and Sociology* 40(2):37–50.

Komarovsky, Mirra. 1962. *Blue-Collar Marriage.* New York: Random House.

Kornblum, William. 1974. *Blue Collar Community.* Chicago: University of Chicago Press.

Kotler, Milton. 1969. *Neighborhood Government: The Local Foundations of Political Life.* Indianapolis: Bobbs-Merrill.

Kowinski, William. 1985. *The Malling of America.* New York: William Morrow.

Krannich, Richard S., and Craig R. Humphrey. 1983. "Local Mobilization and Community Growth: Toward an Assessment of the 'Growth Machine' Hypothesis." *Rural Sociology* 48(1):60–81.

Krieger, Martin H. 1970. "Six Propositions on the Poor and Pollution." *Policy Sciences* 1:311–324.

Kristof, Nicholas D. 1984. "New Era in Service Exports?" *New York Times,* October 24, sec. D, pp. 1,2.

Krohn, Roger, Berkeley Fleming, and Marilyn Manzer. 1977. *The Other Economy: The Internal Logic of Local Rental Housing.* Toronto: Peter Martin Associates.

Kroll, Cynthia. 1981. "Local Distributional Effects of Energy Developments: Boomtown in the Northern Great Plains." Ph.D. dissertation, Department of City and Regional Planning, University of California, Berkeley.

Kucera, Clair L. 1978. *The Challenge of Ecology,* 2d ed. St. Louis: Mosby.

Kucinich, Dennis J. 1978. "Kucinich Defies 'Urban Populism.'" *Cleveland Press,* October 3, sec. A, p. 9.

Lake, Laura M. 1983. "The Environmental Mandate: Activists and the Electorate." *Political Science Quarterly* 98(Summer):215–233.

Lamarche, Francois. 1976. "Property Development and the Economic Foundations of the Urban Question." Pp. 85–118 in C. G. Pickvance (ed.), *Urban Sociology: Critical Essays.* New York: St. Martin's Press.

Lamb, David. 1983. "Once-Lovely Cairo Turns to Ugliness." *Los Angeles Times,* June 15, pp. 1,8,9.

Laska, Shirley B., and Daphne Spain (eds.). 1980. *Back to the City: Issues in Neighborhood Renovation.* New York: Pergamon.

Lasswell, Harold. 1936. *Politics: Who Gets What, When, How*. New York: McGraw-Hill.

Lauber, V. 1978. "Ecology and Elitism in American Society: The Fallacy of the Post-Materialist Hypothesis." Paper presented at the 32d annual meeting of the Western Political Science Association, Los Angeles, March 16–18.

Lave, Lester B., and Eugene P. Seskin (eds.). 1977. *Air Pollution and Human Health*. Baltimore: Johns Hopkins University Press.

Leach, Edmund Ronald. 1976. *Social Anthropology: A Natural Science of Society*. London: British Academy.

Lefebvre, Henri. 1970. *La Revolution Urbaine*. Paris: Gallimard.

Lehmann, Nicholas. 1985. "Change in the Banks." *Atlantic Monthly* 256(2):60–68.

Lester, Marilyn. 1971. "Toward a Sociology of Public Events." Master's thesis, Department of Sociology, University of California, Santa Barbara.

Lever, Janet. 1983. *Soccer in Brazil: Sports' Contribution to Social Integration*. Chicago: University of Chicago Press.

Levine, Adeline Gordon. 1982. *Love Canal: Science, Politics and People*. Lexington, Mass: D. C. Heath.

Levine, Martin P. 1980. "The Ghetto: Towards a Reconceptualization." Paper presented at the 75th annual meeting of the American Sociological Association, August 29. Boston.

Levison, Andrew. 1974. *The Working Class Majority*. New York: Coward, McCann and Geoghegan.

Levy, Steven, and Robert K. Arnold. 1972. "An Evaluation of Four Growth Alternatives in the City of Milpitas, 1972–1977." Technical Memorandum Report. Palo Alto, Calif.: Institute of Regional and Urban Studies.

Lewis, Dan A., and Michael G. Maxfield. 1980. "Fear in the Neighborhoods: An Investigation of the Impact of Crime." *Journal of Research in Crime and Delinquency* 17(2):160–189.

Lewis, Dan A., and Greta Salem. 1983. *Crime and Urban Community: Towards a Theory of Neighborhood Security*. Evanston, Ill.: Center of Urban Affairs, Northwestern University.

Lewis, Geoffrey. 1985. "Wherever GM Puts Saturn, It's Going to Get a Sweet Deal." *Business Week*, April 1, pp. 36–37.

Lewis, Paul. 1984. "Europeans Keeping to Building Plans on Nuclear Power." *New York Times*, January 23, p. 24.

Lewis, Richard. 1972. *The Nuclear Power Rebellion*. New York: Viking.

Lewis, Tamar. 1984. "Cynicism Cited in Plan's Loss." *New York Times*, June 14, sec. I, p. 42.

Ley, David. 1974. *The Black Inner City as Frontier Outpost*. Washington, D.C.: Association of American Geographers.

Ley, David, and J. Mercer. 1980. "Locational Conflict and the Politics of Consumption." *Economic Geography* 56:89–109.

Licht, Judy. 1983. "The Nuclear Waste Lottery." *Re:Sources* 6(3):1–7.

Lieberson, Stanley. 1980. *A Piece of the Pie: Blacks and White Immigrants since 1800*. Berkeley and Los Angeles: University of California Press.

Liebow, Elliot. 1967. *Tally's Corner*. Boston: Little, Brown.

Lineberry, Robert. 1977. *Equality and Urban Policy: The Distribution of Urban Public Services*. Beverly Hills, Calif.: Sage.

Linsky, Arnold S. 1965. "Some Generalizations concerning Primate Cities." *Annals of the Association of American Geographers* 55(September):506–513.

Lipton, S. Gregory. 1977. "Evidence of Central City Revival." *Journal of the American Planning Association* 45:136–147.

Livingston, Laurence, and John A. Blayney. 1971. "Foothill Environmental Design Study: Open Space vs. Development." Final report to the City of Palo Alto. San Francisco: Livingston and Blayney.

Lo, Clarence Y. H. 1984. "Mobilizing the Tax Revolt: The Emergent Alliance between Homeowners and Local Elites." Pp. 293–328 in Richard Ratcliff (ed.), *Research in Social Movements, Conflict, and Change*, vol. 6. Greenwich, Conn.: JAI Press.

Lofland, Lyn. 1973. *A World of Strangers*. New York: Basic Books.

Logan, John R. 1976a. "Industrialization and the Stratification of Cities in Suburban Regions." *American Journal of Sociology* 82(2):333–348.

Logan, John R. 1976b. "Notes on the Growth Machine: Toward a Comparative Political Economy of Growth." *American Journal of Sociology* 82(2):349–352.

Logan, John R. 1978. "Growth, Politics, and the Stratification of Places." *American Journal of Sociology* 84(2):404–415.

Logan, John R. 1983a. "The Disappearance of Communities from National Urban Policy." *Urban Affairs Quarterly* 19(1):75–90.

Logan, John R. 1983b. "Worker Mobilization and Party Politics: Revolutionary Portugal in Perspective." Pp. 135–150 in Lawrence Graham and Douglas Wheeler (eds.), *In Search of Modern Portugal*. Madison: University of Wisconsin Press.

Logan, John R., and O. Andrew Collver. 1983. "Residents' Perceptions of Suburban Community Differences." *American Sociological Review* 48(3):428–433.

Logan, John R., and Reid Golden. Forthcoming. "Suburbs and Satellites: Two Decades of Change." *American Sociological Review.*

Logan, John R., and Mark Schneider. 1981a. "The Stratification of Metropolitan Suburbs, 1960–1970." *American Sociological Review* 46(2):175–186.

Logan, John R., and Mark Schneider. 1981b. "Suburban Municipal Expenditures: The Effects of Business Activity, Functional Responsibility, and Regional Context." *Policy Studies Journal* 9:10–39.

Logan, John R., and Mark Schneider. 1982. "Governmental Organization and City/Suburb Income Inequality 1960–1970." *Urban Affairs Quarterly* 17(3):303–318.

Logan, John R., and Mark Schneider. 1984. "Racial Segregation and Racial Change in American Suburbs, 1970–1980." *American Journal of Sociology* 89(4):874–888.

Logan, John R., and Moshe Semyonov. 1980. "Growth and Succession in Suburban Communities." *Sociological Quarterly* 21(1):93–105.

Logan, John R., and Linda Brewster Stearns. 1981. "Suburban Racial Segregation as a Non-Ecological Process." *Social Forces* 60(1): 61–73.

Lohr, Steve. 1984. "Singapore's Link to Chicago." *New York Times,* September 7, pp. 31,34.

London, Bruce. 1980. "Gentrification as Urban Reinvasion: Some Preliminary Definitional and Theoretical Considerations." Pp. 77–92 in Shirley B. Laska and Daphne Spain (eds.), *Back to the City: Issues in Neighborhood Renovation.* New York: Pergamon Press.

Long, Norton. 1958. "The Local Community as an Ecology of Games." *American Journal of Sociology* 64:251–261.

Los Angeles Times. 1982. "Developers Double Vote Contributions in State Race." *Los Angeles Times,* March 31, sec. I, p. 26.

Losch, August. 1954. *The Economics of Location.* New Haven, Conn.: Yale University Press.

Love, Sam. 1972. "Ecology and Social Justice: Is There a Conflict?" *Environmental Action* 4:3–6.

Lowe, P. D. 1977. "Amenity and Equity: A Review of Local Environmental Pressure Groups in Britain." *Environment and Planning* 9(1): 35–58.

Lubasch, Arnold. 1977. "Ban Lifted on U.S. Aid to Hartford Suburbs." *New York Times,* August 16, p. 36.

Luckingham, Bradford. 1983. "Phoenix: The Desert Metropolis." Pp. 309–327 in Richard M. Bernard and Bradley R. Rice (eds.), *Sunbelt Cities: Politics and Growth since World War II.* Austin: University of Texas Press.

Lueck, Thomas J. 1984. "Connecticut Growth Makes Its Economy One of Best in U.S." *New York Times,* September 18, sec. A, p. 1, sec. B, p. 5.

Luger, Michael. 1984. "Federal Tax Incentives as Industrial and Urban Policy." Pp. 201–234 in Larry Sawers and William K. Tabb (eds.), *Sunbelt/Snowbelt: Urban Development and Regional Restructuring.* New York: Oxford University Press.

Lydenberg, Steven D. 1980. *Bankrolling Ballots Update 1980: The Role of Business in Financing Ballot Question Campaigns.* New York: Council on Economic Priorities.

Lynch, Kevin. 1960. *The Image of the City.* Cambridge, Mass.: MIT Press.

Lyon, Larry, Lawrence G. Felice, M. Ray Perryman, and E. Stephen Parker. 1981. "Community Power and Population Increase: An Empirical Test of the Growth Machine Model." *American Journal of Sociology* 86(6):1387–1400.

McCaull, Julian. 1976. "Discriminatory Air Pollution." *Environment* 18(2):26–32.

McCombs, Maxwell E., and Donald Shaw. 1972. "The Agenda Setting Function of Mass Media." *Public Opinion Quarterly* 36:176–187.

McConnell, Grant. 1966. *Private Power and American Democracy.* New York: Random House.

McGarry, T. W. 1985. "Irish Will March to Four Different Drummers." *Los Angeles Times,* March 14, sec. II, pp. 1,3.

McGee, T. G. 1967. *The Southeast Asian City: A Social Geography of the Primate Cities of Southeast Asia.* London: G. Bell.

McKenzie, R. D. 1922. "The Neighborhood: A Study of Local Life in the City of Columbus Ohio—Conclusion." *American Journal of Sociology* 27:780–799.

McKenzie, R. D. 1933. *The Metropolitan Community.* New York: McGraw-Hill.

McKenzie, R. D. (1926) 1961. "The Scope of Human Ecology." Pp. 30–36 in George A. Theodorson (ed.), *Studies in Human Ecology.* Evanston, Ill.: Harper and Row.

McKown, Ted. 1980. "Executives Protest County Curb on Industrial Growth." *Santa Barbara News Press,* January 20, sec. A, p. 4.

McLemore, David. 1984. "Prospect of N-Waste Dump Stirs Fear, Anger in Hereford." *Dallas Morning News,* December 26, sec. A, pp. 1,7.

McMillan, T. E., Jr. 1965. "Why Manufacturers Choose Plant Locations vs. Determinants of Plant Location." *Land Economics* 41(3):239–246.

Magdoff, Harry. 1966. *The Age of Imperialism.* New York: Monthly Review Press.

Maguire, Miles. 1985. "Boondoggle or Marvel: Tenn-Tom Waterway Locks Open." *Baltimore Sun,* January 13, sec. D, p. 1.

Maita, Stephen. 1985. "S.F.'s Real Estate King." *San Francisco Chronicle,* July 22, sec. I, pp. 22,23,31.

Makielski, Stanislaw J. 1966. *The Politics of Zoning: The New York Experience.* New York: Columbia University Press.

Malecki, E. J. 1980. "Corporate Organization of R&D and the Location of Technological Activities." *Regional Studies* 14(3):219–234.

Mandel, Ernest. 1975. *Late Capitalism.* Atlantic Highlands, N.J.: Humanities Press.

Mandelker, Daniel. 1971. *The Zoning Dilemma.* Indianapolis: Bobbs-Merrill.

Mansbridge, Jane J. 1980. *Beyond Adversary Democracy.* New York: Basic Books.

Mar, Don. 1984. "Chinese Immigrants and the Ethnic Labor Market." Unpublished Ph.D. dissertation, Department of Economics, University of California, Berkeley.

Marcuse, Peter. 1981. "The Targeted Crisis: On the Ideology of the Urban Fiscal Crisis and its Uses." *International Journal of Urban and Regional Research* 5(3):330–355.

Marglin, Stephen A. 1974. "What Do Bosses Do?" *Review of Radical Political Economics* 6(2):60–112.

Margolis, Julius. 1957. "Municipal Fiscal Structure in a Metropolitan Region." *Journal of Political Economy* 65(June):225–236.

Markusen, Ann. 1978. "Class, Rent and Sectoral Conflict: Uneven Development in Western U.S. Boomtowns." *Review of Radical Political Economics* 10(3):117–129.

Markusen, Ann. 1980. "City Spatial Structure, Women's Household Work, and National Urban Policy." *Signs* 5(3):23–44.

Markusen, Ann R. 1984. "Class and Urban Social Expenditure: A Marxist Theory of Metropolitan Government." Pp. 82–101 in William K. Tabb and Larry Sawers (eds.), *Marxism and the Metropolis.* New York: Oxford University Press.

Markusen, James R. 1979. "Elements of Real Asset Pricing: A Theoretical Analysis with Special Reference to Urban Land Prices." *Land Economics* 55(2):153–166.

Martin, L. G. 1975. "The 500: A Report on Two Decades." *Fortune* 41:238–241.

Marx, Karl. 1967. *Capital* (3 volumes). New York: International Publishers Edition.

Masotti, Louis H., and Jeffrey K. Hadden (eds.). 1973. *The Urbanization of the Suburbs.* Beverly Hills, Calif.: Sage.

Massey, Doreen. 1984. *Spatial Divisions of Labor: Social Structures and the Geography of Production*. New York: Methuen.

Maurer, Richard, and James Christenson. 1982. "Growth and Non-growth Orientations of Urban, Suburban and Rural Mayors: Reflections on the City as a Growth Machine." *Social Science Quarterly* 63(June):350–358.

Mazie, Sara Mills, and Steve Rowlings. 1973. "Public Attitude toward Population Distribution Issues." Pp. 603–615 in Sara Mills Mazie (ed.), *Population Distribution and Policy*. Washington, D.C.: Commission on Population Growth and the American Future.

Melosi, Martin. 1983. "Dallas-Fort Worth: Marketing the Metroplex." Pp. 162–195 in Richard M. Bernard and Bradley R. Rice (eds.), *Sunbelt Cities: Politics and Growth since World War II*. Austin: University of Texas Press.

Mercer, Lloyd J., and W. Douglas Morgan. 1982. "An Estimate of Residential Growth Controls' Impact on House Prices." Pp. 189–215 in M. Bruce Johnson (ed.), *Resolving the Housing Crisis: Government Policy, Decontrol, and the Public Interest*. San Francisco: Pacific Institute for Public Policy Research.

Metropolitan Council of the Twin Cities Area. 1976. *Modest-Cost Housing in the Twin Cities Metropolitan Area*. St. Paul, Minn.: Metropolitan Council of the Twin Cities Area.

Meyer, Richard. 1984. *Running to Shelter*. New York: Public Citizen Press.

Meyer, Richard. 1985. "Tax Shelters Abuse the System." *Los Angeles Times,* March 14, sec. II, p. 5.

Meyerson, Martin, and Edward C. Banfield. 1955. *Politics, Planning and the Public Interest*. New York: Macmillan.

Michelson, William H. 1976. *Man and His Urban Environment*. Reading, Mass.: Addison-Wesley.

Mier, Robert, and Scott E. Gelzer. 1982. "State Enterprise Zones: The New Frontier?" *Urban Affairs Quarterly* 18:39–52.

Milbrath, Lester W. 1965. *Political Participation; How and Why Do People Get Involved in Politics?* Skokie, Ill.: Rand McNally.

Miller, Gary. 1982. *The Lakewood Plan and the Politics of Municipal Incorporation*. Cambridge, Mass.: MIT Press.

Miller, Jay. 1981. "Assessing Residential Land Price Inflation." *Urban Land* 40(3):16–20.

Mills, C. Wright. 1956. *The Power Elite*. New York: Oxford University Press.

Mills, C. Wright. 1959. *The Sociological Imagination*. New York: Oxford University Press.

Mills, C. Wright, and Melville Ulmer. 1970. "Small Business and Civic Welfare." Pp. 124–154 in Michael T. Aiken and Paul E. Mott (eds.), *The Structure of Community Power*. New York: Random House.

Mingione, Enzo. 1981. *Social Conflict and the City*. New York: St. Martin's Press.

Mintz, Beth, and Michael Schwartz. 1981a. "Interlocking Directorates and Interest Group Formation." *American Sociological Review* 46(6):851–867.

Mintz, Beth, and Michael Schwartz. 1981b. "The Structure of Intercorporate Unity in American Business." *Social Problems* 29(2):87–103.

Mintz, Beth, and Michael Schwartz. 1985. *The Power Structure of American Business*. Chicago: University of Chicago Press.

Mitchell, Daniel J. B. 1983. "International Convergence with U.S. Wage Levels." Working Paper Series 57, Institute of Industrial Relations, University of California, Los Angeles.

Mitchell, John L. 1984. "Thousands of Dollars Fueling Beverly Hills Hotel Campaigns." *Los Angeles Times,* November 4, sec. W, p. 1.

Mitchell, Robert Cameron. 1979. "Silent Spring/Solid Majorities." *Public Opinion* 2(August-September):16–21.

Mohl, Raymond A. 1984. "Miami: The Ethnic Cauldron." Pp. 58–99 in Richard M. Bernard and Bradley R. Rice (eds.), *Sunbelt Cities: Politics and Growth since World War II*. Austin: University of Texas Press.

Mollenkopf, John. 1976. "The Postwar Politics of Urban Development." *Politics and Society* 5(3):247–295.

Mollenkopf, John. 1981. "Community and Accumulation." Pp. 319–338 in Michael Dear and Allen J. Scott (eds.), *Urbanization and Urban Planning in Capitalist Society.* New York: Methuen.

Mollenkopf, John. 1983. *The Contested City*. Princeton, N.J.: Princeton University Press.

Molotch, Harvey. 1967. "Toward a More Human Human Ecology." *Land Economics* 44(June):336–341.

Molotch, Harvey. 1969. "Racial Change in a Stable Community." *American Journal of Sociology* 75(2):226–238.

Molotch, Harvey. 1970. "Oil in Santa Barbara and Power in America." *Sociological Inquiry* 40(Winter):131–144.

Molotch, Harvey. 1972. *Managed Integration: Dilemmas of Doing Good in the City.* Berkeley and Los Angeles: University of California Press.

Molotch, Harvey. 1976. "The City as a Growth Machine." *American Journal of Sociology* 82(2):309–330.

Molotch, Harvey. 1979. "Capital and Neighborhood in the United States." *Urban Affairs Quarterly* 14(3):289–312.

Molotch, Harvey. 1980. "Media and Movements." Pp. 71–93 in Mayer Zald and John McCarthy (eds.), *The Dynamics of Social Movements*. Cambridge, Mass.: Winthrop.

Molotch, Harvey. 1984. "Romantic Marxism: Love Is (Still) Not Enough." *Contemporary Sociology* 13(2):141–143.

Molotch, Harvey, and Joseph Kasof. 1981. "The Impacts of Land Use Constraint: Environmentalism, Speculation and the Housing Crisis." Paper presented at meeting of the American Sociological Association, New York, August 31.

Molotch, Harvey, and Marilyn Lester. 1974. "News as Purposive Behavior: On the Strategic Use of Routine Events, Accidents, and Scandals." *American Sociological Review* 39(1):101–113.

Molotch, Harvey, and Marilyn Lester. 1975. "Accidental News: The Great Oil Spill as Local Occurrence and National Event." *American Journal of Sociology* 81(2):235–260.

Montanelli, Indro. 1970. "For Venice." Pp. 8–22 in International Fund for Monuments, *Venice in Peril*. New York: International Fund for Monuments.

Morain, Dan. 1985. "S.F. Moves: Yuppies In, the Poor Out." *Los Angeles Times*, April 3, sec. I, pp. 1,3,22.

Moriarty, Barry M. 1980. *Industrial Location and Community Development*. Chapel Hill: University of North Carolina Press.

Mormino, Gary R. 1983. "Tampa: From Hell Hole to the Good Life." Pp. 138–161 in Richard M. Bernard and Bradley R. Rice (eds.), *Sunbelt Cities: Politics and Growth since World War II*. Austin: University of Texas Press.

Moses, L., and H. Williamson. 1967. "The Location of Economic Activity in Cities." *American Economic Review* 57(2):211–222.

Moskowitz, Milton, Michael Katz, and Robert Levering. 1980. *Everybody's Business, an Almanac: The Irreverent Guide to Corporate America*. San Francisco: Harper and Row.

Moss, William G. 1977. "Large Lot Zoning, Property Taxes, and Metropolitan Area." *Journal of Urban Economics* 4(4):408–427.

Moulaert, Frank, and Patricia W. Salinas (eds.). 1983. *Regional Analysis and the New International Division of Labor: Applications of a Political Economy Approach*. Boston: Kluwer-Nijhoff.

Mueller, Eva. 1961. *Location Decision and Industrial Mobility in Michigan, 1961*. Ann Arbor: Survey Research Center, University of Michigan.

Muller, Peter O. 1982. *Contemporary Suburban America*. Englewood Cliffs, N.J.: Prentice-Hall.

Mumford, Lewis. 1961. *The City in History.* New York: Harcourt.

Murray, Richard. 1980. "Politics of a Boomtown." *Dissent* 27(4):500–504.

Musgrave, P. B. 1975. "Direct Investment Abroad and the Multinationals: Effects on the United States Economy." Subcommittee on Multinational Corporations, Committee on Foreign Relations, U.S. Senate, 94th Congress, 1st Session (August). Washington, D.C.: Government Printing Office.

Muth, Richard. 1969. *Cities and Housing.* Chicago: University of Chicago Press.

Muth, Richard, and Elliot Wetzler. 1976. "The Effect of Constraints on Housing Costs." *Journal of Urban Economics* 3(1):57–67.

Myrdal, Gunnar. 1944. *An American Dilemma: The Negro Problem and Modern Democracy.* New York: Harper.

Nakase, T. 1981. "Some Characteristics of Japanese-Type Multinationals Today." *Capital and Class* 13:61–98.

Narvaex, Alfonso. 1984. "11-Term Congressman Assesses Loss." *New York Times,* November 11, sec. A, p. 40.

Nathan, Richard P., Allen D. Mannel, Susannah E. Calkins, and Associates. 1975. *Monitoring Revenue Sharing.* Washington, D.C.: Brookings Institute.

Nathan (Robert R.) Associates. 1968. *Industrial and Employment Potential of the United States-Mexico Border.* Washington, D.C.: U.S. Department of Commerce, Economic Development Administration.

National Institute for Advanced Studies. 1983. "Market Generated Displacement" (draft report). Washington, D.C.: National Institute for Advanced Studies.

Navin, Thomas A., and Marian V. Sears. 1955. "The Rise of a Market for Industrial Securities." *Business History Review* 29(1):105–138.

Neiman, Max, and Ronald O. Loveridge. 1981. "Environmentalism and Local Growth Control: A Probe into the Class Bias Thesis." *Environment and Behavior* 13(6):759–772.

Nelson, Kathryn P. 1979. *Recent Suburbanization of Blacks: How Much, Who and Where?* Washington, D.C.: U.S. Department of Housing and Urban Development.

Nelson, Kathryn P. 1980. "Recent Suburbanization of Blacks." *Journal of the American Planning Association* 46(3):287–300.

Nelson, Kathryn P. 1984. "Distressed Cities and Migration." Paper presented at the 79th annual meeting of the American Sociological Association, San Antonio, August 27–31.

Nelson, Ralph Lowell. 1959. *Merger Movements in American Industry,*

1895–1956. Princeton, N.J.: Princeton University Press.

Nelson, Robert H. 1977. *Zoning and Property Rights*. Cambridge, Mass.: MIT Press.

Netzer, Dick. 1966. *Economics of the Property Tax*. Washington, D.C.: Brookings Institute.

Newman, Sandra J., and Michael Owen. 1980. "Residential Displacement in the U.S., 1970–77." U.S. Department of Housing and Urban Development, Office of Policy Development and Research.

Newson, Michael DeHaven. 1971. "Blacks and Historic Preservation." *Law and Contemporary Problems* 36(Summer):423–431.

Newton, Kenneth. 1975. "American Urban Politics: Social Class, Political Structure and Public Goods." *Urban Affairs Quarterly* 11:241–264.

Newton, Kenneth. 1976. "Feeble Governments and Private Power: Urban Politics and Policies in the United States." Pp. 37–58 in Louis Masotti and Robert Lineberry (eds.), *The New Urban Politics*. Cambridge, Mass.: Ballinger.

Newton, Kenneth. 1978. "Conflict Avoidance and Conflict Suppression: The Case of Urban Politics in the United States." Pp. 76–93 in Kevin Cox (ed.), *Urbanization and Conflict in Market Societies*. Chicago: Maaroufa Press.

New York Times. 1981. "Mormons Reject the MX Missile in Their Backyard." *New York Times,* May 10, sec. D, p. 4.

New York Times. 1984a. "Some Affluent Jersey Towns Bow to Court and Accept Low-Income Homes." *New York Times,* February 29, sec. A, p. 1, sec. B, p. 5.

New York Times. 1984b. "California's Split on the Unitary Tax." *New York Times,* September 18, sec. D, p. 4.

New York Times. 1984c. "Census Report Shows Rise in Foreign-Born Americans." *New York Times,* October 21, sec. A, p. 60.

New York Times. 1984d. "Plan for Nuclear Dump Divides Dakota Town." *New York Times,* November 4, sec. A, p. 76.

New York Times. 1985. "Spreading Stardust in Europe." *New York Times,* November 11, sec. A, p. 26.

Nguyen, Liem T., and Allan B. Henkin. 1982. "Vietnamese Refugees in the United States: Adaptation and Transitional Status." *Journal of Ethnic Studies* 9(4):101–116.

Nicholas, James C. 1981. "Housing Costs and Prices under Growth Control Regulation." *Journal of the American Real Estate and Urban Economics Association* 9(4):384–396.

Nishioka, Hisao, and Gunter Krumme. 1973. "Location Conditions,

Factors and Decisions: An Evaluation of Selected Location Surveys." *Land Economics* 49:195–205.

Noland, E. William. 1962. "The Role of Top Business Executives in Urban Growth." Pp. 226–259 in Francis S. Chapin, Jr., and Shirley F. Weiss (eds.), *Urban Growth Dynamics*. New York: Wiley.

Novak, Thomas P., and J. Richard Udry. 1983. "Indicators of Quality of Life as a Function of Skin Color in Egypt and Thailand." Paper presented at the 78th annual meeting of the American Sociological Association, Detroit, Michigan, August 31–September 4.

Noyelle, Thierry J. 1983. "The Implications of Industry Restructuring for Spatial Organization in the United States." Pp. 113–133 in Frank Moulaert and Patricia W. Salinas (eds.), *Regional Analysis and the New International Division of Labor*. Boston: Kluwer-Nijhoff.

Oakland, William H. 1977. "Local Taxes and Intraurban Industrial Location: A Survey." Pp. 13–30 in George F. Break (ed.), *Metropolitan Financing and Growth Management Policies: Principles and Practices* (proceedings of a symposium sponsored by the Committee on Taxation, Resources and Economic Development at the University of Wisconsin-Madison, 1974). Madison: University of Wisconsin Press.

O'Connor, James. 1973. *The Fiscal Crisis of the State*. New York: St. Martin's Press.

O'Connor, Michael. 1984. "A Modern Dilemma: Contrast and Conflicts in Miami Beach's Deco District." *Art and Antiques,* May, pp. 43–49.

Offe, Claus. 1982. *Structural Problems of the Capitalist State*. London: Macmillan.

Oliver, Melvin. 1984. "The Urban Black Community as Network: Toward a Social Network Analytic Perspective." Unpublished paper, Department of Sociology, University of California, Los Angeles.

Oliver, Melvin, and Mark A. Glick. 1982. "An Analysis of the New Orthodoxy on Black Mobility." *Social Problems* 29(5):511–523.

Oliver, Melvin, and James Johnson, Jr. 1984. "Inter-Ethnic Conflict in an Urban Ghetto: The Case of Blacks and Latinos in Los Angeles." Pp. 57–94 in Richard Ratcliff (ed.), *Research in Social Movements, Conflict, and Change* (vol. 6). Greenwich, Conn.: JAI Press.

Oreskes, Michael. 1984. "State Offers Loan to Bail Out Yonkers." *New York Times,* March 29, sec. B, p. 3.

Orlebecke, Charles J. 1982. "Administering Enterprise Zones: Some Initial Observations." *Urban Affairs Quarterly* 18(1):31–38.

Osofsky, Gilbert. 1963. *Harlem: The Making of a Ghetto*. New York: Harper and Row.

Ostrom, Elinor. 1983. "The Social Stratification-Government Inequality

Thesis Explored." *Urban Affairs Quarterly* 19(1):91–112.

Pack, Howard, and Janet Rothenberg Pack. 1978. "Metropolitan Fragmentation and Local Public Expenditures." *National Tax Journal* 31(4):349–361.

Pahl, Raymond Edward. 1969. "Urban Social Theory and Research." *Environment and Planning* 1:143–154.

Pahl, Raymond Edward. 1970. *Whose City? and Other Essays on Sociology.* London: Longman.

Pahrump Valley (Nev.) Times Star. 1985. "Nuclear Testing Moratorium Would Affect 8000 at NTS." *Pahrump Valley (Nev.) Times Star,* April 26, p. 4.

Palmer, Donald, and Roger Friedland. Forthcoming. "Corporation, Class and City System." In Mark Mizruchi and Michael Schwartz (eds.), *The Structural Analysis of Business.* New York: Cambridge University Press.

Palmer, Donald, Roger Friedland, and Amy Roussell. 1985. "Corporate Headquarters and Business Service Activity." Unpublished manuscript, Graduate School of Business, Stanford University.

Palmer, Donald, Roger Friedland, and Jitendra Singh. n.d. "Ties, Links and Interdependence: The Determinants of Stability in a Corporate Interlock Network." Unpublished manuscript, Graduate School of Management, Stanford University.

Palmer, Donald, Roger Friedland, P. Devereaux Jennings, and Melanie Powers. 1984. "Testing a Political Economy Model of Divisionalization in Large U.S. Corporations." Paper presented at the 44th annual meeting of the Academy of Mangement, Boston. August 12–15.

Park, Robert E. 1952. *Human Communities: The City and Human Ecology.* New York: Free Press.

Park, Robert E. 1967. "The City: Suggestions for the Investigation of Human Behavior in the Urban Environment." Pp. 1–46 in Robert E. Park, Ernest W. Burgess, and Roderick D. McKenzie (eds.), *The City.* Chicago: University of Chicago Press.

Park, Robert E., and Ernest W. Burgess. 1921. *Introduction to the Science of Sociology.* Chicago: University of Chicago Press.

Parke, Robert, Jr., and Charles Westoff (eds.). 1972. *Aspects of Population Growth Policy* (report of the U.S. Commission on Population Growth and the American Future, vol. 6). Washington, D.C.: Commission on Population Growth and the American Future.

Parker, R. Andrew. 1982. "Local Tax Subsidies as a Stimulus for Development: Are They Cost-Effective? Are They Equitable?" *City Almanac* 16(5–6):8–15.

Pashigian, B. Peter. 1982. "Environmental Regulation: Whose Self-Interests Are Being Protected?" Center for the Study of the Economy and the State, University of Chicago.

Pearce, Diana. 1976. "Black, White and Many Shades of Gray: Real Estate Brokers and Their Racial Practices." Ph.D. dissertation, University of Michigan.

Pearson, Harry. 1957. "The Economy Has No Surplus: Critique of a Theory of Development." Pp. 320–341 in Karl Polanyi, M. Arensberg, and Harry Pearson (eds.), *Trade and Market in the Early Empires: Economies in History and Theory.* New York: Free Press.

Peet, Richard. 1975. "Inequality and Poverty: A Marxist-Geographic Inquiry." *Annals of the Association of American Geographers* 65:564–571.

Peet, Richard. 1980. "The Consciousness Dimension of Fiji's Integration into World Capitalism." *Pacific Viewpoint* 21:91–115.

Peet, Richard. 1982. "International Capital, International Culture." Pp. 275–302 in Michael Taylor and Nigel Thrift (eds.), *The Geography of Multinationals.* London: Croom Helm.

Peiser, Richard B. 1981. "Land Development and Regulation: A Case Study of Dallas and Houston, Texas." *Journal of the American Real Estate and Urban Economics Association* 9(4):397–417.

Perez, L. A., Jr. 1975. "Tourism in the West Indies." *Journal of Communication* 25(2):136–143.

Perin, Constance. 1977. *Everything in Its Place.* Princeton, N.J.: Princeton University Press.

Perlez, Jane. 1983. "Tax Break Zones Face Tough Fight." *New York Times,* Dec. 18, sec. A, p. 12.

Perrow, Charles. 1970. "Departmental Power and Perspectives in Industrial Firms." Pp. 59–89 in Mayer Zald (ed.), *Power in Organizations.* Nashville, Tenn.: Vanderbilt University Press.

Perrow, Charles. 1984. *Normal Accidents.* New York: Basic Books.

Perry, David C., and Alfred J. Watkins. 1977. "People, Profit, and the Rise of the Sunbelt Cities." Pp. 277–306 in David C. Perry and Alfred J. Watkins (eds.), *The Rise of the Sunbelt Cities.* Beverly Hills, Calif.: Sage.

Peters, Thomas J., and Robert H. Waterman, Jr. 1982. *In Search of Excellence: Lessons from America's Best-Run Companies.* New York: Harper and Row.

Peterson, George E. 1973. "The Property Tax and Low-Income Housing Markets." Pp. 107–124 in George E. Peterson (ed.), *Property Tax Reform.* Washington, D.C.: Urban Institute.

Peterson, George E. 1976. *Federal Tax Policy and Urban Development.* Washington, D.C.: Urban Institute Working Paper.

Peterson, George E. 1978. "Capital Spending and Capital Obsolescence—The Outlook for Cities." Pp. 49–74 in Roy Bahl (ed.), *The Fiscal Outlook for Cities: Implications of a National Urban Policy*. Syracuse, N.Y.: Syracuse University Press.

Peterson, Paul E. 1981. *City Limits*. Chicago: University of Chicago Press.

Phelan, James, and Robert Pozen. 1973. *The Company State* (Ralph Nader's Study Group report on DuPont in Delaware). New York: Grossman.

Philpott, Thomas. 1978. *The Slum and the Ghetto*. New York: Oxford University Press.

Piore, Michael. 1970. "Jobs and Training." Pp. 53–83 in Samuel H. Beer and Richard E. Barringer (eds.), *The State and the Poor*. Cambridge, Mass.: Winthrop.

Pirenne, Henri. 1925. *Medieval Cities: Their Origins and the Revival of Trade*. Princeton, N.J.: Princeton University Press.

Pitt, Leonard. 1966. *The Decline of the Californios*. Berkeley and Los Angeles: University of California Press.

Pittas, Michael. 1984. "The Arts Edge: Revitalizing Economic Life in California's Cities." Speech presented at a conference sponsored by the California Economic Development Commission Local Government Advisory Committee, Santa Barbara, July 15.

Piven, Francis Fox, and Richard A. Cloward. 1971. *Regulating the Poor: The Functions of Social Welfare*. New York: Random House.

Polanyi, Karl. 1944. *The Great Transformation: The Political and Economic Origins of Our Time*. Boston: Beacon Press.

Pollock, Dale, and Al Delugach. 1984. "Fox Moving to Raise Cash in Wake of Big Losses." *Los Angeles Times*, November 29, pp. 1,6.

Pope, Leroy. 1982. "Environmentalists Accused of Subverting Movement of Industry to Sunbelt, West." *Los Angeles Times*, November 18, sec. C, p. 6.

Popper, Frank J. 1981. *The Politics of Land-Use Reform*. Madison: University of Wisconsin Press.

Portes, Alejandro. 1981. "Modes of Structural Incorporation and Present Theories of Labor Immigration." Pp. 279–297 in Mary M. Kritz, Charles B. Keely, and Silvano M. Tomasi (eds.), *Global Trends in Migration: Theory and Research on International Population Movement*. New York: Center for Migration Studies.

Portes, Alejandro. 1982. "Immigrants' Attainment: An Analysis of Occupation and Earnings among Cuban Exiles in the United States." Pp. 91–111 in Robert M. Hauser (ed.), *Social Structure and Behavior: Essays in Honor of William Hamilton Sewell*. New York: Academic Press.

Portes, Alejandro, and John Walton. 1976. *Urban Latin America: The Political Condition from Above and Below.* Austin: University of Texas Press.

Portes, Alejandro, and John Walton. 1981. *Labor, Class and the International System.* New York: Academic Press.

Poulantzas, Nicos. 1973. *Political Power and Social Classes.* London: New Left Books.

Pred, Allan Richard. 1966. *The Spatial Dynamics of U.S. Urban-Industrial Growth, 1800–1914; Interpretive and Theoretical Essays.* Cambridge, Mass.: MIT Press.

Pred, Allan Richard. 1976. "The Interurban Transmission of Growth in Advanced Economies: Empirical Findings versus Regional Planning Assumptions." *Regional Studies* 10(2):151–171.

Pred, Allan Richard. 1977. *City Systems in Advanced Economies: Past Growth, Present Processes, and Future Development Options.* London: Hutchinson.

Pred, Allan Richard. 1980. *Urban Growth and City Systems in the United States, 1840–1860.* Cambridge, Mass.: Harvard University Press.

Price, Kent A. 1984. "U.S. Food and Fiber—Abundance or Austerity?" *Resources* No. 76 (Spring):2–20.

Priest, Donald. 1980. "Regulatory Reform, Housing Costs and Public Understanding." *Urban Land* 39(4):3–4.

Pritchett, Clayton. 1977. "The Effect of Regional Growth Characteristics on Regional Housing Prices." *Journal of the American Real Estate and Urban Economics Association* 5(2):189–208.

Protash, William, and Mark Baldasarre. 1983. "Growth Policies and Community Status: A Test and Modification of Logan's Theory." *Urban Affairs Quarterly* 18(3):397–412.

Public Administration Times. 1984. "Cap on Business IDB's Pushed for States, Cities." *Public Administration Times,* March 15, pp. 1,3.

Public Opinion. 1982. "Environmental Update." *Public Opinion* 5(1):32.

Purnick, Joyce. 1984. "H.R.A. Sees 25% of People in City Below Poverty Line." *New York Times,* December 12, sec. B, p. 3.

Qadeer, M. A. 1981. "The Nature of Urban Land." *American Journal of Economics and Sociology* 40(2):165–182.

Quante, Wolfgang. 1976. *The Exodus of Corporate Headquarters from New York City.* New York: Praeger.

Rainwater, Lee. 1970. *Behind Ghetto Walls: Black Families in a Federal Slum.* Chicago: Aldine.

Rainwater, Lee, Richard P. Coleman, and Gerald Handel. 1959. *Work-*

ingman's Wife: Her Personality, World and Life Style. New York: Oceana.

Rankin, Jerry. 1981. "New Business Groups Making Waves in Local Political Waters." *Santa Barbara News Press,* May 21, sec. B, p. 1.

Rankin, Jerry. 1982. "Big Spenders Don't Always Win at Polls." *Santa Barbara News-Press,* August 4, sec. B, p. 1.

Ratcliff, Richard E. 1979. "Banks and the Command of Capital Flows: An Analysis of Capitalist Class Structure and Mortgage Disinvestment in a Metropolitan Area." Pp. 129–159 in Maurice Zeitlin (ed.), *Classes, Class Conflict and the State.* Cambridge, Mass.: Winthrop.

Ratcliff, Richard E. 1980. "Banks and Corporate Lending: An Analysis of the Impact of the Internal Structure of the Capitalist Class on the Lending Behavior of Banks." *American Sociological Review* 45(4):553–570.

Ratcliff, Richard E., Mary Beth Gallagher, and K. S. Ratcliff. 1979. "The Civic Involvement of Bankers: An Analysis of the Influence of Economic Power and Social Prominence in the Command of Civic Policy Positions." *Social Problems* 26:298–313.

Redburn, Tom, and Sandra Blakeslee. 1979. "Sohio Calls Off Long Beach Oil Terminal Plan." *Los Angeles Times,* March 14, pp. 1,29.

Reich, Robert. 1983. *The Next American Frontier.* New York: Penguin.

Relph, E. 1976. *Place and Placelessness.* London: Pion.

Remy, Dorothy, and Larry Sawers. 1984. "Urban Industrial Decline and the Dynamics of Sexual and Racial Oppression." Pp. 128–151 in Larry Sawers and William K. Tabb (eds.), *Sunbelt/Snowbelt: Urban Development and Regional Restructuring.* New York: Oxford University Press.

Rex, John A., and Robert Moore. 1967. *Race, Community and Conflict: A Study of Sparkbrook.* Oxford, England: Oxford University Press.

Rice, Bradley R. 1983. "If Dixie Were Atlanta." Pp. 31–57 in Richard M. Bernard and Bradley R. Rice (eds.), *Sunbelt Cities: Politics and Growth since World War II.* Austin: University of Texas Press.

Rice, Leslie. 1982. "Defending the Barriers and Bays" *Re:Sources* 2 (4):4.

Rich, Richard. 1980. "The Dynamics of Leadership in Neighborhood Organizations." *Social Science Quarterly* 60:570–587.

Richardson, Dan. 1976. *The Cost of Environmental Protection.* New Brunswick, N.J.: Rutgers University Press.

Rick, William B. 1978. "Growth Management in San Diego." *Urban Land* 37(4):3–5.

Ricks, David, and Ronald Racster. 1980. "Restrictions on Foreign Ownership of U.S. Real Estate." *Real Estate Review* 10(1):111–115.

Risen, James. 1984. "Auto World Theme Park to Close." *Los Angeles Times*, June 12, sec. IV, p. 1.

Rivera, Nancy. 1983a. "High Tech Firm Picks Austin over San Diego." *Los Angeles Times*, May 18, sec. IV, pp. 1,2.

Rivera, Nancy. 1983b. "Fewer Able to Afford Homes, Survey Says." *Los Angeles Times*, September 23, sec. III, p. 1.

Roberts, Steven B. 1985. "Why It's Easier to Scratch a Back than Bite a Bullet." *New York Times*, March 17, sec. E, p. 5.

Roderick, Kevin. 1984. "Cities Play Hardball to Lure Teams." *Los Angeles Times*, June 30, sec. I, pp. 1,24.

Romes, David. Forthcoming. "Networks and Efficacy in Local Political Processes." Ph.D. dissertation, University of California, Santa Barbara.

Rose, Harold M. 1982. "The Future of Black Ghettos." Pp. 138–148 in Gary Gappert and Richard V. Knight (eds.), *Cities in the Twenty-first Century*. Beverly Hills, Calif.: Sage.

Rose, Jerome, and Robert E. Rothman (eds.). 1977. *After Mount Laurel: The New Suburban Zoning*. New Brunswick, N.J.: Center for Urban Policy Research.

Rosen, Bernard C. 1959. "Race, Ethnicity, and the Achievement Syndrome." *American Sociological Review* 24(1):47–60.

Rosenbaum, Nelson. 1978. "Growth and Its Discontents: Origins of Local Population Controls." Pp. 43–61 in Judith May and Aaron Wildavsky (eds.), *The Policy Cycle*. Beverly Hills, Calif.: Sage.

Rosenblatt, Robert. 1979a. "Alternative Plans Face Same Obstacles." *Los Angeles Times*, March 14, sec. I, p. 1.

Rosenblatt, Robert. 1979b. "Sohio Chairman Calls Oil Project Now Hopeless." *Los Angeles Times*, March 28, sec. I, p. 3.

Rosenfeld, Raymond. 1980. "Who Benefits and Who Decides? The Uses of Community Development Block Grants." Pp. 211–234 in Donald B. Rosenthal (ed.), *Urban Revitalization*. Beverly Hills, Calif.: Sage.

Rosenstiel, Thomas B. 1985. "'Killing Fields' Writer Loses N.Y. Times Column, to Be Reassigned." *Los Angeles Times*, August 21, sec. I, p. 21.

Ross, Christopher. 1982. "Regional Patterns of Organizational Dominance: 1955–1975." *Sociological Quarterly* 23(2):207–219.

Ross, Robert, and Kent Trachte. 1983. "Global Cities and Global Classes: The Peripheralization of Labor in New York City." *Review* 6(3):393–431.

Rossi, Peter. 1955. *Why Families Move*. Glencoe, Ill.: Free Press.

Rossi, Peter, and Robert Dentler. 1961. *The Politics of Urban Renewal*. New York: Free Press.

Rothman, David. 1971. *The Discovery of the Asylum*. Boston: Little, Brown.

Roweis, Shoukry T., and Allen J. Scott. 1978. "The Urban Land Question." Pp. 38–75 in Kevin R. Cox (ed.), *Urbanization and Conflict in Market Societies*. London: Methuen.

Rowles, Graham D. 1980. *Prisoners of Space? Exploring the Geographical Experiences of Older People*. Boulder, Colo.: Westview Press.

Royko, Mike. 1971. *Boss: Richard J. Daley of Chicago*. New York: Dutton.

Rubin, Lillian B. 1972. *Busing and Backlash: White against White in an Urban School District*. Berkeley and Los Angeles: University of California Press.

Rubin, Lillian B. 1976. *Worlds of Pain: Life in the Working-Class Family*. New York: Basic Books.

Rudel, Thomas K. 1983. "Managing Growth: Local Governments and the Social Control of Land Use." Unpublished ms., Department of Human Ecology, Rutgers University.

Rudzitis, Gundars. 1982–83. "Rural Attitudes towards Growth and Energy Development: A Texas Example." *Journal of Environmental Systems* 12:249–263.

Rugman, Alan, and Lorraine Eden (eds.). 1985. *Multinationals and Transfer Pricing*. New York: St. Martin's Press.

Ryon, Ruth. 1984. "Rights Grant Gains Favor in Renewals." *Los Angeles Times,* July 8, sec. VII, p. 1.

Sabatier, Paul A., and Daniel Mazmanian. 1983. *Can Regulation Work?* New York: Plenum.

Safire, William. 1981. "Poletown Wrecker's Ball." *New York Times,* April 30, sec. A, p. 31.

Sagalyn, Lynne B., and George Sternlieb. 1973, *Zoning and Housing Costs: The Impacts of Land Use Controls on Housing Price*. New Brunswick, N.J.: Rutgers University Center for Urban Policy Research.

Sahagun, Louis, and Allan Jalon. 1984. "Cities Battle to House Technology Museum." *Los Angeles Times,* November 29, sec. IV, pp. 1,4.

Samuelson, Paul. 1942. "The Business Cycle and Urban Development." Pp. 6–17 in Guy Greer (ed.), *The Problems of Cities and Towns*. Cambridge, Mass.: Harvard University Press.

San Francisco Chronicle. 1984. "Reagan's Hometown Offers Bounty to Lure More Business to the Area." *San Francisco Chronicle,* May 10, p. 4.

Santa Barbara News Press. 1984. "Lowering the Boom." *Santa Barbara News Press,* June 21, sec. E, p. 12.

Sassen-Koob, Saskia. 1984. "The New Labor Demand in Global Cities." Pp. 139–172 in Michael Peter Smith (ed.), *Cities in Transformation: Class, Capital, and the State.* Beverly Hills, Calif.: Sage.

Sawhill, Isabel, and John Palmer. 1984. *The Reagan Record: An Assessment of America's Changing Domestic Priorities.* Washington, D.C.: Urban Institute.

Saxenian, Annalee. 1984. "The Urban Contradictions of Silicon Valley: Regional Growth and the Restructuring of the Semiconductor Industry." Pp. 163–200 in Larry Sawers and William K. Tabb (eds), *Sunbelt/Snowbelt: Urban Development and Regional Restructuring.* New York: Oxford University Press.

Saxton, Alexander. 1971. *The Indispensable Enemy.* Berkeley and Los Angeles: University of California Press.

Schanberg, Sydney H. 1984. "Reagan's Homeless." *New York Times,* February 4, sec. A, p. 19.

Schattschneider, Elmer Eric. 1960. *The Semisovereign People.* New York: Holt, Rinehart and Winston.

Scheiber, Harry N. 1973. "Urban Rivalry and Internal Improvements in the Old Northwest, 1820–1860." Pp. 135–146 in Alexander Callow, Jr. (ed.), *American Urban History: An Interpretive Reader with Commentaries,* 2d ed. New York: Oxford University Press.

Schenectady Gazette. 1984a. "Japan Warns States to Go Easy on Tax." *Schenectady Gazette,* February 11, p. 36.

Schenectady Gazette. 1984b. "17 Gulf Coast Cities Vie for 3,500-Sailor Base." *Schenectady Gazette,* November 24, p. 7.

Schenectady Gazette. 1985. "U.S. Judge Bans Westway Construction." *Schenectady Gazette,* August 8, p. 40.

Schill, Michael H., and Richard P. Nathan. 1983. *Revitalizing America's Cities: Neighborhood Reinvestment and Displacement.* Albany: State University of New York Press.

Schmedel, Scott R. 1985. "Tax Report." *Wall Street Journal,* February 27, p. 1.

Schmenner, Roger W. 1975. "City Taxes and Industry Location." Ph.D. dissertation, Yale University.

Schmenner, Roger W. 1982. *Making Business Location Decisions.* Englewood Cliffs, N.J.: Prentice-Hall.

Schmidt, William E. 1984. "Suburbs' Growth Pinches Atlanta." *New York Times,* April 24, sec. A, p. 14.

Schnaiberg, Allan. 1980. *The Environment: From Surplus to Scarcity.* New York: Oxford University Press.

Schneider, Mark, and John R. Logan. 1981. "The Fiscal Implications of Class Segregation: Inequalities in the Distribution of Public Goods and Services in Suburban Municipalities." *Urban Affairs Quarterly* 17(1):23–36.

Schneider, Mark, and John R. Logan. 1982a. "The Effects of Local Government Finances on Community Growth Rates: A Test of the Tiebout Hypothesis." *Urban Affairs Quarterly* 18(1):91–105.

Schneider, Mark, and John R. Logan. 1982b. "Suburban Racial Segregation and Black Access to Local Public Resources." *Social Science Quarterly* 63(4):762–770.

Schneider, Mark, and John R. Logan. 1983. "Fiscal Implications of Black and Low Income Suburbanization, 1970–1980" (Working Paper No. 7). Albany, N.Y.: Rockefeller Institute.

Schneider, Mark, and John R. Logan. 1984. "Fiscal Disparities and the Location of Firms in Suburban Regions." Paper presented at the annual meeting of the International Studies Association, Atlanta, Georgia, April.

Schnore, Leo F. 1961. "The Social and Economic Characteristics of American Suburbs." *Sociological Quarterly* 4(2):122–134.

Schoenberger, Erica, and Amy K. Glasmeier. 1980. "Selling the MX: The Air Force Asks Nevada to Move Over." *Progressive* (May), pp. 16–21.

Schrage, Michael. 1984. "Pentagon High-Tech Role Debated." *Los Angeles Times*, October 23, sec. IV, pp. 3, 4.

Schultze, Charles. 1977. *The Public Use of Private Interest*. Washington, D.C.: Brookings Institute.

Schulze, Robert O. 1961. "The Bifurcation of Power in a Satellite City." Pp. 19–80 in Morris Janowitz (ed.), *Community Political Systems*. Glencoe, Ill.: Free Press.

Schurmann, Franz. 1983. "The Deamericanization of America." Talk delivered to the Department of Sociology, University of California, Santa Barbara, May 16.

Schwartz, Seymour I., and Robert Johnson. 1979. "Suburban Growth Management and Metropolitan Housing Needs: An Emerging Conflict." *Urban Interest* 1(Fall):81–87.

Schwartz, Seymour I., et al. 1979. *The Effect of Growth Management on New Housing Prices: Petaluma, California*. Davis: Institute of Governmental Affairs, University of California, Davis.

Scott, Allen J. 1982. "Locational Patterns and the Dynamics of Industrial Activity in the Modern Metropolis." *Urban Studies* 19(2):111–142.

Secter, Bob. 1986. "Philadelphia's Mayor Goode Apologizes for Deaths, Fire in MOVE Confrontation." *Los Angeles Times*, March 10, sec. I, p. 8.

Seidel, Stephen R. 1978. *Housing Costs and Government Regulations:*

Confronting the Regulatory Maze. New Brunswick, N.J.: Center for Policy Research.

Seley, John, and Julian Wolpert. 1975. "A Strategy of Ambiguity in Locational Conflicts." Pp. 275–300 in Kevin R. Cox, David R. Reynolds, and Stein Rokkan (eds.), *Locational Approaches to Power and Conflict*. New York: Halsted Press.

Selznick, Philip. 1949. *TVA and the Grass Roots*. Berkeley and Los Angeles: University of California Press.

Sengstock, Mary C. 1983. "Functions and Dysfunctions of Ethnic Self-Employment: Detroit Iraqui-Chaldeans as a Case Study." Paper presented at the 78th annual meeting of the American Sociological Association, Detroit, Michigan, August 31–September 4.

Seppa, Nathan. 1982. "Reagan Overrides Public Referendum" *Re:Sources* 4(2):3.

Shefer, Daniel. 1970. "Comparable Living Costs and Urban Size: A Statistical Analysis." *Journal of the American Institute of Planners* 36(November):417–421.

Shlay, Anne B., and Denise DiGregorio. 1983. "Same City, Different Worlds: Examining Gender and Work Based Differences in Perceptions of Neighborhood Desirability." Paper presented at the 78th annual meeting of the American Sociological Association, Detroit, Michigan. August 31–September 4.

Shlay, Anne B., and Robert P. Gilroth. 1984. "Gambling on World's Fairs: Who Plays and Who Pays." *Neighborhood Works* 7(August): 11–15.

Shlay, Anne B., and Peter H. Rossi. 1981. "Putting Politics into Urban Ecology: Estimating Net Effects of Zoning." Pp. 257–286 in Terry N. Clark (ed.), *Urban Policy Analysis: Directions for Future Research*. Beverly Hills, Calif.: Sage.

Shonfield, Andrew. 1965. *Modern Capitalism: The Changing Balance of Public and Private Power*. London: Oxford University Press.

Sierra Club of San Diego. 1973. "Economy, Ecology, and Rapid Population Growth." San Diego: Sierra Club.

Sills, David L. 1975. "The Environmental Movement and Its Critics." *Human Ecology* 3(1):1–41.

Silver, Hilary. 1984. "Regional Shifts, Deindustrialization, and Metropolitan Income Inequality." Paper presented at the 79th annual meeting of the American Sociological Association, San Antonio, Texas, August 27–31.

Simison, Robert L. 1980. "Consumers Power Will Continue to Build Nuclear Plant in Michigan Despite Woes." *Wall Street Journal*, March 7, p. 12.

Sing, Bill. 1985. "Airline Chief Barred from Fare Talks." *Los Angeles Times,* July 13, sec. IV, p. 1.

Sjoberg, Gideon. 1955. "The Preindustrial City." *American Journal of Sociology* 60:438–445.

Skelton, George. 1979. "Stunned Brown Tries to Blame Oil Firm: Sohio Case Could Be Black Eye for Him Nationally in Any Quest for Presidency." *Los Angeles Times,* March 14, sec. I, pp. 3,31.

Smith, I. J. 1982. "The Role of Acquisition in the Spatial Distribution of the Foreign Manufacturing Sector in the United Kingdom." Pp. 221–252 in Michael Taylor and Nigel Thrift (eds.), *The Geography of Multinationals.* Cambridge: Cambridge University Press.

Smith, Michael Peter, and Marlene Keller. 1983. "Managed Growth and the Politics of Uneven Development in New Orleans." Pp. 126–166 in Susan Fainstein (ed.), *Restructuring the City.* New York: Longman.

Smith, Reginald. 1984. "Willie Brown's Big Income Revealed in State Report." *San Francisco Chronicle,* March 7, p. 12.

Smith, Reginald. 1985. "Downtown Plan OKd on Quick 6-to-5 Vote." *San Francisco Chronicle,* September 11, pp. 1,16.

Smith, V. Kerry. 1976. *Economic Consequences of Air Pollution.* Philadelphia: Ballanger.

Snow, Robert. 1983. "The New International Division of Labor and the U.S. Workforce: The Case of the Electronics Industry." Pp. 39–69 in June Nash and Maria P. F. Kelley (eds.), *Women, Men, and the International Division of Labor.* Albany: State University of New York Press.

Soja, Edward. 1985. "The Assertion of Space in Social Theory." Presentation to the Department of Sociology, University of California, Santa Barbara, February 6.

Soja, Edward, Rebecca Morales, and Goetz Wolff. 1983. "Urban Restructuring: An Analysis of Social and Spatial Change in Los Angeles." *Economic Geography* 59(2):195–230.

Sollen, Robert. 1983a. "Cities Say Yes, Ventura County No, to Oil Lease Sale." *Santa Barbara News Press,* July 27, sec. B, p. 3.

Sollen, Robert. 1983b. "Measure Defeat Followed Pattern of Other Elections." *Santa Barbara News Press,* December 10, sec. D, pp. 1,2.

Sonquist, John A., and Tom Koenig. 1975. "Examining Corporate Interconnections through Interlocking Directorates." Pp. 53–83 in Tom R. Burns and Walter Buckley (eds.), *Power and Control: Social Structures and Their Transformation.* London: Sage.

Sovani, N. V. 1964. "The Analysis of Overurbanization." *Economic Development and Cultural Change* 12(2):113–122.

Sowell, Thomas. 1981. *Ethnic America.* New York: Basic Books.

Spaulding, Charles. 1946. "Housing Problems of Minority Groups in Los Angeles County." *Annals of the American Academy of Political and Social Sciences* 248:220–225.

Spaulding, Charles. 1951. "Occupational Affiliations of Councilmen in Small Cities." *Sociology and Social Research* 35(3):194–200.

Squires, Gregory. 1984. "Capital Mobility versus Upward Mobility: The Racially Discriminatory Consequences of Plant Closings and Corporate Relocations." Pp. 152–162 in Larry Sawers and William K. Tabb (eds.), *Sunbelt/Snowbelt: Urban Development and Regional Restructuring*. New York: Oxford University Press.

Stack, Carol. 1974. *All Our Kin*. New York: Harper and Row.

Stahura, John M. 1982. "Status Transition of Blacks and Whites in American Suburbs." *Sociological Quarterly* 23(1):79–93.

Stammer, Larry. 1977. "Brown Signs Bill to Speed LNG Facility." *Los Angeles Times*, September 17, sec. II, p. 1.

Stanback, Thomas M., Jr., and Thierry J. Noyelle. 1982. *Cities in Transition: Changing Job Structures in Atlanta, Denver, Buffalo, Phoenix, Columbus, Ohio, Nashville, and Charlotte*. Totowa, N.J.: Allanheld, Osmun.

Stanback, Thomas M., Jr., Peter Bearse, Thierry J. Noyelle, and Robert Karasek. 1981. *Services: The New Economy*. Totowa, N.J.: Allanheld, Osmun.

Stanfield, R. 1977. "The Human Renewal." *National Journal* 9:290.

Stanford Research Institute. 1964. *City of Industry: Its Economic Characteristics and Significance, 1957–1970*. South Pasadena, Calif.: Stanford Research Institute.

Steidtmann, Nancy. 1985. "Citizen Lesher: Newspaper Publisher." *Bay Area Business Magazine* IV(October 3):14–18.

Steinberg, Stephen. 1981. *The Ethnic Myth: Race, Ethnicity and Class in America*. Boston: Beacon Press.

Stephens, John D., and Brian P. Holly. 1980. "The Changing Pattern of Industrial Corporate Control in the Metropolitan United States." Pp. 161–180 in Stanley D. Brunn and James O. Wheeler (eds.), *The American Metropolitan System: Present and Future*. New York: Wiley.

Stern, Robert N., and Howard Aldrich. 1980. "The Effect of Absentee Firm Control on Local Community Welfare: A Survey." Pp. 162–181 in John J. Siegfried (ed.), *The Economics of Firm Size, Market Structure and Social Performance: Proceedings of a Conference Sponsored by Bureau of Economics, Federal Trade Commission*. Washington, D.C.: Government Printing Office.

Sternlieb, George, and James W. Hughes. 1983a. *The Atlantic City Gamble*. Piscataway, N.J.: Center for Urban Policy Research.

Sternlieb, George, and James W. Hughes. 1983b. "The Uncertain Future of the Central City." *Urban Affairs Quarterly* 18:455–484.

Stinchcombe, Arthur L. 1965. "Social Structure and Organizations." Pp. 142–193 in James March (ed.), *Handbook of Organizations*. New York: Rand McNally.

Stinchcombe, Arthur L. 1983. *Economic Sociology*. New York: Academic Press.

Stodden, J. R. 1973. "Their Small Size Costs Banks Business of Larger Companies." *Federal Reserve Bank of Dallas Business Review,* October, pp. 6–7.

Stone, Clarence N. 1976. *Economic Growth and Neighborhood Discontent: System Bias in the Urban Renewal Program of Atlanta*. Chapel Hill: University of North Carolina Press.

Stone, Clarence N. 1981. "Community Power Structure—A Further Look." *Urban Affairs Quarterly* 16(4):505–515.

Stone, Clarence N. 1982. "Social Stratification, Non-Decision-Making and the Study of Community Power." *American Politics Quarterly* 10(3):275–302.

Stone, Clarence N. 1984. "City Politics and Economic Development: Political Economy Perspectives." *Journal of Politics* 46(1):286–299.

Stoneman, Colin. 1975. "Foreign Capital and Economic Growth." *World Development* 3(1):11–26.

Storey, David J. 1981. "New Firm Formation, Employment Change and the Small Firm." *Urban Studies* 18(3):335–345.

Storper, Michael, and Richard Walker. 1983. "The Theory of Labor and the Theory of Location." *International Journal of Urban and Regional Research* 7(1):43.

Storr, Richard J. 1966. *Harper's University: The Beginnings*. Chicago: University of Chicago Press.

Stout-Wiegand, Nancy, and Robert Trent. 1983. "Sex Differences in Attitudes toward New Energy Resource Developments." *Rural Sociology* 48(4):637–646.

Stuart, Darwin, and Robert Teska. 1971. *Who Pays for What: Cost Revenue Analysis of Suburban Land Use Alternatives*. Washington, D.C.: Urban Land Institute.

Stull, William J. 1974. "Land Use and Zoning in an Urban Economy." *American Economic Review* 64(3):337.

Stutz, Frederick. 1981. "Explaining Geographic Variations in Housing Prices." Unpublished paper, Department of Geography, San Diego State University.

Summers, Gene F., and Kristi Branch. 1984. "Economic Development and Community Social Change." *Annual Review of Sociology* 10:141–166.

Summers, Gene F., et al. 1976. *Industrial Invasion of Nonmetropolitan America: A Quarter Century of Experience*. New York: Praeger.

Sundquist, James. 1975. *Dispersing Population: What America Can Learn from Europe*. Washington, D.C.: Brookings Institute.

Suttles, Gerald. 1968. *The Social Order of the Slum: Ethnicity and Territory in the Inner City*. Chicago: University of Chicago Press.

Suttles, Gerald. 1972. *The Social Construction of Communities*. Chicago: University of Chicago Press.

Swanstrom, Todd. 1981. "The Crisis of Growth Politics: Cleveland, Kucinich, and the Challenge of Urban Populism." Ph.D. dissertation, Princeton University.

Swanstrom, Todd. 1985. *The Crisis of Growth Politics: Cleveland, Kucinich, and the Challenge of Urban Populism*. Philadelphia: Temple University Press.

Swierenga, Robert P. 1966. "Land Speculator 'Profits' Reconsidered: Central Iowa as a Test Case." *Journal of Economic History* 26(1): 1–28.

Szelenyi, Ivan. 1983. *Urban Inequalities under State Socialism*. New York: Oxford University Press.

Tabb, William K. 1984a. "Economic Democracy and Regional Restructuring: An International Perspective." Pp. 403–416 in Larry Sawers and William Tabb (eds.), *Sunbelt/Snowbelt*. New York: Oxford University Press.

Tabb, William K. 1984b. "The Failures of National Urban Policy." Pp. 255–269 in William K. Tabb and Larry Sawers (eds.), *Marxism and the Metropolis*, 2d ed. New York: Oxford University Press.

Tabb, William K. 1984c. "The New York City Fiscal Crisis." Pp. 298–322 in William K. Tabb and Larry Sawers (eds.), *Marxism and the Metropolis*, 2d ed. New York: Oxford University Press.

Tabb, William K. 1984d. "A Pro-People Urban Policy." Pp. 367–382 in William K. Tabb and Larry Sawers (eds.), *Marxism and the Metropolis*, 2d ed. New York: Oxford University Press.

Taeuber, Karl. 1983. "Racial Residential Segregation in Twenty-eight Cities, 1970–1980" (Working Paper No. 83–12). Madison: University of Wisconsin, Center for Demography and Ecology.

Taeuber, Karl, and Alma Taeuber. 1965. *Negroes in Cities*. Chicago: Aldine.

Taggart, Harriett, and Kevin Smith. 1981. "Redlining: An Assessment of the Evidence in Metropolitan Boston." *Urban Affairs Quarterly* 17(1):91–107.

Takagi, Dana. 1985. "Class and Community Politics in San Francisco." Presentation to the Department of Asian American Studies, University of California, Santa Barbara.

Tanzer, Michael. 1968. *The Sick Society*. Chicago: Holt, Rinehart and Winston.

Taplin, Ruth. 1984. "Women in World Market Factories: East and West." Paper presented to the Society for the Study of Social Problems, San Antonio, Texas. August 24–26.

Taylor, Graham. 1915. *Satellite Cities*. New York: Appleton.

Taylor, Michael, and Nigel Thrift. 1982. *The Geography of Multinationals*. London: Croom Helm.

Terrell, Paul. 1976. *The Social Impact of Revenue Sharing*. New York: Praeger.

Thackray, John. 1984. "Service Management's Second Coming." *Management Today,* June, pp. 56–69, 129–133.

Thomlinson, Ralph. 1969. *Urban Structure: The Social and Spatial Characteristics of Cities*. New York: Random House.

Thorngren, B. 1970. "How Do Contact Systems Affect Regional Development?" *Environment and Planning* 2(4):409–427.

Thunen, Johann Heinrich von. 1826. *Der Isolierte Staat in Beziehung auf Landwirtschaft und Nationökonomie* [The Isolated State]. Hamburg: Perthes.

Thurow, Lester. 1980. *The Zero-Sum Society*. New York: Basic Books.

Thurow, Lester. 1984. "The Disappearance of the Middle Class." *New York Times,* February 5, sec. F, p. 3.

Thurow, Lester. 1985. "Retooling the Mainstream." *Resources* 80(2):1–9.

Tiebout, Charles M. 1956. "A Pure Theory of Local Expenditures." *Journal of Political Economy* 64(October):416–424.

Tilly, Charles. 1974. "The Chaos of the Living City." Pp. 86–107 in Charles Tilly (ed.), *An Urban World*. Boston: Little, Brown.

Tilly, Charles, Louise Tilly, and Richard Tilly. 1975. *The Rebellious Century, 1830–1930*. Cambridge, Mass.: Harvard University Press.

Tocqueville, Alexis de. 1945. *Democracy in America,* vol. 1. New York: Vintage Books.

Tomkins, Calvin. 1983. "The Art World: Dallas." *New Yorker* 59(17): 92–97.

Tonnies, Ferdinand. 1887 (1963). *Community and Society*. [Gemeinschaft und Gesellschaft.] Charles P. Loomis, trans. and ed. New York: Harper.

Tournier, Robert E. 1980. "Historic Preservation as a Force in Urban Change: Charleston." Pp. 173–186 in Shirley Laska and Daphne Spain (eds.), *Back to the City: Issues in Neighborhood Renovation*. New York: Pergamon.

Trent, Robert B., and Nancy Stout-Wiegand. 1984. "The Perceived Benefits of Local Industrial Development: A Replication and Extension."

Paper presented at the 79th annual meeting of the American Sociological Association, San Antonio, Texas, August 27–31.

Trillin, Calvin. 1976. "U.S. Journal: Rockford, Illinois—Schools without Money." *New Yorker* 52(38):146–154.

Trillin, Calvin. 1979. "U.S. Journal: Atlantic City, N.J.—Assemblage." *New Yorker* 54(47):44–48.

Trillin, Calvin. 1981. "U.S. Journal: San Diego. Thoughts While Riding a Trolley toward Tijuana." *New Yorker* 57(43):129–138.

Tuchman, Gaye. 1972. "Objectivity as Strategic Ritual: An Examination of Newsmen's Notions of Objectivity." *American Journal of Sociology* 77(4):660–679.

Tuchman, Gaye. 1978. *Making News: A Study in the Construction of Reality.* New York: Free Press.

Tumulty, Karen, Dale Pollock, Al Delugach, Robert Dallos, and Harry Anderson. 1981. "The Takeover of Fox: A Drama of Wealth, Intrigue and Passion." *Los Angeles Times,* August 2, sec. VI, pp. 1–5.

Turner, D. M. 1977. *An Approach to Land Values.* Berkhamsted (U.K.): Geographical Publications.

United States Bureau of the Census. 1979. *1977 Survey of Minority-owned Business Enterprises: Black.* Washington, D.C.: Department of Commerce, Bureau of the Census, Government Printing Office.

United States Bureau of the Census. 1982a. *Provisional Estimates of Social, Economic and Housing Characteristics.* Washington, D.C.: Government Printing Office.

United States Bureau of the Census. 1982b. *Statistical Abstract of the United States, 1982–1983,* 103d ed. Washington, D.C.: Government Printing Office.

United States Bureau of the Census. 1983a. *Current Population Reports.* Series P-20. Washington, D.C.: Government Printing Office.

United States Bureau of the Census. 1983b. *Statistical Abstract of the United States.* 104th ed. Washington, D.C.: Government Printing Office.

United States Bureau of the Census. 1984. *Consolidated Federal Funds Report, Fiscal Year 1983.* Washington, D.C.: Government Printing Office.

United States Department of Commerce, Bureau of Economic Analysis. 1985. "Selected National Income and Product Accounts Tables." *Survey of Current Business* 65(5):7.

United States Department of Housing and Urban Development. 1978. *A Summary Report of Current Findings from the Experimental Housing Allowance Program.* Washington, D.C.: Office of Policy Development and Research, HUD.

United States Minority Business Development Agency. 1982. *Minority*

Business Enterprise Today: Problems and Their Causes. Washington, D.C.: Minority Business Development Agency.

United States President's Commission on Housing. 1981. *Interim Report.* Washington, D.C.: President's Commission on Housing, Government Printing Office.

United States President's Committee on Urban Housing. 1969. *A Decent Home: Report.* Washington, D.C.: Government Printing Office.

Useem, Bert. 1980. "Solidarity Model, Breakdown Model, and the Boston Anti-Busing Movement." *American Sociological Review* 45(June): 357–369.

Valentine, Betty Lou. 1978. *Hustling and Other Hard Work.* New York: Free Press.

Van Liere, Kent D., and Riley Dunlap. 1980. "The Social Bases of Environmental Concern: A Review of Hypotheses, Explanations and Empirical Evidence." *Public Opinion Quarterly* 44(2):181–197.

Vartabedian, Ralph. 1984. "For California, 1983 Was Year of the Merger." *Los Angeles Times,* May 20, sec. V, p. 1.

Vaughn, Robert J. 1979. *State Taxation and Economic Development.* Washington, D.C.: Council of State Planning Agencies.

Verba, Sidney, and Norman H. Nie. 1972. *Participation in America: Political Democracy and Social Equality.* New York: Harper and Row.

Vernon, Raymond. 1975. "Foreword." In Duane Kujawa (ed.), *International Labor and the Multinational Enterprise.* New York: Praeger.

Vidich, Arthur J., and Joseph Bensman. 1960. *Small Town in Mass Society: Class, Power and Religion in a Rural Community.* Garden City, N.Y.: Doubleday.

Villarejo, Don. 1982. "The California Water Project." Paper presented at a conference of the University of California Committee on Appropriate Technology, "Sustaining the Lands," Santa Barbara, May 21.

Von Eschen, Donald, Jerome Kirk, and Maurice Pinard. 1971. "The Organizational Substructure of Disorderly Politics." *Social Forces* 49(4):529–544.

Wade, Richard C. 1959. *The Urban Frontier: The Rise of Western Cities, 1790–1830.* Cambridge, Mass.: Harvard University Press.

Wald, Matthew. 1983. "Shoreham Epitomizes the End of an Atomic Era." *New York Times,* December 8, sec. A, p. 18.

Waldbott, George. 1978. *Health Effects of Environmental Pollutants.* St. Louis: Mosby.

Walker, Bruce. 1979. "Income Distribution, City Size and Urban Growth: A Comment." *Urban Studies* 16(3):341–343.

Walker, Richard A. 1974. "Urban Ground Rent: Building a New Conceptual Framework." *Antipode* 6(1):51–58.

Walker, Richard A. 1978. "Two Sources of Uneven Development under Advanced Capitalism—Spatial Differentiation and Capital Mobility." *Review of Radical Political Economics* 10(3):28–38.

Walker, Richard A. 1981. "A Theory of Suburbanization: Capitalism and the Construction of Urban Space in the United States." Pp. 383–429 in Michael Dear and Allan J. Scott (eds.), *Urbanization and Urban Planning in Capitalist Society*. New York: Methuen.

Walker, Richard A., and Michael K. Heiman. 1981. "Quiet Revolution for Whom?" *Annals of the Association of American Geographers* 71(1):67–83.

Walker, Richard A., and Matthew J. Williams. 1982. "Water from Power: Water Supply and Regional Growth in the Santa Clara Valley." *Economic Geography* 58(2):95–119.

Wallerstein, Immanuel. 1974. *The Modern World System: Capitalist Agriculture and the Origins of the European World-Economy in the Sixteenth Century*. New York: Academic Press.

Wallerstein, Immanuel. 1979. "Class Formation in the Capitalist World Economy." Pp. 222–230 in Immanuel Wallerstein, *The Capitalist World Economy*. New York: Cambridge University Press.

Walton, John. 1970. "A Systematic Survey of Community Power Research." Pp. 443–464 in Michael Aiken and Paul Mott (eds.), *The Structure of Community Power*. New York: Random House.

Walton, John. 1982. "The International Economy and Peripheral Urbanization." Pp. 119–136 in Norman Fainstein and Susan Fainstein (eds.), *Urban Policy under Capitalism*. Beverly Hills, Calif.: Sage.

Ward, Sally. 1984. "Trends in the Location of Corporate Headquarters: Changing Patterns of Metropolitan Dominance in the 1970s." Paper presented at the 79th annual meeting of the American Sociological Association, San Antonio, Texas, August 31–September 4.

Warner, Sam Bass. 1973. *Streetcar Suburbs*. Cambridge: MIT Press.

Warner, Sam Bass, and Colin Burke. 1969. "Cultural Change and the Ghetto." *Journal of Contemporary History* 4:173–188.

Warren, Bill. 1975. "How International Is Capital?" Pp. 135–141 in Hugo Radice (ed.), *International Firms and Modern Imperialism*. Harmondsworth, England: Penguin Books.

Warren, Donald. 1975. *Black Neighborhoods: An Assessment of Community Power*. Ann Arbor: University of Michigan Press.

Warren, Robert D. 1966. *Government in Metropolitan Regions: A Reappraisal of Fractionated Political Organization*. Davis: Institute of Governmental Affairs, University of California.

Warren, Roland. 1963. *The Community in America*. Chicago: Rand McNally.

Wayne, Leslie. 1984. "America's Astounding Job Machine." *New York Times*, June 17, sec. C, pp. 1,25.

Wayslenko, Michael J. 1980. "Evidence of Fiscal Differentials and Intrametropolitan Firm Location." *Land Economics* 56(3):339–348.

Wayslenko, Michael J. 1981. "The Location of Firms: The Role of Taxes and Fiscal Incentives." Pp. 155–190 in Roy Bahl (ed.), *Urban Government Finance: Emerging Trends*. Beverly Hills, Calif.: Sage.

Weiler, Conrad. 1978. *Achieving Social and Economic Diversity in Inner City Neighborhoods through Increased Demand for City Housing by Middle-Income Persons*. Washington, D.C.: National Association of Neighborhoods.

Weinstein, Bernard L., and Robert E. Firestine. 1978. *Regional Growth and Decline in the United States*. New York: Praeger.

Weinstein, James. 1968. *The Corporate Ideal in the Liberal State, 1900– 1918*. Boston: Beacon Press.

Weitzman, Lenore J. 1981. "The Economics of Divorce: Social and Economic Consequences of Property, Alimony and Child Support Awards." *UCLA Law Review* 28(August):1251.

Wellman, Barry. 1979. "The Community Question: The Intimate Networks of East Yorkers." *American Journal of Sociology* 84(5):1201– 1231.

Wenzlick, Roy. 1966. "Raw Land Values in Metropolitan Areas." *Real Estate Analyst* 35(December):42.

White, Charles Langdon, and Edwin J. Foscue. 1964. *Regional Geography of Anglo-America*. New York: Prentice-Hall.

White, Michelle. 1978. "Self-Interest in the Suburbs: The Trend toward No-Growth Zoning." *Policy Analysis* 4(Spring):185–203.

White, Morton, and Lucia White. 1962. *The Intellectual versus the City*. Cambridge, Mass.: Harvard University Press.

Whitt, J. Allen. 1982. *Urban Elites and Mass Transportation: The Dialectics of Power*. Princeton, N.J.: Princeton University Press.

Whyte, William F. 1943. *Street Corner Society*. Chicago: University of Chicago Press.

Wienk, Ronald E., et al. 1979. *Measuring Racial Discrimination in American Housing Markets*. Washington, D.C.: U.S. Department of Housing and Urban Development, Office of Policy Development and Research, Division of Evaluation, Government Printing Office.

Wiesenthal, Eric. 1984a. "City Ordinance Regulates Plant Relocations." *Public Administration Times*, February 15, p. 3.

Wiesenthal, Eric. 1984b. "Aid Cut, Service Hike Send Cities for Help." *Public Administration Times*, March 15, p. 5.

Wiesenthal, Eric. 1984c. "States Take Initiative in Enterprise Zone Laws." *Public Administration Times*, June 1, pp. 1,8.

Willhelm, Sidney M. 1962. *Urban Zoning and Land-Use Theory.* New York: Free Press.

Willhelm, Sidney M. 1970. *Who Needs the Negro?* Cambridge, Mass.: Schenkman.

Williams, James, Andrew Sofranko, and Brenda Root. 1977. "Change Agents and Industrial Development in Small Towns: Will Social Action Have Any Impact?" *Journal of the Community Development Society* 8(1):19–29.

Williams, Lena. 1984. "Yonkers Settles Its Suit on Housing Segregation." *New York Times,* February 8, p. 32.

Williams, Oliver, and C. R. Adrian. 1963. *Four Cities: A Study of Comparative Policy Making.* Philadelphia: Temple University Press.

Williams, Oliver, Harold Herman, Charles Liebman, and Thomas Dye. 1965. *Suburban Differences and Metropolitan Policies.* Philadelphia: University of Pennsylvania Press.

Williams, Peter R. 1976. "The Role of Institutions in the Inner London Housing Market: The Case of Islington." *Transactions of the Institute of British Geographers* 1(1):72–82.

Williamson, Oliver. 1975. *Markets and Hierarchies.* New York: Free Press.

Wilson, James Q. (ed). 1980. *The Politics of Regulation.* New York: Basic Books.

Wilson, Kenneth L., and Alejandro Portes. 1980. "Immigrant Enclaves: An Analysis of the Labor Market Experiences of Cubans in Miami." *American Journal of Sociology* 86(2):295–319.

Wilson, William. 1978. *The Declining Significance of Race.* Chicago: University of Chicago Press.

Wilson, William. Forthcoming. *Hidden Agenda: Race, Urban Social Dislocations, and Public Policy.* Chicago: University of Chicago Press.

Wirth, Louis. 1928. *The Ghetto.* Chicago: University of Chicago Press.

Wolf, Peter. 1981. *Land in America: Its Value, Use and Control.* New York: Pantheon.

Wolfe, Alan. 1981. *America's Impasse: The Rise and Fall of the Politics of Growth.* New York: Pantheon.

Wolinsky, Leo. 1984. "Cities Fatten Budgets on Redevelopment Law." *Los Angeles Times,* sec. I, pp. 1,3,30.

Wood, Robert. 1958. *Suburbia: Its People and Their Politics.* Boston: Houghton Mifflin.

Wood, Robert. 1961. *1400 Governments: The Political Economy of the New York Metropolitan Region.* Cambridge, Mass.: Harvard University Press.

Worster, Donald. 1982. "Hydraulic Society in California: An Ecological

Interpretation." *Agricultural History* 56(July):503–515.

Worthington, Richard. 1984. "Is There Any Such Thing as High Tech?" Paper presented to the annual meeting of the Society for the Social Studies of Science, Ghent, Belgium, November 16.

Wyner, Allen. 1967. "Governor-Salesman." *National Civic Review* 61(February):81–86.

Yago, Glenn. 1983. "Urban Transportation in the Eighties." *Democracy* 3(1):43–55.

Yago, Glenn. 1984. *The Decline of Transit: Urban Transportation in German and U.S. Cities, 1900–1970*. New York: Cambridge University Press.

Yago, Glenn, Hyman Korman, Sen-Yuan Wu, and Michael Schwartz. 1984. "Investment and Disinvestment in New York, 1960–1980." *Annals of the American Academy of Political and Social Science* 475(September):28–38.

Yancey, William L., Eugene P. Ericksen, and Richard N. Juliani. 1976. "Emergent Ethnicity: A Review and Reformulation." *American Sociological Review* 41(3):391–403.

Yinger, John, George Galster, Barton Smith, and Frederick Eggers. 1978. *The Status of Research into Racial Discrimination and Segregation in American Housing Markets*. Washington, D.C.: Department of Housing and Urban Development.

Yoo, Kisook. 1981. "Corporate Resource Access Strategies and the Local Community." Ph.D. dissertation, Department of Sociology, State University of New York at Stony Brook.

Young, Ken, and John Kramer. 1978. "Local Exclusionary Policies in Britain: The Case of Suburban Defense in a Metropolitan System." Pp. 229–251 in Kevin R. Cox (ed.), *Urbanization and Conflict in Market Societies*. Chicago: Maaroufa Press.

Zacchino, Narda, and Bill Boyarsky. 1982. "Big Business Gets Revenge." *Los Angeles Times,* October 29, sec. I, pp. 1,20.

Zald, Mayer N., and Roberta Ash. 1966. "Social Movement Organizations: Growth, Decay and Change." *Social Forces* 44(March):327–341.

Zald, Mayer, and John D. McCarthy (eds.). 1979. *The Dynamics of Social Movements: Resource Mobilization, Social Control and Tactics*. Cambridge, Mass.: Winthrop.

Zax, Leonard A., and Jerold S. Kayden. 1983. "The New Jersey Court Opens a New Chapter in Exclusionary Zoning." *National Law Journal* 5(March 14):11.

Zeigler, L. H. 1961. *The Politics of Small Business*. Washington, D.C.: Public Affairs Press.

Zeitlin, Maurice. 1974. "Corporate Ownership and Control: The Large Corporation and the Capitalist Class." *American Journal of Sociology* 79(5):1073–1119.

Zeitlin, Maurice. 1984a. *The Civil Wars in Chile; or, The Bourgeois Revolutions That Never Were*. Princeton: Princeton University Press.

Zeitlin, Maurice. 1984b. "High Wages Are *Not* Industry's Trouble." *Los Angeles Times*, October 8, sec. II, p. 5.

Zeitlin, Maurice, W. Lawrence Neuman, and Richard Ratcliff. 1976. "Class Segments: Agrarian Property and Political Leadership in the Capitalist Class of Chile." *American Sociological Review* 41(December):1006–1029.

Zorbaugh, Harvey. (1926) 1961. "The Natural Areas of the City." Pp. 45–49 in George A. Theodorson (ed.), *Studies in Human Ecology*. Evanston, Ill.: Harper and Row.

Zunz, Olivier. 1982. *The Changing Face of Inequality: Urbanization, Industrial Development, and Immigrants in Detroit, 1880–1920*. Chicago: University of Chicago Press.

Name Index

Neiman, M., 82, 221, 222
Nelson, K. P., 287
Nelson, R. L., 264
Netzer, D., 186
Newman, S. J., 102
Newson, M. DeH., 115
Newton, K., 180, 199
New York Times, 73, 77, 173n, 191n, 213, 244n, 252, 269, 273, 274
Nguyen, L. T., 126
Nicholas, J. C., 279n
Nie, N. H., 221
Nishioka, H., 186
Noland, E. W., 204
Novak, T. P., 126
Noyelle, T. J., 207, 261, 262, 282

O'Connor, J., 282n
O'Connor, M., 276
Offe, C., 251
Oliver, M., 105, 126, 131, 141
Oreskes, M., 193
Oropesa, R. S., 137
Osofsky, G., 114, 116, 128, 129, 131
Ostrom, E., 195
Owen, M., 102

Pahl, R. E., 138, 138n, 148
Palmer, D., 84, 134, 204, 206, 259, 261, 262, 284; et al., 106, 262, 266
Palmer, J., 282
Pang, W. N., 186, 259
Park, R. E., 6, 7, 112
Parke, R., Jr., 97
Pashigian, B. P., 218
Pearce, D., 129
Pearson, H., 26
Peet, R., 19, 255
Peiser, R. B., 279n
Perez, L. A., Jr., 255
Perin, C., 20, 157
Perrow, C., 164, 264
Perry, D. C., 281
Peters, T. J., 263
Peterson, G. E., 177, 246
Peterson, P. E., 33, 41, 62, 70, 85, 151, 179, 292
Phelan, J., 168
Philpott, T., 116, 128
Piore, M., 282n
Pirenne, H., 125n
Pitt, L., 128

Pittas, M., 76
Piven, F. F., 139
Polanyi, K., 23, 28, 216, 226n
Popper, F. J., 159, 162, 164
Portes, A., 124, 125, 126, 255, 256, 274, 285, 285n, 289
Poulantzas, N., 251
Pozen, R., 168
Pred, A. R., 22, 201, 203n, 261
Prewitt, K., 188, 221
Price, K. A., 226
Priest, D., 159
Protash, W., 160, 190, 221
Public Administration Times, 177
Public Opinion, 228
Purnick, J., 287
Puryear, D., 167
Pusey, A., 191

Qadeer, M. A., 10, 24
Quante, W., 259

Racster, R., 236
Rainwater, L., 167; et al., 104
Rankin, J., 229, 230
Ratcliff, R. E., 206; et al., 106
Redburn, T., 234
Reich, R., 264
Relph, E., 18
Remy, D., 283
Rex, J. A., 148
Rice, B. R., 80, 139, 211
Rice, L., 227
Rich, R., 135
Richardson, D., 279n
Rick, W. B., 279n
Ricks, D., 236
Riemer, R., 128
Risen, J., 77
Rivera, N., 76, 206n
Roark, J. L., 128
Roderick, K., 79, 80
Romes, D., 10
Rose, H. M., 288
Rose, J., 192n
Rosen, B. C., 126
Rosenfeld, R., 172
Rosenstiel, T. B., 73
Ross, C., 201, 259
Ross, R., 282, 287, 287n
Rossi, P., 42, 75, 142, 158, 168
Rothman, D., 152
Rothman, R. E., 192n

Subject Index

Compositor:	Graphic Composition
Printer:	McNaughton-Gunn
Binder:	McNaughton-Gunn
Text:	$^{10}/_{12}$ Times Roman
Display:	Goudy Bold